South Coast Shipwrecks

off East Dorset and Wight 1870–1979

David Wendes

Dedicated to the memory of no less than 1,875 lives lost in the sinkings described in this book.

Published in 2006 by David Wendes, Wight Spirit Charters, PO Box 502, Eastleigh, SO50 0BU.

ISBN 0-9554592-0-6 / 978-0-9554592-0-7 — Paperback edition
0-9554592-1-4 / 978-0-9554592-1-4 — Hardback edition

Printed by BAS Printers
1 Premier Way, Abbey Park Estate, Romsey, Hampshire SO51 9DQ

Introduction

The 176 shipwrecks contained in this book are those which lie, or are thought to lie, in the area bounded between 1° and 2° west, and as far south as about 50° 3′ north (in the west of the area), and 50°10′ north (in the east of the area). Not included are the wrecks which lie inshore to the east and south east of the Isle of Wight. Very approximately, this book covers wrecks in the area south, west and south east of the Isle of Wight and as far south as the mid Channel traffic separation zone, with a line drawn south from Anvil Point in the west, and Hayling Island in the east providing the boundaries.

The wrecks cover the period 1870 to 1979 and are produced in date order. The vast majority are steam ships though large sailing ships, submarines and motor ships are included. Vessels such as dumb barges, pleasure yachts and speedboats, small commercial sailing ships, hovercraft, mulberry harbours and aircraft are not included save for one or two examples where the wreck is charted and identified. Details of wrecks which lie in the westbound shipping lane in the middle of the English Channel have not, with a few exceptions, been dived on and investigated by me. Anyone who has seen the numbers of large ships steaming at 20 knots in line abreast over these wreck sites will understand the reasons why. However, if the wreck was reported lost in the area, details can be found in this book. The final chapter lists positions of some unidentified wrecks.

I have made extensive use of the records contained in the National Archives at Kew as well as in many reference libraries throughout the United Kingdom and other parts of the world. I have used these records as the original source documents and the information for each ship is as accurate as those original records. For the sake of historical accuracy, nothing has been added nor any part exaggerated though amendments and adjustments have been made to make the record more readable. The events recorded here are, therefore, based on contemporary newspaper accounts, Admiralty reports, survivor's reports, war diaries, courts martial and reports of courts of enquiry.

Nearly all wrecks in this book have been positively identified and the reader may wish to note that at the end of each chapter, mention is made of how the identity of the wreck was determined, or at the very least, why a name has been attributed to it. In most cases this is straightforward – the recovery of a ship's bell or builder's nameplate was all that was necessary. In other cases, identification is less positive, and hinges on location, size of the vessel, cargo and so on, and is based on circumstantial evidence. Where identification has not been made by the author, other reputable and trusted sources have been used.

The position of each wreck is also recorded, firstly in terms of the original report, e.g. 6 miles south of the Needles Lighthouse, followed by an accurate position in WGS84 GPS of where the wreck actually is, if known.

A huge amount of information has been obtained during nearly 35 years of diving and research, and it is impractical for it all to be included here. For example, information such as crew lists and personal details of those who died is not, as a rule, included, but may be available from my records should any reader require it. Having obtained so much knowledge and information over the years, and correctly identified so many wrecks, I wanted to ensure this knowledge is passed on, and the result is this book. I have worked hard to minimise mistakes but any which occur are mine. I trust they are minor. The author can be contacted through www.wightspirit@btinternet.com., or PO Box No. 502.

Acknowledgements

I would like to thank Roger Bayzand of Lymington and Dave Saywell of Poole for sharing their local knowledge of wrecks in the area, and for taking me to so many of them, thus enabling me to acquire details of each site and to correctly identify them. Thanks also to Martin Woodward of Bembridge for providing positions for many charted and uncharted wrecks, many of which, if not already identified by him, I was able to identify. His help has been especially useful and is much appreciated

For translating foreign material, I would like to thank Richard Beszant (French), Christa Mounce and Anke Otto (German), Sophia Exelby (Danish, Swedish and Norwegian) and to Victor Turon of Barcelona for all his assistance with U-boat information from the publication Der Krieg zur See, der Handelskrieg mit U-booten. E N Taylor of Gosport was especially helpful in providing photographs of obscure steamers.

Thanks also to Hamish Morrison for his photographic work for the colour section in this book, and Brian Tinsen of Dtek Systems Ltd for the loan of photographic equipment.

I have made use of the services of numerous libraries, archives, records offices and museums not only in the UK but across the world, and in particular I would like to acknowledge the assistance provided by staff at the National Archives, Kew, National Maritime Museum, Greenwich, Southampton Reference (Special Collections) Library, Weymouth Library, Dorset, World Ship Society, Imperial War Museum, London, Norsk Sjøfarts-museum, Oslo, Norway, Rijksmuseum, Amsterdam, Maritiem Museum, Rotterdam, Nationaal Scheepvaarts-museum, Antwerp, Sofartsmuseet, Denmark, Handels-og Sofartsmuseet på Kronborg, Helsingor and Deutsches Schiffahrtsmuseum, Bremerhaven.

Great care has been taken to properly credit the photographs published in this book. It was not possible to ascertain the origins of a few of the more obscure images and the author apologises if the publication of any image is in breach of copyright. No such breach is intended.

I would like to thank my fellow divers, past and present, who helped to fill in the gaps in my knowledge with descriptions of what they have seen on wrecks, and by recovering items through which it was possible to identify wrecks and eliminate others.

I would also thank those who have allowed me to photograph items which are shown in the colour section.

Lastly, and by no means least, I thank my long suffering wife Ann for her support. She has patiently endured the many hours I have spent researching, writing letters, cleaning artefacts and for "holding the fort" while I was diving.

Wreck identification

Anyone who is serious about researching wrecks ought to follow some basic principles in the quest to correctly locate and identify them. As a start it is very helpful – though not necessarily essential – to know the names of the ships to be researched. It cannot be stressed enough that thorough prior research not only saves time in the long run, but pays dividends when wrecks are located and identified. It is also immensely rewarding. My area of research has focussed almost entirely on iron and steel ships, mostly steamships, though the reader will find some sailing ships, warships and motor ships in this book, all of which were lost in the period 1870 to 1979.

The researcher may have certain wrecks in mind when commencing enquiries and it is certainly of great help first to have a good idea of what wrecks are thought to lie in a particular area. At the earliest opportunity one should attempt to narrow the research as much as possible. A starting point might be through the Shipwreck Index of the British Isles which lists nearly all ships lost around the British Isles. Additionally, the Hydrographic Office can supply much detail about known or charted wrecks but frequently a wreck may be uncharted or unknown, charted as unidentified or it may be wrongly identified. In the process of my own research I have discovered numerous instances where wrecks are either wrongly identified or are not located where they are said to be. It is therefore vital for the researcher to conduct his own research and not rely on what has been done before. Frequently, incorrect information – often published in good faith – is merely copied and reproduced as fact without first being subjected to further scrutiny. Mistakes have been copied and re-copied. The researcher has to be prepared to spend considerable time in libraries, museums and archives, and expend time, money and effort in writing to potential sources of information in order to obtain the detail required. Land based research may comprise the following:

Lloyd's Register of Shipping. This annual publication is extremely useful because almost every merchant ship is listed, and remains so for the extent of its life. There are, however, some exceptions, which may include vessels which were built and almost immediately lost and which did not therefore merit an entry in the Register. Some vessels may apparently disappear from the Register years before they were actually sunk, and this can sometimes be explained when there is a change of name. In addition, some vessels do not appear in the Register at all for reasons which are not always obvious.

The Register lists ships alphabetically and contains a wealth of information including where, when and by whom the ship was built, the dimensions and tonnage, details of the machinery, name changes, port of registry, owners and so on. In the case of the shipbuilder or engine manufacturer, if their records survive and can be traced, much additional information can be obtained by pursuing enquiries through the archives.

Mercantile Navy List. This is also an annual publication which relates only to British registered merchant vessels, both steam and sail. Some vessels which do not appear in Lloyd's Register of Shipping may be found in the Mercantile Navy List. The information contained within the List is not as detailed as in Lloyd's Register but nonetheless further useful material may be found.

Newspapers, books and other publications. Old newspapers are a rich source of information about shipping losses and their importance should not be underestimated. The Times frequently carried reports of shipping casualties but for more detail it is necessary to research newspapers local to where the casualty took place. It is also worth pursuing such research from sources close to the ship's port of registry, as often crew members originated from those ports and therefore there would have been local interest in the loss. Do not, however, expect to find much information if the ships or wrecks you are researching were lost in either the First or Second World Wars, as publication of details of British losses was not permitted. A weekly newspaper, Lloyd's List, contains a section on shipping casualties and is also worthy of research, particularly for some of the information contained in the reports from the late 19th century.

Many shipping casualties resulted in a court of enquiry being held. Unfortunately such reports were heavily weeded for the 19th century and the majority no longer survive in their original form though some can be found abbreviated in local newspapers, published at the time of the enquiry but many months after the sinking. Some very useful extracts can be found in the Board of Trade Wreck Returns from the late 19th to early 20th centuries.

Many shipping publications such as Sea Breezes, the Mariners Mirror, Motor Ship, Shipbuilding and Shipping Record, The Siren and others survive and these too can be useful sources.

Finally, it is always worth reading books on shipping company histories as they may contain photographs and information which cannot be obtained from other sources.

The National Maritime Museum in Greenwich has a very comprehensive library covering all aspects of ships and shipping and research should be pursued there. Further, a comprehensive selection of annually arranged wreck reports and enquiries, maritime books and magazines, Lloyd's Registers of Shipping, the Mercantile Navy List, newspapers and other publications can be viewed at the excellent Special Collections section at Southampton Reference Library. The quality and range of material is regarded as second only to the National Maritime Museum in Greenwich and the researcher is recommended to make use of the facilities there.

The National Archives. Based in south west London, the National Archives contain an almost overwhelming amount of information on almost every subject relating to the history of the country. Fortunately, shipping and related records are well represented whether in connection with the Royal Navy or Merchant Navy. In particular there is much detail available concerning shipping losses during the two world wars. Survivors' reports and information concerning the activities of German submarines provide a great deal of very useful information, as can reports from the Auxiliary Patrol of the First World War. Courts martial can usually be located here as well as operational information concerning the activities of warships. It will be necessary to attend the Archives in person to view documents though much can now be done to narrow the search by using the internet to identify which documents the researcher wishes to examine.

Enquiries abroad. The researcher should be prepared to conduct research abroad since many ships or wrecks were not British built or owned. Museums, libraries and archives around the world also contain a great deal of information. It is worth mentioning that the Norwegian records are most comprehensive; in particular their survivors reports for the First World War, and their photographic archive is excellent. The use of Lloyd's Register of Shipping as an aid to research is clearly illustrated here since the Register will contain details of foreign owners and ports of registry. It is then a matter of identifying potential sources abroad and writing to them for the information sought.

U-boat logs/war diaries. Towards the end of the Second World War, the allies overran Tambach Castle near Coburg, Germany. There they found the entire records of the German Navy 1850–1945. These were seized and brought to London where they were registered and arranged in sequence. Over a considerable period of time the records were filmed on microfilm. Copies of those microfilms are available to the researcher. Records which proved particularly interesting and useful in my research concerned the war diaries of German U-boats during the First World War. The diaries vary somewhat in their content but they do contain information about attacks on merchant shipping. Importantly from a research point of view is that the location of the attack is given with such accuracy as was possible at the time. As an example, the U-boat commander who sank the SS *Britannia* in 1917 provided a position which proved uncannily accurate to where the wreck lies today. Some entries contain some remarkable comments, such as those written by the commander of the U-boat which sank the mine carrier SS *Eleanor* in 1918, who wrote in his diary the words spoken by the sole survivor, "*Thank God if your souls are saved, these are all mines.*" The British records confirm that the survivor, Barton Hunter, admitted to the Admiralty that he had given this information to the Germans.

Copies of microfilm can be ordered from the US National Archives and Records Service.

Photographs and plans. A determined, committed and persistent researcher should be able to locate and obtain some plans and photographs of ships when they were in service. This may prove extremely difficult or impossible for some 19th century ships, because either no photographs were taken or if they were they no longer exist or cannot be located. Sometimes, if all else fails, it may be helpful to obtain a photograph or plan of a sister ship. Photographs are especially useful in identifying wrecks, providing enough of the structure of the wreck survives. It merely becomes a question of comparing what is seen on the image with what can be seen on the wreck. Studying the image with a magnifying glass may reveal certain features such as types of construction, and shapes, sizes and locations of fixtures and fittings. A photograph may reveal whether the ship had a well-deck or awning deck, or whether it was a turret deck vessel. It may prove crucial, for example, to note any unusual features, such as the design of the masts, or where, what type and how the anchors are stowed. In some cases it is possible to determine exactly where the bell is located, and even if the ship's name is painted or made up of welded or brass letters. Care should be taken in the use of photographs and plans, however, as changes and alterations made later during a ship's life may cause the researcher to be misled.

Photographs and plans may be obtained, in particular, through the National Maritime Museum, and both the Imperial War Museum and the World Ship Society have extensive photograph collections. To research further it will be necessary to know who the shipbuilder was, and then try to locate the builder's records. These may be held by libraries, archives, museums, companies which took over the previous shipping company, or private individuals.

Builder's records. Although much still survives, a huge amount has been destroyed or lost. Some builder's records are almost complete while others are practically non-existent. In order to make progress in locating these records the researcher will find it particularly useful to refer to Modern British Shipbuilding, a Guide to Historical Records, which lists many of the builders and gives details of what survives and where it is located. Frequently these records are now held in county archives or museums. However, even this excellent publication can become out of date, as since it first appeared, some archives have been moved elsewhere, and shipping companies gone into receivership. The National Maritime Museum in Greenwich may be able to assist in locating records. Occasionally, records such as First Yard Reports can be obtained of a ship; such records contain a great deal of detail which may be helpful in the subsequent identification of a wreck.

Diving on wrecks. There are numerous ways in which to identify wrecks. Armed with the knowledge first gleaned from shore based research, the diving researcher stands a very good chance of making correct wreck identifications. It may be necessary to rely on these methods particularly if the bell or builder's plate cannot be found or has already been recovered by another, and who has chosen to keep the discovery secret or not to share the information.

Use your eyes. First and foremost the ability to remember what's been seen underwater and to recall it later is a distinct advantage. Using a video camera is even better. The diver should note, for example, how many boilers there are, whether they are single or double ended, conventional or Yarrow design. Is there a donkey boiler and if so, what design is it? Is the machinery fitted amidships or aft? Is the engine a compound two cylinders, a triple expansion three cylinders or a six cylinders diesel? Are there two engines? If there are no engines, is the wreck a sailing ship or a barge? Whether it's steam or sail, are there deadeyes on the wreck which would indicate a sailing ship or an early steam ship in the transition period from sail to steam?

How many holds are there and what style are the winches? How does the wreck lie – on its port side, upside down, bows to the south? What do you estimate the tonnage is? Is there any cargo? What is it? Can you bring a sample up? How many davits are there? Where are they? What type of anchors are there? What condition is the wreck in? Are the hull plates welded or riveted? Is the wreck's general state consistent with being a loss from the First or Second World War? Do you think it's older or more recent? Why? Is there damage which might indicate how the ship was lost? Are the hull plates blown inwards or outwards? Are there bullet holes in the ship's fittings suggesting a Second World War loss? How do these features fit in with your research so far?

Ship's bell. Recovery of a ship's bell usually leads to the identification of a wreck. Assuming the bell is marked (some are not), it may bear the current or previous name of the ship, and often has the port of registry and year of build engraved or in relief in the brass. Occasionally the bell may bear the bell maker's name and this in itself may lead to further research. Bells are normally located on the bridge, on the fo'c'sle and in the crow's nest. Sailing ships have a bell on or near the fo'c'sle and at the stern close to the stern steering wheel. Some U-boat commanders of the First World War took bells as trophies before sinking their victims with bombs. Whether or not they did so may be recorded in the archives.

The sailing ship *Waitara,* SS *Cuba,* ST *Michael Clements,* SS *Inger,* SS *Aparima,* SS *Start,* among many others, were identified when their bells were found.

Builder's nameplates. On most steam or motor ships, the builder's nameplate is located on the front of the bridge. Usually oval or rectangular, occasionally circular, these nameplates bear the name and occupation of the builder and where the builder is located, sometimes a yard number, year and, rarely, the name of the ship. The SS *Tweed,* SS *Fallodon* and the SS *Messina* were identified in this way.

Engine builder's nameplate. The engine builder may very well be different to the shipbuilder. Nameplates from the engine room may be similar to builder's plates but care should be taken when researching. The number on the engine plate will be different to the number on the shipbuilder's plate. This is an important distinction and in conducting research it should be clearly stated whether the number is an engine or ship number.

Maker's plates of brass may be found on boilers including donkey boilers. The dates on these may be important, since Lloyd's Register of Shipping will usually record the fact of when the machinery including boilers was manufactured. Any changes will also be recorded, such as when a new donkey boiler was fitted. The new boiler should bear a nameplate with the name of the maker and the year. An entry in the Register will give the year of change and if this corresponds with the nameplate then identification may be made. Even if no change has taken place the date and makers name may be compared with the information from Lloyd's Register of Shipping.

The Dutch steamer *Betsy Anna* was identified from the nameplate from her donkey boiler, and the SS *Lapwing* was identified by her engine nameplate.

Ship's crockery & cutlery. Crockery or cutlery bearing the shipping company name or crest may be the only items found on a wreck which can identify it. Knowledge of previous ship ownership obtained through prior research is most useful as it can lead to identification. The clipper *Smyrna,* the sailing barque *Simla* and steamers *Fluent* and *Luxor* were all initially identified through ship's crockery.

Ship's steering gear. A number of identifications have been made through recovery of both bridge and stern steering gear. On bridge steering pedestals the manufacturers name and town can be found engraved on the top cover. Crucially, serial numbers and dates may also be present. The researcher then has to locate the maker's records and, with a little luck, the wreck may be properly identified. The SS *Olivine* and SS *Braatt II* were both identified using this method. On some bridge steering positions which pre-date pedestals, maker's plates can lead to identification even where there is no serial number. The steering nameplate from the SS *Cuba* revealed the name of the German builder and the year, and since the *Cuba* was the only vessel lost which was built by that builder, identification was confirmed.

The centre hub of the ship's wheel on the bridge may also contain evidence of the name of the ship and port of registry. Most steamers had an emergency steering position fitted at the stern above the rudder. These too may have a brass hub cover which may give builder's details or, in the case of early steamers, the builder's nameplate itself may have been fitted to the stern steering wheel. The SS *Clarinda* was identified in this way.

Official number. Each British ship, when completed, was allocated a unique official number. This number was cut into the main frame on the inside of the hatch coaming of number 2 hold, just forward of the bridge. The cutting was usually done with a cold chisel and the letters and numbering were substantial. Very occasionally, and if the main frame has survived reasonably well, it may be possible to discern the number and through it, the name of the ship.

Signal letters. As well as having an official number, each vessel was also allocated a unique four letter signal code. In the days before radio, the only means of communicating with a land station or another vessel at sea was through Morse code, flags or light signals. Upon receipt the signal letters could be checked against a master index and the ship identified. By using signal letters there could be no confusion with other vessels of the same name or description. Again, very occasionally, signal letters have been found stamped on items of brass and this has lead to identification.

Ship's name. Some wrecks have been identified through welded or brass letters on the bow and/or stern. Examples include the SS *Venezuela*, SS *Borgny* and SS *Avanti*. The *Venezuela* also had the previous port of registry, Buenos Aires, in brass letters on the stern. Other ships had the name in brass letters across the front of the bridge. The diver should look for loose letters lying in the wreck since it is almost certain they will have fallen off.

Ship's fittings. Wrecks may be identified through any number of ship's fittings ranging from clocks, barometers and telegraphs to compasses, lamps and so on. Maker's plates may be found on electric motors and pumps. Many fittings were given serial numbers and there is a remote chance that if the company or its archives still survive, the records of sale or allocation may also have survived. Careful cleaning is essential so as not to cause any damage. A clue to the subsequent identity of the Italian steamer SS *Derna* came from examination of a bridge steering wheel, where an Italian name had been scratched into the brass. Very occasionally a ship's name may be found on small brass plates attached to steam pressure gauges, though this is usually the case only with Royal Navy vessels. Ship's logs, notably Walker logs, bear serial numbers and if they are still legible, the ship can be traced through Walker's themselves, who continue to trade. Rarely, capstan covers are made of brass and these too can bear the maker's name and serial number as in the case of the SS *Tweed*. Ships' portholes – or, more correctly, scuttles – are another potential clue as the manufacturer's name can sometimes be found stamped in the brass. In addition, a ship may have had her name stamped into the brass backplate of a scuttle. The SS *Aparima* is an example.

Ship's ensigns. I know of two instances where a ship's ensign has survived in the seabed, both from ships which had lain on their sides. The ensigns had become buried in the seabed only to be revealed many years later. The survival of such flags may indicate no more than the nationality of a ship but this in itself can eliminate other possible ships.

Armament. In researching ships lost in the First and Second World Wars, details of any armament should be known. The weight of the projectile and gun are usually recorded, i.e. 12 pounder, 12 cwt (weight of projectile 12 pounds, weight of gun 12 hundredweight). A small brass nameplate fitted on the breech will record these details as well as who the gun maker was. It is helpful to know how many guns there were and where they were fitted. Shell cases have quite a lot of information stamped into their bases, not only of their calibre but more importantly their date of manufacture. These clues are all useful in trying to identify a wreck. However, care should be taken because if the ship was not sunk through war causes, the fact that it was armed may not be recorded in the report of the sinking. Both the SS *Myrtlegrove* and RMS *Mendi* were fitted with defensive stern guns but they were not lost through war causes and no mention is made of their guns in reports from the time. More in-depth research revealed their armament.

Cargo. Sometimes the cargo alone can lead to identification. However, particularly during the First World War so many vessels carried coal or were in ballast that this method is not easy unless the cargo is unusual. The Dutch schooner *Fenna* and the British SS *Eleanor* had such distinctive cargoes that they could not have been any other vessels. It may help to bring up a small sample – iron ore can easily be confused with coal.

Personal effects. In the haste to abandon a sinking ship personal effects were often left behind and though it is rare indeed to find small, personal items it is not impossible. Engravings in watches and rings, or nameplates on travelling cases could identify a crew member or passenger which in turn could identify the ship. Rarely, even paper material can survive if the conditions for preservation have been right. Gunners often kept their belongings in chests close to the gun, and these very often contained the owner's details including service number on brass nameplates. The names of a ship's gunners are often recorded in the archives.

Submarines and U-boats. U-boats are best identified by clearing away marine growth from the propellers, usually around the hub or close to the base of the blades. The number of the U-boat may then be revealed. Take care, however, because as the First World War progressed spares were taken from unserviceable boats to be fitted for operational use on others. Second World War boats have been identified through numbers found stamped on equipment such as range finders or binoculars. British submarines can usually be identified by their names in brass letters fitted to each side of the bridge.

Measurements. Sometimes it is necessary to use a tape to measure the dimensions of a wreck. This is not easy especially where the wreck has broken up but it can nonetheless help to eliminate other possible wrecks on grounds of size. The wreck known as the *Reindeer/Clyde/Spyros* was finally identified as the *Spyros* after archaeologists obtained accurate measurements. Measuring the cylinder bores of steam engines is also possible, and can be conclusive in proving a wreck's identity. This is because steam engines were manufactured individually and tailored to each particular vessel. As a result, they all have differences, some more subtle than others, but differences nevertheless. These differences can be measured and compared with the details contained in Lloyd's Register of Shipping.

One other method which might be adopted is to use an auger to take a vertical sample through the silt or cargo of the wreck. Analysis of the sample will indicate the presence or absence of certain substances which may help to identify a cargo.

Tower Hill Memorial. Located at Tower Hill, London, is a substantial memorial dedicated to those men and women who lost their lives in the Merchant Navy during the two World Wars. Their names are listed under the names of their ships. In an adjacent building are the registers which provide details of the deceased. This information may be particularly useful for those researching the loss of family members as it provides information such as that for the SS *South Western*. An example is "Horace Edward Newton, 15, Deck Boy, son of Robert William and Bessie Alice Newton. Born Portswood."

Final note. Some wrecks are easy to identify. Others may have a complete absence of readily accessible material or artefacts and it may prove to be a long and difficult process to achieve identification. If the serious researcher is properly equipped with as much information as possible and applies that information to what is seen on the seabed then chances of success are good. The message is to research thoroughly first, rely only on reputable sources of information, conduct your own dives and keep notes. In difficult cases narrow down the area of research and work out what's there through a process of elimination.

SS *Normandy*
Collision 17 March 1870

Paddle steamer *Normandy*, from an oil painting. Courtesy National Railway Museum, York.

On the *Normandy's* penultimate voyage a few days before she was lost, Henry Beckford Harvey, the Company's oldest captain was in discussion with a passenger and said, "The company want me to retire on a pension, but I have a presentiment I shall die in the service." Described as having "a large vermillion face, white whiskers and eyes with a good and brave expression" Captain Harvey did indeed die in the service of the Company just four days later.

The paddle steamer *Normandy*, owned by the London and South Western Railway Company, was a fast ship for her time, described as "a splendid paddle steam ship." It was said she was a strongly built vessel "of great power in proportion to her tonnage" no doubt illustrated by her ability to make almost 16 knots at full speed. She was "one of the swiftest and strongest of the Company's fleet." She was "perfectly seaworthy in every respect, well found and equipped."

Normandy's regular voyage was from Southampton to the Channel Islands and return. On 16 March 1870 *Normandy* was berthed at Southampton where she was laden with a general cargo and a consignment of mail. About 33 passengers embarked for the passage to Jersey. Around midnight, the ship slipped her moorings and headed down Southampton Water and the Solent towards the Needles.

In the early hours on the morning, *Normandy* passed the Needles and shaped a course towards Jersey at half speed. The weather was fine and clear and the ship was steaming at about 8 knots, her crew attesting "she never does go so fast of a night as she does during the day." The passengers and those members of the crew who were not on watch retired to their quarters for the remainder of the voyage.

Thick fog was already causing concern to the crew of the fully laden steamer *Mary* which was proceeding up the Channel for London. She had reduced her speed considerably, her master Captain Robert Stranack, estimating she was doing no more than 1 or 2 knots against the ebb tide. As an added precaution to prevent collision, her steam whistle was sounded at frequent intervals through the night and the navigation lamps were kept properly trimmed and illuminated. It may have been of no consequence but one of her masthead lamps had been lowered, adjusted and was in the process of being raised again when disaster loomed out of the fog. The *Normandy* and the *Mary* were about to collide.

The *Normandy* had been making good time towards Jersey when the vessel unexpectedly ran into a bank of thick fog, and rain had begun to fall. Visibility had gone from good to poor and varied from about a quarter of a mile to no more than 20 yards. Concerned about the reducing visibility the officer in charge sent a look-out man below to rouse Captain Harvey, who was in his cabin. Before he had time to appear on the bridge, the red navigation light of a ship was seen only 200 yards away off *Normandy's* starboard side. The helmsman later described seeing a bright white light low down, just above the red light, which was *Mary's* masthead lamp being raised. Although the *Mary's* engines were put full astern and her steering wheel hard to port, there was insufficient time to slow her headway, and her bows crashed into the *Normandy* just abaft the starboard paddle box, smashing the starboard lifeboat and carrying away rigging, stanchions and davits, leaving a gaping hole the size of a door, allowing the sea to surge into the ladies cabin. The *Mary* struck twice more before she passed clear of *Normandy's* stern. Immediately before the collision Captain Harvey on the *Normandy* ordered the helm hard to starboard and after the collision he had the engines stopped and ordered the ship's remaining two boats to be lowered. With a capacity of 32 persons between them it was inevitable there would be loss of life as there were more than 60 souls aboard the *Normandy*. Nevertheless Captain Harvey ordered "Ladies first" and filled the boats with survivors.

Boats were lowered from the *Mary* to assist in rescue, in response to calls for help from the Normandy's crew to "send a boat; the ship is sinking." The two boats full of survivors from the *Normandy* pulled towards the *Mary* as Captain Harvey had instructed them to do, saying "pull away to the other steamer at once." They soon met one of *Mary*'s boats manned by five of her crew. "Go to our ship, save some of the souls, the ship is going down" they were told, but the answer was "We must go back and receive orders from the Captain." Returning to the *Mary* a voice called out "Shall I go on Sir?" and the reply came "Yes, what did I send you for?" In the event, despite searching in the dark and fog, no more survivors were picked up. The only evidence found of the Normandy was a few pillows and timber.

The *Mary*, herself in a sinking condition with her bows stove in, managed to remain afloat and limp into Southampton where the survivors were disembarked

Among those lost were a nurse caring for four young children, all aged under four, Captain Harvey and six or seven crew, three soldiers and a number of residents of Southampton and the Channel Islands. In all, 35 lives were lost. The disaster had an enormous impact on Southampton and the Channel Islands, with all the steamers in Southampton Docks flying their flags at half mast, and "there is a great gloom over the town." A disaster fund was set up to provide for the bereaved and orphaned.

The Court of Enquiry held at Greenwich in April 1870 concluded that the Officer in Charge of the *Normandy* should have slowed his engines and not entered the fog at high speed across the track of both inward and outward bound vessels. The evidence was that the engines were not slowed until after the collision. As a result, the *Normandy* violated the regulations which state, "Every steamship when approaching another ship so as to involve risk of collision, shall slacken her speed or if necessary stop and reverse and every steamship shall, when in a fog, go at a moderate speed." Accordingly the actions of those on the Normandy were at fault and solely to blame for the collision. The court saw fit, however, to comment on "the irresolute conduct of the second mate of the *Mary* when despatched by the master to render assistance to the *Normandy*. There seemed to be no valid reason for his return to his own ship without carrying out the orders he had received from his master. Had he obeyed those orders and proceeded in the first instance as requested to do so by the crews of the *Normandy's* boats – although the *Normandy* had disappeared in the fog – more lives might possibly have been saved."

The wreck of the *Normandy* was first located during a survey in the 1950's but it remained uncharted until the first decade of the 21st century. The midships section containing the boilers and engines is remarkably intact and upright, while the stern and bow sections have been reduced to seabed level, where the outline of the hull can just be seen. The remains of the large paddle wheels survive. Seabed depth is about 46 metres.

Name: *Normandy*. **Former name(s):** None.
Vessel type: Paddle steamer.
Builder: J Ash & Company, Cubitt Town, Millwall.
When completed: 1863.

Machinery built by: J Stewart, Poplar.
Tonnage: 550 tons gross.
Dimensions: Length: 210′. **Breadth:** 24′.
Depth of holds: 14′.
Official number: 44911. **Yard number:** –
Signal letters: – **Last port of registry:** Southampton.
Ship description: Paddle steamer. 1 deck 2 masts, schooner rigged. Iron hull 2 funnels. Straight stem. Berths for 130 passengers.
Machinery description: Compound engines of 225 nominal horse power. 2 boilers.
Career and ownership: Built for and owned by the London and South Western Railway Company. Served on the Channel Islands run for 7 years. In 1868 she earned substantial salvage in the case of the dismasted French schooner *Paul et Louis*. *Normandy* towed the vessel to Jersey. *Normandy* was under Government contract to carry mails and bonds to and from the Channel Islands.
Destination and cargo: Southampton for Jersey with passengers, mails and general cargo.
Date sunk: 17 March 1870.
How sunk: Collision in fog with the steamer *Mary*.
Reported position of loss: Variously as 19, 20, 25 and 30 miles west-south-west of the Needles.
Actual position of wreck: 50° 22.68′ north, 001° 55.87′ west.
Orientation/height: Stands 4 metres in 46 metres on seabed of large pebbles and shingle.
How identity of wreck proved: Ship's crockery bearing company crest. Wreck is of a paddle steamer and only *Normandy*, a paddle steamer, is known to have been lost in the area.

SS *Lapwing*
Collision 1 July 1872

In 1868 the Cork Steam Ship Company ordered three new steamers from a Newcastle shipbuilder, Palmer's Company Ltd. They were named *Lapwing, Tern* and *Widgeon.* All three were subsequently lost by collision – *Widgeon* going first in 1871, followed by *Lapwing* in 1872. *Tern*, by sheer coincidence, was involved in a collision with the steamer *Clarinda* in 1885, which sank not far from where the *Lapwing* was lost, before *Tern* herself was lost in 1887.

Lapwing was engaged in the general cargo and passenger trade between Liverpool and Rotterdam. On 29 June 1872 she departed Liverpool under the command of Captain Cullen "a most experienced and skilful commander" and with a full general cargo and four passengers. The voyage had been without incident. On the night of Sunday 30 June *Lapwing* was approaching the Isle of Wight in wind conditions of south west force 5–6, but otherwise the weather was fine with a slight haze.

The iron sailing barque *Abbey Holme* had departed London for Brisbane with a full general cargo and she was taking full advantage of the fresh breeze blowing from the south west. Tacking down Channel, her crew had sighted the oncoming *Lapwing* and had hailed her and received the answer "All right" but *Lapwing* carried on, failing to give way in good time to the sailing ship. At the last moment the master of the *Abbey Holme*, Captain Robinson, put his helm hard down in an attempt to lessen the shock of the inevitable collision. The barque struck the *Lapwing* with terrific force on the port side aft, "cutting her right down" and in the process destroying the port lifeboat. The shuddering of the impact dislodged the funnel which toppled over and came crashing down, smashing the starboard lifeboat, leaving only the ship's dinghy as a means of rescue. This small boat was capable of carrying no more than three persons, and Lapwing had a crew of 19 and four passengers.

As soon as the collision occurred and while the two ships were locked together, the *Lapwing's* engineer, a stewardess and the quartermaster scrambled aboard the *Abbey Holme* before the two ships separated, and were thus saved. Working in Lapwing's engine room, oiling the cylinders, was a 38 year old Portuguese fireman called Henry Emanuel. On hearing a violent crash and seeing the engine room fill with steam, he thought one of the boilers had burst. Emanuel recalled, "the concussion was so great that for some moments I was quite bewildered, and only recovered my presence of mind when I found the engine room full of water."

Meanwhile, boats were lowered from the *Abbey Holme* at the request of Captain Cullen who shouted out "Barque ahoy! You had better lower your boats and save us before we all go down!" He then ordered the survivors on the *Lapwing* to make for the ship's dinghy, which though only fit for three persons, was nevertheless made to accommodate seven. The dinghy was boarded by Captain Cullen, the ship's carpenter and by the pilot and his daughter and other members of the crew. As the Captain ordered the painter to be cut the *Lapwing* went down; the dinghy and all those in it were pulled under water and drowned. Emanuel found a lifejacket and resolved to wait his fate when he witnessed the drownings as the *Lapwing* lurched heavily to starboard and disappeared, taking him down with the suction. He regained the surface minus his lifejacket; his ship had gone and the *Abbey Holme* was nowhere to be seen. Being a good swimmer, he paddled around and found some wooden grating to cling to, until a bale of cotton, part of the ship's cargo, floated within reach. Exhausting himself by trying to lie on top of it as it rolled and swirled around, he had to abandon his attempts in favour of another more suitable bale. He finally managed to clamber upon it, but by daybreak the bale had absorbed water and with him astride it, it was a foot beneath the surface, but just sufficiently buoyant to keep him afloat.

On the evening of 1 July 1872, 18 hours after the *Lapwing* had disappeared, and in an utterly exhausted and hypothermic state Henry Emanuel was saved by the Sunderland steamer *Lady Annie,* which chanced upon him and his bale of cotton, and he was pulled alive from the sea. Apart from him and the three crew who jumped aboard the *Abbey Holme*, three others were saved from floating bales of cotton. One was found on 2 July by a fishing smack, and two more by the ship

Rhine. These were the only survivors from the *Lapwing*.

In the days following the loss of the ship, more than 58 bales of cotton were picked up, as well as nine mahogany logs and a bale of wool floating in the sea off the Isle of Wight.

The wreck of the *Lapwing* lies in 40 metres of water. Lying across the tide, her engines lie hard over to starboard and are fitted as far aft as it is possible to be. Forward of the main boiler and donkey boiler, the wreck is very broken, spread out and low to the ground.

Name: *Lapwing*. **Former name(s):** None.
Vessel type: Steam ship with sails.
Builder: Palmer's Company, Jarrow on Tyne, Newcastle.
When completed: 1868.
Machinery built by: Palmer's Company Ltd, Jarrow on Tyne, Newcastle. Engine No 146.
Tonnage: 841 tons gross.
Dimensions: Length: 212′. **Breadth:** 28′.
Depth of holds: 17′.
Official number: 58547. **Yard number:** –
Signal letters: HCRV. **Last port of registry:** Cork.
Ship description: Iron hull screw steamer.
Machinery description: Compound 2 cylinders. 1 boiler, 1 donkey boiler. Machinery fitted aft. 90 horse power.
Career and ownership: Built for and owned by the Cork Steam Ship Company (Ebenezer Pike) and engaged on the Liverpool to Rotterdam route transporting general cargo and passengers.
Destination and cargo: Liverpool for Rotterdam with full general cargo including bales of cotton and baulks of mahogany.
Date sunk: 1 July 1872.
How sunk: Collision with the sailing barque *Abbey Holme*.
Reported position of loss: Variously as 12–15 miles west of the Isle of Wight, and 18 miles off St Catherine's Point.
Actual position of wreck: Not disclosed.
Orientation/height: Lies 000°/180°. Engine stands 5 metres in 40 metres on shingle seabed.
How identity of wreck proved: Engine maker's nameplate recovered.

SS *Woodham*

Broke down and blown ashore 2 March 1873

SS *Woodham* aground off Chilton Chine. Courtesy Martin Woodward.

"A fine screw steamship, handsomely built" was the description given to the Norwegian steamer *Woodham* after she had drifted ashore on the south coast of the Isle of Wight. She had been on voyage from Newcastle for New York with a cargo of coals and soda and when about 20 miles south of St Catherine's Point, in rough seas, her propeller shaft broke and disabled her machinery. A passing ship, the steamer *South Roberts,* took the *Woodham* in tow for an agreed sum of £500, a very substantial amount of money at the time. The agreement was for the disabled ship to be towed to Spithead where repairs could be effected. However, the unfavourable sea conditions hampered the salvage operation and in the rising sea the tow broke three times. Undeterred, the crews of the two vessels attached the hawser for a fourth time, but when that too broke, they knew their chance of winning the battle had gone. The *South Roberts*, seeing the crew of the *Woodham* in no immediate danger, continued on their voyage to Cardiff.

Woodham was left to the mercy of wind and waves, "beating about for a number of hours" until finally, during the early hours of 2 March 1873, she finally came ashore and stranded about half a mile out to sea from Chilton, Isle of Wight on a rock known as Chilton Calf. The shipwrecked crew fired distress signals and ignited some paraffin in such quantities that spectators on shore thought the ship was well ablaze.

The Brighstone Grange lifeboat was launched at low water after being towed by its team of horses along the beach to a point opposite the wreck, and on reaching the *Woodham*, found the shipwrecked crew in the ship's boats. In strong winds and driving snow, with tremendous swells sweeping the wreck, the lifeboat coxswain implored the shipwrecked crew to leave their boats and come aboard the lifeboat, which they did not a moment too soon. Breaking seas soon smashed *Woodham's* boats but 18 crew were rescued and brought safely to land. The ship's master and first mate refused to leave their ship despite being urged to do so, and the lifeboat was recovered from the sea and rehoused. Hardly had this been done when further signals of distress were seen on the *Woodham*, and the lifeboat was called out again in worsening conditions. The seas had become higher with driving rain and snow, and "waves rolling in mountain high and dashing with great force onto the steep ridges of beach at the foot of the chine."

It proved impossible to launch the lifeboat from its previous position and the team of horses towed the lifeboat on its transporting carriage from Brighstone to Chilton Chine and down to the beach where, in the darkness and bitter weather "men were up to their waists and horses up to their flanks in water." In spite of these appalling conditions the lifeboat managed to get away and was soon alongside the *Woodham,* taking off the master and first mate just as seas were almost sweeping right over the stranded ship. By the time the lifeboat reached shore, "the horses were spent, they were hard at it from 6 in the morning until 3 in the afternoon." No lives were lost and the lifeboat coxswain, James Buckett, was awarded the RNLI silver medal for gallantry.

Efforts to salvage the wrecked ship came to nothing as "water flows into her as high inside as out and she must be considerably lightened before getting off." In the event the ship became a total loss, after her sails, running gear and stores were landed.

The wreck must lie in shallow water of 6 metres or less in rocky/rough ground.

Name: *Woodham.* **Former name(s):** None.
Vessel type: Steamship with sails.
Builder: J P Denton, Hartlepool.
When completed: May 1869.
Machinery built by: G Clark, Sunderland.
Tonnage: 980 tons gross.
Dimensions: Length: 209′. **Breadth:** 30′.
Depth of holds: 15′ 6″.
Official number: 62757. **Yard number:** –
Signal letters: JCTM. **Last port of registry:** Christiania (Oslo).
Ship description: Iron screw steamer, spar decked.
Machinery description: Compound 2 cylinders. 98 horse power.
Career and ownership: Owned by Winge & Company, Christiania, who took over ownership from R Young in 1873. The owners had tried to start a direct emigrant route from Christiania to Quebec but the competition from the big liners was too strong. In 1872 *Woodham* sailed to Livorno, Italy, and was the first steamer to go there. She was also the first to go to Egypt in the same year, on both occasions carrying coal cargo.
Destination and cargo: Newcastle for New York with coals and soda.
Date sunk: 2 March 1873.
How sunk: Broke down and in a disabled condition was blown ashore and wrecked.
Reported position of loss: On a rock called Chilton Calf, Chilton Chine, Isle of Wight, 400 yards offshore and east of Hardman Rock.
Actual position of wreck: Approximate position 50° 38.00′ north, 001° 25.50′ west.
Orientation: –
How identity of wreck proved: Not located but any wreckage of a steamer in the vicinity of Chilton Calf can only be the *Woodham.*

Author's note: There is some doubt as to the accuracy of the technical specifications. *Woodham* was a ship owned by the Norwegians in 1873. However, *Woodham* continues to appear in Lloyd's Register post 1873, even stating a new boiler was fitted in 1874 after the ship had been wrecked. Accordingly, it is thought there may have been two ships named *Woodham* built around the same time. Care should be taken in interpreting the technical information.

SS *Vera*
Collision 31 January 1874

SS *Vera*. Courtesy Danish Maritime Museum, Helsingør.

The circumstances surrounding the loss of the steamer *Vera* and the vessel with which she collided, the sailing barque *Hagda,* went unreported in the British press and it was not until the late 1990's that their fates became known.

A diver exploring a "hanger" or "fastener" – in fisherman's parlance, an obstruction on the seabed, found himself on an old, iron steamship. Finding the area where the bridge had collapsed, he recovered and later cleaned the centre brass hub of the ship's steering wheel. The mystery was solved when the name *Vera* was revealed, and the port of registry, Elsinore.

According to Danish records, the only information available was that the two vessels collided in the English Channel, the *Hagda* sinking first, and the *Vera* after a period of some 12 hours.

The wreck believed to be the *Vera* lies in 46 metres of water. She is broken but much remains on the seabed, her single boiler, two smaller donkey boilers and compound engine being the highest parts. The engine lies over to port while the stern leans over to starboard. The reason the wreck is only believed to be the *Vera* is because the GPS position written down by the diver was subsequently lost, and the wreck in the position given below is in the immediate vicinity.

Name: *Vera.* **Former name(s):** None.
Vessel type: Steamship with sails.
Builder: Norddeutsche Schiffsbau Gesellschaft, Kiel, Germany.
When completed: May 1873.
Machinery built by: Schweffgel & Company, Kiel, Germany.
Tonnage: 662 tons gross.
Dimensions: Length: 187′. **Breadth:** 27′.
Depth of holds: 14′ 6″.

Official number: – **Yard number:** –
Signal letters: NKHJ. **Last port of registry:** Elsinore.
Ship description: Iron screw steamer. 1 deck and spar deck.
Machinery description: Compound 2 cylinders vertical direct acting steam engines. 1 single ended boiler. 100 horse power.
Career and ownership: Owned by the SS Vera Company Ltd, Elsinore, Denmark.
Destination and cargo: –
Date sunk: 31 January 1874.
How sunk: Collision with the sailing barque *Hagda*.
Reported position of loss: English Channel.
Actual position of wreck: 50° 23.36′ north, 001° 58.17′ west.
Orientation/height: Stands about 4 metres on a stony and shingle seabed, bows to the west.
How identity of wreck proved: Recovery of hub of ship's wheel bearing the name *Vera*. It is not confirmed that the hub was recovered from the wreck in the position given. The wreck of a sailing ship, which may or may not be the *Hagda*, is in position 50° 27.44′ north, 002° 04.14′ west, orientated 000°/180°.

SS *Newbiggin*
Ran aground 3 April 1880

On the night of 2 and 3 April 1880, dense fog prevailed in the English Channel. Steaming up Channel was the North Shields registered steamer, the *Newbiggin.* She was to become the first steamship to fall victim to the Atherfield Ledges on the south coast of the Isle of Wight, an area which had seen many earlier shipwrecks.

Losing her bearings in the fog, the *Newbiggin* ran aground and stuck fast on Atherfield Ledge, a series of three ledges forming shoal waters. When news of the stranding came through, Lloyd's agent attended the scene and reported "Left this wreck at 1pm on 4 April owing to heavy sea. Water is up to the top of the cylinders and level forward. Engine room bulkhead gone. The deck is up. Cabin dry but water running in aft. Landed 41 bales of wool, sound, and 2 lifeboats. Arrangements made to salve all possible. Master remains on the spot. Wind west, strong."

Salvage operations continued in the days following, with some cargo saved as well as stores and fittings from the ship, but the *Newbiggin* became a total loss and was eventually abandoned.

The wreck of this vessel lies in the rocky ground which characterises Atherfield Ledge, along with the scattered remains of a number of other iron hulled and wooden ships. Depths where wreckage lies is in the region of 6 metres.

Name: *Newbiggin.* **Former name(s):** None.
Vessel type: Steamship with sails.
Builder: W Pile & Company, Sunderland.
When completed: 1872.
Machinery built by: W Pile & Company, Sunderland.
Tonnage: 1366 tons gross.
Dimensions: Length: 229′. **Breadth:** 32′.
Depth of holds: 24′ 3″.
Official number: 65442. **Yard number:** –
Signal letters: LKSW. **Last port of registry:** North Shields.
Ship description: Iron screw steamer.
Machinery description: Compound 2 cylinders. 120 horse power.
Career and ownership: Owned by Geoffrey Robinson Dawson, Blyth.
Destination and cargo: Odessa for Dunkirk with grain, rape seed and wool.
Date sunk: 3 April 1880.
How sunk: Ran aground in thick fog.
Reported position of loss: Atherfield Ledge, Isle of Wight.
Actual position of wreck: Approximate: 50° 36.44′ north, 001° 22.10′ west.
Orientation/height: Lies among rocks in 6–8 metres.
How identity of wreck proved: Not proved but contemporary reports from 1880 confirm the *Newbiggin* was the ship involved.

SS *Claremont*
Ran aground 27 January 1881

Lloyd's agent based on the Isle of Wight at Cowes reported on 28 January 1881 that a tug had returned from the site of the stranding of the steamer *Claremont* at Whale Chine, on the south coast of the island, and that she was "ashore there, broadside to the beach, position very bad. Seas making clean breach over her. Crew were apparently landed, no boats being visible on board."

The *Claremont* had been proceeding up the English Channel when she encountered dense fog and a heavy sea. Losing her bearings in the darkness and poor visibility, she ran into shoal water just to the west of Whale Chine. The crew of 19 all managed to get clear in the ship's boats, some reaching land unaided, others being picked up after searches by various lifeboats. All the men were saved. The outlook for the *Claremont*, however, was very different.

It was reported that there was little chance of salvage, and later that day on 28th she was rapidly going to pieces in the heavy ground swell then running. *Claremont* quickly became a total wreck and her master was subsequently punished for the loss of the ship, his certificate being suspended for six months.

Wreckage in Chale Bay from Atherfield Ledge to St Catherine's Point, which includes Whale Chine, moves in storm conditions. Some pieces have been known to move as much as a quarter of a mile during a winter. Other parts cover and uncover in the sand and shingle, but the depths in which some of the *Claremont's* remains lie are about 6 metres.

Name: *Claremont.* **Former name(s):** None.
Vessel type: Steam brig with sails.
Builder: Backhouse & Dixon, Middlesbrough.
When completed: 1871.
Machinery built by: Blair & Company Ltd, Stockton.
Tonnage: 1129 tons gross.
Dimensions: Length: 226′. **Breadth:** 30′ 2″.
Depth of holds: 17′.
Official number: 62622. **Yard number:** –
Signal letters: KGLD. **Last port of registry:** Newcastle.
Ship description: Iron screw steamer.
Machinery description: Compound 2 cylinders. 99 horse power.
Career and ownership: *Claremont* was the first vessel blown ashore at South Shields during the great storm of 21 December 1876, but she was refloated several days later. Owned in 1878 by W Wilson & Company, and from 1880 by Fisher, Renwick & Company.
Destination and cargo: Vallerigan for Middlesbrough with a cargo of iron ore and copper ore.
Date sunk: 27 January 1881.
How sunk: Ran aground in dense fog.
Reported position of loss: About 100 yards west of Whale Chine.
Actual position of wreck: Approximate position is 50° 36.08′ north, 001° 20.58′ west.
Orientation/height: Such wreckage as remains is flattened on a sand and shingle seabed in about 6 metres.
How identity of wreck proved: Contemporary reports from 1881 identify the *Claremont* in this position.

SS *Essen*
Ran aground 6 March 1881

SS *Essen* aground at Rocken End near St Catherine's Point. Courtesy St Catherine's Quay Museum, Blackgang Chine.

Thick fog covered the coast of the Isle of Wight as the German steamer *Essen* proceeded up Channel in March 1881. She had come from Bilbao and was making for Rotterdam, but she was hopelessly off course. This was not altogether surprising, as her master later recalled "fog has been so dense the whole voyage that we had not had an observation since leaving Bilbao." At 3am on 6 March in appalling visibility and a heavy sea, with a south west wind blowing on to a lee shore, *Essen* ran ashore just to the west of St Catherine's Point at a place known as Rocken End. She stranded at high water and was soon embedded in the sand, but as the tide receded her crew simply walked ashore unharmed.

Essen, heavily laden with a full cargo of iron ore, quickly filled with water and it was feared at an early stage the ship would become a total wreck. Nevertheless, hopes were entertained of saving the ship and salvaging materials, and work commenced to salve as much as possible. The situation did not look good. She was broadside to the sea and the wind and sea continued from the south west. Within a day or two her hull had been buried in sand to a depth of 11 feet. She was almost high and dry at low water, but her engine room and holds had filled with water and it soon became obvious that the ship was finished.

Since 1881, the cliffs at Rocken End have receded through natural erosion, and the beach has advanced, so that the remains of the *Essen* lie in 5 or 6 metres of water. She has been flattened by decades of storms and ground swells.

Name: *Essen.* **Former name(s):** None.
Vessel type: Steamship with sails.
Builder: Nrddtsh Shipyard, Kiel, Germany.
When completed: January 1874.
Machinery built by: Schwffel & Howldt, Kiel, Germany.
Tonnage: 1248 tons gross.
Dimensions: Length: 240′. **Breadth:** 32′.
Depth of holds: 21′.
Official number: – **Yard number:** –
Signal letters: LCDN. **Last port of registry:** Kiel.
Ship description: Iron screw steamer.
Machinery description: Compound inverted 2 cylinders. 125 horse power.
Career and ownership: Owned by Fred Krupp.
Destination and cargo: Bilbao for Rotterdam with a cargo of iron ore.
Date sunk: 6 March 1881.
How sunk: Ran aground in thick fog.
Reported position of loss: Rocken End, just west of St Catherine's Point.
Actual position of wreck: Approximate position is 50° 34.71′ north, 001° 18.56′ west.
Orientation/height: Wreckage is flattened on a rock, sand and shingle seabed in about 6 metres.
How identity of wreck proved: Contemporary reports from the time identify the *Essen* in this position.

Schooner *Fenna*
Foundered 11 March 1881

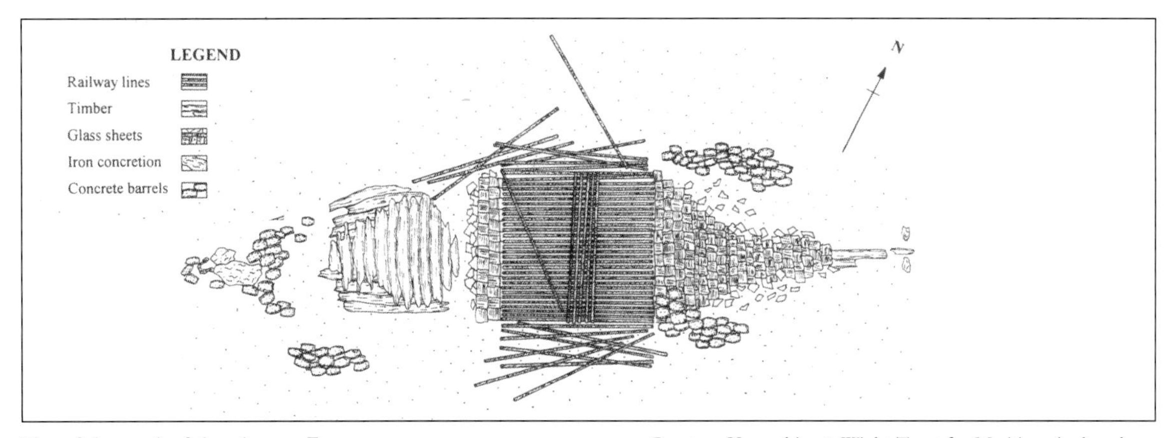

Plan of the wreck of the schooner *Fenna*. Courtesy Hampshire & Wight Trust for Maritime Archaeology.

The first anyone knew that the schooner *Fenna* had been lost was when her crew arrived in the ship's boat in Poole Bay. Heading for the red light which glowed in the dark and which turned out to be the end of Bournemouth Pier, they received refreshments and directions to Poole, where the master and four crew subsequently landed.

Their tale was that their ship, bound down Channel, had experienced heavy gales and the *Fenna* began to leak. The water gained so much that the ship became disabled and waterlogged. The crew consulted the master and it was agreed that their only hope was to abandon the *Fenna* and take to the ship's boat. Unseen, *Fenna* later filled completely and sank.

A few days after the ship had gone down, the master of the steamer *Ventnor*, William Gardner, reported passing a sunken wreck with one mast projecting, about 2 miles west by north of the Needles Lighthouse. This was the *Fenna*.

The wreck of the *Fenna* lies in about 24 metres of water and is like an oasis in the desert. The surrounding seabed is flat, but the wreck stands up to provide shelter for a variety of life. Her cargo of railway lines, barrels and cases of sheet glass are clearly evident in the wreck, and some of the bottom of the hull is still visible. She appears to have sunk in an upright position. She is a safe, easy dive.

Name: *Fenna*. **Former name(s):** None.
Vessel type: Schooner.
Builder: At Hoogezand.
When completed: 1863.
Machinery built by: –
Tonnage: 172 tons gross.
Dimensions: Length: – **Breadth:** –
Depth of holds: –
Official number: – **Yard number:** –
Signal letters: – **Last port of registry:** –
Ship description: Wooden 2 masted schooner.
Machinery description: –
Career and ownership: Owned by J A Hooites, Hoogezand.
Destination and cargo: Amsterdam for Messina and Trieste with 230 tons of cargo including bar iron, iron in barrels, sheet glass in cases.
Date sunk: 11 March 1881.
How sunk: Became leaky and waterlogged and foundered in heavy weather.
Reported position of loss: 20 miles from land. Wreck reported 2 miles west by north of the Needles.
Actual position of wreck: 50° 38.44′ north, 001° 40.47′ west.
Orientation/height: Stands 2.5 metres in 24 metres on a flat, shingle seabed.
How identity of wreck proved: Type of cargo is very distinctive and the position of the wreck is close to where the projecting mast was reported in 1881.

SS *Wheatfield*
Ran aground 31 December 1882

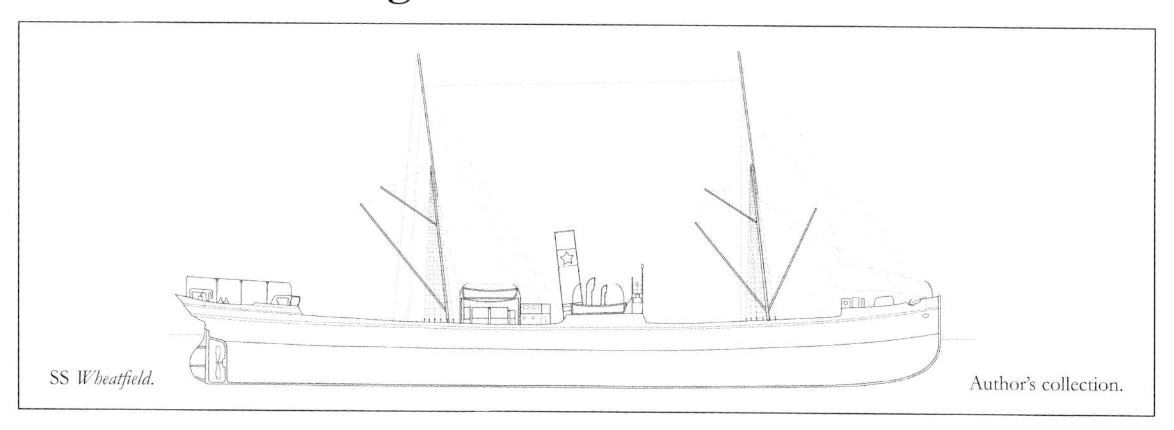
SS *Wheatfield*. Author's collection.

The wrecking of the steamer *Wheatfield* proved to be a welcome event for the local people of Blackgang, Isle of Wight. The ship carried a full cargo of foodstuffs and this was too good an opportunity to miss. Her loss was in familiar circumstances; she was caught up in the curse of the south coast of the Isle of Wight, dense fog.

About 7.40pm on New Year's Eve, 1882, the *Wheatfield* ran ashore about 100 yards to the west of the *Essen,* at Rocken End, not far from St Catherine's Point. Her crew of 26 hands saved themselves in the ship's boats and there was no loss of life. It was reported the next morning, "the steamer now (7am) lies with her head to the westward entirely covered at half tide. Her deck is exposed to the sea and her mainmast and funnel have gone by the board. Should the weather remain as it is, which is doubtful, the prospects for salvage are favourable, the beach being strewn with sacks of flour washing out of her holds. It seems likely the *Wheatfield* will become a total wreck. Wind west south west, moderate, thick fog and rain."

As the day wore on, the *Wheatfield* became a total wreck. The hull broke up and disappeared and much cargo had washed ashore. Flour, tinned meat and oil cake was washing about in the surf and being cast ashore, a great deal being lost "for want of labour to get it up the cliffs."

The remains of the *Wheatfield* lie in about 6 metres of water, a boiler, riddled with holes, being most prominent. The remainder of the wreck has been flattened, with wreckage crushed and forced into crevices and gullies. Her bell is in the Spyglass Inn at Ventnor.

Name: *Wheatfield*. **Former name(s):** None.
Vessel type: Steam ship with sails.
Builder: Palmers Company Ltd, Newcastle.
When completed: May 1879.
Machinery built by: Palmers Company Ltd, Newcastle.
Tonnage: 1963 tons gross.
Dimensions: Length: 270′. **Breadth:** 35′ 3″.
Depth of holds: 24′.
Official number: 81552. **Yard number:** –
Signal letters: SNVF. **Last port of registry:** London.
Ship description: Iron screw steamer.
Machinery description: Compound inverted 2 cylinders. 200 nominal horse power.
Career and ownership: Owned by Hunting & Pattison.
Destination and cargo: New York for Leith with general cargo including flour, tinned meat and oil cake.
Date sunk: 31 December 1882.
How sunk: Ran aground in dense fog.
Reported position of loss: Rocken End, west of St Catherine's Point, 100 yards west of the *Essen*.
Actual position of wreck: Close position 50° 34.02′ north, 001° 18.92′ west.
Orientation/height: Flattened except for a boiler standing about 2 metres.
How identity of wreck proved: Contemporary reports from 1882 identify the *Wheatfield* and its position of loss.

SS *Iduna*
Collision 26 May 1883

On the morning of 25 May 1883, the steamer *Iduna* was off St Catherine's Point, experiencing one of the Channel's troublesome thick fogs. She was heading down Channel for Malaga having departed the north east of England a few days earlier. Heading towards her was the 603 ton barque *Zadok*, on her voyage from Iquique for Hamburg with a cargo of nitrate of soda. At 7.10am the two vessels met in the fog, the *Zadok* running into the *Iduna,* carrying away *Zadok's* jibboom and stoving in her bows.

The unfortunate steamer was severely damaged, but her crew of 19 hands just had sufficient time to rescue some of their belongings before abandoning the *Iduna* and making off in the ship's boats, later landing at Ventnor. Their ship subsequently disappeared.

The wreck of the *Iduna* lies more or less with the tide in 40 metres of water. The stern section as far forward as the boilers is upright and intact, while the bow section lies on its starboard side. Large lumps of coal in the wreck are evidence of her cargo. The highest part of the wreck is the machinery, her engines standing up about 5 metres off the seabed. Great care should be taken when diving this wreck on high water. It is important to take full advantage of slack water. As the tide turns, a strong vortex of water develops across the stern section, catching out the unwary by preventing ascent. Should this happen the diver will have to allow himself to be carried well clear of the wreck before the vortex weakens to allow ascent.

Name: *Iduna.* **Former name(s):** None.
Vessel type: Steam ship with sails.
Builder: T & W Smith, North Shields.
When completed: March 1868.
Machinery built by: Ouseburn Engineering Works, Newcastle. Engine No 184.
Tonnage: 859 tons gross.
Dimensions: Length: 214′ 7″. **Breadth:** 29′ 3″.
Depth of holds: 17′ 7″.
Official number: 56095. **Yard number:** –
Signal letters: HCPM. **Last port of registry:** Newcastle.
Ship description: Iron screw steamer. 3 masts.
Machinery description: Compound inverted 2 cylinders. 2 single ended boilers. 120 horse power.
Career and ownership: Owned in 1882 by Elliotts, Lowry & Dunford. In 1883 owned by J Elliott, Newcastle upon Tyne.
Destination and cargo: South Shields for Malaga with a cargo of coal.
Date sunk: 26 May 1883.
How sunk: Collision in dense fog with the sailing barque *Zadok*.
Reported position of loss: Off St Catherine's Point.
Actual position of wreck: 50° 25.03′ north, 001° 25.68′ west.
Orientation/height: Lies 090°/270°. Stands 5 metres on a shingle seabed.
How identity of wreck proved: Ship's bell and engine builder's nameplate recovered.

Sailing ship *Waitara* Collision 22 June 1883

Sailing barque *Waitara*. Courtesy National Maritime Museum, Greenwich.

Many lives were lost when two iron sailing ships owned by the same company came into collision in the English Channel on the night of 22 June 1883. The ships, the *Waitara*, 883 tons, and the 1053 ton *Hurunui*, were owned by the New Zealand Shipping company based in Christchurch, New Zealand. According to reports, the two ships left London at about the same time, both being bound for New Zealand ports with full general cargoes.

On 19 June 1883 both ships departed Gravesend. The *Waitara,* under the command of her master Kennedy Webster, had a crew of 25 hands, 16 passengers and a stowaway. Dropping off her pilot at Dover, *Waitara* set sail down Channel against a fresh south westerly breeze and all seems to have proceeded normally. The *Hurunui*, under the command of her master Captain Hazlewood, being a bigger ship, had a larger crew of 30, as well as two passengers and two stowaways. She too dropped her pilot off at Dover and commenced to beat down Channel under full sail. The ships had frequently been in sight of each other as they sailed down Channel and both were well aware of the other's presence, but during the evening of 22 June the conditions for those on watch had deteriorated as "the weather was thick with rain" and "the moon was hidden in the mist." Crucially, this occurred at a time when the vessels had come into close range of each other when about 25 miles south east of Portland Bill.

Waitara was sailing on the port tack and heading west-north-west, when the red light of another ship, which proved to be that of the *Hurunui,* was sighted about a mile and a half distant. Her lookout man immediately reported this, since it was the duty of the *Waitara* to give way to the other ship. There was no response from the second officer to his report, and he repeated it again a minute later. There was even a suggestion that it was necessary for the report to be made a third time before the second officer came to deal with the report. The *Hurunui* was on a starboard tack and under the rules for preventing collisions at sea, *Waitara* had to give way. When the second officer eventually became aware of the impending danger – possibly after the third time the lookout man made his report – he ordered evasive action to be taken and waved the binnacle lamp to indicate to the other ship that she had been seen. The ship's captain, Mr Webster, who was asleep below, was summoned but by the time he reached the deck *Hurunui* was almost upon them.

Hurunui was heading south-south-east on the starboard tack when her lookout sighted the glow of the green starboard light from *Waitara.* Although the chief mate was on watch, the ship's master had just gone below to check the chart when he heard that the green light of the *Waitara* had been sighted. At once, he came up on deck and ordered the ship to be "luffed up to the wind" and for the chief mate to go forward and blow the ship's fog horn. Seeing the reassuring sight of the *Waitara's* binnacle lamp being waved, the *Hurunui* maintained her starboard tack, close hauled to the wind.

What *Hurunui's* master did not know was the dithering which then took place on board *Waitara*, with first the helm being altered, and then returned to its position. No obvious and decisive action was taken. When it became clear that a collision was inevitable, the *Hurunui's* master ordered the ship's helm hard down in a desperate attempt to lessen the shock of the impact, but *Hurunui* struck *Waitara* hard on her starboard side just abaft the main rigging. Bouncing back a second time, she then struck her again just forward of the break of the poop. A passenger on *Hurunui* recalled, "about 10.15 soon after we retired for the night, I was awakened by a sudden shock, and at the same time the captain burst into the cabin and ordered everyone on deck. A large vessel was at our bows, and its white ports stood out plainly in the dark night" ...... "I rushed below to wrap up in case we might have to use the boats. I was not down a minute and when I returned the ship had already disappeared." Another passenger said, "it did not seem to crash but to break through the side like so much cardboard."

Efforts to rescue survivors were immediately put into effect from the *Hurunui,* with her boats being lowered to save any lives they could and after a thorough search six or seven persons were rescued. In the event, the master of the *Waitara* and some of her crew had succeeded in scrambling aboard the *Hurunui's* bows while the two ships were briefly locked together. The *Waitara* sank too quickly for there to be many survivors, and 14 crew and 12 passengers were lost, carried down with their ship. Of the original 42 people on board, only 12 crew and four passengers survived.

At the formal investigation into the loss of the *Waitara*, the full circumstances of the collision were examined and the court came to its conclusion. It blamed the second officer of the *Waitara,* who was on watch in the moments leading up to the collision, as, "he appears . . . to have been walking on the weather side of the poop talking to one of the passengers, which was no doubt the reason why the report had to be repeated two, if not three times, before he heard it." The court continued, "the chief blame for the collision rests with the second officer of the *Waitara*, but he was unfortunately drowned." They went on to blame the master of the *Waitara* for "having left the deck when the vessel was in the Channel, heading for the land, and on the port tack, instead of being, as he ought to have been, on deck, attending to the navigation of the vessel." In the opinion of the court, he was guilty of great negligence.

The wreck of the *Waitara* lies in about 60 metres of water. She is more or less upright, but leans to starboard. Some of her cargo has spilled from the hull onto the seabed off the starboard side of the wreck. The bow section is most prominent but the wreck becomes less so until the stern area, which does not stand much above the seabed. The wreck still contains a great deal of cargo in the form of bottled goods, crockery, flagons, glassware and so on.

Name: *Waitara.* **Former name(s):** *Hindostan.*
Vessel type: Sailing barque.
Builder: J Reid, Port Glasgow.
When completed: November 1863.
Machinery built by: –
Tonnage: 883 gross.
Dimensions: Length: 191′ 3″. **Breadth:** 31′ 4″.
Depth of holds: 20′ 9″.
Official number: 47634. **Yard number:** –
Signal letters: VPKM. **Last port of registry:** Lyttelton, New Zealand.
Ship description: Iron sailing barque.
Machinery description: –
Career and ownership: As *Hindostan*, the ship was owned by the British & Eastern Shipping Company Ltd, and registered in Liverpool until 1874. She then became the first ship owned by the New Zealand Shipping Company in 1874 when she was renamed *Waitara.*
Destination and cargo: London for Wellington with general cargo and 16 passengers.
Date sunk: 22 June 1883.
How sunk: Collision with the sailing ship *Hurunui.*
Reported position of loss: 20 to 25 miles south east of Portland Bill.
Actual position of wreck: 50° 14.54′ north, 001° 54.39′ west.
Orientation/height: Lies 130°/310°. Stands 6 metres on a seabed of shingle. Bows to the north west.
How identity of wreck proved: Ship's bell recovered.

SS *Ferncliffe*
Collision 19 September 1883

The first news of the "shocking disaster off the Needles" came when the German steamer *Habsburg* docked at Southampton, having earlier come across four ship's boats off the Needles containing the master, family and crew from the Italian barque *Fratelli Gaggino*, numbering 15 all told. The *Fratelli Gaggino,* on a voyage from Dunkirk for Cardiff in ballast had been sailing in clear weather when the French pilot on board reported that a big steam vessel was upon them. Before they could alter her course "she crashed into her bulwarks and sailed away." The barque immediately filled and sank in less than half an hour in a position reported as 15 miles south of Durleston off Anvil Point.

The steamer turned out to be the 547 ton ship *Ferncliffe.* Her crew said that on sighting the barque, which was on a course which would take her clear of the *Ferncliffe,* she suddenly altered course when very close at hand and almost immediately collided with their ship. In the impact, *Ferncliffe's* funnel was carried away and a hole some 7 feet square was caused amidships by the bows of the *Fratelli Gaggino.* All hands were quickly on *Ferncliffe's* deck and every effort was made to keep her afloat.

Ferncliffe's master, Captain Sewell, knowing his ship was badly damaged, decided to run for Poole. Steaming at full speed the crew of 12 "worked most earnestly in their endeavours to save the vessel." All their work, however, was in vain, as water gained inside the ship. After striving for nearly 3 hours and making a distance of some 10 miles, the crew realised they had lost the battle, and they took to the boats and watched as their ship sank.

Ferncliffe settled in a completely upright position, her foremast above the water, "a matter of some curiosity and speculation on the part of the many passengers by the local steamboats between Bournemouth and Swanage." The position was marked to warn other vessels but it was doubted if anything could be salved.

The wreck of the *Ferncliffe* has been shown on the chart for many years, it making its first appearance around 1885. However, it has acquired the name of a ship sunk in the Second World War, the *Leny,* which struck a mine and sank in a position very close by. Many divers believe they have dived the *Leny* when in fact the wreck is the *Ferncliffe.* The remains lying on the seabed in 16 metres are largely buried in the seabed, though a boiler, propeller shaft and some plating and minor machinery is evident.

Name: *Ferncliffe.* **Former name(s):** None.
Vessel type: Steam ship with sails.
Builder: Palmer's Company, Sunderland.
When completed: June 1883.
Machinery built by: J Gilmour & Company, Glasgow.
Tonnage: 547 tons gross.
Dimensions: Length: 165′. **Breadth:** 26′ 3″
Depth of holds: 12′ 7″.
Official number: 83589. **Yard number:** –
Signal letters: HLMS. **Last port of registry:** Maryport.
Ship description: Iron screw steamer.
Machinery description: Compound inverted 2 cylinders. 80 horse power.
Career and ownership: Owned by J Melmore & Company, Maryport.
Destination and cargo: Workington for Newhaven with 600 tons of steel rails.
Date sunk: 19 September 1883.
How sunk: Collision with Italian sailing barque *Fratelli Gaggino.*
Reported position of loss: 5 miles south of Christchurch.
Actual position of wreck: 50° 38.80′ north, 001° 52.60′ west.
Orientation/height: Lies 000°/180°. Stands about 2 metres in 16 metres on a soft seabed of mud, sand and shingle.
How identity of wreck proved: Position of wreck corresponds with charted position in 1885.

SS *Castle Crag*
Ran aground 14 December 1883

The nearly new steamer *Castle Crag* was the second of three steamships to be wrecked on Brook Ledges, Isle of Wight, and the presence of thick fog was again partly to blame for the subsequent loss of this ship.

At the Court of Enquiry which was held to determine the circumstances of loss, the court ruled that, in their opinion, the ship "was supplied with proper and sufficient compasses" and that the master, Captain Auguste Arendrup, took bearings to verify his position when off the Casquets, but he "did not then and thereafter set and steer proper courses as he did not make due allowance for the strong spring ebb tide." The court continued, "the master was not justified in proceeding at full speed with the square sail set without first taking any precaution to verify the position of his vessel. He should certainly have used the lead, have slackened his speed and taken in sail." The master "had committed a grave error of judgement in not making sufficient allowance for the strong spring ebb tide and the master was in default for not using his lead and proceeding in thick weather at full speed and with sail set." The punishment was that Captain Arendrup had his certificate suspended for six months.

Castle Crag had left Odessa for Antwerp on 20 November 1883 with a crew of 31 hands and a cargo of grain and cattle. The voyage had proceeded normally and the ship's position was fixed on 13 December when a sighting of the Casquets light was made. In the early hours of 14 December, the chief officer was on watch and had expected to have sighted St Catherine's light by about 2am. The weather had become hazy and threatening and as a result, Captain Arendrup was called from his berth. By 3am the haze had thickened to dense fog and a slight alteration of course was made, Captain Arendrup remaining on the bridge throughout. Full speed was maintained when suddenly land and breakers was sighted. Although the helm was put hard down, almost immediately afterwards the *Castle Crag* bumped onto the Brook Ledge on the south coast of the Isle of Wight, and came to a stop. She began to settle and fill with water and the crew made preparations to abandon ship. Seas began sweeping over the ship and signals of distress were fired. Within a very short time, Brook lifeboat was launched, the sea at this time described as "one sheet of rolling, breaking and tumbling white waves, breaking clean over the lifeboat."

On board *Castle Crag*, the crew had taken to the main rigging and lashed themselves on to await rescue. The lifeboat, having been rowed the half mile to the wreck, was unable to come alongside the ship, and the crew had to jump into the sea and be hauled aboard the lifeboat. Eighteen men were rescued in this way when a huge wave pitched the lifeboat hard up against the *Castle Crag*. Five more men took their chances and jumped into the lifeboat, and these were all landed safely. Although "the waves ran like mountains" the lifeboat returned to the wreck and successfully took off the remaining nine men including the captain and all the officers.

In the days following, the ship was surveyed by divers and declared not in a fit state to float. Salvage operations were commenced and valuable stores, gear and cargo were recovered. At some time the ship had slewed round so her head faced the south west, and the bad weather continued, hampering efforts to survey the vessel properly. The Liverpool Salvage Association reported, "boarded *Castle Crag* this morning. Blowing too hard, with bad sea, to survey properly, but from what could be seen, little hope of saving the vessel. Engines and boilers disturbed, funnel up 18″, water throughout inside level with outside. Ship very low in the water." Five days after the stranding, it was reported the ship had broken across the boilers and was breaking in two at the engine space. She had become a total loss.

The wreck of the *Castle Crag* lies in 6–9 metres of water in among the rocks and gullies of Brook Ledge. A prominent capstan and two hawse pipes are all that remain of the bow section, but both boilers are there, one at right angles to the other as well as a great deal of mainly flattened hull plating. There is a large, humpbacked rock in the centre of the wreck, the boilers on the south west side, and the remains of machinery and condenser tubes on the north east side. It is clear that this is the rock upon which the *Castle Crag* settled and broke in two. Evidently the ship's bell was recovered soon after the ship was abandoned and is on display in the village of Brighstone.

Some refer to this wreck as *Castle Craig* but *Castle Crag* is the correct name.

Name: *Castle Crag.* **Former name(s):** None.
Vessel type: Steam ship with sails.
Builder: W Richardson & Company, Newcastle.
When completed: September 1883.
Machinery built by: W Richardson & Company, Newcastle.
Tonnage: 2428 tons gross.
Dimensions: Length: 301′. **Breadth:** 37′ 2″.
Depth of holds: 27′ 4″.
Official number: – **Yard number:** –
Signal letters: – **Last port of registry:** Liverpool.
Ship description: Iron screw steamer. 1 deck. Spar deck.
Machinery description: Compound 2 cylinders. 300 horse power. 2 single ended boilers.
Career and ownership: Owned by Castle Crag Steam Ship Company Ltd.
Destination and cargo: Odessa for Antwerp with 3000 tons of wheat, barley, maize, oil cake, feathers and 175 cattle.
Date sunk: 14 December 1883.
How sunk: Ran aground in thick fog.
Reported position of loss: Brook Ledge half a mile offshore.
Actual position of wreck: 50° 38.01′ north, 001° 27.12′ west.
Orientation/height: Lies 240°/040°. Stands no more than 1 metre in 6–9 metres on seabed of rock and rock gullies and shingle.
How identity of wreck proved: Contemporary reports say the wreck stranded half a mile from shore with her bows to the south west. Wreck lies in this position.

Sailing barque *Simla*
Collision 25 January 1884

Simla in her days as a P & O steamer before conversion to a sailing ship. Courtesy National Maritime Museum, Greenwich.

On a January night in 1884, two large sailing ships found themselves on a collision course about 25 miles west south west of the Needles. The Australian clipper ship *City of Lucknow* was bound from Port Adelaide for London with a cargo of wool, sailing up Channel with a crew of 28 hands. The other vessel was the former P & O ship *Simla*, now converted to a four masted sailing barque, on voyage London for Sydney with a full general cargo. She had on board some 50 persons all told, including two passengers, under the command of Captain Malcolm Nicholson.

About 8pm on Friday 25 January 1884, "the weather at the time being very thick and squally, with heavy seas running, the two vessels, one on her course up Channel and the other down, were sighted, and before they could steer clear of each other they came in collision, the *Simla* being struck amidships, and some of her boats stove in. She rebounded, but struck a second time, carrying away the two main masts of the *Simla*, her mizzen and foretop masts, and her jibboom, the wreckage smashing her boats." According to Captain James Macdonald of the *City of Lucknow*, they had made a very good passage from Australia of 84 days and when some 18 miles south of Anvil Point, the night was "as dark as pitch and very threatening. A light was seen ahead and then the ships met with a heavy crash." The ships remained locked together for 10 or 15 minutes, and through this many were saved – perhaps as many as 30 in number.

In a stroke of good fortune, the steamer *Guernsey* was in the vicinity and saw signals of distress, and reaching the scene rescued a number of survivors in boats. Although remaining on the spot for some hours, "the violence of the storm preventing any further assistance being rendered" the *Guernsey* put into Yarmouth where the survivors were landed. They reported at the time they left the *Simla*, she had about 9 feet of water in her holds, and that the captain and his wife and child and some of the crew had managed to escape to the *City of Lucknow* while the two vessels were in contact with each other.

A passing steamer, the *Nicholas Vagliano*, came across 23 survivors and saved them all. She then stood by the stricken *Simla* and attempted to get her under tow. By midday on the 26 January, with the storm still raging, Captain Macdonald could see from the *City of Lucknow* that the *Simla* was still afloat and heading towards Southampton though it was not clear if she was being blown along or if she was under tow.

News that the *Simla* had finally sunk came when the *Nicholas Vagliano* arrived in Dunkirk with some of *Simla's* survivors. Although they had been close to the Isle of Wight, the towing operation could not cope with the weather, and *Simla* was abandoned to her fate.

In the days following, huge quantities of debris appeared off the Sussex coast. Among the cargo washed ashore were "twelve 36 gallon casks of wine, 2 pianos, perfume, money, jewellery, furniture of every description. A monkey came ashore alive. Cognac, rum, whiskey and gin and quantities of brandy in bottles." This set the scene for unparalleled drunkenness, with casks being broached and "all the scum of Brighton got scent of the plunder" with some "drinking spirits from their hats, and afterwards were lying on the grass, some, I am afraid, dying, and others nearly so." A complaint was made to the police for more assistance, as "the policemen here could do nothing with 200 to 300 roughs."

The wreck of the *Simla* lies upright in 40 metres of water south of St Catherine's Point. Although the hull has collapsed outwards and is fairly flat, a great deal of cargo remains piled up in the wreck, including two small shunting steam trains, packs of corrugated iron, barrels, crockery, bottles; some containing foodstuffs, other containing alcohol, tiles, glass, rolls of lead and so on.

Name: *Simla.* **Former name(s):** None.
Vessel type: Sailing barque.
Builder: Tod & McGregor, Glasgow.
When completed: 1854.
Machinery built by: –
Tonnage: 2288 tons gross.
Dimensions: Length: 330′ 2″. **Breadth:** 39′ 8″. **Depth of holds:** 26′ 7″.
Official number: 13952. **Yard number:** 70.
Signal letters: LKDC. **Last port of registry:** Glasgow.
Ship description: Iron 4 masted sailing barque.
Machinery description: –
Career and ownership: Originally owned by P & O as a steamer and launched on 30 January 1854. Employed on the Southampton to Alexandria route, later Suez to Calcutta service. In 1854 she was requisitioned as a transport (No 118) for the Crimea war. When returned to commercial service she was chartered to European & Australian Royal Mail Company for whom she completed 3 sailings. In 1878 her machinery was removed and she was converted as a sailing vessel. In September she was sold to Devitt & Moore, London, who owned her at the time of loss.
Destination and cargo: London for Sydney with full general cargo.
Date sunk: 25 January 1884.
How sunk: Collision with the clipper ship *City of Lucknow.*
Reported position of loss: Position of collision 18 miles south of Anvil Point, and 25 miles west south west of the Needles.
Actual position of wreck: 50° 29.97′ north, 001° 21.56′ west.
Orientation/height: Lies 160°/340°. Stands 3–4 metres on hard chalk seabed.
How identity of wreck proved: Ship's crockery from her P & O days.

SS *Messina*
Collision 14 May 1885

SS *Messina*, from an oil painting. Author's collection.

The German steamer *Messina* left Lisbon on 10 May 1885, bound for Hamburg with a cargo of 1200 tons of iron ore. She carried a crew of 22 hands and one passenger. About 9pm on the evening of 14th, she was steaming eastwards in fine, clear weather, on a smooth sea with a breeze from the north. The ship's master, evidently satisfied all was well, left the deck and retired to the chart-room to lie down, leaving the ship in control of the chief officer, whose watch consisted of three AB's and the boatswain. The *Messina* continued on her course at her top speed of 8 ½ knots. Sighting the light from Durlston Head off her port side just over an hour later, the ship was well on its way to reaching its destination.

Steaming towards the *Messina* was a much larger vessel, the 2544 ton *Numida,* a British steamer bound from London for New York with 1800 tons of cargo. She was steaming at her top speed of 9 ½ knots steering west by north, and her estimated position about 8pm on the evening of 14 May was 16 or 17 miles off St Catherine's Point. Her master, like the master of the *Messina,* decided to go to his cabin to lie down, leaving his ship in the charge of the chief officer and his watch.

The events which followed were subject to some scrutiny from the subsequent Court of Enquiry, hearing as they did from those on board the *Numida,* and from the survivors of the *Messina,* as "it is said, and with truth, that both these stories cannot be true."

Those on watch on both ships were aware of the other's presence, as their respective navigation lamps were lit and clearly visible. Each saw the masthead lamps of the other ship, but as they closed each other, their green and red lamps came into view. The *Numida* maintained her course, as she was bound to do, but the *Messina* failed to alter hers in time in order to avoid the inevitable collision. *Messina's* master immediately rushed on deck as soon as he heard someone shout, "hard a'port" and heard the whistle blowing. By the time he reached the bridge he saw the *Numida* on a collision course only two ship's lengths away. Ordering all crew on deck, the *Numida* then crashed into *Messina's* port side about 30 feet from the stern, cutting into her some 10 or 12 feet. In an instant, eight crew members clambered aboard the *Numida,* while a further five men jumped overboard and were quickly picked up. The damage was so severe that *Messina* went to the bottom in less than 3 minutes. The *Numida* remained on the spot until daylight amid a great quantity of wreckage but no more survivors were found. Ten men had perished.

What was established with certainty at the Court of Enquiry was that the two vessels were approaching each other in a crossing situation, and that in those circumstances, it was the duty of the vessel which had the other on its starboard side to give way. Since the *Messina* had the *Numida* on her starboard side, *Messina* was under a duty to give way. The Court ruled that in every respect the fault for the collision lay with the *Messina*. She had failed to alter course as required by the regulations for preventing collisions at sea, and she had failed to ease her engines, or stop and reverse if necessary. Finally, she had improperly ported her helm and together, these failings brought about the collision.

The wreck of the *Messina* lies upright in 50 metres of water. Her engines and single boiler plus donkey boiler are the highest parts of the wreck. Not much of the hull stands up. There is a large hump of cargo forward of the boilers which appears to be coal, but is in fact iron ore. A spare propeller lies off to starboard aft of the engines. Some kind of pressure vessel is fitted on top of the boiler. An iron cannon, probably the signal gun, lies off the bows.

Name: *Messina.* **Former name(s):** None.
Vessel type: Steam ship with sails.
Builder: Denton Gray & Company, West Hartlepool.
When completed: August 1872.
Machinery built by: T Richardson & Sons, West Hartlepool.
Tonnage: 1063 gross.
Dimensions: Length: 230′ 5″. **Breadth:** 29′ 8″.
Depth of holds: 17′.
Official number: – **Yard number:** –
Signal letters: RDLQ. **Last port of registry:** Hamburg.
Ship description: Iron screw steamer. 2 decks.
Machinery description: Compound inverted 2 cylinders. 1 single ended boiler. 110 horse power.
Career and ownership: Owned by R M Sloman & Company, Hamburg.
Destination and cargo: Lisbon to Hamburg with 1200 tons iron ore and 1 passenger.
Date sunk: 14 May 1885.
How sunk: Collision with SS *Numida.*
Reported position of loss: 25 miles south west of St Catherine's Point.
Actual position of wreck: 50° 18.45′ north, 001° 49.28′ west.
Orientation/height: Stands 5 metres on flat sandy/shingle seabed.
How identity of wreck proved: Ship's bell and builder's nameplate recovered.

SS *Olive Branch*
Collision 5 June 1885

When the steamer *Olive Branch* was lost her passing did not attract a great deal of interest. A brief entry in the local newspapers reported, "During a dense fog on Friday morning and when about 30 miles off St Catherine's Point, the steamer *Olive Branch* collided with the SS *Tudor Prince* from Taganrog for Lynn. The *Olive Branch* sank in about 10 minutes. Her crew, 22 in number, saved themselves by lowering their boats and getting on board the *Tudor Prince*. The *Tudor Prince*, which received serious damage, proceeded towards the Island and anchored at the Motherbank whence she subsequently came up to Southampton for repairs. She is now in the Docks."

There is no information as to whether or not this wreck has been located or identified.

Name: *Olive Branch*. **Former name(s):** None.
Vessel type: Steam ship with sails.
Builder: W Doxford, Sunderland.
When completed: September 1881.
Machinery built by: W Doxford, Sunderland.
Tonnage: 1728 gross.
Dimensions: Length: 260′. **Breadth:** 36′.
Depth of holds: 18′ 5″.
Official number: 84993. **Yard number:** –
Signal letters: WDQF. **Last port of registry:** Sunderland.
Ship description: Iron screw steamer. 1 iron deck.
Machinery description: Compound inverted 2 cylinders. 2 single ended boilers. 160 horse power.
Career and ownership: Owned by Nautilus Steamship Company Ltd, Sunderland.
Destination and cargo: Sunderland for Palermo with coal and gas fittings.
Date sunk: 5 June 1885.
How sunk: Collision with the SS *Tudor Prince*.
Reported position of loss: 25 to 30 miles south west of the Owers Light Vessel.
Actual position of wreck: Not known.
Orientation/height: –
How identity of wreck proved: –

SS *Clarinda*
Collision 17 October 1885

The night of Saturday 17 October 1885, was a clear, bright, moonlit night. That two steamers should come into contact and collide in such clear visibility is surprising, particularly as it was reported "both ships were distinctly visible to each other."

About 7pm, the two ships, the *Tern,* sister ship to the ill fated *Lapwing* sunk only a few miles away in 1872, and the *Clarinda* were 12–13 miles south west of St Catherine's Point. The *Tern* was bound up Channel from Liverpool for Rotterdam, while the *Clarinda* was also steaming up Channel bound from Cardiff for Cronstadt.

The *Tern* was in the process of overtaking the *Clarinda* and "on endeavouring to pass, the *Clarinda* was struck amidships, and sunk about an hour afterwards." The 16 crew from *Clarinda* were picked up by the *Tern,* which proceeded to Southampton in a damaged condition. Exactly how these two ships allowed themselves to manoeuvre in such a close quarters situation is not reported, though *Clarinda's* master, J McGovern, made a statement to the Board of Trade so presumably some sort of enquiry was held.

The wreck of the *Clarinda* lies in 40 metres of water. She is upright but broken and much of her hull has collapsed outwards. Some sections of plating are 20 or 30 metres away from the main body of the wreck. The two boilers and engines are the highest parts.

Name: *Clarinda.* **Former name(s):** None.
Vessel type: Steam ship with sails.
Builder: W Doxford & Company, Sunderland.
When completed: 1871.
Machinery built by: G Clark, Sunderland.
Tonnage: 1075 gross.
Dimensions: Length: 220′ 1″. **Breadth:** 30′ 4″.
Depth of holds: 17′.
Official number: 62629. **Yard number:** –
Signal letters: KLVF. **Last port of registry:** Sunderland.
Ship description: Iron screw steamer.
Machinery description: Compound 2 cylinders. 2 single ended boilers. 98 horse power.
Career and ownership: Owned by G J Hay.
Destination and cargo: Cardiff for Cronstadt with coal cargo.
Date sunk: 17 October 1885.
How sunk: Collision with SS *Tern.*
Reported position of loss: 12–13 miles south west of St Catherine's Point.
Actual position of wreck: 50° 27.86′ north, 001° 39.67′ west.
Orientation/height: Lies 140°/320° bows to the south east. Stands 5 metres on hard shingle/chalk seabed.
How identity of wreck proved: Builder's nameplate recovered.

SS *Cormorant*
Ran aground 21 December 1886

SS *Cormorant* with hard hat diver on deck. Courtesy St Catherine's Quay Museum, Blackgang Chine.

The *Cormorant* was a large steamer of the 1880's, owned by the Bird Line, and she came to grief like so many others on the south coast of the Isle of Wight in thick fog. She had departed New Orleans on 27 November 1886 with a cargo of cotton, heading for the German port of Bremerhaven. The voyage was uneventful until 7am on the morning of 21 December when the vessel reached the vicinity of the Isle of Wight. A dense fog prevailed and it was only when the fog momentarily lifted that the ship's master, Captain Lowe discovered that his ship was within a mere 50 yards of land. Despite putting the engines in reverse, the ship ran on to the shallows and grounded just to the west of Whale Chine.

At first, there were high hopes the vessel would be refloated. Although she had grounded at high water, she was bows on to the shore and the weather was calm with a light breeze from the north. All that was needed was to lighten her at the bows by removing cargo and towing her off with tugs. These arrangements were put into effect and a great deal of cotton in bales was lowered by using the ship's derricks, and dragged up the cliffs by teams of horses. Anchors were laid offshore by coastguards and attempts were made to use them and the ship's own power to back her off the beach. In the absence of the awaited tugs, *Cormorant* remained fast, held by her bow section which hung onto the seabed.

During the night of 21/22 December, the fog persisted and in a bizarre occurrence, an unidentified ship lost her bearings and actually rammed the *Cormorant* on her starboard side forward, leaving her figurehead on the deck. She backed away in the night and was seen in the morning at anchor in the bay.

Within 24 hours of the stranding, however, the weather deteriorated, with a fresh breeze springing up from the south west, sending rising seas into Chale Bay. The ship's position worsened and she swung broadside to the beach and took on a list to starboard. The wind freshened to a gale, and *Cormorant* laboured heavily in the surf. Two tugs by now had arrived but could not proceed in the conditions. By the afternoon of 22 December, the sea was making clean breaches across the stranded ship, her decks were open to the sea and water flowed in and out of her. Despite this, more cotton was salvaged, but much of the ship's fittings and stores washed out of her and the vessel soon became a complete loss.

The wreck was sold by auction and work continued on her for some years.

At the subsequent Court of Enquiry, evidence emerged that the ship's compasses were inaccurate by as much as 11°. This, combined with the fact that depth soundings were not taken in the poor visibility, led to the stranding and total loss of the ship. The Court took into account Mr Lowe's "long and meritorious service" and "high character" but could not ignore that "by reckless conduct on this occasion he had lost a very large and valuable ship." The master's certificate was suspended for 6 months.

The remains of *Cormorant* still lie near Whale Chine in about 6 metres of water. She is much flattened and from time to time parts cover and uncover.

Name: *Cormorant.* **Former name(s):** None.
Vessel type: Steam ship.
Builder: Barclay Curle & Company, Glasgow.
When completed: May 1881.
Machinery built by: Barclay Curle & Company, Glasgow.
Tonnage: 2255 gross.
Dimensions: Length: 315′. **Breadth:** 35′ 7″.
Depth of holds: 25′ 4″.
Official number: 84923. **Yard number:** –
Signal letters: VWGC. **Last port of registry:** Leith.
Ship description: Iron screw steamer.
Machinery description: Compound inverted 2 cylin-

SS *Cormorant* aground near Whale Chine. Courtesy St Catherine's Quay Museum, Blackgang Chine.

SS *Cormorant's* stores and equipment being removed. Courtesy St Catherine's Quay Museum, Blackgang Chine.

ders. 230 nominal horse power.
Career and ownership: Owned by Seater, White & Company of the Bird Line.
Destination and cargo: New Orleans for Bremerhaven with 1200 tons of cotton in bales.
Date sunk: 21 December 1886.
How sunk: Ran aground in thick fog.
Reported position of loss: Ladder Chine and Whale Chine, Chale Bay.
Actual position of wreck: Approximate position 50° 36.12′ north, 001° 20.50′ west.
Orientation/height: Flattened wreckage on a seabed of sand and gravel in about 6 metres.
How identity of wreck proved: Contemporary reports and photographs show where the vessel was wrecked.

SS *Flaxmoss*
Foundered 30 October 1887

The *Flaxmoss* was a small ship – only 286 tons gross – and she would succumb to appalling weather in late October 1887, in tempestuous sea conditions produced by force 10 winds from the west-north-west. But, in all likelihood she would have reached her destination had she been properly loaded and secured.

Flaxmoss had come from Guernsey, where she had loaded a cargo of 325 tons of broken granite, as well as an additional 23 tons of coal for her bunkers. It must have been clear to her master that she was overloaded; indeed, her Plimsoll mark was underwater, and some weight ought to have been taken out of her before she proceeded on her voyage. The ship set sail on 29 October with her cargo and with a crew of ten hands and a seaman as passenger, and when off Cap La Hague on the French coast, steered a course for Beachy Head. The wind was moderate from the south west but as the day wore on, it gained in strength, producing a very heavy sea. As night came on the wind increased to such an extent that the ship's master, James Boor, deemed it necessary to heave-to. His vessel then steered bows on to the wind and sea, and some sails were taken in. Despite these measures, the remaining sails were blown out and one of the booms began swinging from side to side, damaging the bridge.

At 3am on the 30th with her engines going at dead slow, *Flaxmoss* was swamped by a huge sea which swept over her, carrying away her navigation lamps. Then the wind changed direction, blowing very hard from the west-north-west, and bringing more heavy seas crashing onto the ship. The forward hatch was stoved in and water flooded below, then the main hatch was also smashed in. It must have been at this point that the master wished he had ensured the hatches were secured with the iron cross beams with which she had been supplied. They had been left off, probably stowed below in the bunker space.

The crew worked desperately and managed to cover the open hatches with sails, and this undoubtedly saved the ship for the time being. By 6am, *Flaxmoss* was still lying-to and it seemed she would weather the storm, but then the bridge steering chain broke. Two men were sent to the stern to control the ship from the aft steering position, but another enormous wave fell upon them, carrying away the steering wheel and very nearly washing the men overboard. With the deck flooded with water, it became obvious to the crew that the ship could not survive. They jumped into the ship's boat, waiting for the *Flaxmoss* to sink beneath them, and hoping they would float clear.

To everyone's surprise, the water on her decks cleared, and the crew then set about repairing the broken steering chain. This was achieved and once again *Flaxmoss* headed bows into the storm. Preparations were made to ready the ship's pinnace but this was carried away by another roller, while the ship's lifeboat was stoved in by yet more heavy seas. The final straw came when water continued to increase in her holds, and wreckage became tangled in *Flaxmoss's* propeller. Unable to maintain her position the ship went beam on to the sea, and fell into the troughs, awaiting the end.

By good fortune, a Dutch barque, the *Neptunus*, came upon the *Flaxmoss*, no doubt in response to the distress flag flying from her mast. Seeing there were no boats left on the *Flaxmoss,* the barque lowered its own boat, and manoeuvred close to the doomed ship. In an incredible feat of seamanship and with great difficulty, the boat from *Neptunus* managed to reach the *Flaxmoss* and rescue every man on board.

Flaxmoss remained afloat for another hour and her crew watched from the *Neptunus* as she finally sank.

At the Court of Enquiry, Captain James Boor was judged to have allowed his ship to proceed to sea when too deeply laden, and his certificate was suspended for 6 months.

There is no information as to whether the wreck of the *Flaxmoss* has been found and identified.

Name: *Flaxmoss.* **Former name(s):** None.
Vessel type: Steam ship with sails.
Builder: Scott & Sons, Bowling.
When completed: 1883.
Machinery built by: J & T Young, Ayr.
Tonnage: 286 gross.
Dimensions: Length: 139′ 7″. **Breadth:** 22′ 2″.
Depth of holds: 10′ 5″.

Official number: 89131. **Yard number:** –
Signal letters: – **Last port of registry:** King's Lynn.
Ship description: Iron screw steamer. 1 iron deck. Schooner rigged.
Machinery description: Compound 2 cylinders. 1 single ended boiler. 50 horse power.
Career and ownership: Owned by the Flaxmoss Steam Ship Company (Charles Eyre Wise, Boal Wharf, King's Lynn, manager).
Destination and cargo: Guernsey for London with 325 tons of broken granite and 1 passenger.
Date sunk: 30 October 1887.
How sunk: Foundered in storm conditions.
Reported position of loss: 10 miles south of St Catherine's Point.
Actual position of wreck: Not known.
Orientation/height: –
How identity of wreck proved: –

Clipper ship *Smyrna*
Collision 28 April 1888

"*Smyrna*, painted with green sides, white figureheads, white blocks and white lower masts, bowsprit and yardarms, and gold stripe and gold scrollwork, was the admiration of sailors wherever she went." So ran a contemporary description of her from the 1880's.

The *Smyrna* (see colour plate on p. 145) was launched as a wool clipper, trading to and from Australia. Her usual routine was to sail out with a general cargo and return with a cargo of wool. Indeed, it was on 24 April 1888 that the *Smyrna,* under the command of her master Captain Thomas Taylor, departed London with a crew of 28 hands and a full general cargo, bound for Sydney, New South Wales. *Smyrna* was taking advantage of the good sailing breeze which was blowing as she glided along the English Channel, leaving St Catherine's Point away off her starboard bow. On 28 April 1888 and under full sail, she was making good progress, but then she entered thick fog.

Steaming from Bilbao with a cargo of iron ore was the nearly new steamer *Moto*, under the command of Captain Henry Digman. *Moto* was making her way to Newcastle when she too entered the fog in the English Channel. About 10.30am Captain Digman was on the bridge of the *Moto* with his brother, who was the chief mate. Two men were at the ship's wheel when suddenly out of the gloom, and rapidly approaching from off their port bow, came the *Smyrna,* still under full sail. *Moto's* whistle was sounded and her engines put hard astern, a situation which evolved over some minutes, until the *Moto* was almost stopped. Despite these efforts, a collision was unavoidable and *Smyrna* was struck near the main rigging, and a great hole torn in her side.

Some crewmen from the *Smyrna* were able to jump aboard the *Moto* and were saved, and *Moto's* boats were lowered to attempt to rescue any survivors. *Smyrna* herself soon went under; some say in as little as 4 minutes. In the debris washing around the site, some survivors were holding on to hencoops and other floating material, while others had managed to secure lifebuoys. Three men were seen to go down with their ship, only to resurface and be rescued. One crewman, an old man, was seen running around the deck frantically, but he could not be saved. In all, 12 men from the *Smyrna* were drowned.

According to the newspaper Leeds Mercury "Newcastle steamers on their way from Bilbao to this country with ore have an evil reputation for assertion of their right of way at sea under any circumstances. It seems to be understood in the trade that close shaving in passing other vessels is a necessity in navigation. We shall not pretend, in advance of the Board of Trade enquiry, with its consequences of costs and personal compensation, to affirm that the sinking of the ship *Smyrna*, off the Needles, on Saturday morning, was due to recklessness; but it was clearly the duty of the steamer *Moto* to keep clear of the other vessel if she could. The weather, it is said, was thick, but vision could go a long way in look-out ahead, because the *Smyrna* was sighted under full sail on the port bow, and the *Moto's* engines were reversed for 3 or 4 minutes. The latter fact alone implies that there was a good interval between the vessels when they sighted each other."

The Board of Trade agreed that the fault for the collision lay entirely with the *Moto.* Considerable sums of money were awarded to *Smyrna's* owners and to the owners of the cargo, and to the dependants of those who lost their lives, as well as to surviving crew members.

The wreck of the *Smyrna* lies in about 55 metres of water. Despite her age, she is in good condition, with parts of the stern standing 6 metres high. Her bows lie over to port, with her cutwater – part of her clipper bows – clearly evident. Mast and spars lie along the port side of the wreck, which is stuffed full of a wide variety of cargo. Glassware, crockery, bottled goods, grindstones, packs of corrugated iron, 2 gallon flagons, stoneware ink jars, and so on. In a truly memorable dive in the mid 1990's, underwater horizontal visibility of 30 metres was recorded, allowing both sides of the wreck and the seabed beyond to be seen, showing the wreck to lie in a huge depression, probably scoured out by the presence of the wreck itself.

Name: *Smyrna.* **Former name(s):** None.
Vessel type: Clipper sailing ship.
Builder: Walter Hood, Aberdeen.
When completed: October 1876.
Machinery built by: –

Tonnage: 1372 gross.
Dimensions: Length: 232′ 3″. **Breadth:** 38′ 5″.
Depth of holds: 22′ 2″.
Official number: 70457. **Yard number:** –
Signal letters: QKCP. **Last port of registry:** Aberdeen.
Ship description: Iron clipper ship. 3 masts. 2 decks.
Machinery description: Small donkey boiler in wreck port side amidships.
Career and ownership: Owned by G Thompson & Company, Aberdeen Line. Her best voyage was from Sydney to London in 1887, taking 96 days. Launched as a wool clipper.
Destination and cargo: London for Sydney with full general cargo.
Date sunk: 28 April 1888.
How sunk: Collision with the SS *Moto*.
Reported position of loss: 16 miles south east of Anvil Point.
Actual position of wreck: 50° 18.97′ north, 001° 29.93′ west.
Orientation/height: Lies roughly 000°/180°. Stands 5–6 metres. Wreck lies across the tide, bows to the south, on a hard, chalk seabed covered with gravel.
How identity of wreck proved: Ship's crockery and builder's nameplate recovered.

SS *Cleddy*
Collision 20 December 1889

"Terrible collision off St Catherine's. Supposed loss of 13 lives. Personal narratives of the survivors." So ran the headlines from the local newspapers when the loss of the steamer *Cleddy* became known. The *Cleddy* had departed Odessa on 3 December 1889 and had landed 158 head of cattle at Malta. From there, she proceeded on her voyage for Antwerp with a cargo of corn. Not long after midnight on 20 December 1889, the *Cleddy* was steaming off St Catherine's Point when she sighted an oncoming three masted steamer. This turned out to be the SS *Isle of Cyprus*, on voyage from the Tyne for Seville with a cargo of coals. In clear conditions with a moderate breeze from the south west, the two vessels were in sight of each other for at least 25 minutes, but still they came into collision.

Giving evidence at the inquest into the deaths of some of his crew, master mariner Captain Thomas Seward told the court he was on watch until midnight and then went to the chart-house, handing command of the *Cleddy* to the chief officer, Alfred Evans. About half an hour later, he heard *Cleddy's* whistle give two blasts and immediately came on deck. He said, "The first I saw was a steamer's masthead and red light about 4 points on my starboard bow. I asked the mate how we got into that position, but got no reply. I asked him how the helm was and he said hard a'starboard. Almost immediately the ship struck us. When the ship struck us I rang the telegraph to stop the engines and gave orders to the chief mate to get out the boats, telling him to get out the starboard lifeboat." He continued, "I went down to the main deck to see what damage was done to our ship. I found we were cut in 10 feet deep, 50 feet from the stern." He said, "I then went on the bridge and found the mate, Alfred Evans, had got the gig out instead of the lifeboat, and the crew were rushing into her. That one boat was not enough to save the lives of the crew." The captain managed to launch the ship's cutter and those remaining on the *Cleddy* managed to escape their sinking ship.

The version of events from the perspective of the *Isle of Cyprus* was that as she was steaming down Channel, she saw the green starboard navigation light of the *Cleddy*. As long as the two ships maintained their respective courses, they would have cleared each other and passed safely. However, James Panton, chief mate of the *Isle of Cyprus*, told the court that the other ship changed course, presenting her red port navigation light. Unsure of her intentions, he ported the helm of his ship but still the ships came together and he ordered the engines to be put full astern. Despite this, a terrific crash occurred, with the *Isle of Cyprus* striking the *Cleddy* on her starboard side abaft the main rigging. In the darkness the ships drifted apart, but all the *Cleddy's* crew managed to leave their sinking ship in two of the ship's boats. They watched as the *Cleddy* sank by the stern 20 minutes after the collision.

The ship's cutter containing the captain and ten men at first kept in touch with the other 13 crew in the ship's gig, but they lost sight of each other in the night. By 3am, the weather had deteriorated, the wind freshening with rain, but by good seamanship the cutter was kept going, eventually coming ashore safely at Bembridge. Of the other boat and survivors, there was no sign, until bodies began to wash ashore around St Catherine's Point. It was assumed the gig had been swamped in St Catherine's Race, and all 13 men had drowned.

The inquest recorded an open verdict on the drowned seamen, the coroner referring to some "incredible" and "not satisfactory" evidence from the crew of the *Isle of Cyprus*. Since those on watch on the *Cleddy* had drowned, it was impossible to ascertain their version of events, and there was insufficient evidence to conclude who was to blame.

The wreck of the *Cleddy* lies in about 42 metres. Her two boilers are the highest parts, with her compound engine lying hard over to starboard. The bow section is skeletal and partly buried and there is hardly any visible wreckage from just forward of the boilers to the bows.

Name: *Cleddy*. **Former name(s):** None.
Vessel type: Steam ship with sails.
Builder: J L Thompson & Sons, Sunderland.
When completed: January 1883.
Machinery built by: J Dickinson, Sunderland.
Tonnage: 2173 gross.
Dimensions: Length: 282′ 5″. **Breadth:** 36′ 6″.

Depth of holds: 23′ 8″.
Official number: 87463. **Yard number:** 187.
Signal letters: HKSP. **Last port of registry:** Cardiff.
Ship description: Iron screw steamer. 2 iron decks.
Machinery description: Compound inverted 2 cylinders. 2 single ended boilers. 250 horse power.
Career and ownership: Owned by J Marychurch & Company.
Destination and cargo: Odessa for Antwerp with a cargo of wheat, maize, barley, linseed and wood.
Date sunk: 20 December 1889.
How sunk: Collision with SS *Isle of Cyprus.*
Reported position of loss: 10 miles south west of St Catherine's Point.
Actual position of wreck: 50° 30.52′ north, 001° 28.06′ west.
Orientation/height: Stands about 4 metres on a gravel seabed in 42 metres.
How identity of wreck proved: Description of wreck fits that of the *Cleddy*. Quantities of grain probably from cargo, found embedded in concretion. Position of wreck is less than 3 miles from her reported position of loss.

SS *Hilda*
Collision 22 March 1895

The *Hilda* was a steam trawler and at the time of loss she was in ballast. She was on voyage from Ostend and it is assumed she was on her way to fishing grounds in the Channel, but as her loss went virtually unreported, no further details are known. What is known is that a collision occurred between the *Hilda* and a vessel named *Petriana*, of London when off St Catherine's Point. The *Hilda* sank but her crew were saved and later landed at Thameshaven.

There is no information on the location or identification of this vessel.

Name: *Hilda.* **Former name(s):** None.
Vessel type: Steam trawler.
Builder: T Charlton, Grimsby.
When completed: July 1892.
Machinery built by: T Charlton, Grimsby.
Tonnage: 169 gross.
Dimensions: Length: 102′. **Breadth:** 20′ 8″.
Depth of holds: 10′ 5″.
Official number: – **Yard number:** –
Signal letters: – **Last port of registry:** Ostend.
Ship description: Iron screw ketch steam trawler. 1 deck.
Machinery description: Triple expansion 3 cylinders. 1 single ended boiler. 55 horse power.
Career and ownership: Owned by J Baels-Mauricx.
Destination and cargo: Ostend – fishing and return – in ballast.
Date sunk: 22 March 1895.
How sunk: Collision with SS *Petriana.*
Reported position of loss: Off St Catherine's Point.
Actual position of wreck: Not known.
Orientation/height: –
How identity of wreck proved: –

SS *Joannis Millas*
Ran aground 11 January 1896

In the early hours of Saturday 11 January 1896, the Greek steamer *Joannis Millas* was steaming up Channel on her voyage from Ibrail for Rotterdam with a cargo of grain. A thick haze prevailed at the time, and in the darkness, hopelessly off course, the ship ran onto the offshore rocks off Chilton on the south coast of the Isle of Wight.

The ship became firmly fixed on the submerged rocks, her forepeak having been pierced, and her forward compartments began to fill with water. With the rise and fall of the tide, the ship began to strain badly, though hopes were entertained that if she could be lightened, she could be pulled clear of the rocks. Tugs and lighters attended the scene and cargo was discharged, and a strong labour force was employed, with more than 600 tons jettisoned over the side.

Three days later, the weather had deteriorated and unsuccessful efforts had been made to tow the ship clear. Her stores, fittings and other gear were removed before the ship was abandoned as a total loss.

The wreck of the *Joannis Millas* lies about half a mile offshore among the rocks and gullies off Chilton. Her 3 cylinder triple expansion engine lies over to starboard and it and the propeller shaft are most prominent, though a great deal of other wreckage remains on site. Both boilers are still there, largely covered under other wreckage, and various frames, beams and pieces of steel hull plating litter the area. She makes and interesting rummage dive, being in 7 or 8 metres depth, though off her stern the depth increases to 9 or 10 metres.

Name: *Joannis Millas* **Former name(s):** None.
Vessel type: Steam ship with sails.
Builder: J L Thompson & Sons, Sunderland.
When completed: November 1889.
Machinery built by: J Dickinson, Sunderland.
Tonnage: 2071 gross.
Dimensions: Length: 284′. **Breadth:** 38′ 1″.
Depth of holds: 18′ 1″.
Official number: – **Yard number:** 256.
Signal letters: HMRC. **Last port of registry:** Argostoli, Cephalonia.
Ship description: Steel screw steamer. 1 deck.
Machinery description: Triple expansion 3 cylinders. 2 single ended boilers. 212 nominal horse power.
Career and ownership: Owned by J Millas & Son.
Destination and cargo: Ibrail for Rotterdam with 3000 tons of barley, rye, wheat and maize.
Date sunk: 11 January 1896.
How sunk: Ran aground in fog.
Reported position of loss: At Chilton on Sudmore Rock.
Actual position of wreck: 50° 37.91′ north, 001° 26.09′ west.
Orientation/height: Lies 070°/250°. Engines stand 2 metres maximum. Lies on rock seabed in 7–8 metres.
How identity of wreck proved: One of 3 steamers lost in the vicinity, this ship was the only one to have a triple expansion engine.

SS *Ceres*
Blown ashore 23 November 1898

The *Ceres* was a small steamer of only 38 tons, and on 23 November 1898 her master, Captain H Doe and two crew, was engaged in loading shingle from the notorious Shingle Bank at Hurst Castle in the western Solent. Exactly what happened is unclear, but a strong wind from the south west, described as a force 7, came up the Solent and blew *Ceres* aground. She became a total loss. A charted wreck in shallow water on the north east end of the Shingle Bank may well be that of the *Ceres*.

Name: *Ceres*. **Former name(s):** None.
Vessel type: Steam barge.
Builder: At Kirkintilloch.
When completed: 1875.
Machinery built by: –
Tonnage: 38 tons gross.
Dimensions: Length: 65′. **Breadth:** 13′ 7″. **Depth of holds:** 4′ 6″.
Official number: 93365. **Yard number:** –
Signal letters: – **Last port of registry:** Liverpool.
Ship description: Iron screw steam barge.
Machinery description: –
Career and ownership: Owned by William E Drewett, Farringford Mills, Freshwater, Isle of Wight.
Destination and cargo: Hurst Castle for an unknown destination with a cargo of shingle.
Date sunk: 23 November 1898.
How sunk: Blown aground in a strong wind.
Reported position of loss: Hurst beach.
Actual position of wreck: 50° 41.89′ north, 001° 33.99′ west.
Orientation/height: Stands 2 metres in 5 metres.
How identity of wreck proved: Not proved but is very close to Hurst beach, as reported when lost.

SS *Netley Abbey*
Collision 4 August 1899

SS *Netley Abbey*. Courtesy Bristol's Museums Galleries & Archives.

On 4 August 1899, the warship HMS *Surprise*, a 1650 ton despatch vessel, was under orders to proceed from Portsmouth to Gibraltar. She had steamed out to Spithead where her compasses were adjusted, and she commenced her journey down the Solent towards the Needles. In fine weather and light winds, her commander, William Fane-Hervey, set a course to take his ship down Channel and increased speed. About 1½ hours later, *Surprise* was in the vicinity of Anvil Point, but there had been a change in the weather. The noise of the explosive fog signal emanating from Anvil Point lighthouse warned of the presence of thick fog, and *Surprise* was steaming into it.

On an opposite course was the 1630 ton steamer *Netley Abbey*, steaming from Cardiff for Cronstadt with a cargo of coal for the Russian government, and under the command of Mr G Lewis. Her voyage had been uneventful until she reached St Alban's Head, when dense fog was encountered. The fog was so thick it was necessary to make a considerable reduction in speed, and *Netley Abbey* crept along with her engines going at dead slow. She had entered the fogbank from the west, as *Surprise* had entered it from the east. As a precautionary measure commander Fane-Hervey ordered his men to their stations to exercise drills of "collision stations" and "abandon ship." He had also ordered the ship's siren to be sounded at regular intervals, but then, about 4.25pm, Fane-Hervey saw dead ahead, and no more than 200 yards distant, the unmistakable shape of a ship emerging from the fog. This was the *Netley Abbey*.

Immediately ordering "full speed astern" and "port helm! Close all watertight doors!" Fane-Hervey anticipated *Surprise* would pass the other ship under her stern. But *Surprise* could not steer clear in time and she struck *Netley Abbey* about amidships on the port side abaft the engine room. Locked together for some 10 minutes, and learning that *Netley Abbey* had no watertight compartments, he evacuated all 22 crew safely across the bridge formed by the two ships. He then ordered his ship to go astern, to break free of the other ship. Soon after doing so, *Netley Abbey* filled and sank by the stern.

A Court-martial was held on board HMS *Victory* where commander Fane-Hervey was charged with "negligently or by default, hazarded or suffered to be hazarded, HMS *Surprise*." Hearing first from the master of the *Netley Abbey*, Mr G Lewis, he told the court that after reducing speed to dead slow, he heard the siren of an approaching ship drawing nearer and ordered his own ship to be stopped in order to locate the source of the siren. Soon after, he sighted the oncoming *Surprise* and rang the telegraph for full speed ahead and gave a long blast on the ship's whistle, at the same time porting his helm. As soon as it became obvious a collision was inevitable, he ordered her engines stopped. Rushing to warn his crew to save their lives as soon as the collision took place, they all came on deck and boarded the *Surprise* by climbing onto her bows as they were embedded in the *Netley Abbey*.

The only part of the charge proved against commander Fane-Hervey was that he had not ordered his ship's engines to be eased when entering the fog. The Court-martial found that the primary cause of the accident was through the bad handling of the *Netley Abbey* in that she did not sound her siren in accordance with regulations, was stopped without way, and lay across the track of vessels passing up and down. Fane-Hervey was admonished and instructed to be more careful in future. That, however, was not the end of the matter, as later the Admiralty admitted liability for the loss of the *Netley Abbey* and conceded both ships shared the blame. They agreed to pay £6,500 to the owners of the *Netley Abbey*.

It is not known if the wreck of the *Netley Abbey* has been located and identified.

Name: *Netley Abbey*. **Former name(s):** None.
Vessel type: Steam ship.
Builder: W Gray & Company, West Hartlepool.
When completed: May 1878.
Machinery built by: T Richardson & Sons, West Hartlepool.
Tonnage: 1630 gross.
Dimensions: Length: 260′. **Breadth:** 34′ 9″.
Depth of holds: 22′ 9″.
Official number: 79383. **Yard number:** –
Signal letters: RSBM. **Last port of registry:** Cardiff.
Ship description: Iron screw steamer, brigantine rigged.
Machinery description: Compound 2 cylinders. 2 single ended boilers. 191 nominal horse power.
Career and ownership: Owned by the Netley Abbey Steamship Company Ltd (Pyman, Watson & Co).
Destination and cargo: Cardiff for Cronstadt with 2300 tons of coal for the Russian government.
Date sunk: 4 August 1899.
How sunk: Collision in fog with HMS *Surprise*.
Reported position of loss: Variously as off St Alban's Head, and Shambles light vessel east by south half south magnetic, about 8 miles.
Actual position of wreck: Not known, but calculating the position of collision from the details contained in the log of HMS *Surprise*, a search commencing in 50° 34.30′ north, 001° 53.10′ west might locate the wreck.
Orientation/height: –
How identity of wreck proved: –

Barquentine *Rosehill*
Collision 14 September 1900

The loss of the iron barquentine *Rosehill* seems to have passed almost unnoticed since local newspapers do not record the event, despite the fact that all those on board lost their lives. *Rosehill* had departed Teignmouth where she had loaded a cargo of China clay in September 1900, and sailed up Channel with her crew of seven hands towards her destination, the Belgian port of Antwerp. Her master, H Langmaid, in reaching the waters south of the Isle of Wight, was sailing against a strong easterly breeze when another ship appeared.

The German steamer *Holtenau*, for reasons unknown, came into collision with the *Rosehill.* So serious was the damage that *Rosehill* sank, and all seven men on board went with her.

A wreck which is almost certainly that of the *Rosehill* lies in 40 metres of water. The wreck is quite flattened and broken, but not spread out. Items of rigging lie on site.

Name: *Rosehill.* **Former name(s):** None.
Vessel type: Sailing ship.
Builder: R Williamson & Son, Harrington.
When completed: August 1875.
Machinery built by: –
Tonnage: 213 tons gross.
Dimensions: Length: 117′. **Breadth:** 22′ 1″.
Depth of holds: 12′.
Official number: 63887. **Yard number:** –
Signal letters: PGSV. **Last port of registry:** Exeter.
Ship description: 3 masted iron barquentine.
Machinery description: –
Career and ownership: Owned by H B Varwell, Exeter.
Destination and cargo: Teignmouth for Antwerp with a cargo of China clay.
Date sunk: 14 September 1900.
How sunk: Collision with SS *Holtenau.*
Reported position of loss: 15 miles west-south-west of St Catherine's Point.
Actual position of wreck: 50° 26.89′ north, 001° 34.37′ west.
Orientation/height: Stands maximum of 1 metre in 40 metres on hard chalk seabed and shingle.
How identity of wreck proved: Wreck is of a small iron sailing ship, its size and location being consistent with that of the *Rosehill.* Large lumps of grey material in the wreck appear to be the remnants of the clay cargo. Reported position of loss is consistent with position of the wreck.

SS *Clyde*
Foundered 25 May 1902

The steamer *Clyde* was on voyage from Aberystwyth for Antwerp with a cargo of lead ore. On 25 May 1902 she called in at Portland to take on coal bunkers and, this operation having been completed, she continued her journey, departing about 1 pm. However, as she was leaving harbour, her hull came into contact with Portland breakwater. It is not recorded what action was then taken, but no doubt checks were made for damage, and as nothing was found to be amiss, *Clyde* carried on.

Unbeknown at the time to Captain Brown, her master, *Clyde* had sustained significant damage to her keel, and she was leaking considerably. Some 8 hours after leaving Portland, and when off the Isle of Wight, it became obvious to all on board that it was not possible to cope with the inflow of water. The decision was made to abandon the vessel, and gathering such personal effects as they could, the captain and crew took to the ship's boats, which were lowered about 10.20pm. Soon after, *Clyde* disappeared, and the crew in their boats cruised around until daybreak, when they were sighted by the Dutch steamer *Flores* and rescued, later being landed at Dover.

There is no information as to whether the *Clyde* has been located or identified.

Name: *Clyde*. **Former name(s):** None.
Vessel type: Steam ship.
Builder: Whitehaven Shipbuilding Company Ltd, Whitehaven.
When completed: December 1880.
Machinery built by: J Jones & Sons, Liverpool.
Tonnage: 307 gross.
Dimensions: Length: 133′ 2″. **Breadth:** 20′ 7″. **Depth of holds:** 11′ 5″.
Official number: 84072. **Yard number:** –
Signal letters: WPMR. **Last port of registry:** Liverpool.
Ship description: Iron screw steamer.
Machinery description: Compound 2 cylinders. 1 single ended boiler. 70 registered horse power.
Career and ownership: Owned by J Crichton.
Destination and cargo: Aberystwyth for Antwerp, via Portland for bunkers, with a cargo of lead ore.
Date sunk: 25 May 1902.
How sunk: Damaged her keel and began to leak, and subsequently foundered.
Reported position of loss: 10 miles off St Catherine's Point.
Actual position of wreck: Not known.
Orientation/height: –
How identity of wreck proved: –

SS *Duncrag*
Foundered 11 April 1904

At less than two years old, the steamer *Duncrag* could have expected to continue trading for a good many years, but the subsequent loss of the ship was, according to the Court of Enquiry, "contributed to by her overladen condition, it was due to the wrongful act of the master alone. The court hereby suspends the certificate of the master, Peter McLachlan, for the period of three months."

Duncrag, a typical steam coaster of the period, had arrived at St Sampson's Harbour, Guernsey from Swansea on 9 April 1904, with a crew of 12 hands. The vessel took on board a cargo of granite stones and when this was completed she attempted to leave harbour, but grounded aft. The fore peak was flooded in order to trim the vessel ready for the next tide, but she had taken on too much water, and was still aground. Pumping out tons of water, she refloated on the next tide and proceeded to sea, but *Duncrag* was in a perilous state. She was overloaded to the tune of 76 tons, the pilot pointing out to Mr McLachlan that her Plimsoll line was submerged.

The voyage to London seems to have gone well enough until 11.30pm on the night of 10 April when Captain McLachlan noticed the ship was behaving abnormally. There was a peculiar movement to her and about 2 feet of water level on the deck. Seas had been coming aboard, breaking over the ship's rail, a situation made worse because she was overloaded, and water was making its way inside the ship. Taking a sounding of the ship's hold and tanks, Captain McLachlan realised there was 4–5 feet of water in her and it became clear something was seriously wrong. Although the bilge injection pumps were working in the holds, it was thought useless to attempt to use the deck pumps, the opinion being that the ship was going to sink.

Around midnight, in a fresh wind from the west-north-west and a moderate sea, the master ordered the ship's boats to be lowered. By now, *Duncrag* was so low in the water that the hatch cover on the well deck was practically submerged. Taking to the boats, the crew stood by until 1.30am, when their ship listed to starboard and foundered stern first. On the afternoon of 11 April, the two boats reached Ventnor, Isle of Wight, with all on board safe and well.

There is no information as to whether the *Duncrag* has been located or identified.

Name: *Duncrag*. **Former name(s):** None.
Vessel type: Steam coaster.
Builder: Bow, McLachlan, Paisley.
When completed: May 1902.
Machinery built by: Bow, McLachlan, Paisley.
Tonnage: 563 gross.
Dimensions: Length: 165′ 2″. **Breadth:** 28′ 2″.
Depth of holds: 12′.
Official number: 115679. **Yard number:** –
Signal letters: TKFQ. **Last port of registry:** Glasgow.
Ship description: Steel screw steam coaster. Well deck. 1 deck. Fitted with electric light.
Machinery description: Compound 2 cylinders. 1 single ended boiler. 78 horse power.
Career and ownership: Owned by Home Trade Steam Carrying Company Ltd (John Gray Frew, 88 Clyde Street, Glasgow, manager).
Destination and cargo: Guernsey for London with granite stones consisting of sets, road metal and chips.
Date sunk: 11 April 1904.
How sunk: Foundered due to taking on water when overloaded.
Reported position of loss: 25 miles south of St Catherine's Point.
Actual position of wreck: Not known.
Orientation/height: –
How identity of wreck proved: –

Steam trawler *Dolores*
Foundered 5 October 1906

In early October 1906, a sale was agreed and completed for the Rye trawler, *Athena*. Bought by a Spanish company and renamed *Dolores,* the vessel was heading for Spain under the command of Senor J Perez. As the vessel steamed down Channel in heavy seas and a south west force 6 wind, she sprang a leak and her captain deemed it necessary to anchor off St Catherine's Point. About 1am on the morning of Friday 5 October 1906, the Niton Coastguard saw signals of distress burning from an anchored vessel west-south-west of the coastguard station. This was *Dolores*. Atherfield lifeboat was called out, but before reaching the casualty, *Dolores* sank about 6.45am. By now her crew comprising five Spaniards and a Frenchman had abandoned her, they landing safely near St Catherine's Point in the ship's boat.

There is no information concerning the location or identification of the wreck of the *Dolores*.

Name: *Dolores*. **Former name(s):** *Athena*.
Vessel type: Steam trawler.
Builder: Built in Wallsend probably by Clelands Shipbuilding Company Ltd.
When completed: 1886.
Machinery built by: –
Tonnage: 67 gross.
Dimensions: Length: 77′. **Breadth:** 17′ 2″.
Depth of holds: 9′.
Official number: 89822. **Yard number:** –
Signal letters: – **Last port of registry:** Rye.
Ship description: Wooden steam trawler.
Machinery description: 17 horse power.
Career and ownership: Owned by Kingsnorth Reeve, Rye, then sold in 1906 to Gosalvez y cia, Alicante, Spain.
Destination and cargo: Rye for Alicante in ballast.
Date sunk: 5 October 1906.
How sunk: Sprang a leak in heavy weather and foundered.
Reported position of loss: Variously as 2, 2½ and 4 miles west-south-west of St Catherine's Point.
Actual position of wreck: Not known.
Orientation/height: –
How identity of wreck proved: –

HMS *Tiger*
Collision 2 April 1908

HMS *Tiger*. Courtesy National Maritime Museum, Greenwich.

HMS *Tiger* was a small but very fast torpedo boat destroyer, part of the Home Fleet based in Portsmouth. She left Portsmouth Harbour in company with other destroyers on the afternoon of Thursday 2 April 1908 to take part in exercises in the Channel south of the Isle of Wight. She and her accompanying destroyers, 12 in number, were to practise night attacks against six battleships and cruisers of the Portsmouth Division of the Home Fleet.

During the evening the vessels were in a position south of St Catherine's Point, proceeding without lights and attempting to close the battleships and cruisers without being seen so as to manoeuvre within striking distance for their attacks. On *Tiger's* bridge was Lieutenant Commander William Middleton, while the majority of the ship's complement was forward and the engine staff were engaged in their duties attending the engines and stokeholds. An initial attack at dusk was successfully concluded, but by 8.15pm all lights on all ships taking part were extinguished. The night was clear but extremely dark.

Giving evidence at a Court-martial aboard HMS *Victory* on 10 and 11 April 1908, witnesses described what happened as a terrible disaster unfolded. Steaming at 20 knots, *Tiger* had been working with HMS *Recruit,* the latter being the leader, when the two ships attacked the larger warships of the Battle Squadron, led by HMS *Prince George,* from their port side. Immediately after *Prince George* had been passed, *Tiger,* instead of following her leader, altered course to port directly across the bows of the 9,800 ton cruiser HMS *Berwick. Berwick,* steaming at 10 knots, struck *Tiger* on her starboard side between the second and third funnels, instantly and completely cutting her in two. Amid a great roar of escaping steam, and flames shooting up above the *Berwick*, the two parts of the ship passed down either side of *Berwick* and after a few minutes, sank.

Engineer-Lieutenant Cecil Edward Vinning of HMS *Tiger* told the court, "It was about 10 past 8, I was standing on the starboard side by the engine room, and had just come up from the dynamo engine. I saw the *Recruit*, whom we were following, on the starboard bow. It was so very dark that I could only see the wake of the vessel. She was turning to starboard. The white foam she left behind was about 30 feet on our starboard beam, so we were turning outside of her. At that moment she fired a Very light, and on the port bow I saw the loom of a large vessel. I crossed to the port side to see what it was. I made it out to be the *Prince George*. We fired a Very light on the port side at the *Prince George*. At no time was our course parallel to that of the *Prince George*. She passed away on our port quarter, when the Very lights were out."

"I remarked to myself, both from the *Recruit* and ourselves, that they were exceedingly dazzling, the night being so exceptionally dark it was impossible to see anything afterwards for a moment." He continued, "I firmly believe myself I saw other Very lights on the port bow after the *Prince George* had appeared. We seemed to make for them. The moment after I was astonished to see the ram of a vessel about 20 feet on our starboard bow from us, just before the beam. At that moment a Very light was fired from the bridge of the *Tiger* just before the collision. The moment after that the ship was struck and the ram of the *Berwick* came through the after stokehold just in front of me. The portion on which I was standing sank to the level of the water and I was enveloped in the wave which came over the side. I went aft as fast as I could." Shortly afterwards, the stern section containing Engineer-Lieutenant Vinning upended and sank.

Captain W C Nicholson of HMS *Berwick*, was asked at the coroner's inquest, "Was the *Tiger* endeavouring to pass between the *Prince George* and your ship?" He replied, "Of course, I do not know what the poor fel lows were doing. We cannot suggest that they deliberately came between us, but the *Tiger* was passing us when we struck her." He told the court that he had seen one destroyer (which must have been the *Recruit*) running past the port side of the *Berwick*. On sighting the *Tiger*, he said he shouted out, "Good Lord, there's another one coming closer. The moment I saw her I knew that a collision was inevitable."

Another witness, Torpedo-Instructor Limming from HMS *Recruit*, expected *Tiger* to follow his ship. He remarked to a Petty Officer as *Tiger* veered away, "Where the dickens is she off to?" The reply was, "I don't know unless she is coming up inside." Inexplicably, *Tiger* had not followed the leader, and the opinion was expressed that the glare of the red Very light had caused those on the *Tiger* to lose sight of *Recruit*, with disastrous consequences.

In the event, 36 sailors lost their lives, but 22 men were picked up alive.

It is not known if the wreckage of *Tiger* has been located and identified, but if the position noted at the time of loss is accurate, she will lie in two pieces in the thick of the westbound shipping lane.

Name: HMS *Tiger*. **Former name(s):** None.
Vessel type: Torpedo boat destroyer.
Builder: Initially, John Brown but the build was taken over by J & G Thompson, Clydebank.
When completed: 19 May 1900.
Machinery built by: –
Tonnage: 400 displacement.
Dimensions: Length: 218′. **Breadth:** 20′ 7″.
Depth: 9′.
Official number: – **Yard number:** –
Signal letters: – **Last port of registry:** Portsmouth based.
Ship description: Steel screw torpedo boat destroyer. 3 funnels. "C" class destroyer.
Machinery description: Triple expansion 3 cylinders on 2 shafts producing 6,400 horse power. 3 Normand boilers. Capable of 30 knots.
Career and ownership: Built as a speculation and purchased by the Admiralty on 31 March 1900.
Armament: 1 × 12 pounder, 5 × 6 pounders. 2 × 18″ torpedo tubes, deck mounted.
Destination and cargo: Portsmouth and return for night exercises off St Catherine's Point.
Date sunk: 2 April 1908.
How sunk: Collision with HMS *Berwick*.
Reported position of loss: 50° 17′ north, 001° 21′ west.
Actual position of wreck: Not known.
Orientation/height: –
How identity of wreck proved: –

SS *Hopedale*
Collision 24 July 1908

Turret deck SS *Hopedale*. Courtesy Bristol's Museums Galleries & Archives.

The *Hopedale* was an unusual vessel in that she was a "turret decked" ship. This was a design intended to legally circumvent the amount of tax required to be paid when passing through the Panama and Suez Canals. The tax was based on the deck area, and turret decked ships were constructed with the upper parts of their hulls curved inwards, leaving a much smaller space for the deck. They proved to be unpopular in practice and as a method of construction, did not really catch on.

During the early hours of Friday 24 July 1908, *Hopedale* was off the Isle of Wight, making her way westwards for Bordeaux with a cargo of coal. A dense fog enveloped the area, when out of the gloom emerged the iron ore carrier SS *Elmsgarth*. *Elmsgarth* struck the *Hopedale* abreast number 3 hatch below the water line. Taking in water rapidly, *Hopedale's* master, Captain Chevins, ordered the ship's boats to be manned, and they then stood by their ship. Eventually, she flooded completely, and the captain and officers left the ship and got into the lifeboats, *Hopedale* sinking immediately afterwards.

The *Elmsgarth*, her bows seriously damaged and her forepeak full of water, took Captain Chevins and his crew on board, and landed them at Portland.

There is no information as to whether the wreck of the *Hopedale* has been found or identified.

Name: *Hopedale*. **Former name(s):** None.
Vessel type: Steam ship.
Builder: W Doxford & Sons, Sunderland.
When completed: 1895.
Machinery built by: W Doxford & sons, Sunderland.
Tonnage: 1746 gross.
Dimensions: Length: 280′. **Breadth:** 38′.
Depth of holds: 18′ 4″.
Official number: 104350. **Yard number:** –
Signal letters: NRVM. **Last port of registry:** Sunderland.
Ship description: Steel screw steamer. Turret deck.
Machinery description: Triple expansion 3 cylinders, 2 single ended boilers. Machinery fitted aft. 180 horse power.
Career and ownership: Owned by Mrs Dolores M Laing, Manor House, Hamble (R C Thompson, manager).
Destination and cargo: Sunderland for Bordeaux with coal.
Date sunk: 24 July 1908.
How sunk: Collision in fog with the SS *Elmsgarth*.
Reported position of loss: Variously as off St Catherine's Point, and 35 miles west-south-west of St Catherine's Point.
Actual position of wreck: Not known.
Orientation/height: –
How identity of wreck proved: –

Steam trawler *Nemrod*
Ran aground 5 February 1910

Steam trawler *Nemrod* aground in Chale Bay. Author's collection.

The Belgian trawler *Nemrod* was a brand new vessel only 16 days old when she came to grief on the south coast of the Isle of Wight. Fully laden with a cargo of fresh fish, she became caught up in the characteristic thick fog which afflicts the area. Around midnight on 5 February 1910 in poor visibility and heavy seas, and having lost her bearings, she ran onto the beach in Chale Bay almost at high water, near Ladder Chine. Her crew later recalled that the vessel was on her way back to Ostend when thick fog came down. At first, they followed the wake of a steamer, and then sighted another light and thought they would follow that. In all likelihood, that light was shining from the land and by following it they ran themselves ashore.

As a signal of distress, her siren was repeatedly sounded and this alerted some fishermen who lived in cottages near the cliff edge. Rushing to the cliff, they could just make out the lights of the *Nemrod* close to shore. Realising the great danger which must have faced the crew, the fishermen climbed down the cliffs in the darkness and reached the ship amid waves washing up to the base of the cliff. Hailing the vessel, they heard shouts from the water and concluded, rightly as it turned out, that some of the crew had taken to the lifeboat to escape the wreck. Then, an answer came from the *Nemrod*, shouting, "six men in boat." Quickly a rope was thrown to the men on the beach, and the four crewmen who had remained on board were pulled through the surf to safety. The rest of the crew, by now missing from the scene, later came ashore safely at Ventnor.

Later that day three tugs arrived and one of them, the Swedish tug *Belos,* attached a towing line to the *Nemrod.* At the first attempt in pulling the *Nemrod* clear on a falling tide, the tow parted and the wrecked vessel was abandoned. She had by now swung broadside to the beach and taken on a heavy list to starboard, her deck to the sea, and continually washed by the breakers.

Within 24 hours, her position had become hopeless, and though she was visible at low water, at high water she was practically submerged. Fish washed out of her hold, and much was salvaged by local people who had a rare opportunity to go home with turbot, plaice, cod and haddock, using the fish baskets washed out of the wreck.

Although hopes were entertained that the vessel might be saved, in the event she was blasted apart with dynamite to remove some of her metal fittings. Described as beautifully fitted out and with hardly a scratch on her paintwork, it was a sad sight to see such a fine vessel being smashed by the sea.

Nemrod's remains lie scattered along Chale Bay east of Ladder Chine, though it is impossible to determine which piece of wreckage came from which ship. Her bell is in Blackgang Chine Theme Park.

Name: *Nemrod* **Former name(s):** None.
Vessel type: Steam trawler.
Builder: Cook, Wellington & Gemmell Ltd, Beverly, Hull.
When completed: 1910.
Machinery built by: –
Tonnage: 125 gross.
Dimensions: Length: – **Breadth:** –
Depth of holds: –
Official number: – **Yard number:** –
Signal letters: **Last port of registry:** Ostend.
Ship description: Steel steam trawler.
Machinery description: Triple expansion 3 cylinders. 1 single ended boiler. 60 horse power.
Career and ownership: Vessel handed over to owners on 22 January 1910 for completion. Owned by H P Asperlagh, Belgium.
Destination and cargo: Ostend for fishing in the Irish Sea and return. 70 tons of fish on board.
Date sunk: 5 February 1910.
How sunk: Ran aground in thick fog.
Reported position of loss: 200 yards east of Walpen Chine, Chale Bay.
Actual position of wreck: Not determined with any accuracy but approximate position is 50° 35.40′ north, 001° 19.25′ west.
Orientation/height: Flattened remains move east and west each winter.
How identity of wreck proved: Position of loss accurately reported at the time.

SS *Daylesford* and schooner *Puhlin* Collision 1 April 1911

The presence of dense fog off St Catherine's Point in April 1911 was once again instrumental in the loss of two ships, they being the British steamer *Daylesford* and the Russian schooner *Puhlin*. *Daylesford* had been laid up in dry dock for a considerable time at her home port of Leith, along with a number of other steamers, and only ten days previously she had come through an overhaul. Setting out on her first voyage of the season under the command of her master, Captain Colley, the vessel came to Blyth where she loaded her cargo of coal and coke which was to be shipped to a Spanish port.

By the early hours of Saturday 1 April 1911, *Daylesford* was approaching the vicinity of the Isle of Wight in dense fog. Unknown to her, she was in close proximity to another vessel, the 307 ton Russian schooner *Puhlin,* heavily laden with a cargo of logwood. Looming out of the fog, neither vessel had time to avoid the other and between 6.30am and 7am the two ships collided, with *Puhlin* ramming the after part of the *Daylesford.*

It became immediately apparent that the *Daylesford* was severely and fatally damaged, and nothing could be done to save the ship. Her engine room staff managed to escape just in time, in only their shirts and trousers, but all 18 crew made it on deck, and just in time to clamber aboard the *Puhlin.* As soon as they had done so, *Daylesford* settled right down in the water, and was gone. No more than 5 minutes had elapsed since the collision.

Aboard the *Puhlin,* things were not much better. Her master, Captain Wentenberg, realised his ship was also in danger of sinking, but, as she had a cargo of wood, he expected she would remain afloat. Working hard at the pumps they managed to keep her going, fighting against the inrush of water. *Puhlin* made some headway towards the land, and at about 4pm a Danish steamer, the *Vulcan*, came across them. Her master declined to take the *Puhlin* in tow but agreed to take off the crew from the *Daylesford*, later landing them safely at Dover.

Puhlin remained afloat for another 2 hours, but eventually succumbed to the rising water. Her crew escaped in the ship's boats just before their ship heeled over and sank 2 or 3 miles off St Catherine's Point. Her nine crew later made it safely ashore.

A wreck believed to be that of the *Daylesford* has been located in 46 metres of water. The wreck is broken and contains a coal cargo. She has similar machinery to that of the *Daylesford* and her design is consistent with a steamer built in the 1880's. The highest parts are the engines and boilers. The location of the wreck of the *Puhlin* is unknown.

Name: *Daylesford.* **Former name(s):** None.
Vessel type: Steam ship.
Builder: R Thompson & Sons, Sunderland.
When completed: November 1882.
Machinery built by: T Clark & Company, Newcastle.
Tonnage: 1406 gross.
Dimensions: Length: 240′ 7″. **Breadth:** 34′ 1″. **Depth of holds:** 17′.
Official number: 85024. **Yard number:** –
Signal letters: HBTR. **Last port of registry:** Leith.
Ship description: Iron screw steamer. Well deck.
Machinery description: Compound 2 cylinders. 2 single ended boilers. 175 nominal horse power.
Career and ownership: Owned by New Line Steam Ship Company Ltd (Richard Mackie & Company, managers).
Destination and cargo: Blyth for Torre de Mar, Spain, with a cargo of coal and coke.
Date sunk: 1 April 1911.
How sunk: Collision in thick fog with the schooner *Puhlin.*
Reported position of loss: Variously as 20 miles off St Catherine's, and 17 miles south east of St Catherine's Point.
Actual position of wreck: 50° 22.27′ north, 001° 16.22′ west.
Orientation/height: Lies 090°/270°. Stands about 4 metres in 46 metres on shingle seabed on chalk.
How identity of wreck proved: Not confirmed but location, cargo and description of wreck fits that of the *Daylesford.*

SS *Derna*
Collision 10 December 1912

It was not until two days after the Italian steamer *Derna* had gone to the bottom that her true identity became known. Then, on 12 December 1912, on the south coast of the Isle of Wight, near Brook, a ship's boat was washed up bearing the name *Derna,* Genova. In the boat was the body of a man with a broken neck, dressed only in a jersey. Other wreckage came ashore in large quantities near St Catherine's Point, comprising part of the ship's bridge attached to which was the ship's wheel bearing the name *Derna,* together with her compass, bell and bridge rails. It was clear there had been a terrible disaster.

On 9 December 1912, Captain Guy Gaunt, Royal Navy, had taken the new battleship HMS *Centurion* from Plymouth for 30 hours of trials in the English Channel. The trials were to test the ship at moderate power between the Lizard and Portland. Soon after 5.30am, with the trials almost completed, *Centurion,* displacing 23,000 tons, was steaming at 19 knots off St Alban's Head down Channel towards Plymouth. The weather was clear but the night was very dark.

Captain Gaunt, just before he left the bridge to go to the chart-room, said to the officer of the watch, Lieutenant Boyes, "Keep me fully informed of everything and give all traffic plenty of room." Retiring to the chart room, he had been resting for perhaps 4 minutes when he heard a noise and felt a shock, and a sailor reported to him, "Ship's in collision, sir." Arriving on *Centurion's* upper bridge, Gaunt saw a steamer, showing two white lights, which was then abreast *Centurion's* bridge. "Her stern seemed to be towards us and she came very close to the quarterdeck. I jumped down on to the superstructure and tried to hail her but escaping steam at that moment deafened everything." He went on, "The unknown steamer gave a blast on her siren and seemed to turn away. I slewed this ship round towards her but saw no signs of her. Searchlights were switched on and kept going until daylight. I kept the ship on the spot, keeping a sharp look-out until daylight broke when, seeing no trace of her or of wreckage, I shaped course at 7.23 for Plymouth."

Members of the ship's company on *Centurion's* deck reported seeing the approaching steamer, but not before she was under their bows, and before assistance could be rendered, the ship had sunk. One crew member reported seeing a man jump from the steamer in a desperate attempt to reach *Centurion's* bow, but missed his footing and fell into the water.

Seaman Pearce, giving evidence at the Court-martial of Captain Gaunt and her officer of the watch Lieutenant Boyes in May 1913, said, "I was starboard look-out in the morning watch on 10 December. About 5 minutes before we struck a steamer I reported, 'Two lights burning dimly about 2 points off the starboard bow.' I did not see any more until we got near the ship then I shouted out, 'A big black patch, sir!' to the officer of the watch. As we came towards the ship she seemed to alter course towards us and we struck her just on her port bow. She appeared to be an ordinary tramp steamer, very high out of the water. Her propeller was showing." The ship must have been steaming down Channel on a broadly similar heading as *Centurion,* and the 600 foot battleship just ran her over.

The unknown steamer proved to be the *Derna*, and further proof came with the discovery of a port hand navigation lamp, still burning, which was found on *Centurion's* starboard net platform, 103 feet aft of the bows. The lamp bore a maker's name and serial number, and from that it was established that the lamp had been sold in Hamburg to a ship named *Girgenti, Derna's* former name, in 1903.

The Court-martial concluded by acquitting Captain Gaunt of all charges, but Lieutenant Boyes was found to be at blame for the collision in that "he had failed to appreciate the doubtful conditions in which the *Centurion* was placed with regard to the steamer, when lights were seen which did not clearly indicate her course or intention, and in that he failed to report to the Captain that a ship's lights were in sight which were of a doubtful nature." For the offence of endangering the *Centurion,* Lieutenant Boyes was reprimanded. There were no survivors from *Derna's* crew of 36.

The wreck which is almost certainly the *Derna* lies in a position remarkably close to that reported at the time by the *Centurion.* Her two boilers are the highest parts, the engine block being almost upended. The stern area is somewhat flattened.

Name: *Derna.* **Former name(s):** *Girgenti* ex *Danby.*
Vessel type: Steam ship.
Builder: Ropner & Sons, Stockton.
When completed: August 1890.
Machinery built by: Blair & Company Ltd, Stockton.
Tonnage: 2260 tons gross.
Dimensions: Length: 272′ 1″. **Breadth:** 38′ 9″.
Depth of holds: 18′ 1″.
Official number: 98491. **Yard number:** –
Signal letters: RNBS. **Last port of registry:** Genoa.
Ship description: Steel screw steamer. Well deck.
Machinery description: Triple expansion 3 cylinders. 2 single ended boilers. 201 nominal horse power.
Career and ownership: Owned by J Merryweather & Company in 1900 as *Danby.* 1903 sold to Rob M Sloman and renamed *Girgenti.* 1912 sold to Mezzano Shipping Company, Genoa, and renamed *Derna.*
Destination and cargo: Memel (Lithuania) to Port Talbot in ballast.
Date sunk: 10 December 1912.
How sunk: Collision with HMS *Centurion.*
Reported position of loss: 10 miles off Anvil Point, and 50° 27′ north, 002° 01′ west.
Actual position of wreck: 50° 27.22′ north, 002° 00.28′ west.
Orientation/height: Lies 160°/340°. Stands 5 metres in 40 metres on pebble/shingle and sand seabed.
How identity of wreck proved: Wreck is in position very close to that reported in 1912. A secondary ship's wheel, made of brass has been recovered. Scratched in the brass was an Italian name, Gerolimo Oliveri. It has not been established if he was a member of *Derna's* crew or not. Otherwise the description of the vessel fits that of the *Derna.*

Pilot boat *Solent*
Collision 11 December 1912

The *Solent* was one of the latest additions to the pilot fleet operated by Trinity House, and as she was based at Southampton, she was a vessel frequently in demand. About 11am on the morning of Wednesday 11 December 1912, *Solent* was cruising around under sail west of the Needles, awaiting the arrival of the 7457 ton troopship HMS *Dufferin*, inward bound from India. When *Dufferin* was about 4 miles west-south-west of the Needles, she signalled for a pilot, and *Solent*, picking up the signal, made for the warship.

Rough seas made life difficult for the crew of the *Solent*, but she closed the bigger ship with the intention of putting a pilot aboard. However, as she drew close to the *Dufferin* and was about to turn to launch her boat to put the pilot aboard, she mis-stayed and ran in under the lee side of the troopship, which bore down upon her carrying away her mast and rigging and smashing a large hole in her starboard side. Immediately, she began to settle down.

The pilot, a man named Watson, who was due to take the *Dufferin* in to Southampton, succeeded in climbing through one of *Dufferin's* portholes, but the five other men on *Solent* had to abandon ship quickly and escape in the ship's boat. In very difficult conditions, they were soon picked up by the *Dufferin* before the *Solent* sank some 35 minutes after the collision.

There is no information as to whether the wreck of the *Solent* has been located or identified.

Name: *Solent*. **Former name(s):** None.
Vessel type: Motor & sail auxiliary ketch.
Builder: John Cran & Company, Leith.
When completed: 1910.
Machinery built by: William Beardmore & Company Ltd.
Tonnage: 49 tons gross.
Dimensions: Length: 62′ 9″. **Breadth:** 18′.
Depth of holds: 9′ 6″.
Official number: 131752. **Yard number:** –
Signal letters: HSBG. **Last port of registry:** Southampton.
Ship description: Steel screw motor vessel. Motor auxiliary ketch.
Machinery description: Paraffin motor, 2 cylinders. 38 horse power.
Career and ownership: Owned by the Corporation of Trinity House, Tower Hill, London (Arthur Owen, manager).
Destination and cargo: Southampton for the western Solent on pilot duties, with 2 pilots and 4 crew.
Date sunk: 11 December 1912.
How sunk: Collision with HMS *Dufferin*.
Reported position of loss: About 4 miles west-south-west of the Needles.
Actual position of wreck: Not known.
Orientation/height: –
How identity of wreck proved: –

SS *Olivine*
Captured by U-boat and torpedoed 4 April 1915

SS *Olivine*. Courtesy Glasgow University Archives.

Olivine was a steam coaster which departed St Sampsons, Guernsey, on 4 April 1915, bound for Calais. She carried a crew of 12 hands. When she had reached a position about mid Channel late in the afternoon, steaming at 8 knots, a submarine was sighted on the surface about half a mile distant, making directly for the steamer. This was the German U-boat, *U-33*, under the command of Kapitänleutnant Gansser.

The U-boat had hoisted a signal, indicating the *Olivine* to stop and immediately abandon ship. The master, Captain Archibald Lamont, was on the bridge trying to make out what the signal said, when the U-boat came within hailing distance, steaming up alongside *Olivine's* starboard quarter. One of the officer's gave orders that the master and crew had 10 minutes to take to the boats and get clear, as the ship was going to be sunk. In a few minutes, the impatient U-boat crew, dissatisfied with the time being taken to abandon ship, called out, "5 minutes are up! Look alive and get clear of the ship!" No doubt intimidated by the manned gun on *U-33's* foredeck, and other crew on the casing armed with rifles, Captain Lamont had no choice but to comply.

All hands got away safely, and a few minutes later a torpedo from *U-33* was fired, but missed. Another was fired and this struck the ship on her starboard quarter, and in 2 minutes, she went to the bottom, stern first, the mizzen mast and funnel being blown away by the explosion. The survivors were later picked up by a patrol boat.

The Admiralty, unimpressed with the actions of Captain Lamont, complained that he had acted very tamely and made no real effort to save his vessel. However, in seeking further explanation, it became clear that Captain Lamont had not been privy to the Admiralty's instructions to "turn bow to the enemy before he gets too close, and make straight for him." Accordingly, no blame was attached to him for the loss of his ship.

The wreck of the *Olivine* lies in an upright and fairly

intact condition in 72 metres of water, with her cargo of granite piled in her holds. The engine room area is a mess, consistent with torpedo damage.

Name: *Olivine*. **Former name(s):** None.
Vessel type: Steam coaster.
Builder: J Shearer & Son, Glasgow.
When completed: March 1902.
Machinery built by: Muir & Houston Ltd, Glasgow.
Tonnage: 634 tons gross.
Dimensions: Length: 185′ 2″. **Breadth:** 29′ 2″.
Depth of holds: 10′ 8″.
Official number: 114028. **Yard number:** –
Signal letters: TGRW. **Last port of registry:** Glasgow.
Ship description: Steel screw 3 masted steam coaster. Well deck. Fitted with electric light.
Machinery description: Triple expansion 3 cylinders. 1 single ended boiler. 91 registered horse power. Machinery fitted aft.
Career and ownership: Owned by William Robertson, 45 West Nile Street, Glasgow.
Armament: Unarmed.
Destination and cargo: Guernsey for Calais with 751 tons of granite.
Date sunk: 4 April 1915.
How sunk: Captured by *U-33* and torpedoed.
Reported position of loss: 30 miles south of St Catherine's Point.
Actual position of wreck: 50° 13.05′ north, 001° 01.30′ west.
Orientation/height: Lies 160°/340°. Stands 6 metres on shingle seabed.
How identity of wreck proved: Bridge steering position recovered bearing a serial number which proved the steering gear had been sold for the *Olivine*.

Steam drifter *Waterlily*
Collision 23 July 1915

Waterlily was hired by the Admiralty to become part of the Auxiliary Patrol Force and to act as a net vessel, the intention being to form anti-submarine barriers using special wire nets. She was based at Poole.

On 23 July 1915, *Waterlily* was somewhere off St Alban's Head when a collision took place involving her and an accompanying vessel, the steam trawler *Ouse*, another hired vessel attached to the Auxiliary Patrol. How and why the collision took place is unclear, but the cause was said to be that the pilot in charge of the *Ouse* thought that the *Waterlily* was endeavouring to supply information regarding speed and course to be steered. No further information was given and it is assumed the two vessels came together so severely that *Waterlily* suffered such serious damage that she took on water and sank.

During the 1980's a fisherman snagged some gear on an obstruction which was found to be a wreck. Divers recovered a builder's nameplate which identified the wreck as the remains of the *Waterlily*. Not much stands up apart from her boiler, though her wooden ribs are evident.

Name: *Waterlily*. **Former name(s):** None.
Vessel type: Steam drifter.
Builder: Henry Reynolds, Oulton Broads, Lowestoft.
When completed: 1907.
Machinery built by: William Burrell, Great Yarmouth.
Tonnage: 82 tons gross.
Dimensions: Length: 85′. **Breadth:** 18′ 6″.
Depth of holds: 8′ 8″.
Official number: 124651. **Yard number:** –
Signal letters: – **Last port of registry:** Banff.
Ship description: Wooden screw steam drifter.
Machinery description: Compound 2 cylinders. 1 single ended boiler. 75 indicated horse power.
Career and ownership: Owned in 1910 by John May, Buckpool. Hired as an Admiralty drifter, No 2171, port number BF595, and commissioned in May 1915.
Armament: Unarmed.
Destination and cargo: On anti-submarine duties. No cargo.
Date sunk: 23 July 1915.
How sunk: Collision with the steam trawler *Ouse*.
Reported position of loss: Off St Alban's Head.
Actual position of wreck: 50° 31.25′ north, 001° 52.60′ west.
Orientation/height: Stands about 3 metres on rough seabed.
How identity of wreck proved: Builder's nameplate recovered.

SS *Algerian*
Mined 12 January 1916

SS *Flintshire*, later renamed *Algerian*. Author's collection.

During the third week of October 1915, the newly completed minelaying U-boat, *UC-5*, under the command of Oberleutnant zur See Herbert Pustkuchen, was operating to the east of the Isle of Wight off the Nab Light Vessel, where she laid a number of mines. Having "sown her eggs" she motored west, arriving off the Needles where the rest of her mines, probably four in number, were sown, then returning empty to her base in Zeebrugge. The Needles mines remained undetected until 12 January 1916, when the large steamer *Algerian,* steaming at about 10 knots, reached a position about 2½ miles south west of the Needles. The time was 10.15am.

Suddenly, a loud explosion was heard on the starboard side of the ship abreast number 2 hatch, close to the bridge. Her master, Captain John Ring, told an investigation team that he had just left the bridge, telling the Third Officer, "Keep a careful lookout and let me know if anything is sighted, at once." No sooner had he entered the chart room when the whole ship shook with the force of the explosion, blowing the hatch covers off and sending ballast as high as the masthead. *Algerian* began to settle at once and it was thought she would soon sink. Ordering the crew to take to the ship's boats, but telling them to remain close by, Captain Ring remained the only man on board as he inspected his ship for damage.

In number 2 hold, water was gaining rapidly. On the starboard side of the hull, the ship's plates were buckled and corrugated, extending from the main deck to the water line. Number 1 hold was flooding too, and Captain Ring decided he would have to abandon ship. Standing by the vessel as she settled by the head, listing to port, it became apparent after some time that she seemed to have stabilised, and that she was being kept afloat by the integrity of her bulkheads. Re-boarding his ship, Captain Ring called for volunteers to assist in saving her, as three Admiralty drifters had now arrived on the scene. He intended to coax his ship to Southampton or to beach her in the Solent. Towing cables were attached to two of the drifters and after much difficulty, *Algerian's* head was turned and she started her journey to the Solent

The Needles were passed by noon, and with a flood tide pushing them along, a speed of 3 knots was achieved. It began to look as though the ship might be saved, when off Hurst Castle the ship sheered badly. New arrangements had to be adopted to control *Algerian*, and the tow carried on. By 2pm, with water continuing to rise, steam steering power was lost and she became less manageable. With only a short distance left to go before the ship could be beached within the relative safety of the Boom Defence area, set up to deter U-boats, Commander Harold, officer in charge of the Boom Defence, ordered, "Captain! You'll have to let go an anchor!" Captain Ring protested this would strain the *Algerian* too much, and so it proved to be. Within 15 minutes of being anchored, *Algerian* flooded completely, heeled over to port and disappeared.

The wreck of the *Algerian* still stands 7 or so metres high. Her hull plates are very thin and some can be easily bent. She was dispersed in the early 1920's and it is hard to recognise what's what. A boiler is evident but the rest of the wreck is covered in marine growth making recognition difficult. She is also a collection point for rubbish discarded in the Solent. The wreck can be dived safely in the summer on good neap tides in settled weather when up to 6 metres visibility can be expected. Spring tides and bad weather, particularly heavy rain, will reduce visibility to practically zero, and so should be avoided. Great care is also needed due to the high numbers of yachtsmen sailing in the Solent.

Name: *Algerian*. **Former name(s):** *Flintshire*.
Vessel type: Steam ship.
Builder: Sunderland Shipbuilding Company Ltd.
When completed: June 1896.
Machinery built by: North East Marine Engineering Ltd, Sunderland.
Tonnage: 3837 tons gross.
Dimensions: Length: 361′. **Breadth:** 45′ 2″.
Depth of holds: 19′ 9″.
Official number: 105833. **Yard number:** 183.
Signal letters: PHTJ. **Last port of registry:** Liverpool.
Ship description: Steel screw steamer. 1 deck and spardeck. Clipper bow. Fitted with wireless.
Machinery description: Triple expansion 3 cylinders. 2 single ended boilers. 345 nominal horse power.
Career and ownership: Built for Jenkins & Company, London, as *Flintshire*. 1907, sold to Royal Mail Steam Packet Company, London. 1913 taken into ownership of Ellerman Lines and renamed *Algerian*. Managed by the Hall Line.
Armament: Unarmed.
Destination and cargo: Cowes for Avonmouth in ballast on government charter.
Date sunk: 12 January 1916.
How sunk: Struck a mine laid by *UC-5*.
Reported position of loss: Near Cowes.
Actual position of wreck: 50° 46.07′ north, 001° 20.35′ west.
Orientation/height: Stands about 7 metres in 22–25 metres on a shingle seabed.
How identity of wreck proved: Contemporary reports show the wreck sank in the position indicated.

Steam trawler *Albion II* Mined 13 January 1916

After the steamer *Algerian* had been lost after striking a mine from an undetected minefield south west of the Needles, orders were given to the Auxiliary Patrol to sweep the area to clear it of mines. The trawler *Albion II*, accompanied by another, the *Zena Dare*, commenced sweeping operations on the morning of the 13 January. Receiving orders to amend the area to be swept, *Albion II* hauled in her kite, an underwater device designed to work with the sweeping wire, when the ship's mate saw a mine on the kite wire itself. Immediately halting the lift, the vessel's master, Captain Clark Mead, looked for the mine but could not see it. The kite wire was slackened, the intention being to try to slip the mine onto the sweeping wire, where it could be cut free and destroyed.

Hauling again on the kite wire, nothing was seen, and Captain Mead ordered the sweep wire to be winched in. Immediately, an explosion occurred, throwing everyone off their feet, the signal boy being thrown from the bridge onto the deck. Checking that everyone was alright and ordering the boat to be readied for lowering, Captain Mead quickly went aft and asked the engineer Charles Neller how the ship was below. He said, "The seacocks are blown out and the engine room flooring has lifted." "Is she making any water?" asked Captain Mead. "Yes, it's up over the crank pits." Within a minute or two the water was gaining rapidly.

Frederick Morgan, second hand, questioned at the subsequent Court of Enquiry, was asked, "There was no attempt made to save the ship?" He said, "No, it was impossible." Asked why, he said, "The water was coming in and the steam pumps were no good." "How far off land were you?" Morgan replied, "About a mile and a half." Also giving evidence, Charles Neller, the first engineer, told the court, "The explosion was on the port side of the keel in the fore part of the engine room, just abaft the boiler. I went to find out what damage was done, as I thought that the boiler bottom had been pierced as the engine room was full of steam, but it was the cold water running in and coming into contact with the hot boiler . . . and the seacock was blown off the ship's side. The flooring of the engine room was all blown up. The water was then running in the furnaces."

Fifteen minutes after the explosion, Captain Clark and his crew of 12 men left their sinking ship, and boarded the *Zena Dare*. Thirty minutes later, in rough seas and a fresh breeze, *Albion II* went down. The minefield laid by the *UC-5* had claimed its second victim.

The wreck of the *Albion II* has been charted as an obstruction for some time, more or less where Frederick Morgan estimated she was in 1916. The most prominent parts are the boiler and triple expansion engine. Most of the wreck lies under a layer of shingle, though parts of the hull, and a larger part of the bows, stand up. A gun mounting lies just forward of the boiler.

Name: *Albion II.* **Former name(s):** None.
Vessel type: Steam trawler.
Builder: Smiths Dock, North Shields.
When completed: December 1907.
Machinery built by: W V V Lidgerwood.
Tonnage: 240 tons gross.
Dimensions: Length: 120′ 3″. **Breadth:** 21′ 6″.
Depth of holds: 11′ 7″.
Official number: 127410. **Yard number:** 363.
Signal letters: HPSL. **Last port of registry:** Milford.
Ship description: Steel screw steam trawler.
Machinery description: Triple expansion 3 cylinders. 1 single ended boiler. 68 registered horse power.
Career and ownership: Built for the Pater Steam Trawling Company. Milford port No M219. Hired by the Admiralty in August 1914 (No 139) for service as a minesweeper, and attached to the Portsmouth area.
Armament: 1 × 3 pounder gun.
Destination and cargo: Portsmouth for the Needles area to sweep for mines and return.
Date sunk: 13 January 1916.
How sunk: Mined by *UC-5*.
Reported position of loss: About 1½ miles off land.
Actual position of wreck: 50° 38.35′ north, 001° 34.28′ west.
Orientation/height: Stands about 3 metres on shingle seabed.
How identity of wreck proved: Description of wreck fits that of the *Albion II*, complete with gun mounting, and witnesses reported her position of loss as 1½ miles off the land, which is where she is.

SS *Asger Ryg*
Torpedoed 6 April 1916

SS *Asger Ryg*. Courtesy Bristol's Museums Galleries & Archives.

From time to time, entire ships and their crews simply disappear, one such vessel being the Danish steamer *Asger Ryg*. She left the Tyne for Algiers on 4 April 1916, and was last heard of after she had passed Beachy Head. When one of the ship's lifeboats, bearing the name *Asger Ryg*, was found floating off St Catherine's Point four days later, it was obvious something terrible had happened. The empty lifeboat was badly damaged, and that damage was consistent with some kind of explosion.

It is likely that the *Asger Ryg* was torpedoed by Oberleutnant zur See Herbert Pustkuchen in the coastal U-boat, *UB-29*. He wrote in his log, "On the night of the 6th April, surface torpedo attack against a steamer of about 4000 tons without hull markings. Torpedo hit. Saw what was believed to be the ship sinking. Name and nationality unknown." Pustkuchen was later promoted posthumously from Oberleutnant to Kapitänleutnant.

The discrepancy in the estimation of tonnage was not unusual among U-boat commanders, who sometimes overestimated the size of their victims when engaged in submerged, night attacks.

There is no information to say whether the wreck of the *Asger Ryg* has been found or identified.

Name: *Asger Ryg*. **Former name(s):** *Mimi Horn*.
Vessel type: Steam ship.
Builder: Schömer & Jensen, Tønning.
When completed: 1902.
Machinery built by: Schömer & Jensen, Tønning.
Tonnage: 1134 tons gross.
Dimensions: Length: 218′ 1″. **Breadth:** 33′.
Depth of holds: 13′ 4″.
Official number: – **Yard number:** –
Signal letters: NJMD. **Last port of registry:** Copenhagen.
Ship description: Steel screw steamer. 1 deck and well deck.
Machinery description: Triple expansion 3 cylinders. 92 nominal horse power.
Career and ownership: Owned by Dampskibs Actieselskabet, Skjalm Hvide (Marius Nielson & Sön, managers).
Armament: Unarmed.
Destination and cargo: The Tyne for Algiers with 1275 tons of coal.
Date sunk: 6 April 1916.
How sunk: Torpedoed by *UB-29*.
Reported position of loss: None.
Actual position of wreck: Not known.
Orientation/height: –
How identity of wreck proved: –

Sailing vessel *Jacques Cartier* Scuttled by bombs 3 August 1916

Little is known about the loss of the French schooner *Jacques Cartier*. This is almost certainly because the survivors, relatively safe in the ship's boats, headed directly back for France, since that was their home country and in any case, it was closer than England. Accordingly, there is no survivor's account of the loss of the ship.

What is known is that the *Jacques Cartier* was in the central part of the English Channel south of the Isle of Wight on 3 August 1916. The steamer *Sphene* was not far away and her crew reported that, about 1 pm, a loud noise was heard in the vicinity. They soon spotted a German U-boat on the surface, which was the small coastal U-boat, the *UB-18,* under the command of Oberleutnant zur See Otto Steinbrinck, in the act of sinking a sailing vessel. According to U-boat records, the *Jacques Cartier* was stopped by gunfire from the *UB-18,* the crew ordered to abandon ship, and then scuttling charges were placed on board which exploded and sank the ship. As soon as this had been accomplished, *UB-18* headed away at full speed towards the *Sphene.*

The wreck of a fairly small sailing ship lies in mid Channel in about 63 metres of water. Some of her timbers are blackened, possibly as a result of burning, and the size of the wreck fits that of the *Jacques Cartier*.

Name: *Jacques Cartier*. **Former name(s):** None.
Vessel type: Sailing vessel.
Builder: G Gautier, St Malo.
When completed: 1911.
Machinery built by: –
Tonnage: 259 tons gross.
Dimensions: Length: 116′ 5″. **Breadth:** 25′ 8″. **Depth of holds:** 12′ 7″.
Official number: – **Yard number:** –
Signal letters: JPRC. **Last port of registry:** St Malo.
Ship description: Wooden 3 masted schooner.
Machinery description: –
Career and ownership: Owned by Boscher.
Armament: Unarmed.
Destination and cargo: Not known.
Date sunk: 3 August 1916.
How sunk: Stopped by *UB-18* and scuttling charges placed on board.
Reported position of loss: 25 miles north of Cherbourg.
Actual position of wreck: 50° 03.70′ north, 001° 47.21′ west.
Orientation/height: Stands about 3 metres in 66 metres on shingle seabed.
How identity of wreck proved: Not proved but position agrees with that provided by *UB-18*, and is not far from the wreck of the SS *Sphene* from where *Jacques Cartier* was seen to sink.

SS *Sphene*
Captured and scuttled with bombs 3 August 1916

SS *Sphene*. Courtesy E N Taylor collection.

Sphene was a 740 tons steam coaster which sailed from Honfleur on 2 August 1916, bound for Newport, Wales. Her voyage was briefly interrupted by the appearance of thick fog, and she anchored in Havre Roads until it lifted. In a smooth sea and fine weather, she steamed away again on her journey until she had gone as far as about 25 miles north of Cherbourg. Unknown to her crew, the small coastal U-boat, *UB-18*, under the command of Oberleutnant zur See Otto Steinbrinck, was on war patrol in mid Channel, on the lookout for ships to sink.

About 1pm on 3 August, *Sphene's* crew were alerted by a loud noise. Looking around to determine the source, a German U-boat was seen on the surface away off their port beam, in the process of sinking a sailing ship about 2 miles to the southward. This turned out to be the *Jacques Cartier*, a French vessel of 259 tons. *UB-18* then approached *Sphene*, firing her deck gun, a shell landing in the water just 30 yards ahead of her bows.

Sphene's master, 48 year old Richard Stirling, ordered the engines stopped and told the crew to take to the boats. *UB-18* drew up, ordering Captain Stirling and three men to board the U-boat. Then, a German submariner loaded four bombs in one of *Sphene's* boats, and rowed across to the ship and boarded her. Attaching the bombs before and abaft the bridge, he quickly made a search of the chart room before setting the timing fuses on the bombs, and getting clear of the ship. Ten minutes later, the bombs exploded, and *Sphene* heeled over to starboard, going down by the bows. For several minutes, her stern was tipped up in the air, before rising up, the ship then going down head first. Ordered back to their boats, Captain Stirling and his crew watched as the *UB-18* made off, the survivors later being rescued by French torpedo boats.

The wreck of the *Sphene* lies in 66 metres of water in the mid Channel separation zone. Her large single boiler and engine are the highest part, with the stern section containing the machinery being the most interesting parts of the wreck. Forward of the boiler she is much more broken.

Name: *Sphene.* **Former name(s):** None.
Vessel type: Steam coaster.
Builder: A Rodger & Company, Port Glasgow.
When completed: September 1902.
Machinery built by: A Rodger & Company, Port Glasgow.
Tonnage: 740 tons gross.
Dimensions: Length: 195′ 4″. **Breadth:** 30′ 1″. **Depth of holds:** 11′ 1″.
Official number: 115710. **Yard number:** –
Signal letters: TQKF. **Last port of registry:** Glasgow.
Ship description: Steel screw 3 masted steam coaster. 1 deck and well deck.
Machinery description: Triple expansion 3 cylinders. 1 single ended boiler. Machinery fitted aft. 99 registered horse power.
Career and ownership: Owned by William Robertson, 45 West Nile Street, Glasgow.
Armament: Unarmed.
Destination and cargo: Honfleur for Newport, Wales, in ballast.
Date sunk: 3 August 1916.
How sunk: Stopped by gunfire from *UB-18* and captured. Scuttled by bombs placed on board.
Reported position of loss: Variously as 26 miles south west of St Catherine's Point, and 25 miles north of Cherbourg.
Actual position of wreck: 50° 06.93′ north, 001° 38.73′ west.
Orientation/height: Lies 000°/180°. Stands about 5 metres on hard chalk seabed and shingle.
How identity of wreck proved: Ship's bell recovered.

SS *Badger*
Captured and scuttled with bombs, then gunfire
3 August 1916

The *Badger* was a small steam coaster of only 89 tons, but her size did not prevent her becoming another victim of the submarine war. Departing Jersey for Portsmouth, *Badger* was in the vicinity of both the *Sphene* and the *Jacques Cartier* when she became the third vessel sunk on 3 August 1916. In common with the other two, *Badger* was stopped by gunfire. *UB-18* fired her deck gun, and *Badger's* master, Captain Thomas Harvey, stopped his ship. The U-boat came alongside and ordered Captain Harvey and the four crew to immediately get into the ship's boat. Doing as they were told, the U-boat commander, Oberleutnant zur See Otto Steinbrinck was heard to say, "Set the charge for six minutes." One of the U-boat's crew then went to *Badger's* engine room with a scuttling charge.

Captain Harvey said, "The crew of the submarine were very excited and because we were told to get straight into the boat, we didn't have time to save any of our clothing or money. The submarine then went away to a distance of about half a mile, and we were told to stay clear of the *Badger*. When the bomb went off it didn't sink my vessel, so the submarine returned and fired five shots from about 50 yards, sending my vessel to the bottom."

A charted wreck lying in 66 metres in the mid Channel separation zone is thought to be the *Badger*.

Name: *Badger*. **Former name(s):** None.
Vessel type: Steam coaster.
Builder: Not known, but built at Hamilton Hill, Glasgow.
When completed: 1894.
Machinery built by: Not known.
Tonnage: 89 tons gross.
Dimensions: Length: 66′. **Breadth:** 18′ 3″.
Depth of holds: 8′ 5″.
Official number: 102688. **Yard number:** –
Signal letters: – **Last port of registry:** Portsmouth.
Ship description: Steel screw steam coaster.
Machinery description: 15 horse power, probably 2 cylinder compound engine.
Career and ownership: 1909, owned by the Glasgow Steam Coasters Company Ltd, 142 St Vincent Street, Glasgow. At the time of loss owned by Thomas H Harvey, Stamshaw Chemical Works, Portsmouth.
Armament: Unarmed.
Destination and cargo: Jersey for Portsmouth with 80 tons of oil and coal tar.
Date sunk: 3 August 1916.
How sunk: Stopped by gunfire and captured by UB-18. Scuttling charge placed on board, then finished off with gunfire.
Reported position of loss: 50° 06′ north, 001° 38′ west.
Actual position of wreck: 50° 05.58′ north, 001° 35.62′ west. It is possible the wreck in position 50° 05.44′ north, 001° 48.82′ west may be the *Badger*.
Orientation/height: Stands about 4 metres on a hard seabed.
How identity of wreck proved: Not proved but the wreck, its description and position broadly fits that of the *Badger*.

SS *Spiral*
Stopped by gunfire, captured and scuttled with bombs
4 August 1916

SS *Spiral*. Courtesy Norwegian Maritime Museum/Nylands verksted.

Oberleutnant zur See Otto Steinbrinck in *UB-18* had not quite finished his war patrol when he spotted the British steamer *Spiral* in a position estimated at about 40 miles west-south-west of St Catherine's Point. It was about 7.30am on the morning of 4 August 1916, when *Spiral* was steaming down Channel at about 8 ½ knots. Her master, Captain Nathan Bradley, had previously gone below, having been on deck most of the night, leaving control of the ship to his chief officer. Suddenly, a U-boat was sighted on the surface no more than ¼ mile away off the port quarter.

In clear weather and a calm sea, *UB-18* opened fire with her deck gun, the shell falling 20 feet ahead of the *Spiral*. Hearing the noise, Captain Bradley guessed what was going on, and quickly destroyed the ship's secret sailing instructions and confidential papers before going on deck. There, the U-boat hailed *Spiral's* crew, the commander, Steinbrinck, shouting out, "Get into your boats!" Being unarmed and completely at the mercy of the U-boat at point blank range, Captain Bradley had no option but to obey, and *Spiral* was abandoned by her crew of 20.

UB-18 approached *Spiral's* boats, and demanded the ship's papers. Captain Bradley at first denied having any papers, but a revolver was pointed at his head, and Otto Steinbrinck told him, "Don't be reckless." At this point, the ship's register, bills of lading, manifest and some personal papers were handed over. Meanwhile, some of the German submariners had boarded *Spiral*, removing various provisions as well as her clocks and barometers, and evidently placing their bombs inside her hull.

After *Spiral* was left for the last time, three internal explosions were heard, but these had not caused enough damage to sink her. Some time later, *UB-18* returned and put an officer on the abandoned ship, presumably to lay additional charges. After he left, a further explosion took place, and *Spiral* began to sink by the stern, taking a list to port, before finally disappearing for good.

A wreck thought to be that of the *Spiral* lies in 55 metres of water just north of the westbound shipping lane. The wreck has settled towards her port side, the engines and two boilers being prominent, though the bow section has broken off and stands completely vertical some 7 or 8 metres high. She remains a substantial wreck, with debris lying along her port side.

Name: *Spiral.* **Former name(s):** None.
Vessel type: Steam ship.
Builder: Nylands Vaerksted, Christiania.
When completed: 1906.
Machinery built by: Nylands Vaerksted, Christiania.
Tonnage: 1342 tons gross.
Dimensions: Length: 245′ 6″. **Breadth:** 36′ 5″.
Depth of holds: 16′ 5″.
Official number: 135919. **Yard number:** –
Signal letters: JLWR. **Last port of registry:** West Hartlepool.
Ship description: Steel screw steamer, schooner rigged. 1 deck.
Machinery description: Triple expansion 3 cylinders. 2 single ended boilers. 160 nominal horse power.
Career and ownership: Built for Hj Siegwarth, Norway. 1907/8 owned by Acties-Spiral. 1912 owned by Acties, Oceanb (J P Pederson & Son, managers). 1916 owned by Minnie Steam Ship Company (E A Casper, Edgar & Company, managers).
Armament: Unarmed.
Destination and cargo: Tyne for Bordeaux with 1858 tons of coal.
Date sunk: 4 August 1916.
How sunk: Stopped by gunfire from *UB-18*, captured and scuttling charges placed on board.
Reported position of loss: 40 miles west-south-west of St Catherine's Point.
Actual position of wreck: 50° 17.75′north, 001° 55.22′ west.
Orientation/height: Lies 090°/270°, bows to the east. Stands up to 8 metres in 55 metres on shingle seabed.
How identity of wreck proved: Not proved, but there are similarities between what can be seen on the wreck in comparison with photographs of the ship. Description of wreck is broadly consistent with that of the *Spiral.* The bridge steering position has been recovered, manufactured in Hull, bearing markings which suggest it had been in Scandinavian ownership. A number of names of Scandinavian origin are scratched in the brass of the ship's wheel. There is even a date of 21 July 1916. It is possible the wreck in the position given is in fact the *Norma.*

SS *Barbara*
Sunk by gunfire 20 October 1916

The British steamer *Barbara* was a substantial vessel of 3740 tons gross, built in 1897. She was unarmed, and had little prospect of escape when she was attacked by a surfaced U-boat, the *UB-40,* under the command of Oberleutnant zur See Hans Howaldt. *Barbara* had departed Philadelphia on 27 September 1916, bound for West Hartlepool, and the voyage had proceeded without incident until the ship was in a position estimated as about 25 miles south of St Catherine's Point, Isle of Wight.

About 4.25pm on 20 October, *Barbara* was steaming in an easterly direction at about 7 knots. The weather was fine and clear. All seemed well until a surfaced U-boat was sighted on an opposite course, steaming towards the ship no more than 2 miles distant. Ahead of *Barbara* was another steamer, the Spanish ship *Victor de Chavarri*, a neutral. She had been stopped by the *UB-40* and evidently given a choice – return to Bilbao or be sunk. That wasn't much of a choice, and the *Victor de Chavarri* did indeed go about, and made her way unmolested back down the Channel, but not before she took *Barbara's* survivors with her.

UB-40 came to within about a mile of *Barbara* and put a shell across her bows. The engines were stopped and all the crew comprising 32 hands took to the ship's boats. Then, the U-boat began to shell the ship, averaging a shot per minute interspersed with more rapid fire. *Barbara's* master, William Mayne, estimated more than 30 rounds had been fired at her.

Around 5.20pm in the gloom of that October evening, *Barbara* filled and disappeared. Half an hour later, the *Victor de Chavarri* picked up all the survivors safely and, some days later, landed them safely at Bilbao.

A wreck which may be that of the *Barbara* lies in about 82 metres of water in mid Channel off the Isle of Wight. The wreck lies on its starboard side with the bows almost upside down. The boilers have rolled out. This is a substantial wreck which stands some 9 or 10 metres off the seabed.

Name: *Barbara.* **Former name(s):** None.
Vessel type: Steam ship.
Builder: Furness Withy & Company Ltd, West Hartlepool.
When completed: February 1897.
Machinery built by: W Alland & Company Ltd, Sunderland.
Tonnage: 3740 tons gross.
Dimensions: Length: 340′. **Breadth:** 47′ 1″.
Depth of holds: 19′ 2″.
Official number: 106959. **Yard number:** –
Signal letters: PNQJ. **Last port of registry:** West Hartlepool.
Ship description: Steel screw steamer, schooner rigged. Spar deck.
Machinery description: Triple expansion 3 cylinders. 2 single ended boilers. New donkey boiler 1911. 299 nominal horse power.
Career and ownership: Owned by Kent Steam Ship Company Ltd (S Watson, manager).
Armament: Unarmed.
Destination and cargo: Philadelphia for West Hartlepool with 6000 tons of refined sugar.
Date sunk: 20 October 1916.
How sunk: Stopped by *UB-40* and sunk by gunfire.
Reported position of loss: 25 miles south of St Catherine's Point.
Actual position of wreck: 50° 12.05′ north, 001° 06.54′ west.
Orientation/height: Lies 070°/250° and stands 9 to 10 metres in 82 metres.
How identity of wreck proved: Not proved, but the wreck is large and substantial, as was *Barbara*, and is in the right area.

Steam drifter *Fame*
Ran aground 22 October 1916

Fame was a steam drifter which had been part of the fishing fleet based at Whitby. As the First World War progressed, she was commissioned and hired by the Admiralty to become part of the southern Auxiliary Patrol Force, where she would be utilised as a net defence drifter. The vessel left North Shields on 18 October 1916 shortly after the Admiralty requisitioned her. The records from the Auxiliary Patrol indicate what happened as the *Fame* headed for her new port:

"About 6.45am on 22 October 1916, the drifter *Fame*, on passage from North Shields for Poole, ran ashore on the Hook Sands at the entrance to Poole Harbour. It is feared she will become a total loss as her bows are now under water and a heavy sea is breaking over her. All the crew have been saved. As soon as the weather moderates every endeavour will be made to salve her." However, soon after another report said, "The drifter *Fame,* stranded on the Hook Sands, is now commencing to break up and her salvage is regarded as hopeless. A heavy sea is breaking and has been breaking over her since 24th instant and the pumping out and lifting operations had to be abandoned. All fittings that could be got at have been salved."

The final report said, "*Fame* now a total loss. Every endeavour was made to salvage her but the continuous gales which have prevailed since her stranding put a stop to all operations. She has now sunk from 3 to 4 feet into the sand, her holds and engine room are filling with sand and she is gradually breaking up."

A Court-martial was convened for the trial of *Fame's* captain, skipper Arthur Geoffrey Holmes, but the result is not known.

The wreck of the *Fame* remains on the Hook Sands, her single boiler and triple expansion engine being the highest parts. She is upright and covers and uncovers with sand. Her engine room telegraph was found in the wreck, not in its usual position on the forward end of the engine, starboard side, but in the engineer's vice. Whether this was relevant to the loss of the ship may never be known.

Name: *Fame*. **Former name(s):** None.
Vessel type: Steam drifter.
Builder: Not known, but built in Leith.
When completed: 1901.
Machinery built by: Not known.
Tonnage: 68 tons gross.
Dimensions: Length: 77′ 5″. **Breadth:** 18′ 3″.
Depth of holds: 8′ 4″.
Official number: 113357. **Yard number:** –
Signal letters: – **Last port of registry:** Banff.
Ship description: Wooden screw steam drifter.
Machinery description: Triple expansion 3 cylinders. 1 single ended boiler. 18 horse power.
Career and ownership: Port number WY71. Managed by William Slater, Buckpool, Banff. Commissioned and hired by the Admiralty in October 1916 as a net defence drifter based with the southern Auxiliary Patrol Force in Poole.
Armament: Unarmed.
Destination and cargo: North Shields for Poole.
Date sunk: 22 October 1916.
How sunk: Ran aground on the Hook Sands during a south easterly gale.
Reported position of loss: On the Hook Sands.
Actual position of wreck: 50° 40.75′ north, 001° 55.98′ west.
Orientation/height: Stands about 3 metres in 6 metres on sand seabed.
How identity of wreck proved: Contemporary reports show *Fame* was lost on the Hook Sands and this is the only wreck there which fits the description.

SS *Inger*
Stopped by gunfire, captured, scuttled with bombs and sunk by gunfire 11 December 1916

SS *Inger*. Courtesy Bristol's Museums Galleries & Archives.

Inger was a Danish steamer which departed Gandia, Spain on 1 December bound for London with a cargo of fresh fruit. Her master, Captain Mads Skou, said that on 11 December 1916 the ship was some 15 miles south-south-west of St Catherine's Point when a U-boat appeared on the surface about 2 miles away. This was the minelayer, *UC-18*, under the command of Oberleutnant zur See Wilhelm Kiel. The U-boat had hoisted a signal which Captain Skou could not at first read, and it was not until a shell was fired across *Inger's* bows that he realised the U-boat wanted him to stop.

When *Inger* had come to a standstill, another signal from *UC-18* ordered, "Bring your papers over to my ship." Obeying this instruction, the ship's papers were conveyed to the U-boat, where Oberleutnant Kiel questioned Captain Skou, saying, "Why don't you stop when I signal?" No answer was made. Kiel then examined the ship's papers and said, "You are bound for London?" Skou replied, "Yes." Kiel said, "Well, I must sink your ship." Skou responded, "You are not allowed to do that as fruit is not contraband. I call that a luxury cargo." Kiel answered, "No, it's not luxury. It is food stuff and that is contraband. In any case you are bound for London and I must sink you." Skou protested, saying, "It is a shame the way you are going on" and Kiel answered, "I am very sorry, but it is war time. We have to carry out our instructions, and have received orders to sink anything that could possibly assist England." By now, some of *UC-18's* crew had carried out Kiel's orders and three bombs were taken aboard the *Inger* and placed inside the hull. Rowing clear with some provisions taken from the *Inger,* the bombs exploded, causing the ship to heel over to port. She then sank very slowly by the stern, the U-boat steaming around her, firing seven rounds at her fore part. She took 1 ½ hours to sink.

When *Inger* had disappeared, *UC-18* approached the 15 crew in the ship's boats. Captain Skou asked to be towed in, but was told, "No. I can't do that. St Catherine's Lighthouse is north-north-east 23 miles." *UC-18* then slipped away and the survivors headed for land, later being picked up by another Danish steamer, the *Anna Maersk*.

The wreck of the *Inger* lies in 55 metres of water many miles from where she was reported lost. Her engines and boilers are the highest parts. She is more or less upright but has collapsed to port and is quite broken, with much of her bow section buried.

Name: *Inger.* **Former name(s):** None.
Vessel type: Steam ship.
Builder: A/S Kjobenhavens Flydedock og Skibsvaerft, Copenhagen.
When completed: March 1908.
Machinery built by: A/S Kjobenhavens Flydedock og Skibsvaerft, Copenhagen.
Tonnage: 786 tons gross.
Dimensions: Length: 211′ 2″. **Breadth:** 30′ 7″. **Depth of holds:** 13′ 1″.
Official number: – **Yard number:** –
Signal letters: NQSL. **Last port of registry:** Esbjerg.
Ship description: Steel screw steamer. 1 deck.
Machinery description: Triple expansion 3 cylinders. 2 single ended boilers.
Career and ownership: Owned by Dampskselsk Vesterhavet (J Lauritzen, managers).
Armament: Unarmed.
Destination and cargo: Gandia for London with fresh fruit.
Date sunk: 11 December 1916.
How sunk: Stopped by gunfire and captured by *UC-18*. Scuttling charges placed on board. Finished off by gunfire.
Reported position of loss: 15 miles south-south-west, and 23 miles south-south-west of St Catherine's Point.
Actual position of wreck: 50° 21.78′ north, 001° 06.35′ west.
Orientation/height: Lies roughly 000°/180°, bows to the south. Stands about 5 metres in 55 metres on a seabed of hard clay and shingle.
How identity of wreck proved: Bridge bell recovered.

SS *Norma*
Stopped by gunfire, captured, scuttling charges and gunfire 14 January 1917

SS *Vulcan*, later renamed *Norma*. Courtesy Danish Maritime Museum, Helsingør.

The *Norma* was under Danish ownership but on charter for the British Government when she departed Valencia, Spain, for London on 30 December 1916 with a cargo of fruit and general cargo. By the time she reached Finisterre in the Bay of Biscay, she had encountered very heavy weather, labouring in high seas in force 10 winds from the north east. The next day the winds eased, but came back with a vengeance the day after. Gusts of hurricane strength brought a great deal of water on board, causing her deck cargo to shift, and though strenuous efforts were made to re-secure it some went overboard. Reaching Ushant, the winds again moderated, but more deck cargo was lost, and the crew of 19 were no doubt relieved when they reached Falmouth, where they took on 50 tons of coal bunkers. Departing Falmouth on 13 January 1917, *Norma* steamed east up the English Channel. Reaching an area in the central part of the Channel, Norma's first officer, Styrmand Svarrer was on watch on the bridge when he saw a U-boat off the starboard bow. The master, Captain Jens Nielsen Jepsen, was notified immediately and he arrived on the bridge. The U-boat had hoisted some signals, but at first their meaning could not be determined. Then, a shot was fired across Norma's bows, and then another, and the ship heaved-to. By now, the signal from the U-boat was understood, it saying, "Bring your papers onboard." Captain Jepsen boarded one of the ship's boats and did as he was ordered. Inspecting the papers, the U-boat commander then ordered Captain Jepsen to remain with him on board while two German submariners rowed across to Norma and placed external bombs against the ship's hull and *Norma's* crew were given 10 minutes to get clear of their ship. Captain Jepsen protested against the German's intention to sink his ship, saying, "Fruit is not contraband" to which the German officer replied, "The

English could very well eat oranges." Meanwhile the remainder of *Norma's* crew boarded the ship's boats and abandoned her.

On their return to the U-boat, the German crew brought with them a sack of rations, the ship's chronometer, Captain Jepsen's new sextant and other instruments, ship's flag and papers, and other items. Captain Jepsen was allowed to rejoin his crew while the bombs exploded, and the U-boat finished *Norma* off with four rounds fired from her deck gun. Fifteen minutes later, she went to the bottom, stern first.

The U-boat was the coastal submarine *UB-37*, under the command of Oberleutnant zur See Paul Gunther. Within hours of sending Norma to the bottom, *UB-37* and all her crew were lost in action with the Q-ship *Penshurst* a few miles to the eastward.

It is not known if the wreck of the *Norma* has been located and identified. There was a possibility that the wreck thought to be the *Spiral* is in fact the *Norma*, but *Spiral* had a triple expansion engine and *Norma* a compound engine.

Name: *Norma*. **Former name(s):** *Vulcan* ex *Gulf of Akaba*.
Vessel type: Steam ship.
Builder: Railton Dixon & Company, Middlesbrough.
When completed: December 1883.
Machinery built by: Blair & Company Ltd, Stockton.
Tonnage: 1997 tons gross.
Dimensions: Length: 275′. **Breadth:** 37′ 8″.
Depth of holds: 19′.
Official number: 87400. **Yard number:** –
Signal letters: NJTC. **Last port of registry:** Copenhagen.
Ship description: Iron screw steamer. Well deck. Fitted with electric light. New donkey boiler 1894.
Machinery description: Compound inverted 2 cylinders. 2 single ended boilers. 210 nominal horse power.
Career and ownership: Built as the *Gulf of Akaba* and owned by the Greenock Steam Ship Company Ltd. 1898 sold to Akties Gulf of Akaba (Blom & Ohlsen) (Norway). 1899 renamed *Vulcan* and owned by Dpskslsk. Vulcan (C P Jensen) (Copenhagen). 1917 renamed *Norma*.
Armament: Unarmed.
Destination and cargo: Valencia for London with a cargo of onions, oranges and wine.
Date sunk: 14 January 1917.
How sunk: Stopped by gunfire, captured, scuttled with bombs and finished off with gunfire by *UB-37*.
Reported position of loss: 50° 13′ north, 002° 00′ west, and 50° 27′ north, 001° 38′ west.
Actual position of wreck: Not known, though it is possible the wreck in position 50° 17.75′ north, 001° 55.22′ west, is in fact the *Norma*, and not, as thought, the *Spiral*.
Orientation/height: –
How identity of wreck proved: –

UB-37

Sunk by gunfire and depth charges 14 January 1917

At 3.50pm on Sunday 14 January 1917, one of Britain's Q ships, the steamer *Penshurst,* disguised as an unarmed steamer, was steaming in the central part of the mid English Channel. Steering an easterly course, a U-boat was sighted off the port beam, heading towards the ship. Five minutes later, when about 3000 yards off, the U-boat fired a shot which fell short. *Penshurst's* commander, Captain F H Grenfell, Royal Navy, ordered "stop engines" and got the ship's boats away with the "abandon ship" party. This was no more than a ruse to convince the Germans the ship had been abandoned, the intention being to lure the U-boat within close range. The ship would then reveal her own guns manned by crew hidden on board and, with the element of surprise on their side, open fire on the U-boat.

The U-boat did indeed come within range. Commander Grenfell observed, "The submarine closed rapidly on this bearing, firing at intervals, and when within about 700 yards she turned as though to cross ahead of us. I reserved fire, thinking she was going round to the boats, which were on our port quarter, and that I should get her at close range on our port beam. However, she stopped in this position, exposing her broadside, and quickened her rate of fire (all told she fired 14 rounds), evidently with the intention of sinking us from this position by gunfire." Grenfell continued, "It was now that we were hit twice in rapid succession. The first hit broke an awning ridge pole, the second struck the angle of the lower bridge, cutting the engine room telegraph connections . . . This shot, also, I regret to say, killed the gunlayer and loading number of the 6 pounder gun and also wounded the breech worker and signalman standing by to hoist the white ensign."

"On perceiving the submarine's intention, I opened fire at 4.24pm. The first shot from the 12 pounder gun hit the base of the conning tower and caused a large explosion as though ammunition had been exploded. Large parts of the conning tower were seen to be blown away, and a big volume of black smoke arose from it. The second shot from the 12 pounder hit a little abaft the conning tower and also visibly caused damage to the hull. The starboard 3 pounder hit the lower part of the conning tower certainly 4 times and probably twice more. The submarine sank by the stern, her bows coming appreciably out of the water."

Penshurst then steamed over the spot, dropped depth charges, and a large quantity of oil rose to the surface. The submarine was the *UB-37*, and she disappeared taking her commander, Oberleutnant zur See Paul Gunther and 21 men with her.

The wreck of a U-boat believed to be that of the *UB-37* lies in 62 metres less than 2 miles from the reported scene of the action. Pretty much intact, her conning tower is gone and she has a slight list to starboard. Her upper torpedo bow cap is open, in the "ready" position, and a quantity of both spent and "ready use" ammunition lies adjacent to where the conning tower would have been. Her gun is still bolted to the deck. A hatch cover aft of the conning tower is open, the lid lying on the seabed. Her net cutter at the bows is clearly visible.

Name: *UB-37.* **Former name(s):** None.
Vessel type: U-boat.
Builder: Blohm & Voss.
When completed: 1916.
Machinery built by: Daimler, Korting or Benz.
Tonnage: Displacement tonnage: 263 surfaced, 292 submerged.
Dimensions: Length: 36.1 metres. **Breadth:** 4.4 metres. **Draught:** 3.7 metres.
Official number: – **Yard number:** –
Signal letters: – **Last port of registry:** Part of the Flanders Flotilla.
Ship description: Coastal UBII series boat.
Machinery description: Equipped with twin diesel and twin electric motors.
Career and ownership: Ordered in July 1915. Conducted operations in the English Channel.
Armament: 2 bow torpedo tubes for 4 × 50cms torpedoes. 1 × 5cms deck gun.
Destination and cargo: Left Bruges on 2 January 1917 to wage war on merchant shipping in the English Channel.

Date sunk: 14 January 1917.
How sunk: Gunfire from the British Q ship *Penshurst* and then depth charges.
Reported position of loss: Variously as 25 miles north-east by north of Cap la Hague, and 50° 09′ north, 001° 46′ west.
Actual position of wreck: 50° 10.30′ north, 001° 38.36′ west.
Orientation/height: Lies 070°/250°. Stands about 6 metres in 62 metres on hard shingle seabed.
How identity of wreck proved: Not proved, but position of wreck is quite close to that reported in 1917. Evidence on site shows the boat was at action stations when lost. Size of wreck fits that of a UBII series vessel.

SS *Cuba*
Collision 18 February 1917

SS *Cuba*. Courtesy Norwegian Maritime Museum.

The *Cuba* was a Norwegian steamer of 731 tons under the command of Captain Anders Hansen. On 16 February 1917, *Cuba* departed Bristol, bound for Kastrup via Blyth with a cargo of saltpetre. Passing Portland Bill on the way up Channel in calm seas and reasonably clear weather about 9.30pm on the 17th, the voyage was progressing normally. However, by the early hours of the next day, fog had descended and Captain Hansen was obliged to reduce his ship to half speed, and operate her steam whistle to warn other vessels.

On *Cuba's* bridge with Captain Hansen was the second mate, Karl Sørbø, who said, "I had been on duty since 12 o'clock. There was some mist, but later it became more clear. About 2.15am I could see a steamship passing in the same direction off our starboard side, but when the ship was some way ahead, her lights disappeared, and I thought it was once more becoming foggy. 5–10 minutes passed and I could hear whistle signals off to starboard and I thought it was the ship which had just passed us."

Half an hour later at 2.45am, visibility had worsened considerably and Captain Hansen was in thick fog. Aware of the close proximity of the other ship, he ordered the second mate, "Stop engines." Immediately afterwards the red port hand navigation lamp of an oncoming vessel was sighted. Instantly, the helmsman tried to take avoiding action, as did the other ship which sounded her whistle three times, indicating she was operating astern propulsion. These actions were not enough, however, and *Cuba* was rammed amidships on her starboard side. Water gushed into the stoke hold and *Cuba* took an instant list to starboard, her crew rushing on deck to escape their vessel which was sinking beneath their feet. Having no time to save anything, Captain Hansen and his crew of 13 just managed to get clear in the ship's boats, watching *Cuba's* navigation lamps extinguish as the ship went under.

Rowing clear of the site, the crew reached the other ship which turned out to be another Norwegian vessel, the SS *Kronprins Olav*, where they were all taken aboard. The visibility had been good until the *Kronprins Olav* entered a fog bank, and they had been in fog for half an hour before the collision occurred. She was on voyage from Rouen for Methil in ballast and her master admitted he had been steaming at full speed.

Subsequently, blame for the collision and loss of the *Cuba* was ascribed to "a combination of fog, and that the *Kronprins Olav* went into it at great speed, therefore the blame must lie with her."

The wreck of the *Cuba* lies south of St Catherine's Point in 43 metres of water. She is completely upright, her compound engine being the highest part. Most of the hull has collapsed but she is a good dive.

Name: *Cuba.* **Former name(s):** *Portugal.*
Vessel type: Steam ship.
Builder: Acties Gesell "Weser," Bremen.
When completed: August 1883.
Machinery built by: Acties Gesell "Weser," Bremen.
Tonnage: 731 tons gross.
Dimensions: Length: 189′ 6″. **Breadth:** 27′ 1″. **Depth of holds:** 17′ 9″.
Official number: – **Yard number:** –
Signal letters: HFLJ. **Last port of registry:** Porsgrund.
Ship description: Iron screw steamer. 2 decks. Schooner rigged.
Machinery description: Compound 2 cylinders. Engine No 203, actiengesellschaft. 1 single ended boiler (new 1893). 110 horse power.
Career and ownership: Built as *Portugal* and owned by Oldenburger Portugiesische Dampfschff Gesellsc. 1889 owned by A Juell, Christiania, and renamed *Cuba.* 1899 owned by Ths S Falck, 1916 owned by Akties Seil & Damp and 1917 same owners but managed by Akties Hansen & Hermansen.
Armament: Unarmed.
Destination and cargo: Bristol for Kastrup with a cargo of saltpetre.
Date sunk: 18 February 1917.
How sunk: Collision with the *SS Kronprins Olav.*
Reported position of loss: 6 miles south of St Catherine's Point.
Actual position of wreck: 50° 29.64′ north, 001° 19.05′ west.
Orientation/height: Lies 135°/315°, bows to the east. Stands 5 metres in 43 metres on a hard chalk seabed and shingle.
How identity of wreck proved: Ship's bell, steering maker's nameplate and engine nameplate recovered.

RMS *Mendi*
Collision 21 February 1917

RMS *Mendi*. Courtesy E N Taylor collection.

At 7am on the morning of 21 February 1917, the commanding officer of HM trawler *Grenadier* received a signal, "Assist sinking steamer 12 miles south of St Catherine's. Dense fog. Proceed with all possible despatch, courses various."

At 8.15am, the schooner *Sydney* came within hailing distance of the *Grenadier* and reported hearing cries at 6am, to the southward. Fifteen minutes later, *Grenadier* came across wreckage of bunker hatches, spars and other debris. Nosing through the wreckage, *Grenadier* reported, "Sighted bodies of negroes dressed in military uniform floating with the aid of life-belts. A considerable number hanging onto tank rafts. Majority had their heads under water, their life-belts were made fast too low around their bodies, about the middle. Searched thoroughly, but on investigation, there was not a live person amongst them. I estimate there were from 300 to 400 bodies. Amongst them were five white men, two of them apparently stewards, had their heads above water and well back, and arms outstretched as if they had been swimming on their backs. Hauled them aboard and found they were dead, no papers of identification on them." The officer continued, "Sighted a large raft with three negroes lying on it, one perfectly naked, with the exception of a singlet. They were dead. Picked up two lifebuoys, name on them 'Mendi' of Liverpool painted on. Also a binocular box as used on a bridge, binoculars inside, with the name 'Mendi' engraved on them."

The British and African Steam Navigation Company's steamer *Mendi* was under charter to the British government from autumn 1916. Early in 1917, she departed a South African port, having on board 1500 tons of government cargo and an African labour battalion of five officers, 17 non-commissioned officers and 802 South African troops. The *Mendi* herself was manned by a crew of 89 hands making a total of 913 persons on board. During the voyage to the United Kingdom, exercises were frequently carried out at fire and boat stations, and the labour battalion received instruction and training in releasing liferafts and getting them overboard. Indeed, both crew and troops received daily training and exercises as the voyage proceeded, mustering at their boats stations and rafts and putting on life-belts.

When the *Mendi* began her journey up the Channel after calling at Plymouth on 20 February, she was escorted by the destroyer HMS *Brisk*, which took up station astern. They were making *Mendi's* full speed of 12 knots in light winds and a smooth sea. By 11.30pm that night, the weather became foggy and *Mendi* sounded her whistle at regular intervals. Her master, Captain Henry Arthur Yardley remained on the bridge throughout. As the voyage continued, so the visibility worsened and Captain Yardley wisely reduced speed. At times, her engines were running at dead slow, and this caused difficulty for HMS *Brisk*, who recorded, "Course S 76° E (magnetic). About 6 knots." *Brisk* experienced great difficulty in keeping station on *Mendi* as her speed appeared to fluctuate between 12 and 6 knots according to the density of the fog. At 4.30am *Brisk* ran up alongside *Mendi* and asked her speed by megaphone; the reply was "I am going slow." Both *Mendi* and *Brisk* sounded their whistles once every minute, and heard the sound signals of other ships in the vicinity. Just before 5am, as Captain Yardley went to the chart room to fix his position, the second and fourth officers were on the bridge when they heard the sound of a ship approaching them through the water. *Mendi's* whistle was again sounded, when suddenly the masthead and port navigation lamps of the oncoming steamer were sighted. She was heading directly for *Mendi's* starboard side. The telegraphs were immediately rung, "full speed astern!" and the steering put hard a'starboard, but it was too late. *Mendi* was struck very heavily, at right angles, as the other vessel cut into her by some 20 feet. *Brisk* recorded, "the collision was heard at 4.57am." *Mendi's* consignment of troops were billeted between decks in numbers 1, 2 and 4 holds, and how many perished in the ship is unknown.

The steamer *Darro* was an 11,480 ton ship, more than 500 feet in length, and it was she who struck such a terrible blow to *Mendi's* side. In the chaos and confusion which followed, *Mendi* quickly took a heavy list to starboard, jamming the port side lifeboats, and many men of the labour battalion slid down *Mendi's* deck and fell into one of the boats which had been launched, capsizing it. Captain Yardley, having been knocked over by the force of the collision, ordered all rafts to be put overboard and for everyone to take to the boats and rafts, the crew and troops behaving with commendable discipline. Indeed, ordinary seaman Vincent Capner remarked, "I saw the native troops, under their officers, getting out the rafts, as if at a drill." As *Mendi* finally settled and with the sea nearly level with the bridge, Captain Yardley, wearing a life belt, "walked across to the port side of the ship and entered the water, floating amongst the wreckage, where he was struck on the head by the trunk of the foremast, as the ship righted herself before sinking. Stunned by the blow, he went under the water and came again to the surface and managed to reach one of the rafts which had about 14 to 16 natives hanging on to it. Captain Yardley hung onto the raft until he became unconscious, but some of the troops were already dying from exposure, the water temperature being only 38° Fahrenheit. Other troops dropped off the raft before rescue came."

As for *Darro's* master, Captain Henry Winchester Stump, there is nothing to be said in his favour. At the Court of Enquiry held in July 1917, the court found that, as far as the *Darro* was concerned, "What her full speed was is not easily ascertained. The master stated it was about 12½ knots; the ship's register shows it was estimated at 13 knots; and the entries in the deck log on the morning of the casualty – which have obviously been altered – give it as 15.6 knots before 3am and 12.6 knots afterwards. As the five entries which have been altered were, all of them, originally 13.8, it may be assumed that the actual full speed was somewhere about 14 knots." *Darro* had steamed through the fog at full speed, in appalling visibility, making no sound signals, when she collided with the *Mendi*. As if that was not bad enough, *Darro* reversed her engines, leaving a vast, gaping hole in *Mendi's* side fully open to the sea, and stood off from the casualty, neither lowering boats to aid those from the *Mendi,* nor making any attempt to hail her. Men in the water were making a great deal of noise, shouting and crying out, but Captain Stump still sent out no assistance, despite the shouts being heard for about two hours. Nothing was done to make any attempt to investigate or rescue anyone in the water, an unforgivable and inexcusable decision.

The Court continued, "The facts of the case are such that the Court is unable to find any excuse for the master's inaction. He knew that his powerful ship, going at full speed, had struck another vessel a heavy right-angled blow and, very soon afterwards, that this vessel was the *Mendi* with troops, the crew of which had been compelled to take to the boats. He must have heard, for much longer than he admitted, the cries proceeding from the water, as they were heard generally on board his ship for hours, by competent witnesses on duty. There was nothing to have prevented him from sending away boats . . . he made no inquiries, and took no steps, to ascertain the result of the casualty, remaining in the vicinity and doing nothing for, in all, nearly four hours. Had he got boats out as soon as he knew his vessel was safe, many more lives would, in all reasonable probability, have been saved. In the opinion of the court, his inaction was inexcusable." Captain Henry Stump had his master's certificate suspended for 12 months.

The South African labour battalion were not intended to fight in France, but to work in support of front line troops by carrying out such work as tree felling and cutting up trunks for use in the trenches. They were also employed in the quarries, and in loading and unloading trains of supplies and ammunition. Some carried out work at the docks with a concentration of men at the rail heads and ports, moving much hay and coal.

In unconfirmed reports which is part of South African oral legend, it was said that the Reverend Isaac Dyobha called out to his men, "Be quiet and calm my countrymen, for what is taking place is exactly what you came to do. You are going to die, but that is what you came to do. Brothers, we are drilling the death drill. I, a Xhosa, say you are my brothers. Swazi's, Pondo's, Basuto's, we die like brothers. We are the sons of Africa. Raise your war cries, brothers, for though they made us leave our assegais in the kraal, our voices are left with our bodies." Casting off their boots, the troops stamped the death dance on the deck of the sinking ship. Whether this actually took place is not recorded in any official records, but it is possible that such an event took place.

From a battalion force of 822 men, 615 were lost, in addition to 30 crew members of the *Mendi*. In all, 645 lives were lost, one of the worst maritime disasters in British waters.

The wreck of the *Mendi* lies in about 40 metres of water south of St Catherine's point. She is a substantial wreck, with the port side of her hull, engines and boilers being the highest parts. The gun lies on the seabed close to the stern.

Name: *Mendi.* **Former name(s):** None.
Vessel type: Steam ship.
Builder: Alexander Stephen & Sons, Glasgow.
When completed: June 1905.
Machinery built by: Alexander Stephen & Sons, Glasgow.
Tonnage: 4229 tons gross.
Dimensions: Length: 370′ 2″. **Breadth:** 46′ 2″. **Depth of holds:** 27′.
Official number: 120875. **Yard number:** 407.
Signal letters: HDGP. **Last port of registry:** Liverpool.
Ship description: Steel screw steamer. 2 decks. "Karina" class ship, clincher built, schooner rig, 2 masts, having passenger accommodation for 100 1st class and 70 2nd class.
Machinery description: Triple expansion direct acting vertical inverted 3 cylinders. 4 single ended boilers. 654 nominal horse power.
Career and ownership: Owned by British and African Steam Navigation Company (Elder Dempster & Company Ltd, managers). 1916, requisitioned as an army transport.
Armament: Armed with a defensive stern gun, details not known.
Destination and cargo: South Africa for Plymouth and an undisclosed destination in northern France, with 1500 tons government cargo and a South African labour battalion of 822 men.
Date sunk: 21 February 1917.
How sunk: Collision in dense fog with the SS *Darro.*
Reported position of loss: 10–12 miles south of St Catherine's Point.
Actual position of wreck: 50° 27.50′ north, 001° 20.05′ west.
Orientation/height: Stands about 7 metres in 40 metres on hard, shingle and chalk seabed.
How identity of wreck proved: Ship's crockery recovered.

SS *Glynymel*
Captured and sunk by gunfire and scuttling charges 12 March 1917

The British steamer *Glynymel* departed Rouen bound for Swansea on 11 March 1917. That night, as she steamed in a northerly direction across the English Channel, without lights, she had reached the mid Channel area when, at 3.30am on 12 March and without warning, the ship was struck by two shells fired from a surfaced U-boat. The U-boat was then seen off the port beam, approaching the *Glynymel* and firing her deck gun. This was the *UC-66,* commanded by Oberleutnant zur See Herbert Pustkuchen. His first shot had been accurate, striking the bridge and injuring the mate, while the second shell passed through and destroyed the chart-house. *Glynymel's* master, Captain E Thomas, wasted no time and ordered his crew, "Abandon ship!" While the crew, numbering 15 all told, swung out the boats ready for boarding, Pustkuchen continued to fire, killing the second engineer, Robert Stote, but the rest of the crew managed to get away.

When it became obvious that the crew were abandoning ship, *UC-66* ceased firing, allowing *Glynymel's* crew to row clear. They then watched as *UC-66's* deck gun was put to further use, more rounds striking the ship. Captain Thomas said, "I did not see my ship sink but I heard a heavy thud, and I consider that she was sunk by a torpedo. The enemy did not board us and at 5.30am we were picked up the SS *Farraline.*"

In fact, the *Glynymel* had not been torpedoed at all; she had been boarded by *UC-66's* crew, who had finished her off by placing scuttling charges in her, sending her to the bottom.

There is no information concerning whether the wreck of the *Glynymel* has been found and identified.

Name: *Glynymel.* **Former name(s):** *Maria Regier* ex *Abchurch* ex *Balear.*
Vessel type: Steam ship.
Builder: Strand Slipway Company, Sunderland.
When completed: September 1890.
Machinery built by: North East Marine Engineering Company Ltd, Sunderland.
Tonnage: 1394 tons gross.
Dimensions: Length: 242′ 5″. **Breadth:** 35′.
Depth of holds: 14′ 8″.
Official number: 105776. **Yard number:** –
Signal letters: JBVH. **Last port of registry:** Swansea.
Ship description: Steel screw steamer. 1 deck.
Machinery description: Triple expansion 3 cylinders. 1 single ended boiler. New donkey boiler 1901. 120 horse power.
Career and ownership: 1891 owned as *Balear* by Sociedad General Mallorquina de Palma. 1897 owned by Abchurch Steam Ship Company Ltd (Fenwick Stobart & Company Ltd) as *Abchurch.* Then owned by P Regier and renamed *Maria Regier.* At time of loss owned by Harries Brothers & Company as *Glynymel.*
Armament: Unarmed.
Destination and cargo: Rouen for Swansea in ballast.
Date sunk: 12 March 1917.
How sunk: Gunfire and scuttling charges from *UC-66.*
Reported position of loss: Variously as 15 miles south west of St Catherine's, 23 miles south by west of St Catherine's, and 50° 12.50′ north, 001° 11.00′ west.
Actual position of wreck: Not known.
Orientation/height: –
How identity of wreck proved: –

SS *Pandion*
Collision 15 March 1917

The steamer *Pandion*, 1279 tons, owned and operated by the Cork Steam Ship Company, had departed Rotterdam bound for Manchester with a full general cargo. On 15 March 1917 she passed to the west of the Owers Light Vessel south of Selsey Bill.

Exactly what happened remains a mystery, as no detailed accounts have been located and those that did probably have not survived. What is known is that the *Pandion* came into collision with the government transport and Liverpool registered SS *Northwestern Miller*. The damage inflicted was so severe that the *Pandion* sank, leading to the death of one of her crew of 21 hands.

It is hardly surprising the *Pandion* came off worse: *Northwestern Miller* was a much larger ship of 6504 tons gross.

The wreck of the *Pandion* lies in 38 metres of water, a considerable distance from her reported position of loss. She lies over to starboard, bows to the west; both her boilers have rolled but remain in position forward of the engine, though the port boiler is under the hull plating. The engine block is almost upside down, with the piston con rods horizontal.

Name: *Pandion*. **Former name(s):** None.
Vessel type: Steam ship.
Builder: Swan Hunter & Wigham Richardson Limited, Newcastle upon Tyne.
When completed: May 1904.
Machinery built by: Swan Hunter & Wigham Richardson Limited, Newcastle upon Tyne.
Tonnage: 1279 tons gross.
Dimensions: Length: 255′ 4″. **Breadth:** 33′ 7″. **Depth of holds:** 18′ 6″.
Official number: 115119. **Yard number:** 710.
Signal letters: VRWH. **Last port of registry:** Cork.
Ship description: Steel screw steamer. 1 deck. Well deck. Fitted with electric light.
Machinery description: Triple expansion 3 cylinders. 2 single ended boilers. New donkey boiler 1912.
Career and ownership: Owned by the Cork Steam Ship Company Limited. Launched 18 April 1904 at the Neptune Shipyard. She was intended to work for the carriage of a few passengers and cargo between Liverpool and Dutch and Belgian ports.
Armament: Not confirmed but 12 pounder shell cases lie in the wreck.
Destination and cargo: Rotterdam for Manchester with a full general cargo.
Date sunk: 15 March 1917.
How sunk: Collision with the SS *Northwestern Miller*.
Reported position of loss: 11 miles west of the Owers Light Vessel.
Actual position of wreck: Not disclosed.
Orientation/height: Lies 070°/250°, bows to the west on a hard seabed of shingle. Stands 5–6 metres.
How identity of wreck proved: Not proved but size, description and location indicate this is the *Pandion*.

Sailing ship *Ernest Legouve*
Torpedoed 5 April 1917

Sailing barque *Ernest Legouve*. Courtesy State Library of Victoria, Australia.

The *Ernest Legouve* was a large, steel sailing ship of 2246 tons. On 2 April 1917, she departed Northfleet for Buenos Aires with a cargo of cement in barrels under the command of Captain Le Pannerer. Since Admiralty records relating to shipping casualties for April 1917 appear to have been lost, the details concerning the ship's subsequent loss are somewhat scanty. What is known is that three days after leaving Northfleet, she was still under tow from the tug *Joffre,* presumably due to an absence of wind.

When the two vessels were to the south west of St Catherine's Point, a German U-boat, the *UB-32*, under the command of Oberleutnant zur See Viebeg, fired a torpedo at *Ernest Legouve* without warning. The torpedo found its mark and the ship sank quickly, taking 20 men with her, only the second mate and three other men being saved by the *Joffre*.

The wreck of the *Ernest Legouve* remains a substantial one. She lies half over on her starboard side with the stump of her main mast projecting above the hull. Many barrels of cement are evident in the wreck, and some have spilled onto the seabed. Although this can be regarded as a 40 metre dive on the wreck, as much as 45 metres can be found in the scour.

Name: *Ernest Legouve*. **Former name(s):** None.
Vessel type: Sailing barque.
Builder: Atel & Chantiers de la Loire, Nantes.
When completed: Launched 1 February 1901.
Machinery built by: –
Tonnage: 2246 tons gross.
Dimensions: Length: 276′ 5″. **Breadth:** 44′.
Depth of holds: 22′ 5″.
Official number: – **Yard number:** –
Signal letters: JCTH. **Last port of registry:** Nantes.
Ship description: Steel 3 masted sailing barque.
Machinery description: –
Career and ownership: Built for N & C Guillon, Nantes. 1912 sold to Soc. Nouvelle d'Armament, Nantes.
Armament: Unarmed.
Destination and cargo: Northfleet for Buenos Aires with a cargo of cement.
Date sunk: 5 April 1917.
How sunk: Torpedoed by *UB-32*.
Reported position of loss: 5 miles west by south of St Catherine's.
Actual position of wreck: 50° 31.25′ north, 001° 28. 57′ west.
Orientation/height: Stands about 7 metres in 40–45 metres on shingle and chalk seabed.
How identity of wreck proved: Ship's name in brass letters on bows.

Schooner *Florence Louisa*

Captured by U-boat and scuttled with a bomb 17 May 1917

Schooner *Florence Louisa*. Author's collection.

The 115 ton schooner *Florence Louisa* was chartered to transport a cargo of scrap steel from Rouen, from where she set sail on 16 May 1917, bound for Briton Ferry, near Swansea. Her master, Captain James Prettyman, had charge of the vessel and her crew of three. At first the schooner made reasonable progress across the Channel, but next day, on the morning of 17 May 1917, when seven or eight miles south of the Needles, the wind died away completely, and the vessel became becalmed. With no other means of propulsion, the *Florence Louisa* languished helplessly, waiting for the wind to return.

On patrol in the vicinity was the German U-boat *UB-40*. Under the command of Oberleutnant zur See Hans Howaldt, he was prepared to conduct operations on the surface in broad daylight. His boat had been disguised in order to deceive prying eyes. Captain Prettyman said, "The submarine approached from astern, on the surface . . . a small mast and gaff with brown canvas was rigged up on it to have the appearance of a sail. I saw she had an octopus painted on her bows." He continued, "Four of the submarine crew, wearing white sweaters, questioned us as to our cargo and tonnage. They had a good knowledge of the English language."

Taking to the ship's boat, the crew of *Florence Louisa* watched as a bomb was hung by a clip to the outside of the ship's side and exploded under water. As the stricken schooner settled down, and on the approach of the destroyer HMS *Nymphe, UB-40* disappeared beneath the surface while *Florence Louisa* went down half an hour later. Subsequently, her crew were picked up by a patrol boat and landed at Ventnor.

A small area of wreckage lying in 40 metres is thought to be the remains of the *Florence Louisa,* but the site has yet to be investigated.

Name: *Florence Louisa.* **Former name(s):** None.
Vessel type: Schooner.
Builder: J Gough, Bridgewater.
When completed: 1876.
Machinery built by: –
Tonnage: 115 tons gross.
Dimensions: Length: 86′ 2″. **Breadth:** 22′ 1″.
Depth of holds: 10′ 1″.
Official number: 67970. **Yard number:** –
Signal letters: – **Last port of registry:** Chester.
Ship description: Wooden hulled topsail schooner.
Machinery description: –
Career and ownership: Owned by J Reney.
Armament: Unarmed.
Destination and cargo: Rouen for Briton Ferry with a cargo of scrap steel. **Date sunk:** 17 May 1917.
How sunk: Captured by *UB-40* and scuttled with a bomb.
Reported position of loss: 7–8 miles south of the Needles.
Actual position of wreck: Not disclosed.
Orientation/height: stands 2 metres in 40 metres.
How identity of wreck proved: Not proved.

Steam drifter *Plantin*
Struck a mine and sank 26 April 1917

During the operational war patrol of the German minelaying U-boat, the *UC-72,* under the command of Oberleutnant zur See Ernst Voigt, a minefield was laid off Standfast Point, near Old Harry rocks close to Poole. Her activities in the second week of March 1917 had gone unnoticed, and she slipped away at the end of her tour of duty to leave her mines to do what they would.

On the night of 24 April, *Plantin,* attached to the Auxiliary Patrol Force as a net drifter, had commenced to shoot her nets in a position given as 3 miles south-south-east of Standfast Point. In company with another drifter, the *WPG*, under the command of Lieutenant J P A Richardson, officer in charge of operations, *Plantin* was ordered to haul her nets as she had deployed them in the wrong place. It then appeared that the nets ran out; in fact it was described that they had been torn out, with great rapidity, and *Plantin's* skipper signalled that he had a submarine in his nets. Cutting the footrope and marking the position with a Dan buoy, the *WPG* steamed up and dropped a depth charge over the spot. When it exploded, two further explosions were heard, but nothing came to the surface.

The next morning the position was again depth charged, with no more result, and it was concluded that the strong flood tide had produced the effect of something foul in the nets. Determined to resolve the matter once and for all, Lieutenant Richardson made plans to detonate a large charge electrically over the position the following day. Before this could be carried out, *Plantin* was ordered to remain all night on the spot to keep all traffic clear. In the morning at 6am, she approached the buoyed position where her nets were. As she did so, an explosion occurred under her port quarter and she was blown up and destroyed, it being assumed she had struck a mine which was foul of her nets. Only one man survived the explosion; the skipper and eight ratings being killed in the explosion. None of their bodies were recovered.

Wreckage of what is thought to be *Plantin* lies in about 33 metres of water located quite by chance during a training dive. The main body of the wreck, if it exists, has not been located, but debris including a boiler and copper steam pipe has been found on the rocky seabed. A search along the 30–40 metre contour between Peveril Ledge Buoy and the *Kyarra* should produce results.

Name: *Plantin.* **Former name(s):** None.
Vessel type: Steam drifter.
Builder: McIntosh, Buckie.
When completed: 1912.
Machinery built by: Not known.
Tonnage: 84 tons gross.
Dimensions: Length: 85′ 2″. **Breadth:** 19′.
Depth of holds: 9′ 2″.
Official number: 127351. **Yard number:** –
Signal letters: – **Last port of registry:** Banff.
Ship description: Wooden screw steam drifter.
Machinery description: Not known. 27 horse power.
Career and ownership: Managed in 1916 by Alexander Mair, Portknockie, Banffshire. Port number BF453. Hired by the Admiralty as a net drifter in April 1915.
Armament: 1 × 3 pounder.
Destination and cargo: Net patrol duties off Standfast Point.
Date sunk: 26 April 1917.
How sunk: Struck mine laid by *UC-72.*
Reported position of loss: 3 miles south-south-east of Standfast Point.
Actual position of wreck: Not precisely known.
Orientation/height: Nothing found stands up above the rocky seabed other than a boiler
How identity of wreck proved: Not proved but wreckage is in the area where the explosion took place.

SS *Indutiomare*
Torpedoed 6 July 1917

SS *Indutiomare* waterlogged and under tow. Courtesy collection of Musée Maritime du Quebec.

Lurking in the waters just to the west of St Catherine's Point on the morning of 6 July 1917, Oberleutnant zur See Georg Gerth in the minelaying U-boat *UC-61* was on the lookout for victims to sink. About 7.20am, he sighted the Belgian steamer *Indutiomare,* on voyage up Channel from Swansea for Le Havre. The ship was following its route instructions, which required it to remain close to land before making a direct heading across the Channel to its destination. Remaining submerged with only the tip of his periscope showing above water, Gerth manoeuvred for an attack.

On board *Indutiomare* her master, Captain Alphonse Leenaers was up and about, alert to the hazards which faced shipping in 1917. His ship was steaming east by south at 8 knots in fine weather and good visibility. Suddenly, he saw, only 200 yards away off his starboard bow, the wake of a torpedo heading straight for his ship from the southward. The second mate saw it too and immediately the helm was put hard a'starboard, but the ship could not steer clear in time. The torpedo struck home and exploded, and the vessel was abandoned as she began to sink so quickly. Taking to the boats, 22 men made it to safety, but three were missing.

The sinking was witnessed by those on board the steamer *Nosted*, which was nearby. Her captain saw the ship blow up, stating the ship sank in about 6 minutes, and that no sign of a submarine could be seen.

The wreck of the *Indutiomare* lies in an area of shifting sands very close to the position provided by her captain at the time she was lost. The wreck lists to port, the port boiler being almost buried in sand. The 90mm

SS *Indutiomare.* Courtesy National Maritime Museum, Antwerp.

French field gun lies in her stern, which lies half over on its port side. A large steel ship's wheel is still in position at the stern. The triple expansion engine is the highest part of the wreck.

Name: *Indutiomare.* **Former name(s):** None.
Vessel type: Steam ship.
Builder: W Pickersgill & Sons Ltd, Sunderland.
When completed: 1910.
Machinery built by: MacColl & Pollock Ltd, Sunderland.
Tonnage: 1577 tons gross.
Dimensions: Length: 259′ 2″. **Breadth:** 39′ 2″.
Depth of holds: 17′ 6″.
Official number: – **Yard number:** –
Signal letters: MBJS. **Last port of registry:** Antwerp.
Ship description: Steel screw steamer. 1 deck.
Machinery description: Triple expansion 3 cylinders. 2 single ended boilers. 162 nominal horse power.
Career and ownership: Owned by Antwersche Zeer Maats (Brys & Gylsen Ltd, managers) (Lloyd Royal Belge).
Armament: 90mm French field gun fitted at the stern.
Destination and cargo: Newport for Le Havre with a cargo of coal.
Date sunk: 6 July 1917.
How sunk: Torpedoed by *UC-61*.
Reported position of loss: 50° 34′ north, 001° 26′ west.
Actual position of wreck: 50° 34.39′ north, 001° 26.63′ west.
Orientation/height: Lies 130°/310°. Stands 4–5 metres in 36 metres on seabed of shifting sand, bows to the east.
How identity of wreck proved: Position given by ship's master is very close to where the wreck lies. Gun on the stern is a French field gun, consistent with that carried by *Indutiomare.*

SS *Fluent*
Torpedoed 20 July 1917

SS *Fluent*. Courtesy Memory Lane Photo Gallery, Hull.

The *Fluent* was a 3659 ton ship which, on 20 July 1917, was heading for London from New York. She picked up her escort at Plymouth, which was the trawler *Lord Stanhope*, as well as route instructions and proceeded up Channel. In the evening she was in a position to the south west of the Needles steaming east by south at 8 knots. Her master, Captain Lewis Hutchinson, later reported, "*Fluent* sailed from Plymouth at 7am. When, at 8.10pm she either struck a mine or was torpedoed. Explosion was very violent and seemed to be well underneath the ship. No submarine seen at all or track of torpedo. Engines were stopped on ship being struck . . . waited to see if ship would float, but she began to settle at once and was abandoned."

All 29 hands escaped from the ship, but not before Captain Hutchinson had thrown the ship's papers overboard to prevent them falling into enemy hands.

In the event, the *Fluent* had not struck a mine after all, but had been torpedoed by the minelaying U-boat, the *UC-65*, under the command of Kapitänleutnant Otto Steinbrinck. Earlier in the day, Steinbrinck had sown a minefield off the Needles and then motored west where he carried out a submerged attack on the *Fluent* so successfully that neither his boat nor the track of the torpedo was seen.

Within half an hour of being torpedoed, *Fluent* sank from view, taking her valuable cargo with her.

The wreck of the *Fluent* lies in 40 metres of water, though off the wreck 42 or 43 metres can be found. She leans over and has collapsed to starboard. Her three large boilers are most prominent and are the highest parts of the wreck, the engine lying on its side. Her stern gun lies on the seabed close to the starboard side of the stern. Her aft holds appear empty but the forward holds are stuffed full of what appear to be projectiles. They are in fact harmless steel billets – part of the cargo was described as "round cornered billets."

Name: *Fluent.* **Former name(s):** None.
Vessel type: Steam ship.
Builder: J Priestman & Company, Sunderland.
When completed: November 1911.
Machinery built by: North East Marine Engineering Company Ltd, Sunderland.
Tonnage: 3659 tons gross.
Dimensions: Length: 350′. **Breadth:** 50′ 9″.
Depth of holds: 24′ 4″.
Official number: 132063. **Yard number:** 234
Signal letters: HTQM. **Last port of registry:** Sunderland.
Ship description: Steel screw steamer. 1 deck. Well deck. Fitted with electric light.
Machinery description: Triple expansion 3 cylinders. 3 single ended boilers. 325 nominal horse power.
Career and ownership: Built for an owned by J Westoll.
Armament: 12 pounder, 12 cwt stern gun.
Destination and cargo: New York for London via Plymouth with 6100 tons of cargo comprising oats and including 1413 tons of steel in the form of billets, forgings and ingots for the Ministry of Munitions.
Date sunk: 20 July 1917.
How sunk: Torpedoed by *UC-65.*
Reported position of loss: 10 miles south of Anvil Point, and 50° 26′ north, 001° 52′ west.
Actual position of wreck: 50° 28.86′ north, 001° 51.46′ west.
Orientation/height: Lies 120°/300°, bows to the east. Stands 7 metres in 40 metres on shingle seabed.
How identity of wreck proved: Ship's crockery recovered.

SS *Bishopston*
Torpedoed 4 September 1917

On 3 September 1917, the *Bishopston*, a steamer of some 2513 tons, sailed from Le Havre bound for Portsmouth. She was a new ship, being about a year old, and in the early hours of the next day, the ship was in a position in mid Channel south of the Isle of Wight. The night was clear and calm with a bright moon, and the ship's master, Captain Clifford David, was following his orders to zig-zag the ship as she headed north, steaming at a steady 9½ knots. Quite suddenly at 3.45am, a U-boat was sighted on the surface, partially submerged and at a distance estimated at only 100 yards away. Then the wake of an oncoming torpedo was seen. Although the order was given "hard a'starboard" it was too late and the torpedo slammed into the starboard side of the stern in the after part of number 4 hold, destroying the propeller and after part of the stern. This had been a successful, surfaced attack from the small minelaying U-boat, the *UC-16*, under the command of Oberleutnant zur See Reimarus.

Bishopston settled immediately and the ship was quickly abandoned by her surviving crew of 27 hands This was not a moment too soon, as the ship had vanished entirely within two minutes. Two men were reported missing, presumed drowned.

There is no information concerning whether the wreck of the *Bishopston* has been located and identified.

Name: *Bishopston*. **Former name(s):** None.
Vessel type: Steam ship.
Builder: Clyde Shipbuilding & Engineering Company Ltd, Port Glasgow.
When completed: September 1916.
Machinery built by: Clyde Shipbuilding & Engineering Company Ltd, Port Glasgow.
Tonnage: 2513 tons gross.
Dimensions: Length: 300′. **Breadth:** 44′ 7″.
Depth of holds: 19′ 3″.
Official number: 136138. **Yard number:** –
Signal letters: JNFP. **Last port of registry:** Swansea.
Ship description: Steel screw steamer. 1 deck. Well deck. Schooner rigged.
Machinery description: Triple expansion 3 cylinders. 2 single ended boilers. 251 nominal horse power.
Career and ownership: Owned by Swansea Steamers Ltd (Richards Turpin (Shipping) Ltd, managers).
Armament: 1 × 6 pounder stern gun.
Destination and cargo: Le Havre for Portsmouth in ballast on Admiralty charter.
Date sunk: 4 September 1917.
How sunk: Torpedoed by *UC-16*.
Reported position of loss: 50° 08′ north, 000° 57′ west.
Actual position of wreck: Not known.
Orientation/height: –
How identity of wreck proved: –

SS *Vikholmen*
Torpedoed 10 September 1917

SS *Prima II*, later renamed *Vikholmen*, being launched. Courtesy Nederlands Scheepvaartmuseum, Amsterdam.

The *Vikholmen* was a Norwegian steamer, just over a year old, and quite small at only 494 tons gross. The ship left Cardiff on Thursday 7 September 1917, with a crew of 15 hands, proceeding past Land's End and steaming up Channel until she reached Weymouth, where she anchored to await the remainder of the convoy with which she was to travel. The convoy was due to depart about 10.30pm that night, but the other ships arrived early and the convoy of four ships and two escorts left Weymouth at 9.30pm. Reaching St Alban's Head just after midnight on 10 September, the convoy set a course of south quarter east and headed for Cherbourg. Unknown to them, they were steaming towards a German U-boat, the *UC-71*, under the command of Oberleutant zur See Reinhold Saltzwedel. She was lying on the surface in wait for the approaching convoy.

About 3.30am the convoy was in good formation, keeping about 400 metres clear of each other, and making about 8½ knots. The night was a clear one with bright moonlight and starlight, and the sea was calm. At that time, the skipper of one of the escorts, the *John Lyon*, reported to his commanding officer that he had heard a dull and heavy sound like an explosion, and simultaneously red rockets were seen to have been fired astern. This was *Vikholmen,* which had been torpedoed on her starboard side amidships by *UC-71*.

The torpedo destroyed the engine room and the ship's boats, and the only survivors were the captain, second mate, the helmsman and a few others, who found themselves in the sea as their ship went from under them. Since the ship disappeared completely in 15 seconds, it was assumed the remainder of the crew, eight in number must have drowned in their quarters or been killed by the explosion. The survivors were quickly picked up by one of the escorting trawlers, but searches around the site failed to find any others.

The wreck of the *Vikholmen* lies in about 60 metres of water. She is quite broken, the only prominent parts being the boiler and the small triple expansion engine, with its propeller shaft clear of the seabed. Much of the wreck has a covering of shingle though her coal cargo is still visible.

Name: *Vikholmen.* **Former name(s):** *Prima II.*
Vessel type: Steam ship.
Builder: Arnhem ScheStoomsleephelling My. Arnhem.
When completed: March 1916.

Machinery built by: Arnhem ScheStoomsleephelling My. Arnhem.
Tonnage: 494 tons gross.
Dimensions: Length: 151′ 1″. **Breadth:** 25′ 3″. **Depth of holds:** 11′ 5″.
Official number: – **Yard number:** –
Signal letters: MNSB. **Last port of registry:** Skudesnaes.
Ship description: Steel screw steamer. 1 deck. Well deck. Fitted with electric light.
Machinery description: Triple expansion 3 cylinders. 1 single ended boiler. 58 nominal horse power.
Career and ownership: Owned 1916 by E Euston & Company, Bergen, as *Prima II*. 1917 owned by Akties Vikholmen (O G Gjessen) as *Vikholmen*.
Armament: Unarmed.
Destination and cargo: Cardiff for St Malo with 479 tons of coal.
Date sunk: 10 September 1917.
How sunk: Torpedoed by *UC-71*.
Reported position of loss: 50° 11′ north, 001° 52.50′ west.
Actual position of wreck: 50° 13.53′ north, 001° 55.94′ west.
Orientation/height: Lies 045°/225°. Stands 4 metres in 60 metres on shingle seabed.
How identity of wreck proved: Builder's nameplate recovered.

SS *Hartburn*
Mined 15 October 1917

SS *Hartburn*. Courtesy E N Taylor collection.

The steamer *Hartburn* was on voyage from Manchester for St Helens. On the night of 15 October 1917, at 1am, disaster struck. According to her master, Captain Albert Shelton, "She was suddenly struck by torpedo by submerged submarine without warning, or mined, I cannot say which. Ship began to sink at once, but slowly, and boats were lowered but not manned until upper deck was awash, when ship was abandoned. Ten minutes later, the ship sank." He continued his report, "The vessel was making water so rapidly that it was not considered possible to start the pumps. A portion of the cargo caught fire, just as the boats got clear." *Hartburn*, having sustained serious damage on her starboard side amidships, went down by the head, disappearing from view after 30 minutes.

The sinking of the *Hartburn* was claimed by Oberleutnant zur See Max Schmitz, who, as officer commanding the German minelayer *UC-62*, had sown a minefield in the area where the ship was lost.

Which wreck is the *Hartburn* is not entirely clear. She was lost in the same area as the *Hazelwood* which went down three days later. Both ships were of similar size and dimensions, and which is which has been difficult to determine. A wreck lying on its port side with one of the boilers standing on end and a bomb of Second World War vintage lying on the hull amidships, is probably the *Hartburn*.

Name: *Hartburn*. **Former name(s):** None.
Vessel type: Steam ship.
Builder: Blyth Ship Building Company, Blyth.
When completed: August 1900.
Machinery built by: T Richardson & Sons, Hartlepool.
Tonnage: 2367 tons gross.
Dimensions: Length: 302′ 8″. **Breadth:** 43′ 1″.
Depth of holds: 19′ 9″.
Official number: 110356. **Yard number:** –
Signal letters: SCVF. **Last port of registry:** Swansea.

Ship description: Steel screw steamer. 1 deck. Schooner rigged. Fitted with electric light.
Machinery description: Triple expansion 3 cylinders. 2 single ended boilers. 257 nominal horse power.
Career and ownership: Built for and owned by Tyne & Blyth Steam Ship Owning Company Ltd (Newcastle) (Whitfield & Company, managers). 1915 owned by Richards, Turpin & Company Ltd. 1917 owned by A Capel (W L Scott, managers).
Armament: 12 pounder, 12 cwt stern gun.
Destination and cargo: Manchester for St Helens Roads with 880 tons of hay and 70 tons of railway trucks, on government service.
Date sunk: 15 October 1917.
How sunk: Struck a mine laid by *UC-62*.
Reported position of loss: 10 miles south from Anvil Point, and 50° 25′ north, 001° 54′ west. German position reported as 50° 21′ north, 001° 52′ west.
Actual position of wreck: 50° 26.46′ north, 001° 48.05′ west.
Orientation/height: Lies 010°/190°.
How identity of wreck proved: Not proved.

SS *Hazelwood*
Mined 19 October 1917

SS *Hazelwood.* Courtesy R A Snook/F W Hawks collection.

The British authorities did not know that on 13 October 1917, *UC-62*, under the command of Oberleutnant zur See Max Schmitz, had laid a minefield offshore between Anvil Point and the Needles. However, constant precautionary measures were taken and minesweepers were kept active, nine mines being swept in the area on 15 October. Since it was highly likely that a field of 12 mines were laid, the remaining three posed a serious threat to shipping. One of those mines accounted for the *Hartburn;* another would take care of the *Hazelwood.*

Hazelwood, 3120 tons, left the Tyne for Nantes with a cargo of coal on 14 October with her crew of 32. She proceeded down the English Channel, and on the night of 18/19 October, she ran into serious trouble. Exactly what happened will never be known, but at 11.15pm *Hazelwood* transmitted an SOS on her wireless set. It reported, "SOS, 50° 31′ north, 001° 27′ west." No further details came through, but then at 12.15am, another SOS was picked up from the steamer *Estonian,* reporting, "SOS. Vessel sunk 50° 29′ north, 001° 51′ west."

Estonian's master, Captain T Jones, later made a more detailed report, saying, "On Friday 19 October 1917 at 0.30am, distance 22½ miles west of St Catherine's Light in latitude 50° 29′ north, longitude 1° 51′ west, heard persons shouting off starboard bow assumed to be shipwrecked crew, owing to darkness not able to discover their exact position and see them. Sent wireless message immediately to their assistance. Unable to stop ship to rescue crew owing to the danger of being attacked. Proceeded full speed and zig-zagging. Ten minutes later a craft was reported on starboard bow showing no lights, but moving slowly about 500 feet off. Precautions taken instantly. Put helm hard to starboard and brought the suspicious craft right astern and proceeded full speed on zig-zag course. All hands called to stations. Owing to darkness and craft nationality unknown, was not prudent to fire. Proceeded full speed on passage." The unidentified craft was probably the *UC-75* which was on patrol in the area, and which, next day, sank the steamer *Britannia*.

Despite assistance being sent to the scene, and searches conducted through the night and into the morning, nothing was found. Later that day, however, a bag was picked up containing the ship's papers from *Hazelwood* not far from the position reported by the *Estonian*, and the body of *Hazelwood's* steward was found. From the crew of 32 men, none survived. The Admiralty recorded, "No further news has been received and it is now presumed she has gone with all hands – war risk loss."

A wreck believed to be that of the *Hazelwood* lies in about 40 metres quite close to the position reported by the *Estonian*.

Name: *Hazelwood*. **Former name(s):** None.
Vessel type: Steam ship.
Builder: Ropner & Son, Stockton.
When completed: February 1904.
Machinery built by: Blair & Company Ltd, Stockton on Tees.
Tonnage: 3120 tons gross.
Dimensions: Length: 325′. **Breadth:** 48′.
Depth of holds: 23′ 1″.
Official number: 113908. **Yard number:** –
Signal letters: VNGP. **Last port of registry:** Middlesbrough.
Ship description: Steel screw steamer. 1 deck.
Machinery description: Triple expansion 3 cylinders. 2 single ended boilers. 273 nominal horse power.
Career and ownership: Owned by Constantine & Pickering Steam Ship Company.
Armament: 12 pounder, 12 cwt stern gun.
Destination and cargo: The Tyne for Nantes with a cargo of coal.
Date sunk: 19 October 1917.
How sunk: Mined by *UC-62*.
Reported position of loss: Variously as 50° 31′ north, 001° 27′ west (probably, this should read 001° 47′ west, and may either have been wrongly recorded, or, in the confusion of a sinking ship, incorrectly transmitted as 27′ instead of 47′), and 50° 29′ north, 001° 51′ west, or 22 ½ miles west of St Catherine's Light.
Actual position of wreck: *Hazelwood* is probably the wreck in position 50° 28.92′ north, 001° 48.42′ west.
Orientation/height: Stands about 6 metres in 40 metres on shingle seabed.
How identity of wreck proved: Not proved, but the position of the wreck is very close to the position where men were heard shouting in the water.

SS *Britannia*
Torpedoed 19 October 1917

SS *Earl of Aberdeen*, later renamed *Britannia*. Courtesy Memory Lane Photo Gallery, Hull.

The German minelayer, the *UC-75*, was commanded by a most successful submariner, Oberleutnant zur See Johannes Lohs. Later, his command of the *UB-57* led to him sinking many ships. A brief entry in Lohs' log for the early hours of 19 October 1917, reads, "Fired torpedo in surface attack against a lone steamer. Position 50° 29′ north, 001° 46′ west. The ship quickly sank." Lohs had sent to the bottom the 765 ton steamer, *Britannia*.

Like *Hazelwood* before her, none of the crew of 23 survived the sinking, and no information of any kind came through to indicate what had happened to the ship. The Admiralty noted, "There was considerable (submarine) activity on the 18th and 19th October between Portland Bill and the Isle of Wight. Propose to inform . . . the Admiralty have no information . . .."

The only information known was that *Britannia* left Middlesbrough on 16 October 1917, bound for St Malo with a cargo of pig iron. She dropped off her pilot at Deal on the 18th, and proceeded down Channel, never to be heard of again.

The wreck believed to be that of *Britannia* lies in about 40 metres of water. It lies on its port side, both boilers displaced, with the engine also lying on its port side. Some blades are broken off the propeller.

Name: *Britannia.* **Former name(s):** *Earl of Aberdeen.*
Vessel type: Steam ship.
Builder: Hall, Russell & Company, Aberdeen.
When completed: January 1889.
Machinery built by: Hall, Russell & Company, Aberdeen.
Tonnage: 765 tons gross.
Dimensions: Length: 210′. **Breadth:** 30′ 2″.

Depth of holds: 14′ 8″.
Official number: 94527. **Yard number:** 249
Signal letters: LBGJ. **Last port of registry:** Leith.
Ship description: Steel screw steamer. 1 deck.
Machinery description: Triple expansion 3 cylinders. 2 single ended boilers. 200 horse power.
Career and ownership: Owned as *Earl of Aberdeen* by Aberdeen, Newcastle & Hull Steam Company Ltd. At time of loss owned by Leith, Hull & Hamburg Steam Packet Company Ltd (J Currie & Company, managers).
Armament: Unarmed.
Destination and cargo: Middlesbrough for St Malo with a cargo of pig iron.
Date sunk: 19 October 1917.
How sunk: Torpedoed by *UC-75*.
Reported position of loss: German position given as 50° 29′ north, 001° 46′ west.
Actual position of wreck: 50° 28.33′ north, 001° 44.80′ west.
Orientation/height: Stands 4–5 metres in 40 metres on shingle seabed.
How identity of wreck proved: Not proved, but size and description of the wreck fits that of *Britannia.* German position is less than one mile from where the wreck lies.

SS *Baron Garioch*
Torpedoed 28 October 1917

Oberleutnant zur See Karsten von Heydebreck was on patrol in his minelaying U-boat, the *UC-63*, when, on the morning of 28 October 1917, he caught sight of the British steamer, *Baron Garioch*. The weather was fine with light winds, but von Heydebreck chose his position of attack with the sun behind him, and those on board the steamer never saw the track of the approaching torpedo.

The ship was on voyage from Calais and she had first proceeded to St Helens Roads where she received fresh orders to sail for Liverpool. On 28 October 1917 she headed west down Channel and by the morning she was south west of the Needles. About 8.20am, her master, Captain Laurence Leask, was below deck having breakfast, leaving the ship in the charge of the second mate. Suddenly and without warning, an explosion took place on the port side of the ship in the way of number 3 hold. Captain Leask recalled, "The explosion was very violent, blowing away that part of the ship about number 3 hatch, buckling the deck but not blowing a hole in it. The mainmast went by the board." He continued, "The ship suddenly settled by the stern, and sank in about 6 minutes; crew having taken to the starboard boat and after clearing the ship observed Howard, fireman on board, and ordered him to jump into the sea. This he failed to do and went down with the ship. Gunner Herbert Horsley is missing, believed to have been blown from the gun platform by concussion and drowned. All belongings were lost including ship's papers."

Required to provide an explanation as to why he had not been zig-zagging, Captain Leask added, "20 minutes before being struck, two of our own destroyers and an armed trawler passed about 1 ½ miles to seaward of us and were steering nearly the same course. We also had two drifter patrols in sight and, under these conditions, I judged we would be immune from torpedo attack, and dreading the possibility of the enemy having laid mines during the night, I, after serious reflection concluded that the shortest course was the least fraught with danger, so ordered the course west-north-west. I have been in the danger zone since commencement of the war and my ship did not sustain a scratch attributable to myself. I trust this explanation will prove quite satisfactory. I am very anxious to be back on duty again."

The Admiralty did not find the explanation entirely satisfactory, and Captain Leask was cautioned to be more careful in future and carry out Admiralty orders, and not neglect the all important defensive measure of zig-zagging whenever navigationally possible, both by day and by night.

The wreck of the *Baron Garioch* lies in about 38 metres of water. She is more or less upright, the boilers and engine being the highest parts. The barrel of the gun lies just off the stern.

Name: *Baron Garioch*. **Former name(s):** *Kirkstall* ex *Lady Olivia*.
Vessel type: Steam ship.
Builder: William Gray, Hartlepool.
When completed: September 1895.
Machinery built by: Central Marine Engine Works, Hartlepool.
Tonnage: 1831 tons gross.
Dimensions: Length: 265′. **Breadth:** 37′ 6″.
Depth of holds: 17′ 5″.
Official number: 102735. **Yard number:** 505.
Signal letters: PBVK. **Last port of registry:** Ardrossan.
Ship description: Steel screw steamer. 1 deck. Schooner rigged.
Machinery description: Triple expansion 3 cylinders. 2 single ended boilers. 156 nominal horse power.
Career and ownership: Launched as the *Lady Olivia* for the Shipping Agency. While being completed, purchased by J R Cuthbertson and renamed *Kirkstall* for S W Furness, West Hartlepool. 1896 sold to J Guthie, West Hartlepool. 1898 sold to West Hartlepool Steam Navigation Company Ltd. 1908 purchased by Kelvin Shipping Company and renamed *Baron Garioch*. Owned at the time of loss by H Hogarth & Sons. Attacked on 31 January 1917 by *UC-32* who claimed to have sunk her.
Armament: 1 × 13 pounder stern gun.
Destination and cargo: Calais for Liverpool via St Helens Roads.

Date sunk: 28 October 1917.
How sunk: Torpedoed by *UC-63*.
Reported position of loss: 5 miles, Anvil Point bearing north west, and 50° 33′ north, 001° 50′ west.
Actual position of wreck: 50° 31.38′ north, 001° 45.85′ west.
Orientation/height: Stands about 6 metres in 38 metres on shingle seabed.
How identity of wreck proved: Ship's bell recovered.

SS *Redesmere*
Torpedoed 28 October 1917

SS *Redesmere.* Courtesy E N Taylor collection.

In the early hours of 28 October 1917, Oberleutnant zur See Hans Howaldt in the coastal U-boat *UB-40,* was in the vicinity of St Catherine's Point looking for targets. About 4am, a steamer was sighted, and she proved to be the 2123 ton *Redesmere*, on voyage for Southampton. With the tide pushing her to the east and in fairly clear weather with a choppy sea, *Redesmere* was making about 9 knots. *UB-40* prepared to attack from a submerged position.

Redesmere was steaming along in the night with all her lights extinguished and with one lookout man on the fo'c'sle, and the master and one of the officers on the bridge. None saw *UB-40* or the wake of the torpedo which was to hit her. Suddenly and completely without warning, she was struck by a torpedo abaft the engine room bulkhead in number 3 hold. *UB-40* had fired a deadly shot, and *Redesmere* disappeared in 90 seconds. The master, Captain David Jackson and five men were the only survivors, they having been thrown into the water. There had been no time even to attempt to launch the ship's boats; she had gone down too quickly taking 19 men with her.

The wreck of the *Redesmere* lies half over on its port side in about 38 metres of water. Her boilers including a donkey boiler standing vertically are the highest parts of the wreck. One of the main boilers stands on end. Her stern gun is still at the stern where the four-bladed propeller has its uppermost blade broken off. Spare propeller nearby.

Name: *Redesmere.* **Former name(s):** None.
Vessel type: Steam ship.
Builder: Sunderland Shipbuilding Company.
When completed: October 1911.
Machinery built by: North East Marine Engineering Company.
Tonnage: 2123 tons gross.
Dimensions: Length: 290′. **Breadth:** 42′ 7″.
Depth of holds: 19′ 5″.
Official number: 124298. **Yard number:** –
Signal letters: HTNL. **Last port of registry:** Manchester.
Ship description: Steel screw steamer. 1 deck. Schooner rigged.
Machinery description: Triple expansion 3 cylinders. 2 single ended boilers. 226 nominal horse power.
Career and ownership: Owned by Watson Steam Ship Company Ltd (H Watson & Sons, managers) and then Bromport Steam Ship Company Ltd (H R Greenhalgh, managers).
Armament: 1 × 12 pounder, 12 cwt stern gun.
Destination and cargo: Barry Dock for Southampton via Falmouth with a cargo of 3600 tons of coal.
Date sunk: 18 October 1917.
How sunk: Torpedoed by *UB-40.*
Reported position of loss: 6 miles west-south-west of St Catherine's Point and 50° 32′ north, 001° 25′ west.
Actual position of wreck: 50° 28.85′ north, 001° 21.22′ west.
Orientation/height: Lies 090°/270°. Stands about 6 metres in 38 metres on hard chalk seabed with a covering of shingle.
How identity of wreck proved: Process of elimination, and the name Watson & Co (name of shipowners) was found engraved on a telescope recovered from the wreck.

Steam drifter *John Mitchell*
Collision 14 November 1917

Steam drifter *John Mitchell*. Courtesy: From the Port of Lowestoft Research Society collection.

Somewhere between Anvil Point and the Needles lies the wreck of the steam drifter *John Mitchell*. While on Admiralty service in November 1917, she came into collision with a steamer, the SS *Bjerka*, and sank. All her crew were saved and brought into harbour.

There is no information as to whether the wreck of the *John Mitchell* has been located and identified.

Name: *John Mitchell*. **Former name(s):** None.
Vessel type: Steam drifter.
Builder: S Richards & Company, Lowestoft.
When completed: 1913.
Machinery built by: Crabtree & Company, Great Yarmouth.
Tonnage: 89 tons gross.
Dimensions: Length: 85′ 5″. **Breadth:** 20′ 2″.
Depth of holds: 9′ 6″.
Official number: 135765. **Yard number:** 188.
Signal letters: – **Last port of registry:** Lowestoft.
Ship description: Wooden screw steam drifter.
Machinery description: Triple expansion 3 cylinders. 1 single ended boiler. 38 horse power (180 indicated).
Career and ownership: Owned by Colonial Fishing Company Ltd, Waveney Chambers, Lowestoft (John Mitchell, Avenue Road, Lowestoft, manager). Hired by the Admiralty as a net drifter from February 1915. Port number LT211, Admiralty number 1065.
Armament: 1 × 3 pounder bow gun.
Destination and cargo: On Admiralty service.
Date sunk: 14 November 1917.
How sunk: Collision with SS *Bjerka*.
Reported position of loss: Variously as 10 miles south east by east from Anvil Point, and 50° 32′ north, 001° 42′ west.
Actual position of wreck: Not known.
Orientation/height: –
How identity of wreck proved: –

Transport SS *Aparima* Torpedoed 19 November 1917

SS *Aparima*. Courtesy Christchurch Harbour Board, New Zealand.

The *Aparima* was the largest ship to be built for her owners, the Union Steam Ship Company of New Zealand. Early in her career she was fitted out to carry horses, carrying as many as 700 or more at a time, housed in specially constructed stalls. She also traded to and from Calcutta and visited many other ports in southern latitudes. On the outbreak of the First World War, *Aparima* was fitted out for use as a troop and horse carrier, sometimes carrying 1000 troops in one voyage, but it was decided her speed was insufficient to continue as a trooper, and she returned to commercial service. During this time, *Aparima* had been the Company's officer training ship; 30 or 40 young cadets voyaging in her at a time. On her penultimate voyage, she had had all her troop fittings removed and loaded a full cargo of foodstuffs for England. Proceeding via Panama, Newport News and New York, she reached London and discharged her cargo in November 1917. It was there she was requisitioned by the Admiralty to go to Cardiff to load coal for an Italian port.

Aparima left London at 2pm on Saturday 17 November 1917. Following her instructions issued by the Admiralty, the ship zig-zagged down Channel from Dungeness. In an intensely dark night, heavily overcast, the ship passed St Catherine's Light and steamed in a westerly direction at 12 knots. Her master, Captain Gerald Doorly, related what happened in a very detailed and lengthy account; "a violent explosion occurred in

Cadet Geoffrey Bargrove.
Courtesy Mrs Dawn Boddington, New Zealand.

the after part of the ship. The time was 0.52am . . . the ship shook heavily with the concussion and settled down immediately by the stern. I hurriedly pricked off the position of the ship on the chart, which was approximately 7 miles south by west ¾ west from Anvil Point. I rushed along to the wireless house on the after part of the boat deck and shouted out the position. Vipan and Wellington 1st and 2nd operators, were in the wireless room as I looked in the door. They only had time to get out 'SOS A' when the sea smashed along and hissed like a boa up to the after part of the boat deck as the stern sank rapidly." He continued, "I scrambled up to the bridge, blew the 'abandon ship' signal on the whistle and rang the engine telegraph to 'stop;' the engines, however, were out of action by that time. I slid down the bridge ladder and fell against the pilot, who remarked that we had 'got it' this time. I told him to get over the side as soon as possible. The ship was now at the angle of about 45°, the stern evidently on the bottom and the funnel just clear of the sea surface. As the darkness was so intense I was unable to see whether any boats were in the water or not, and there was no time to investigate as the water continued on its terrifying roaring onward rush towards the fore part of the ship as the bow settled down. I leapt down on to the fore deck and noticed the starboard boats' painters still fast to the rail . . . I cast two of these adrift, stripped off my coat and sea boots and slung my life belt around me. The fore part of the ship was now sinking rapidly, and as a perfect seething Niagara was madly rushing along past the saloon house, I slid down a line over the starboard side and flopped into the water. My watch stopped at 0.58am."

Gerald Doorly swam away from the *Aparima* until he came across the ship's gig, overcrowded with survivors, and directed them to the boats he had just released before the ship went down. He said, "Presently a sudden glow and smoke belched from the funnel and an eerie moaning rumbled from the boiler room as it became submerged. The ship sank in about 2 minutes after I left her, i.e. at 1am. Then followed the maddening cries of frenzied men struggling in the water. It was all the more dreadful and uncanny on account of the pitch blackness of the night."

Other survivors related what had happened to them, including an AB named V Fox, who said, "Mr McDonald, 2nd officer, was in a boat which had gone under and refloated full of water. McDonald was in it with a broken limb. He was suffering great pain and a few minutes after the ship sank he said, 'I can't stand this, good-bye *Aparima*' and rolled over the side. He was instantly lost in the water." The chief engineer, Mr Rogerson, went to the engine room to try to close the watertight door. It was half closed when the water burst through; the bulkhead bulged out with the volume of water rushing forward, and Rogerson said, "You can't do any more lads, get on deck." In a remarkable example of good fortune, one of the cadets named T Bevan, asleep in the port middle room, woke up, jumped into water up to his neck as the room instantly filled with water, the sudden rush forcing him upwards and expelling him out of a deck ventilator. Incredibly, Cadet Bevan landed in a raft and was saved.

After the survivors had been rescued, the full scale of the disaster emerged. From a crew of 112 men, 56 were lost and 56 saved. Among those lost were 17 cadets, whose ages ranged from 15 to 19 years.

Captain Gerald Doorly. Courtesy Roger Wilson, New Zealand.

Despite the blackness of the night, *Aparima* had been torpedoed in a surface attack by *UB-40*, commanded by Oberleutnant zur See Hans Howaldt.

Years after the ship was lost, Gerald Doorly light-heartedly remarked to his family that on the night the ship was lost, when he found himself swimming in the English Channel, he did not know whether to aim for France or England, but as his command of French was so execrable, he opted for England.

Captain Doorly's watch is now on display in the Christchurch Museum, New Zealand. *Aparima* is a Maori word meaning "hollowed place of the hand."

The *Aparima* lies in 40 metres of water, listing to port. Her three boilers and twin triple expansion engines are the highest parts. Her bows, broken off, used to stand more than 10 metres, but over the years this has collapsed down. The gun is on the seabed off the starboard side at the stern. Off the wreck as much as 43 metres can be found. Her starboard propeller and condensers were salvaged in the 1970's.

Name: *Aparima.* **Former name(s):** None.
Vessel type: Steam ship.
Builder: William Denny, Dumbarton.
When completed: April 1902.
Machinery built by: William Denny, Dumbarton.
Tonnage: 5704 tons gross.
Dimensions: Length: 430′ 5″. **Breadth:** 54′ 3″.
Depth of holds: 28′ 5″.
Official number: 115807. **Yard number:** 659.
Signal letters: TJBN. **Last port of registry:** London.
Ship description: Steel screw steamer. 2 decks and shelter deck. Fitted with wireless. Schooner rigged. Accommodation for 12 passengers.
Machinery description: Twin triple expansion 3 cylinders. 3 single ended boilers. 389 nominal horse power.
Career and ownership: Ordered August 1901, she was delivered on 1 May 1902 at a cost of £90,240. Built for and owned by the Union Steam Ship Company of New Zealand.
Armament: 1 × 4.7″ quick firing stern gun.
Destination and cargo: London for Cardiff in ballast on government service.
Date sunk: 19 November 1917.
How sunk: Torpedoed by *UB-40.*
Reported position of loss: 7 miles west by south ¾ west from Anvil Point.
Actual position of wreck: 50° 29.41′ north, 001° 55.10′ west.
Orientation/height: Lies 135°/315°. Stands 7 metres in 40 metres on shingle seabed.
How identity of wreck proved: Ship's bell, builder's nameplate and ship's crockery recovered. Ship's name in brass letters on bows.

SS *Myrtlegrove*
Collision 23 November 1917

SS *Huelva*, later renamed *Myrtlegrove*. Courtesy E N Taylor collection.

Despite the serious threat posed by German U-boats, the usual marine hazards continued to be ever present. The loss of the steamer *Myrtlegrove* was due to such a hazard – collision – and we have the report from the colliding vessel, the Norwegian steamer *Mineral*, to show what happened:

On 21 November 1917, the *Mineral* departed Le Havre in convoy bound for Swansea. Hugging the French coast under escort, she passed Barfleur lighthouse and shaped a course to go north across the English Channel, heading for St Catherine's Lighthouse. Passing St Catherine's about 2.35am she steered west by north to remain in sight of the Isle of Wight. Although the night was dark, there was sufficient visibility to make out the other ships in the convoy. About 4am the second mate took over watch on the bridge, the ship at that time steaming at 8 knots. No lights from other vessels were visible, apart from those in the convoy. Quite suddenly, however, the red port hand navigation light of an oncoming ship came into view a short distance off *Mineral's* starboard side. The second mate, Morton Mortenson ordered the helmsman, "Hard a'starboard!" and the ship's whistle was sounded to indicate *Mineral* was altering course.

The oncoming ship was the steamer *Myrtlegrove*, and her crew, hearing the *Mineral* and seeing her alter course, made every effort to take avoiding action too. She altered course to port in a desperate attempt to clear the convoy, but by this time, a collision seemed unavoidable, and the second mate ordered, "Full speed astern!" It was too late, and *Mineral* collided very hard with *Myrtlegrove's* starboard side between the foremast and amidships.

It was obvious that the *Myrtlegrove* was likely to sink, and the *Mineral* stood by alongside and took off all the crew. *Myrtlegrove's* master said he would like to remain on the spot and make attempts to tow the ship in daylight, and by 7am the Norwegian steamer *Astrea* had her in tow. Heavily down by the bows, the tow towards safety was commenced. The disabled ship was later sighted by members of the Auxiliary Patrol Force and it was noticed that *Astrea* was towing *Myrtlegrove* by the head against the tide. At 7.45am the tow parted, and a rope was made fast to the trawler *John Abbot.* An attempt was made to tow the ship by the stern into Freshwater Bay and good progress was being made until 8.20am, when the battle was lost and *Myrtlegrove* sank.

The wreck of the *Myrtlegrove* lies in about 41 metres of water. She lies completely on her port side with her boilers having rolled out of the wreck. The bow section is quite broken, but from just forward of amidships to the stern she stands up from the seabed. Depths around the stern are nearer 44 metres, where the gun can be seen level with the seabed.

Name: *Myrtlegrove.* **Former name(s):** *Huelva.*
Vessel type: Steam ship.
Builder: John Readhead, South Shields.
When completed: December 1894.
Machinery built by: John Readhead, South Shields.
Tonnage: 2642 tons gross.
Dimensions: Length: 303′. **Breadth:** 41′ 6″.
Depth of holds: 10′ 1″.
Official number: 104818. **Yard number:** 301.
Signal letters: NPQW. **Last port of registry:** Glasgow.
Ship description: Steel screw steamer. 1 deck.
Machinery description: Triple expansion 3 cylinders. 2 single ended boilers. 252 nominal horse power.
Career and ownership: Built for and owned by English & American Shipping Company Ltd as *Huelva* (C T Bowring & Company, managers). Sold in 1914 to Steam Ship Mary Company Ltd (Alexander & Mair, managers) and renamed *Myrtlegrove.* Government transport number 8206.
Armament: Armed with a stern gun, details not known.
Destination and cargo: Under sealed orders, from Manchester with a cargo of 6 railway wagons and 1187 tons of hay. Almost certainly she was destined for a port in northern France.
Date sunk: 23 November 1917.
How sunk: Collision with SS *Mineral.*
Reported position of loss: 50° 31′ north, 001° 37′ west.
Actual position of wreck: 50° 31.25′ north, 001° 37.67′ west.
Orientation/height: Stands about 8 metres in 44 metres on hard clay seabed covered with shingle.
How identity of wreck proved: Not proved, but position of wreck is very close to that reported in 1917. Wreck is the right size, layout and description to be the *Myrtlegrove.*

SS *Oriflamme*
Mined 25 November 1917

SS *Oriflamme*. Sir W G Armstrong Whitworth & Co Ltd (Tyne & Wear Museums).

The *Oriflamme* was a steam tanker of 3764 tons, and on 9 November 1917 she departed New York for Le Havre fully laden with a cargo of 5000 tons of benzine. She carried a large crew of some 40 officers and men, plus a man employed as a signalman. Her voyage seems to have been uneventful until the early hours of 25 November, when she was in the vicinity of the Isle of Wight. About 05.45am *Oriflamme* approached an area about 9 miles south of the Nab light vessel.

Unbeknown to those on board *Oriflamme,* the *UC-63* had been on operational patrol in the area, and had laid a minefield. Her commander, Karsten von Heydebreck, had chosen wisely: the area was a gathering point for vessels intending to enter Portsmouth.

A report from the Admiralty said, "*Oriflamme* got separated from her convoy and apparently struck an enemy mine in our deep minefield at 6am, then fired a rocket which came back and ignited her foremost benzine tank. She is still afloat 3 miles to the south of the Nab light vessel. Four tugs there. Still on fire forward, blowing hard and nobody on board. Very few casualties. Hope to get her in if weather moderates and fire goes out."

Another report said, "On entering Portsmouth from the eastward *Oriflamme* crossed the prohibited area and was mined; the ship had a cargo of oil and drifted onshore, burning furiously."

As soon as the fire broke out, *Oriflamme* was abandoned, but one man could not be found. Tugs brought the ship into Sandown Bay and when the ship was reboarded, the missing man was found unconscious and rescued. In the event, the ship could not be saved, and she drifted offshore, witnesses on the Isle of Wight noting, "she was towed away to the west, with benzine spilling from her astern, burning, and the whole ship being alight."

When *Oriflamme* reached a position off St Catherine's Point, she was sunk by gunfire from a torpedo boat destroyer as she was a hazard to navigation.

The wreck of the *Oriflamme* lies about a mile south of St Catherine's Point, lying on her starboard side. The seabed of rock around her has been scoured away, and the whole ship seems to have sunk down into it. Her gun pedestal lies just off the stern, but there is no sign of the barrel. Her boilers and engines are the highest parts of the wreck, fitted aft. Around amidships, there is a spare propeller. Swimming down the slope, in about 46 metres, there is a donkey boiler which has rolled clear of the wreck. All around there are items from the ship, showing up green in the light of torches. The rock seabed is scoured clean, with no marine growth, testimony to the abrasive nature and strength of the tide. Diving should be avoided on spring tides: the tide can run in different directions and turns very quickly. Surface marker buoys, when deployed by divers, have been known to disappear horizontally. Oil continued to seep from the wreck well into the 1980's.

Name: *Oriflamme*. **Former name(s):** None.
Vessel type: Steam tanker.
Builder: Armstrong Whitworth & Company Ltd, Newcastle.
When completed: 1899.
Machinery built by: Wallsend Slipway Company Ltd.
Tonnage: 3764 tons gross.
Dimensions: Length: 335′ 7″. **Breadth:** 45′ 9″. **Depth of holds:** 28′6″.
Official number: 110141. **Yard number:** 691.
Signal letters: RFHC. **Last port of registry:** London.
Ship description: Steel screw steam tanker. 2 decks. 3 masts.
Machinery description: Triple expansion 3 cylinders. 284 nominal horse power. Engine number 501.
Career and ownership: Owned by the Oriflamme Steam Ship Company (Lane & Macandrew).
Armament: 1 × 4.7″ quick firing stern gun.
Destination and cargo: New York for Le Havre with 5000 tons of benzine.
Date sunk: 25 November 1917.
How sunk: Mined by *UC-63*, but may have struck a mine laid by our own forces.
Reported position of loss: Not recorded.
Actual position of wreck: 50° 33.24′ north, 001° 17.86′ west.
Orientation/height: Lies 045°/225°. Stands about 7 metres in 40 to 46 metres on a seabed of rock.
How identity of wreck proved: Engine builder's nameplate recovered.

SS *Øiekast*
Torpedoed 10 December 1917

SS *Øiekast*. Courtesy Norwegian Maritime Museum/P E Johnsen.

The *Øiekast* was a Norwegian steamer of 606 tons, and had a crew of 14 hands including the master. On 8 December 1917, *Øiekast* was preparing to depart Rouen for Cardiff. The pilot navigated the ship to Le Havre, where the ship anchored until the next day. At 9am on 9 December 1917, *Øiekast* prepared to depart at number 18 in a convoy of ships. Setting sail into a fresh breeze from the north east, *Øiekast* left the convoy when off Cape Barfleur and headed for the English coast. The sea was rough and the ship had to reduce speed, making 4–6 knots through the water.

By 8am on the morning of 10 December, *Øiekast* was about 25 miles off the French coast, approximately in mid Channel. About 11.40am, the first mate, Tor Elfstrom saw a surfaced U-boat about 5 miles astern. Immediately informing the captain, who came up on deck, orders were given to turn away from the submarine. Despite this, the U-boat quickly overhauled the *Øiekast* and just before midday, it came within range, opening fire on the steamer. The first shot struck the stern house and lamp room, while more shots struck the funnel, and another took out the steering gear.

Her master, Captain Petter Valdussen ordered, "Stop engines!" and "Abandon ship!" Even before this could be accomplished, however, another six or seven shells had been fired at the ship. As the crew got clear, the U-boat continued to fire, expending about 25 shells before the *Øiekast* flooded, listed to port and disappeared from view. The U-boat was the *U-53* under the command of Kapitänleutnant Hans Rose and after dealing with *Øiekast* she departed to chase another steamer.

In their boats, the survivors drifted apart; the master and nine men subsequently landed in Guernsey, while the second mate and three men landed at Portsmouth. One man was lost.

A wreck which might be the *Øiekast* lies in the mid Channel separation zone in about 62 metres of water. The machinery is fitted aft, as was *Øiekast's*. The wreck is of the right size and description. Her boiler and engines are the highest parts. A close examination of her engines is needed to determine the type of engines fitted – there is a suggestion the wreck has a 2 cylinder compound engine, while *Øiekast* had a triple expansion engine.

Name: *Øiekast*. **Former name(s):** *Mascot*.
Vessel type: Steam coaster.
Builder: Bergens Mek Verks, Bergen.
When completed: 1908.
Machinery built by: Bergens Mek Verks, Bergen.
Tonnage: 606 tons gross.
Dimensions: Length: 171′ 1″. **Breadth:** 29′ 1″.
Depth of holds: 12′.
Official number: – **Yard number:** –
Signal letters: MFGW. **Last port of registry:** Porsgrund.
Ship description: Steel screw steamer.
Machinery description: Triple expansion 3 cylinders. 52 nominal horse power.
Career and ownership: As *Mascot*, owned by Actiesmpskslsk Nordsjoen (Rich. Petersen, manager). Owned 1917 by Akties Oiekast (I M Abrahamsen, manager) as *Øiekast*.
Armament: Unarmed.
Destination and cargo: Rouen for Cardiff in ballast, chartered by the French government.
Date sunk: 10 December 1917.
How sunk: Gunfire from *U-53*.
Reported position of loss: About 25 miles north east by east from Cape Barfleur. Some survivors picked up in 50° 06′ north, 001° 28′ west, some 15 or 20 miles east of the position she was sunk. Estimated position of loss in 1917: 50° 06 north, 001° 51 to 58′ west.
Actual position of wreck: 50° 05.31′ north, 001° 51.16′ west.
Orientation/height: Stands about 5 metres in 62 metres on shingle seabed.
How identity of wreck proved: Not proved but description of *Øiekast* fits what can be seen on the wreck (except that clarification is needed on engine type) and the position fits that reported in 1917.

SS *Borgsten*
Torpedoed 19 December 1917

SS *Borgsten*. Courtesy Norwegian Maritime Museum/P E Johnsen.

The Norwegian steamer *Borgsten* departed Rouen for Newport, Wales, at 5am on the morning of Tuesday 18 December 1917. By 1.15pm, Le Havre had been reached and she dropped anchor, waiting to join a convoy across the Channel the next day. On Wednesday 19th, about 10am, the ship was approached by a patrol boat and told to take up position number 14 in the convoy. Departing together that day, the convoy followed the French coast until it reached Barfleur Point, when it steered a northerly heading for St Catherine's Point. The voyage was progressing without incident, *Borgsten* being in the centre of the convoy of about 30 ships.

About 9.40pm that night a violent explosion took place at the stern of the ship. The ship's master, Captain Sverre Crosby, said, "We assumed we had been torpedoed." The engines were stopped and the lifeboats were immediately made ready for launching. Some difficulty was experienced in lowering the starboard boat, and it was then that the first engineer fell overboard. It was about half an hour before he could be rescued, and then the crew realised that the *Borgsten* might not sink after all. Upon inspection, no damage could be discovered in the holds and the engines appeared to be operating normally.

Re-securing the boats, *Borgsten* got under way again, her master saying, "It was our intention to rejoin our position in the convoy. However, during this time we could hear gunfire and could see torpedoes passing us." Captain Crosby went on, "At 11.15 that night, *Borgsten* was struck by a second torpedo which hit on the port side aft. There was a violent explosion and much of the stern was blown apart. The ship started to sink quickly by the stern. We quickly began to get the lifeboats ready for launching but by that time a number of the crew had jumped into the sea of their own volition. About 1 ½ minutes after the explosion the whole of the stern was under water and about this time a U-boat appeared, heading for us on the surface. Someone from the U-boat shouted out and wanted to know the name of our ship and nationality. We were told to come close to the U-boat. We did not obey any of these orders, and the 2nd mate called out, 'We are not going to do that. First of all we are going to save our friends who have fallen into the sea.' Slowly the U-boat headed off towards our sinking ship."

From the crew of 22 men, two lost their lives.

The U-boat was the minelayer *UC-64*, under the command of Oberleutnant zur See Erich Hecht.

There is no information concerning whether the wreck of the *Borgsten* has been found and identified.

Name: *Borgsten.* **Former name(s):** None.
Vessel type: Steam ship.
Builder: Nylands Vaerksted, Christiania.
When completed: 1913.
Machinery built by: Nylands Vaerksted, Christiania.
Tonnage: 1718 tons gross.
Dimensions: Length: 264′ 9″. **Breadth:** 40′ 2″.
Depth of holds: 18′ 6″.
Official number: – **Yard number:** –
Signal letters: MJSW. **Last port of registry:** Christiania.
Ship description: Steel screw steamer. 4 masts. Fitted with electric light.
Machinery description: Triple expansion 3 cylinders. 152 nominal horse power.
Career and ownership: Owned by Akties Borga (Petter Olsen, manager).
Armament: Unarmed.
Destination and cargo: Rouen for Newport in ballast.
Date sunk: 19 December 1917.
How sunk: Torpedoed by *UC-64*.
Reported position of loss: 50° 12′ north, 001° 23′ west, and Cape Barfleur bearing south ½ west 30 miles.
Actual position of wreck: Not known.
Orientation/height: –
How identity of wreck proved: –

SS *Start*
Torpedoed 22 December 1917

SS *Start* on trials. Courtesy Glasgow University Archives.

The losses to the Norwegian merchant fleet continued to grow into late 1917. Early on 22 December the next victim, the steamer *Start*, was sunk through the activities of the German coastal U-boat, the *UB-58*, under the command of Kapitänleutnant Werner Fürbringer. Fürbringer, known as Fips to his comrades, wrote in his log, "3.25am. 50° 28 00′ north, 001° 47 00′ west. Launched torpedo from 400 metres, surface attack, on vessel of approximately 3000 tons. She is hit forward of the funnel; sinks within 40 seconds without leaving a trace except for a huge oil slick. We pursue a steamer, course east. 4.10am, crash dive in front of destroyer which had hooded lights. . .."

The *Start* was not 3000 tons at all; she was only 728 tons, and she disappeared on the night of 22 December 1917. There were only two survivors from the crew of 14, namely the master, Captain Martin Mikkelsen and the second mate, Olaf Berndtsson. Captain Mikkelsen recalled, "We left Swansea on 18th December 1917 . . .. We followed the coast as far as Falmouth where we arrived about 7am on 17th December. We received instructions and we waited hoping we would receive more precise ones. At 9am on the 20th December, we received orders to continue our voyage … but at 4pm we were stopped by an English patrol boat and told to return to Plymouth. At 11.30am on the 21st, we received another order to continue our voyage . . . there was quite a strong breeze blowing from the east-north-east and we encountered quite foggy weather. On 22nd December we passed the Shambles Light Vessel, about 3 miles distant, at which time there was a strong wind and a heavy sea. I gave orders to the 1st mate to steer east ½ south and to light the lights on the starboard side as well as having a man on the bridge as lookout, as we were taking water from forward. I went down to my cabin and stretched out as I hadn't had a break since we'd left Plymouth. I had been on bridge duty all that time."

Captain Mikkelsen continued, "Very quickly I was awakened by a terrific explosion. As soon as this happened I rushed up on deck and the 2nd mate did the same. We saw that the stern had been severely damaged. The ship's boats had also been damaged. The 2nd mate and the two men who were on the bridge asked what they should do as the boats had been carried away by the explosion. The 2nd mate and I both shouted out that we should make for the raft . . .. The ship at this stage was sinking very rapidly. I was on the raft when the ship's mast struck us . . .. I was thrown from the raft under water." Oluf Berndtsson picked up the story, adding, "The raft itself was forced against the mast and did not float away. I fell into the water and was almost dragged under as the ship sank. The raft was entangled in the rigging but I managed to free it. The raft was almost sucked into the funnel but I kicked it out with my feet." After this, Captain Mikkelsen was able to surface and re-boarded the raft. By this time the *Start* had disappeared. It was 1.30am. At 11.30am, frozen stiff with cold, Captain Mikkelsen and Oluf Berndtsson were rescued. The rest of the crew perished.

The wreck of the *Start* lies in 43 metres of water. Her engine lies on its port side, the large single boiler and vertical donkey boiler being the highest parts. The stern section lies half over to port while from the boiler to the bows the wreck is upright. The wreck has collapsed to port. A spare propeller is situated close to the boiler on the starboard side.

Name: *Start.* **Former name(s):** None.
Vessel type: Steam coaster.
Builder: Scott & Sons, Bowling.
When completed: June 1896.
Machinery built by: Ross & Duncan, Glasgow.
Tonnage: 728 tons gross.
Dimensions: Length: 203′. **Breadth:** 29′ 1″.
Depth of holds: 10′ 6″.
Official number: – **Yard number:** 120.
Signal letters: HQNP. **Last port of registry:** Skien.
Ship description: Steel screw steamer. 1 deck. Well deck. 3 masts.
Machinery description: Triple expansion 3 cylinders. 1 single ended boiler. 98 nominal horse power.
Career and ownership: Owned by Actieselskabet Start (J A Larsen).
Armament: Unarmed.
Destination and cargo: Swansea for Rouen with a cargo of 819 tons of coal.
Date sunk: 22 December 1917.
How sunk: Torpedoed by *UB-58*.
Reported position of loss: Master's position given as 4 miles south of St Alban's Head, German position given as 50° 28 00′ north, 001° 47 00′ west.
Actual position of wreck: 50° 28.29′ north, 001° 49.63′ west.
Orientation/height: Stands about 5 metres in 43 metres. Wreck lies in a hollow on seabed of shingle.
How identity of wreck proved: Ship's bell recovered.

SS *Start.* Author's collection.

SS *Hilda Lea*
Torpedoed 23 December 1917

SS *Hilda Lea*. Courtesy Bergens Sjøfartsmuseum, Norway.

The British steamer *Hilda Lea* was taken into Admiralty use as a collier transport in 1917. She departed St Helens Roads, bound for Rouen, on 23 December 1917, shaping a course to take her clear of the Isle of Wight before steaming south towards the French coast. She was able to achieve a respectable 9 ¼ knots and in fine, clear and calm conditions, the ship made good time.

Hilda Lea's master, Captain Andrew Brown, had wisely taken the precaution of placing three of his crew as lookouts; one was on the fo'c'sle, another amidships, and the third was situated aft. His ship was in a convoy of 13 escorted by trawlers, there being eight ships ahead and four astern, and he must have thought his ship was relatively safe. By the time the convoy reached a position about mid Channel, it was 9.15pm at night, and the ship was steaming without lights, though ships were showing dimmed stern lights. Despite these precautions, the German U-boat *UB-35*, under the command of Oberleutnant zur See Karl Stöeter, had seen the oncoming convoy and selected *Hilda Lea* as his next victim. He prepared to attack.

In the calm, clear conditions of that night, he kept his boat concealed at periscope depth while a torpedo was launched. Nothing was seen by the lookouts until it was too late; the track of the torpedo only being seen when it was 50 feet away. Slamming into the ship's port side amidships, well below the water line and probably directly into the engine room, the torpedo exploded. *Hilda Lea* was sinking fast and Captain Brown ordered the ship to be abandoned, the crew taking to the boats, *Hilda Lea* slipping under the sea 5 minutes later. Incredibly, only one man was lost from the crew of 22, supposedly killed in the engine room. The survivors were quickly picked up by one of the escorting trawlers.

There is no information concerning whether the wreck of the *Hilda Lea* has been located and identified.

Name: *Hilda Lea*. **Former name(s):** None.
Vessel type: Steam ship.
Builder: Wilton's Engineering & Slipway Company, Rotterdam.
When completed: November 1916.
Machinery built by: Wilton's Engineering & Slipway Company, Rotterdam.
Tonnage: 1328 tons gross.
Dimensions: Length: 240′ 1″. **Breadth:** 36′ 4″.
Depth of holds: 15′ 9″.
Official number: – **Yard number:** –
Signal letters: WLBD. **Last port of registry:** London.
Ship description: Steel screw steamer. 1 deck.
Machinery description: Triple expansion 3 cylinders. 2 single ended boilers. 186 nominal horse power.
Career and ownership: Owned 1916 by Erik Grant Lea and registered Bergen. Owned 1917 by the Shipping Controller (Cormack, James & Company, Leith, managers) and taken into service as an Admiralty transport collier.
Armament: 1 × 90mm stern gun.
Destination and cargo: St Helens for Rouen with a cargo of 1720 tons of coal.
Date sunk: 23 December 1917.
How sunk: Torpedoed by *UB-35*.
Reported position of loss: 50° 14′ north, 001° 00′ west.
Actual position of wreck: Not known.
Orientation/height: –
How identity of wreck proved: –

SS *Luciston*
Torpedoed 24 December 1917

SS *Red Cross*, later renamed *Luciston*. Courtesy E N Taylor collection.

German submarine activity remained intense in the Channel through the end of 1917, the next victim falling to the minelayer, *UC-71*, under the command of Oberleutnant zur See Ernst Steindorff. He was on operational war patrol in a position about 1 ½ miles south of the Owers Light Vessel when the *Luciston* came into view.

Luciston, a 2877 ton steamer, was loaded with 1000 tons of government stores as she departed Southampton. Clearing the Isle of Wight, by 8pm the ship was well on her voyage, zig-zagging as required by her Admiralty instructions. However, the ship crossed *UC-71's* sights and suddenly, without warning, a torpedo struck the ship on the port side abreast of the foremast, and the ship began to fill.

At first, the crew abandoned ship, but when it became clear the *Luciston* was not in immediate danger of sinking, some returned to give assistance to two tugs and a trawler which had arrived on site. A towing cable was attached and efforts were made to get the ship into safety. All seemed to be going well and high hopes must have been entertained that the ship would survive. The tow proceeded well as the rescue convoy steamed into Spithead and the eastern Solent, but just as safety was almost in reach, the ship was beached on the edge of a sloping bank. The ship subsequently succumbed to the damage, filled completely and sank close to Calshot Spit.

It was hoped that the ship, lying in only 60 feet of water, could be salved, but in 1922 she was worked on and much of her stern section removed. She was later dispersed by explosives as she was a hazard to navigation.

The wreck of the *Luciston* lies in 16 metres of water. She lies just beneath the route taken by high speed passenger craft going to and from the Isle of Wight from Southampton, but she can be dived with proper safety cover and providing the ferries are aware to keep clear. The wreck has been fairly flattened but the machinery stands up.

Name: *Luciston.* **Former name(s):** *Lucincita* ex *Red Cross.*
Vessel type: Steam ship.
Builder: J L Thompson & Sons, Sunderland.
When completed: September 1890.
Machinery built by: Blair & Company, Stockton.
Tonnage: 2877 tons gross.
Dimensions: Length: 316′. **Breadth:** 40′ 6″.
Depth of holds: 20′ 8″.
Official number: 96555. **Yard number:** 266.
Signal letters: LVCH. **Last port of registry:** Glasgow.
Ship description: Steel screw steamer. 1 deck. Schooner rigged.
Machinery description: Triple expansion 3 cylinders. 2 single ended boilers. New donkey boiler 1904. 256 nominal horse power.
Career and ownership: Owned by Luciston Steam Ship Company Ltd (W S Miller & Company).
Armament: 1 × 12 pounder, 12 cwt stern gun.
Destination and cargo: Southampton for Boulogne with 1000 tons of government stores.
Date sunk: 24 December 1917.
How sunk: Torpedoed by *UB-35,* but towed in and sank in Stokes Bay near Calshot Spit.
Reported position of loss: Close to Calshot Spit near Southampton.
Actual position of wreck: 50° 47.99′ north, 001° 18.13′ west.
Orientation/height: Stands about 4 metres in 16 metres on muddy/stony seabed.
How identity of wreck proved: Contemporary reports from 1917 identify the *Luciston* in the position given.

SS *Espagne*
Torpedoed 25 December 1917

SS *Espagne*. Courtesy National Maritime Museum, Antwerp.

The *UC-71* remained active in the area off the Isle of Wight after *Luciston* had been torpedoed, and the next victim would be the Belgian steamer *Espagne*. Oberleutnant zur See Ernst Steindorff conned his boat, submerged at periscope depth, and fired one torpedo at the *Espagne*.

Espagne had departed Le Havre on Christmas Eve 1917, and headed north across the Channel bound for Newport, Wales. Clearing St Catherine's Point about 5.30am, the ship was making about 9 knots as she headed west in a moderate breeze with fine and clear weather. At the ship's wheel was Emile Hintjens, a lamp trimmer who was taking his turn at the helm, supervised by the second mate. About 6.30am, a loud and violent explosion was heard and felt in the ship. When Hintjens recovered from the initial shock, he found himself covered with wreckage. Clearing this away, he quickly made for the starboard lifeboat but it was no longer there. "I found myself in the water and saw one of the hatch covers floating. I got on it and saw two others of the crew on one of the upturned boats." Only three men survived the sudden destruction of the *Espagne*; 21 others lost their lives.

The wreck of the *Espagne* lies in about 38 metres of water. She is very broken and has collapsed to starboard. The boilers are the highest parts, one of which stands on end. The engine lies on its side partially covered with shingle. At the stern the propeller and rudder are still there, with a spare propeller partly buried nearby.

Name: *Espagne*. **Former name(s):** None.
Vessel type: Steam ship.
Builder: Chant Nav. Anversois, Hoboken.
When completed: March 1909.
Machinery built by: North East Marine Engineering Company, Newcastle.
Tonnage: 1463 tons gross.

Dimensions: Length: 235′ 5″. **Breadth:** 36′ 1″. **Depth of holds:** 12′ 3″.
Official number: – **Yard number:** –
Signal letters: MBHL. **Last port of registry:** Antwerp.
Ship description: Steel screw steamer. 1 deck.
Machinery description: Triple expansion 3 cylinders. 2 single ended boilers. 150 nominal horse power.
Career and ownership: Owned by Armament Adolf Deppe.
Armament: Unarmed.
Destination and cargo: Le Havre for Newport in ballast.
Date sunk: 25 December 1917.
How sunk: Torpedoed by *UC-71*.
Reported position of loss: Survivors rescued from 50° 25′ north, 001° 28′ west.
Actual position of wreck: 50° 26.51′ north, 001° 29.57′ west.
Orientation/height: Stands about 4 metres in 40 metres on shingle seabed.
How identity of wreck proved: Ship's bell recovered.

SS *Fallodon*
Torpedoed 28 December 1917

SS *Fallodon*. Courtesy E N Taylor collection.

The *UC-71* continued to be a persistent threat to shipping, and on 28 December 1917 she would take care of yet another ship. This was to be the British steamer *Fallodon*, 3012 tons, on voyage from Le Havre for Glasgow.

Fallodon's master, Captain Alfred Lodge, said, "The ship was steering north west by north at 8½ knots in position 50° 26′ north, 001° 06′ west. It was 5.30pm. There was a fresh north west wind and the sea was rough, but the moon was up. I had 7 men on watch, 3 and an officer on the bridge, two men aft and one on the fo'c'sle." At this moment, Oberleutnant zur See Ernst Steindorff ordered *UC-71* to fire a torpedo. This order was carried out instantly; the torpedo was released and sped towards the *Fallodon*, striking the ship and exploding. Captain Lodge explained the torpedo hit, describing the location as "the after end of the engine room and fore side of the after hold adjoining. A large hole had been made in both sides of the ship, one side being blown inward and the other blown outward."

The damage was too much for the ship to remain afloat, and the *Fallodon* was abandoned, with every one of the crew being saved by taking to the boats. Despite the severity of the damage, it took ¾ hour for the *Fallodon* finally to fill and disappear from view.

The wreck of the *Fallodon* lies across the tide in 39 metres of water. She lies entirely on her port side, the amidships section being the highest part. One boiler has rolled from its original position. The gun is still at the stern. Much of the deck area of the wreck is buried in shingle.

Name: *Fallodon*. **Former name(s):** None.
Vessel type: Steam ship.
Builder: Bartram & Sons, Sunderland.
When completed: November 1903.
Machinery built by: J Dickinson & Sons Ltd, Sunderland.

Tonnage: 3012 tons gross.
Dimensions: Length: 339′. **Breadth:** 48′ 1″.
Depth of holds: 22′ 1″.
Official number: 118348. **Yard number:** –
Signal letters: VHWK. **Last port of registry:** London.
Ship description: Steel screw steamer. 1 deck. Schooner rigged.
Machinery description: Triple expansion 3 cylinders. 2 single ended boilers. 293 nominal horse power.
Career and ownership: Owned by London & Northern Steam Ship Company Ltd (Pyman Brothers Ltd, managers).
Armament: 1 × 12 pounder stern gun.
Destination and cargo: Le Havre for Glasgow in ballast.
Date sunk: 28 December 1917.
How sunk: Torpedoed by *UC-71*.
Reported position of loss: 50° 26′ north, 001° 06′ west.
Actual position of wreck: 50°26.29′ north, 001° 13.16′ west.
Orientation/height: Lies 000°/180°, bows to the south. Stands 8 metres in 39 metres on shingle/gravel seabed.
How identity of wreck proved: Builder's nameplate recovered.

SS *Westville*
Torpedoed 31 December 1917

SS *Westville*. Courtesy E N Taylor collection.

The dubious distinction of sinking the last ship of 1917 fell to Oberleutnant zur See Karl Stöeter in *UB-35*. He had taken advantage of the darkness of New Year's Eve, 1917 and was cruising on the surface off the Needles. In visibility of no more than a mile, at around 5am, Stöeter's lookouts sighted the British steamer *Westville*. *Westville* was steaming at 9 knots, zig-zagging and taking advantage of the 2 knots of tide which was helping her along. Steering a heading described as north west by west ½ west, the ship was following her route instructions by remaining close to the coast.

Westville's master, Captain George Bell, was on the bridge with the first mate, and he had ensured his ship had lookouts on duty, these being one man on the fo'c'sle and one on the bridge. The night was very dark, and no-one was aware that *UB-35* was lining up for a torpedo attack. In the darkness, another ship could be heard nearby, her whistle sounding from time to time, while another had passed close by.

At 5.10am, without warning, a torpedo struck the *Westville* on her port side on the waterline, just abaft amidships. A large hole was created, cutting open the side of the ship and destroying one of the boats in its davits. Unable to send an SOS on the ship's wireless as it had been put out of action by the explosion, Captain Bell ordered the entire ship's company of 30 men to lower the boats and abandon ship. They must have responded to the order with the utmost speed; 4 minutes after the torpedo had struck, *Westville* capsized, finally sinking 20 minutes later. All were rescued by a patrol vessel and landed at Portsmouth.

The wreck of the *Westville* lies in about 40 metres of water, though up to 43 or 44 metres can be found just off the wreck. She lies half over on her port side, her amidships section being the highest part. One of her boilers has rolled out of position while a large section of hull rests against the engine. The bows are quite broken but at the stern the large propeller and gun can be seen. The bridge deck, made of steel, has slipped off the wreck to the seabed. She is known locally as the six mile wreck.

Name: *Westville.* **Former name(s):** None.
Vessel type: Steam ship.
Builder: John Readhead, South Shields.
When completed: August 1913.
Machinery built by: John Readhead, South Shields.
Tonnage: 3207 tons gross.
Dimensions: Length: 335′ 3″. **Breadth:** 47′ 6″. **Depth of holds:** 23′ 5″.
Official number: 133317 **Yard number:** 135.
Signal letters: JCSK. **Last port of registry:** North Shields.
Ship description: Steel screw steamer. 1 deck.
Machinery description: Triple expansion 3 cylinders. 2 single ended boilers. 310 nominal horse power.
Career and ownership: Owned by Ville Steamships Ltd (Balls & Stansfield, managers).
Armament: 1 × 12 pounder, 12 cwt stern gun.
Destination and cargo: Blyth for Blaye with a cargo of 5200 tons of coals.
Date sunk: 31 December 1917.
How sunk: Torpedoed by *UB-35.*
Reported position of loss: 5 miles west-south-west from St Catherine's and 50° 35′ north, 001° 28′ west.
Actual position of wreck: 50° 33.94′ north, 001° 31. 87′ west.
Orientation/height: Lies 130°/310°. Stands 9 metres in 40–43 metres, bows to the south east on shingle seabed. High bank to the east.
How identity of wreck proved: Bridge steering pedestal recovered bearing date of 1913, the year *Westville* was completed.

SS *Asborg*
Torpedoed 3 January 1918

SS *Leonidas*, later renamed *Asborg*. Courtesy Bristol's Museums Galleries & Archives.

As the New Year began, hostilities continued as before, and another Norwegian ship steamed into danger. The *Asborg*, 2751 tons, was under the command of Captain Johannes Johannessen. On 29 December, 1917, *Asborg* departed Newcastle and steamed south on the North Sea. Reaching the English Channel, she shaped a course to take her in a westerly direction towards her intended destination of Leghorn. Everything went well until the ship was approaching St Catherine's Point about 3.30am. Captain Johannessen said, "Everything went very well until 3rd January 1918, when the ship was torpedoed on the port side, probably in the vicinity of the store room hold. At that time St Catherine's Point was about 4 miles distant, the magnetic position being about north west by north. The lifeboats on the port side were totally destroyed and also destroyed was a small skiff which had also been placed on the port side. The crew went to their stations ready to leave the ship on the starboard side. Since the ship was not sinking very rapidly everyone remained on board in the hope that they would be able to save her."

Adding to this account, Halvor Pedersen, first mate, said, "I was on watch on the bridge. I was on the starboard side and was able to make out the light at St Catherine's Point. The weather was slightly foggy when I heard a noise coming from the sea, immediately followed by a loud explosion from the port side. The explosion seemed to come from the middle of the port side somewhere in the vicinity of the transverse hatchway. This was destroyed and I was showered in a column of coal, smoke and water. The ship lurched to starboard and then came back to port, and began to sink. Within a short time the deck was awash although it did not seem to sink further."

In the engine room, stoker Simon Knudsen recalled, "I was on watch in the boiler room. The torpedo struck near the coal chute, and the boiler was moved about 4 feet to starboard. I lost account of what was going on, but regained control of myself when the ship began to take on water. Flames were shooting out of the firebox and I received burns to my left arm."

Thirty-five minutes after the torpedo strike, it now

being clear the ship could not be saved, she sank from view. The entire crew of 25 men got off the ship, into the lifeboats and made for St Catherine's Point.

Asborg had been sunk by the *UC-75* under the command of Oberleutnant zur See Johannes Lohs.

The wreck of the *Asborg* lies in about 28 metres of water. She is upright, with parts of the stern still standing. Forward of her large, single boiler, the wreck is flatter, but much of her cargo of steel lies on the seabed. The boiler and engine are the highest parts of the wreck.

Name: *Asborg*. Former name(s): *Leonidas*.
Vessel type: Steam ship.
Builder: Short Brothers Ltd, Sunderland.
When completed: 1896.
Machinery built by: J Dickinson & Sons Ltd, Sunderland.
Tonnage: 2751 tons gross.
Dimensions: Length: 321′. **Breadth:** 43′ 1″.
Depth of holds: 21′ 9″.
Official number: – **Yard number:** –
Signal letters: WKPD. **Last port of registry:** Christiania.
Ship description: Steel screw steamer. 1 deck.
Machinery description: Triple expansion 3 cylinders. 1 single ended boiler. 252 nominal horse power. New donkey boiler 1909.
Career and ownership: Originally owned by A Embiricos, then owned by Akties To. (Thv. B Heinstein & Sonner, managers), Christiansand.
Armament: Unarmed.
Destination and cargo: Newcastle for Leghorn with a cargo of 450 tons of sheet steel, 10 tons of drums and 2800 tons of coal.
Date sunk: 3 January 1918.
How sunk: Torpedoed by *UC-75*.
Reported position of loss: 3 miles south of St Catherine's Point.
Actual position of wreck: 50° 31.85′ north, 001° 15.80′ west.
Orientation/height: Lies 090°/270°. Stands 7 metres in 28 metres on hard chalk seabed covered with shingle.
How identity of wreck proved: Not proved but description of cargo, and size, layout and position of wreck fits that of the *Asborg*.

HMS *Mechanician*
Torpedoed 20 January 1918

HMS *Mechanician* down by the stern off the Needles. Courtesy National Maritime Museum, Greenwich.

By any standards, the *Mechanician* was a large ship of over 9000 tons. Her size and speed were considered useful for the Admiralty, and she was commissioned into the Royal Navy as an armed ocean escort ship. She must have been a very attractive target for Oberleutnant zur See Karl Stöeter in his boat, the *UB-35*. *UB-35* was on war patrol in the vicinity of the Isle of Wight in the early hours of 20 January 1918 when *Mechanician* came into view. The ship had departed London and was heading down Channel at over 10 knots, zig-zagging as she went, passing close to St Catherine's Point. In a fresh breeze and squally but fairly clear conditions, *Mechanician* was approaching the Needles when *UB-35* attacked. At 2.45am, Stöeter judged his attack, and a torpedo was fired. *Mechanician* was hit on the port side abreast number 6 hatch, killing three engineers and a signalman.

The chief engineer, Walter Clare, RNR, said, "There had been no damage in the engine room though water was breaking through from the deep tank. Returning to the engine room I found that all the firemen had left. I ordered them back down again but only managed to persuade the donkeyman, and with the assistance of three engineers we managed to keep up a full head of steam. Those three engineers subsequently died in the stokehold which had been deserted by the firemen."

Twenty-five minutes after the first attack, Stöeter fired a second torpedo, striking the *Mechanician* in the engine room. A distress signal was sent out and a trawler arrived to investigate, taking off survivors. The damage from the second torpedo was very considerable; the engines were out of action and the steering would not operate. Lifeboats were manned and lowered and most of the survivors abandoned ship, leaving about 30 men on board.

These men were much encouraged by the fact that their ship remained afloat, and with the arrival of two tugs when they were only 3½ miles from the Needles, there was every hope the ship could be saved. However, the weather was bad and a ground swell had developed. Towing cables parted as they reached the entrance to the Needles Channel and with the ship drawing 36 feet aft, it was feared she would ground.

Trying to tow a 9000 ton waterlogged ship with unmanageable steering proved to be too much for the two small tugs, which did their best to save the ship. Driven by wind and sea, and with insufficient power to control her, *Mechanician* went aground on the south western part of the Shingle Bank in the Needles Channel. Soon after, she broke her back and became a total loss. From her large crew of 102, 13 men died in the torpedo attacks.

The wreck of this large ship lies on the edge of the Shingle Bank in about 12 metres of water, though the nature of the Shingle Bank is that there is a constant movement of shingle, sometimes covering and sometimes exposing the wreck. Conditions are not often good enough to dive on her, but in good weather and neap tides she can be dived in safety.

Name: *Mechanician.* **Former name(s):** None.
Vessel type: Steam ship.
Builder: Workman Clark, Belfast.
When completed: October 1900.
Machinery built by: Workman Clark, Belfast.
Tonnage: 9044 tons gross.
Dimensions: Length: 482′. **Breadth:** 57′.
Depth of holds: 31′.
Official number: 113414. **Yard number:** –
Signal letters: RVWG. **Last port of registry:** Liverpool.
Ship description: Steel screw steamer. 2 decks. 4 masts. Fitted with electric light and wireless.
Machinery description: Twin triple expansion 6 cylinders. 2 single ended boilers. 604 nominal horse power.
Career and ownership: Built for and owned by Charente Steam Ship Company Ltd (T & J Harrison, managers). Formerly a Harrison liner. Carried a cargo of mules from Newport News for Egypt for the British Expeditionary force 1916/1917. Transferred to the Liner Section and Commissioned into the Royal Navy as a commissioned armed ocean escort.
Armament: 2 × 6″ guns and 2 × 4″ quick firing guns.
Destination and cargo: London for Plymouth for orders.
Date sunk: 20 January 1918.
How sunk: Torpedoed by *UB-35,* stranded on the Shingle Bank and became a total loss.
Reported position of loss: On the south west Shingle Bank.
Actual position of wreck: Approximate: 50° 39.73′ north, 001° 36.47′ west.
Orientation/height: Lies 090°/270°. Stands up a few metres depending on the movement of shingle.
How identity of wreck proved: Contemporary reports describe the position of loss.

SS *Molina*
Torpedoed 20 January 1918

SS *Molina*. Courtesy Norwegian Maritime Museum.

The Norwegian steamer *Molina* departed Le Havre in convoy bound for Swansea on 21 January, 1918. She had almost completed her crossing of the Channel, and had sighted St Catherine's Light about 3 ½ miles off about 1.30am the next morning. Steaming at about 9 ½ knots, all seemed to be well. The lookouts, one man on the fo'c'sle and two on the bridge, scanned the waves, trying to see through the drizzle and taking advantage of the few glimpses of moonlight. They saw nothing, but a German U-boat had spotted them.

UB-35, having destroyed the *Mechanician* only two days earlier, had the *Molina* in her sights, and a torpedo was fired at the ship.

Her master, Captain Roald Larsen reported, "I was on the bridge with the 2nd mate. We steered north-north-west and immediately there was an incredible explosion at the after end of the ship. The engines stopped at the same time and water started to enter the holds and engine room via the propeller shaft tunnel. The ship started to sink immediately and it could be seen that the whole stern of the ship had been destroyed. The crew took their places in the lifeboats and also in the motorised launch. It was evident *Molina* was sinking quickly by the stern. She remained in a vertical position for a short time and then sank completely."

Gerhard Johnsen, the second mate, added, "I was on watch on the bridge. The weather was good; it was quite clear but overcast and from time to time there was drizzle. I had seen nothing untoward or suspect. After the explosion occurred, the captain blew the whistle and I shouted, 'All men to the boats!' By then, the ship's stern was already underwater. The vessel took on a vertical position with her bows in the air. She remained like that for 10 to 15 minutes before finally disappearing."

The entire crew of 17 men were later picked up by a passing steamer.

The wreck of the *Molina* lies upright in about 36 metres of water. Her after end is much flattened and her bronze propeller, minus two blades, has been salvaged. The engine and boilers are the highest parts of the wreck.

Name: *Molina.* **Former name(s):** None.
Vessel type: Steam ship.
Builder: Nylands Vaerksted, Christiania.
When completed: 1905.
Machinery built by: Nylands Vaerksted, Christiania.
Tonnage: 1122 tons gross.
Dimensions: Length: 229′. **Breadth:** 36′.
Depth of holds: 16′ 9″.
Official number: – **Yard number:** –
Signal letters: MCND. **Last port of registry:** Haugesund.
Ship description: Steel screw steamer. 1 deck. Fitted with electric light.
Machinery description: Triple expansion 3 cylinders. 2 single ended boilers. 109 nominal horse power.
Career and ownership: Owned by J Ringens Rederi Akties (J Ringen, manager).
Armament: Unarmed.
Destination and cargo: Le Havre for Swansea in ballast.
Date sunk: 22 January 1918.
How sunk: Torpedoed by *UB-35.*
Reported position of loss: 50° 32′ north, 001° 20′ west.
Actual position of wreck: 50° 33.82′ north, 001° 29.03′ west.
Orientation/height: Lies 090°/270°. Stands about 6 metres on shingle seabed.
How identity of wreck proved: Ship's bell and builder's nameplate recovered.

SS *Serrana*
Torpedoed 22 but sunk 23 January 1918

Three hours after *Molina* had disappeared, *UB-35* sank the steamer *Serrana*, 3677 tons, under the command of captain Albert George Maskell.

He reported, "On Tuesday 22 January at 4.35am, the weather was fine and clear with a moderate sea. We were 10 miles off St Catherine's Lighthouse proceeding at full speed steering west by north magnetic, making 9 knots. I was on the bridge with the Trinity House pilot, the chief and 3rd mates and one hand at the wheel. One hand was forward and the gunners were aft. No lights were being exhibited."

He continued, "An explosion occurred on the port side amidships with huge clouds of steam and the ship commenced to buckle up amidships and in less than 5 minutes water was washing across the deck amidships. The pilot, one of the hands and myself got onto a raft being cut from one of the boats. One passenger was drowned in endeavouring to get on to the raft and the other passenger was also drowned in apparently trying to reach a boat. Forty other members of the crew were saved in boats, one dying after being landed. Three stokers were killed in the stokehold."

Chief Skipper William Green was at sea in the Auxiliary Patrol Force vessel, the drifter *White Oak*, when he, "heard an explosion and shortly afterwards a rocket was seen. I proceeded full speed towards the position and at 5.35am found the *SS Serrana* apparently in a sinking condition; her boats had just left her. I sighted *Torpedo Boat No 21* and requested she signal, '*SS Serrana* of London … torpedoed … still afloat, crew sent to Poole. I have not enough power to tow and beach her.' Shortly afterwards the tugs *Grappler* and *Walvisch* came up and after we had secured a hawser aft, commenced to tow her by the stern."

With her entire stern post and propeller clear of the water, she reached the Bridge Reef but the tide took control of the ship, and she grounded and later broke her back on the reef. The stern section floated clear on the rising tide and sank.

When the tugs returned to the site the stern section, with only a derrick showing, was lying about 400 yards north west of the lighthouse. The bow section was still on the reef with its foremast still standing.

The two parts of the wreck of the *Serrana* are in the positions described in 1918. The bow section on the Bridge Reef in about 8 metres has been much flattened, and not much stands up. Some cargo remains in her. The stern section, comprising the boilers, engines and after holds, lie in 18 metres. The engine lies on its side. The gun is visible at the stern partly buried in gravel.

Name: *Serrana.* **Former name(s):** None.
Vessel type: Steam ship.
Builder: John Readhead, South Shields.
When completed: September 1905.
Machinery built by: John Readhead, South Shields.
Tonnage: 3677 tons gross.
Dimensions: Length: 353′ 4″. **Breadth:** 47′ 6″.
Depth of holds: 15′ 3″.
Official number: 102609. **Yard number:** 387.
Signal letters: HDMV. **Last port of registry:** London.
Ship description: Steel screw steamer. 1 deck. Schooner rigged.
Machinery description: Triple expansion 3 cylinders. 2 single ended boilers. 350 nominal horse power.
Career and ownership: Built for Scrutton & Sons.
Armament: Armed with 1×4″, stern gun and 2×7.5″, howitzers.
Destination and cargo: London for Barbados with general cargo comprising 500 tons of coal, 300 tons of general cargo and 112 bags of mails.
Date sunk: Torpedoed on 22 January but broke up and sank on 23 January 1918.
How sunk: Torpedoed by *UB-35*.
Reported position of loss: Bridge Reef, the Needles, and 400 yards north west of the Needles.
Actual position of wreck: Bows: 50° 39.62′ north, 001° 36.16′ west. Stern: 50° 39.87′ north, 001° 35.82′ west.
Orientation/height: Bows much flattened with not much standing up in 8 metres on chalk rock seabed. Stern section: highest parts are the boilers. Wreck stands 5 metres in 18 metres on seabed of shingle.
How identity of wreck proved: Contemporary reports identify the location. Ship's bell recovered.

Clipper ship *Smyrna*, from an oil painting. Courtesy Aberdeen Art Gallery.

Builder's nameplate, *Smyrna*. Diameter 456 mm.

Ship's bells

Messina bell. Diameter 254 mm.

Waitara bell.

Michael Clements bell. Diameter 248 mm.

Inger bell. Diameter 100 mm.

Smyrna stern bell. Diameter 230 mm.

Kong Guttorm bell. Diameter 335 mm.

Ship's Crockery

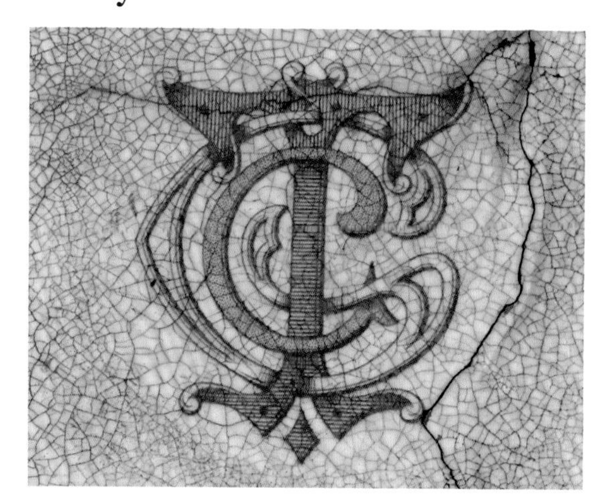

Compagnie Générale Transatlantique, SS *Azemmour*.

P & O, sailing barque *Simla*.

The Moss Steam Ship Company Ltd, SS *Luxor*.

Ship's Crockery

Westoll Line, SS *Fluent*.

Union Steam Ship Company, SS *Aparima*.

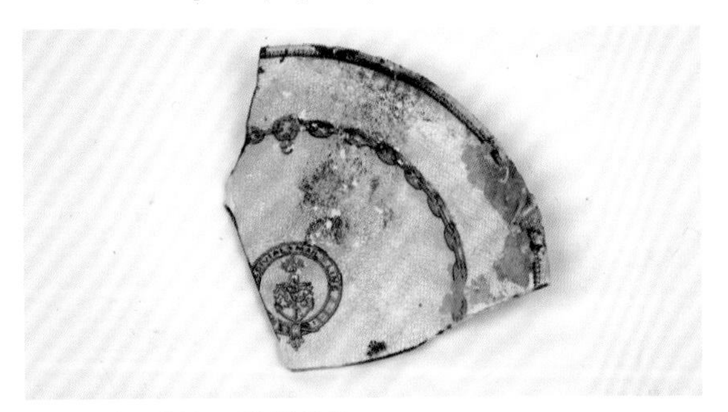

Khedivial Mail Line, SS *El Kahira*.

Cunard Steamship Company Ltd. Found on a drift dive.

Ship's Crockery

The Aberdeen Line, clipper ship *Smyrna*.

British & African Steam Navigation Company Ltd. Elder Dempster & Co Ltd, RMS *Mendi*.

London & South Western Railway Company (Royal Mail), SS *Normandy*.

Nameplates

Engine builder's nameplate, SS *Lapwing*. 327 × 190 mm.

Engine builder's nameplate, SS *Oriflamme*. 606 × 413 mm.

Builder's nameplate, SS *Clarinda*. Diameter 290 mm.

Builder's nameplate, SS *El Kahira*. 510 × 380 mm.

Engine builder's nameplate, SS *Iduna*. 402 × 235 mm.

Capstan cover, SS *Tweed*. Diameter 510 mm.

Telegraphs

SS *Brestois*. Diameter 320 mm.

SS *Clarinda*. Diameter 230 mm.

SS *Spyros*. Diameter 230 mm.

SS *Iduna*. Diameter 365 mm.

Steering pedestals, cover plates

SS *Braatt II*. Diameter 220 mm.

SS *Spiral*. Diameter 263 mm.

SS *Empire Crusader*. Diameter 260 mm.

SS *Olivine*. Diameter 300 mm.

Steering gear

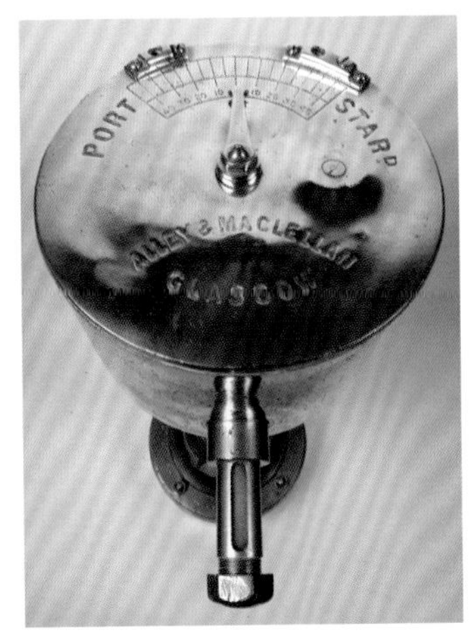

Head of bridge steering pedestal, SS *Sphene*. Height 1060 × 305 mm diameter.

Bridge steering indicator, SS *Cuba*. 275 × 215 mm.

Centre hub cover from stern steering position, SS *Tweed*. Diameter 275 mm.

Bridge equipment

Bridge steering pedestal, SS *Braatt II.*
Height 1010 mm.

Bridge steering pedestal, SS *Sphene.*
Height 1060 mm.

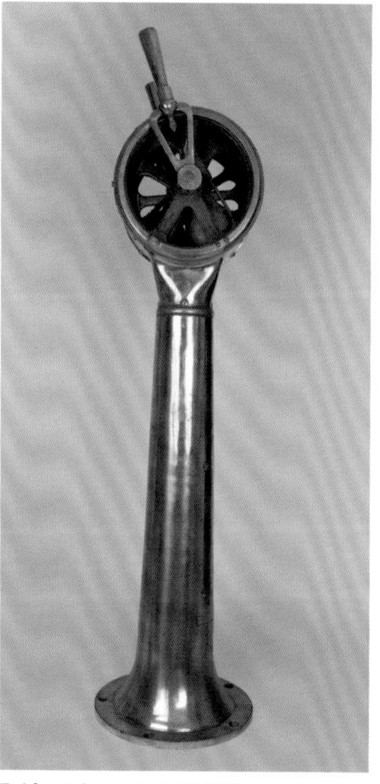

Bridge telegraph, MV *Y48.*
Height 1050 mm.

Bridge telegraph, MV *Guernsey Coast.*
Height 1050 mm.

Sound equipment

SS *Clarinda*. Height 480 mm.

SS *Betsy Anna*. Height 555 mm.

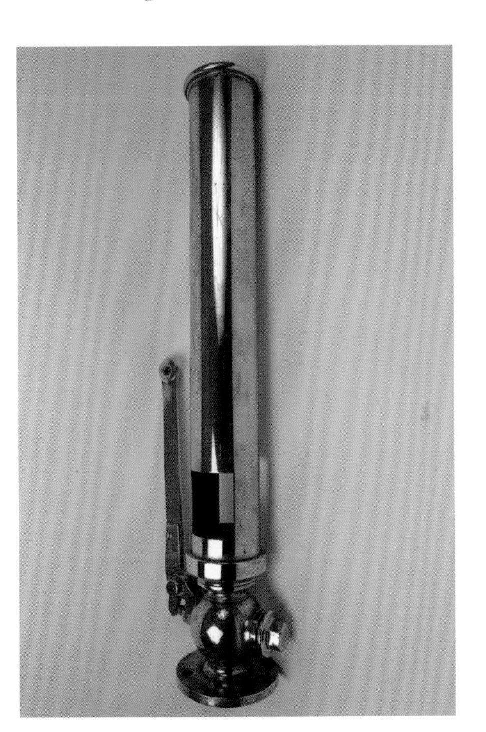

SS *Inger*. Height 840 mm.

MV *Guernsey Coast.*. Length 645 mm.

Engine and machinery fittings

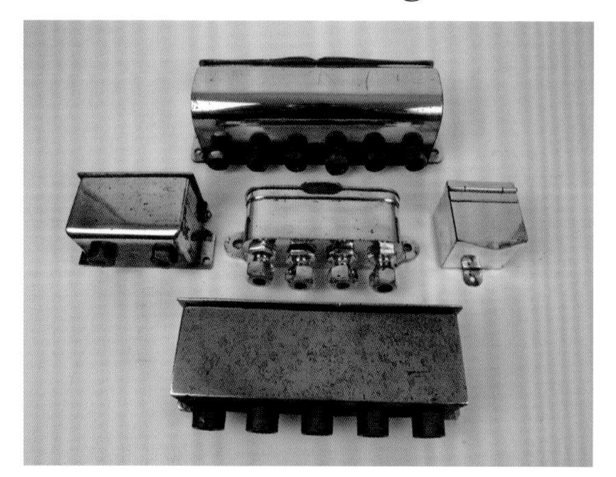

Selection of oil boxes, oiler valves and oil fittings, various wrecks.

Back view of oil box, 350 × 100 mm. SS *Tweed*, and enlargement of the maker's details, J Campbell, maker, Port Glasgow.

Miscellaneous

Selection of steam pressure gauges, various wrecks.

Selection of shell cases, various wrecks.

Engine room nameplates, SS *Empire Crusader*. 150 × 30mm and 212 × 30 mm.

Miscellaneous

Oil lamp, SS *Eleanor*. Height 405 mm.

Compass, unidentified.

Stern compass stand, SS *Clarinda*. Height 660 mm.

Smyrna's general cargo

Selection of crockery. Centre flagon 420 × 220 mm.

Selection of glassware, and two picture frames. Blue bottles 360 mm × 120 mm.

Restored signal gun, SS *Normandy.* Length 860 mm.

Some objects are beyond restoration . . . crushed porthole, sandblasted and de-zincified Chadburn's telegraph, and shellcase.

SS *Aalesund*
Torpedoed 23 January 1918

SS *Aalesund* on the stocks. Courtesy Karmsund Folkesmuseum, Norway.

Aalesund was a small steamer of just over 400 tons, but that did not prevent her becoming a victim of the submarine war. Her story was related by her first mate, Rasmus Thor Rasmussen, who said, "At 10am on the morning of Tuesday 22 January 1918, we left the anchorage of Le Havre and we made our way intending to catch up with the convoy. We did this and took our place as number 4 in the convoy. There were five ships with two torpedo boats and two trawlers. At midnight, the captain went off to get some sleep, and I replaced him as officer on watch. At that time we were in sight of St Catherine's which was north-north-west magnetic. There was quite a breeze from the south west but the night was clear and the sea quite calm."

He continued, "At 1am on the morning of the 23rd, we were hit by a torpedo which exploded about halfway down the ship, making a direct hit on the engine room. Most of the centre of the ship was destroyed including the bridge. The whole ship was full of steam and smoke and it quickly started to settle at the stern and listed severely to port." He added, "I had seen a disturbance in the water … I ran to the wheelhouse to assist the helmsman and then saw the track of the torpedo making its way rapidly to our ship. Two seconds later the explosion took place. There was no way we could have avoided the torpedo."

Continuing his story, Rasmussen said, "I was able to save myself by jumping into the sea and swimming as far away from the ship as possible. As I was swimming I could hear other men crying out in distress but I saw no-one except the 2nd engineer who saved himself by getting on a raft. I could hear cries of 'Help! Help!' and found the 17-year old seaman Bjarne Stakkestad right behind me. Together we tried to cling to a packing case but had to give it up. We were both very cold but just able to swim towards one of the torpedo boats, and we were saved."

Aalesund disappeared in less than 2 minutes, sinking by the stern, her bows high in the air as she took her final plunge to the seabed. From her crew of 12, six men lost their lives. The ship had been torpedoed by the *UC-71* in a submerged attack. Her commander, Oberleutnant zur See Ernst Steindorff, had claimed another victim.

A wreck believed to be that of the *Aalesund* lies in about 43 metres of water off St Catherine's Point. The stern section is completely upside down, the propeller being the highest part of the wreck. From amidships forward the wreck appears to have settled in an upright position, but has collapsed down.

Name: *Aalesund.* **Former name(s):** None.
Vessel type: Steam ship.
Builder: Stavanger Støberi & Dock, Stavanger.
When completed: September 1890.
Machinery built by: Plenty & Son, Newbury.
Tonnage: 414 tons gross.
Dimensions: Length: 146′. **Breadth:** 24′ 6″.
Depth of holds: 12′ 8″.
Official number: – **Yard number:** –
Signal letters: JRFV. **Last port of registry:** Haugesund.
Ship description: Iron screw steamer. 1 deck.
Machinery description: Triple expansion 3 cylinders. 1 single ended boiler. 40 horse power.
Career and ownership: 1904 purchased from Aalesund to Haugesund and owned by Gjaerdsjø & Bakkevig, E Lindø, A Lothe, E H Kongshavn, T Førland, O Bakkevig & S Staalesen. Owned at time of loss by Dampsk. A/S Aalesund (Johan Amundsen).
Armament: Unarmed.
Destination and cargo: Caen for Barry in ballast.
Date sunk: 23 January 1918.
How sunk: Torpedoed by *UC-71*.
Reported position of loss: 50° 23.00′ north, 001° 19.50′ west.
Actual position of wreck: 50° 23.82′ north, 001° 23.65′ west.
Orientation/height: Stern stands about 6 metres in 43 metres on shingle seabed.
How identity of wreck proved: Not proved but reported position of loss is about 2½ miles from the position of the wreck. Size and estimated tonnage are consistent with that of the *Aalesund.*

SS *Avanti*
Torpedoed 2 February 1918

SS *Avanti*. Courtesy Danish Maritime Museum, Helsingør.

On 2 February 1918, Kapitänleutnant Erwin Wassner – known affectionately as Uncle Fritz – was in his coastal U-boat, the *UB-59*, in a position off St Alban's Head. Wassner recorded in his war diary, "On the surface, moved in for an attack on a steamer. Because of the increased revving of the diesels there is so much smoke from the engines that the whole place is full of it. We must turn off the diesels, otherwise there is no visibility. As a result, the boat is too slow to achieve the appropriate distance on the electric motors. Once the smoke has cleared, we discover a steamer heading straight for our boat. We manage to get clear of it on the electric motors and to launch a torpedo against the first steamer. However, it falls in a very acute angle because of our insufficient speed with the electric motors. Immediately after it was launched, we had to dive because of the approach of a second steamer . . .."

After this abortive attack, Wassner continued, "6am, surface torpedo attack against a 3000 ton steamer. Bow shot, first tube, calibre 3 torpedo set to run at 1.5 metres. A hit behind the funnel at a distance of 400 metres. Steamer sinks very quickly, bow first. For a little while, the stern remains above water. Steamer was heavily laden and armed. The billowing smoke from the engines in this attack again endangered the boat. At times it was like moving in thick fog. The engines had to be shut down when we fired the torpedo. At 6.15am there is a boiler explosion. We dive and rest on the seabed."

Wassner had sunk the steamer *Avanti*, 2128 tons, bound from Bilbao for West Hartlepool, loaded with a cargo of iron ore. Only two men survived from her crew of 24. One of the survivors, George Knight, a seaman with the RNVR, was employed as a gunlayer on the ship. He said, "A sudden explosion occurred when I was on watch on the gun platform aft at 6am. The ship broke in half and sank immediately. I was thrown into the air and pitched onto a raft which was then in the water. I saw numbers of the crew in the water swimming and clinging to wreckage but only one, Fransisco Lopez, a Spaniard, managed to reach the raft."

The wreck of the *Avanti* lies in about 40 metres of water. Her boilers, the highest parts of the wreck, have rolled and are upside down, and the engine lies in a tangle on its side. The gun is still in the stern.

Name: *Avanti.* **Former name(s):** None.
Vessel type: Steam ship.
Builder: Akt. Burmeister & Wain, Copenhagen.
When completed: September 1912
Machinery built by: Gutte Hoffaung, Oberhausen.
Tonnage: 2128 tons gross.
Dimensions: Length: 272′ 7″. **Breadth:** 40′.
Depth of holds: 21′ 1″.
Official number: 140271. **Yard number:** –
Signal letters: JRCV. **Last port of registry:** London.
Ship description: Steel screw steamer. 1 deck.
Machinery description: Triple expansion 3 cylinders. 2 single ended boilers. 181 nominal horse power.
Career and ownership: Built for Det. Forenede Dampskibs Selsk, Denmark. 1917 transferred to the Shipping Controller (Lambert Brothers Ltd, managers) on government service.
Armament: 1 × 12 pounder, 12 cwt Japanese stern gun.
Destination and cargo: Bilbao for West Hartlepool via Falmouth with a cargo of 3500 tons of iron ore.
Date sunk: 2 February 1918.
How sunk: Torpedoed by *UB-59.*
Reported position of loss: 50° 34′ north, 002° 2′ west.
Actual position of wreck: 50° 29.90′ north, 001° 55.11′ west.
Orientation/height: Lies 045°/225°. Stands 6 metres in 40 metres on rough seabed with a layer of shingle.
How identity of wreck proved: Ship's bell recovered. Ship's name in brass letters on bow and stern.

SS *Eleanor*
Torpedoed 12 February 1918

One of the most successful of all Germany's submarine commanders of the First World War was Oberleutnant zur See Johannes Lohs. Lohs had had command of the *UC-75*, but he was to make his mark as the officer commanding the coastal U-boat, the *UB-57*. He wrote in his war diary, "In the night of the 11th/12th February, near the Shambles Light Vessel. Surfaced. Fired a calibre 3 torpedo at an armed English steamer. She is hit and sunk. Got the name of the ship as *Eleanor* from a man sitting on a box in the water. No boats had been lowered. The man shouted at us, 'Thank God if your souls are saved! These are all mines!' The cargo was mines for the Mediterranean. 6.20am, fired calibre 3 torpedo at 2000 ton steamer in convoy with many other small steamers. Missed it. Probably too deep since we used a 4 metre setting."

The ship attacked and sunk by Lohs, the *Eleanor*, had departed Immingham on 6 February 1918, bound for Falmouth for orders, and thence to the Mediterranean. The sole survivor was the second mate, Barton Hunter, who recalled, "I had turned in and at about 4am was wakened by an explosion. I ran up on deck and found the vessel was sinking and the boats had been blown away. I went up to the bridge to fire a rocket, and a second explosion occurred, after which the *Eleanor* sank and I found myself on the bridge floating in the sea. It was very dark at the time and I heard shouting from men in the water to send a boat to help them, but I saw no boat and could do nothing to help them." He continued, "After being on the raft [*sic*] for about 15 minutes I saw a vessel coming towards me, and struck a match. She came close to and I saw it was a submarine, very high in the bow, but could not see any other details as it was too dark. Someone hailed from the submarine in very good English but with a foreign accent and asked the name of the ship, what gun she carried, her cargo and port of destination, all of which I correctly gave as I was afraid I would be killed if I refused."

Eleanor, escorted by trawlers, had steamed at full speed towards the west in fine, clear conditions and a smooth sea. She had been torpedoed without warning; none of the four lookouts having given any indication of danger, and she sank almost instantly. Thirty-five men died when she sank.

After the loss of the ship became known to the authorities, other vessels were sent to the scene to pick up debris floating from the wreck. Altogether, 97 mines were picked up, floating on the surface, and taken to Portsmouth for disposal.

The wreck of the *Eleanor* lies upright in 40 metres of water in two main sections. She was easily identified as many mines and depth charges remain, stacked in a large heap just forward of the boilers, rotted out with their explosive content washed away. Another large pile of war cargo lies in the stern section. The boilers and piles of munitions are the highest parts, the engine lying over to port. At the stern the steering quadrant is evident, and the gun lies almost buried, with only the pedestal showing above the shingle.

Name: *Eleanor*. **Former name(s):** None.
Vessel type: Steam ship.
Builder: H S Edwards & Sons, Newcastle.
When completed: November 1888.
Machinery built by: J P Reynolds & Sons, South Shields.
Tonnage: 1980 tons gross.
Dimensions: Length: 270′. **Breadth:** 36′ 5″.
Depth of holds: 19′ 7″.
Official number: 88816. **Yard number:** –
Signal letters: KVNF. **Last port of registry:** South Shields.
Ship description: Steel screw steamer. 1 deck. Well deck. Schooner rigged.
Machinery description: Triple expansion 3 cylinders. 2 single ended boilers. 160 horse power.
Career and ownership: Owned by the Eleanor Steam Ship Company Ltd (J Ridley, Son & Tully). Hired by the Admiralty as a merchant fleet auxiliary in August 1914 (pendant number Y 61).
Armament: 1 × 12 pounder, 12 cwt stern gun.
Destination and cargo: Immingham for the Mediterranean via Falmouth with a cargo of mines and depth charges, together with firing pistols, firing levers, torpedo detonators and other associated paraphernalia.
Date sunk: 12 February 1918.

How sunk: Torpedoed by *UB-57*.
Reported position of loss: 9 miles west by south ½ south from St Catherine's, and 50° 30′ north, 001° 30′ west.
Actual position of wreck: 50° 30.11′ north, 001° 40.41′ west (bow section) and 50° 30.10′ north, 001° 40.38′ west (stern section).
Orientation/height: Lies 100°/280°. Stands 7 metres in 40 metres on seabed of shingle.
How identity of wreck proved: Distinctive cargo of mines and depth charges remain in the wreck. Position of wreck is a few miles west of her reported position of loss.

SS *Borgny*
Presumed mined 26 February 1918

SS Borgny. Courtesy Bergens Sjøfartsmuseum, Norway.

The steamer *Borgny* left Newport, Wales, on 24 February 1918, bound for Rouen with a cargo of coal. Reaching Falmouth, she waited to receive fresh orders, leaving the next day to continue up Channel. She passed Anvil Point about 3.45am on 26 February, keeping the coast in sight, and then started to cross Poole Bay. Her master, Captain Ole Hansen, said, "At 5am that morning the vessel was struck by torpedo on the starboard side close to number 1 hatch. The ship started to sink immediately. The position was about three miles south-south-west of the Needles. At that time I was in the chart room and I immediately went up onto the bridge to ensure that the device for shutting off the steam was closed. I saw a submarine which was about 200 metres away. It dived straight away and I never saw it again. The crew went to their stations and quickly the boats were lowered. Every man who was aboard left safe and sound. The lifeboats got away and stayed some distance away until the *Borgny* sank at about 5.10am that morning."

Another crew member, second mate Adolf Gjerding, said, "I was on watch on the bridge. At 4.45am I thought I saw something black in the water in the vicinity of the port side, but then there was an explosion on the starboard side. From the time of the explosion until the time the water started to come up to the deck was barely 1 or 1 ½ minutes. *Borgny* stayed like that with her stern in the air until 5.5am when it completely disappeared."

Despite Captain Hansen's assertion that he had sighted a submarine, the sinking was never claimed by a U-boat, either through mine or torpedo, and no U-boats were reported as missing, i.e. lost after carrying out an attack. It is presumed that *Borgny* struck a stray, drifting mine which had eluded the minesweepers.

The wreck of the *Borgny* is a popular dive site, lying in about 31 metres of water. She lies on her starboard side with her stern upside down.

Name: *Borgny.* **Former name(s):** None.
Vessel type: Steam ship.
Builder: Akers Mek Verks, Christiania.
When completed: 1909.
Machinery built by: Akers Mek Verks, Christiania.
Tonnage: 1149 tons gross.
Dimensions: Length: 228′ 5″. **Breadth:** 36′ 5″.
Depth of holds: 15′ 8″.
Official number: – **Yard number:** –
Signal letters: MFRL. **Last port of registry:** Christiania.
Ship description: Steel screw steamer. 1 deck. 4 masts.
Machinery description: Triple expansion 3 cylinders. Machinery fitted aft. 111 nominal horse power.
Career and ownership: 1910 owned by Akties Borgaa (P Olson, manager). Under charter to the French government when sunk.
Armament: Unarmed.
Destination and cargo: Newport for Rouen via Falmouth with a cargo of 1466 tons of coal.
Date sunk: 26 February 1918.
How sunk: Presumed to have struck a stray, drifting mine.
Reported position of loss: 3 miles south-south-west of the Needles.
Actual position of wreck: 50° 35.44′ north, 001° 41.72′ west.
Orientation/height: Lies 090°/270°. Stands 7 metres in 31 metres on shingle seabed.
How identity of wreck proved: Brass letters from the bows and stern spelling the ship's name.

SS *Brestois*
Collision 7 March 1918

SS *Brestois*. Author's collection.

The *Brestois* was a small, French steamer, and her loss seems to have aroused little interest; this is entirely understandable when judged against the background of valuable ships, cargoes and crews being destroyed by German U-boats.

Brestois, 348 tons, had departed St Malo bound for Cardiff and on 7 March 1918, she was off the Isle of Wight, no doubt having followed her route instructions from the Admiralty to cross the Channel directly and then keep within sight of land. At some time on 7 March, *Brestois* came into collision with the British steamer *Penmount.* Evidently, the collision was serious and damaged *Brestois* so badly that she sank. Her crew of 18 were all rescued and landed at Poole.

The wreck of the *Brestois* lies in 40 metres of water. She is a small wreck, more or less upright, although the engine lies on its port side, and the bow lies on its starboard side.

Name: *Brestois.* **Former name(s):** None.
Vessel type: Steam coaster.
Builder: McKellar & Company, Dumbarton.
When completed: 1873.
Machinery built by: W King & Company, Glasgow.
Tonnage: 348 tons gross.
Dimensions: Length: 152′ 8″. **Breadth:** 22′.
Depth of holds: 12′.
Official number: – **Yard number:** –
Signal letters: HNMT. **Last port of registry:** Brest.
Ship description: Iron screw steamer. 3 masts.
Machinery description: Compound 2 cylinders. 1 single ended boiler. New boiler 1893. 44 nominal horse power.
Career and ownership: Owned by Chevilotte Freres. Owned at the time of loss by Chargeurs Algeriens Reunis (Jean Stern, owner).
Armament: 1 × 47mm 3 pounder, quick firing stern gun (since raised by the author and donated to the Isle of Wight Shipwreck Museum).
Destination and cargo: St Malo for Cardiff in ballast.
Date sunk: 7 March 1918.
How sunk: Collision with the *SS Penmount.*
Reported position of loss: 7 ½ miles south west by west ½ west of St Catherine's.
Actual position of wreck: 50° 27.45′ north, 001° 31.07′ west.
Orientation/height: Lies roughly 070°/250°. Stands 4 metres, bows to the west, on an undulating chalk rock seabed worn smooth in shifting sand/gravel.
How identity of wreck proved: Bridge telegraph, of an early flat top design, has an additional brass plate, engraved in French, riveted on top of the original English version. 47mm shell cases recovered are French in origin. Description of wreck exactly fits that of the *Brestois.*

SS *Braatt II*
Torpedoed 7 March 1918

SS *Fornjot*, later renamed *Braatt II*. Courtesy Norwegian Maritime Museum/F Edgar Davis.

The *Braatt II* was another Norwegian steamer which would fall victim to a torpedo, this time from the coastal U-boat, the *UB-30*, under the command of Oberleutnant zur See Rhein of the Flanders Flotilla.

The master of the *Braatt II* was Captain Caspar Solberg, and he recalled, "On Wednesday 6 March 1918 at 8am, while we were at Falmouth, we received orders concerning the route we were to follow. Everything went fairly well until Thursday 7 March at 5.20am when an incredible explosion took place. I understood this was a torpedo hit, which must have hit aft as the men in their bunks there were thrown out by the shock onto the deck, and three of them were injured. The engines were stopped immediately and I ordered all the men on deck and to go to their lifeboats, which were quickly put in the water."

In the engine room, the third engineer, named Andersen, said, "I was on watch in the engine room when the explosion took place. I shut the steam off immediately and then went up on deck. When I left the engine room, water was already coming in at a terrific rate through the transmission tunnel. I got into a boat on the starboard side."

Captain Solberg concluded, "As the ship began to sink we abandoned her and, having got some distance away from her, I saw the conning tower of the U-boat which sank us. Ten minutes later my ship sank by the stern."

The wreck of the *Braatt II* lies in 40 metres of water. She lies on her port side, the boilers being the highest parts of the wreck. The bow section has largely rotted away, but there is a great deal of debris along the length of the ship where the wreck has collapsed. The engine lies almost upside down.

Name: *Braatt II*. **Former name(s):** *Trudvang* ex *Stanton* ex *Fornjot*.
Vessel type: Steam ship.
Builder: Fredriksstad Mekaniske Verksted.
When completed: 1914.

Machinery built by: Fredriksstad Mekaniske Verksted.
Tonnage: 1834 tons gross.
Dimensions: Length: 265′. **Breadth:** 42′.
Depth of holds: 20′.
Official number: – **Yard number:** 179
Signal letters: MKRB. **Last port of registry:** Christiania.
Ship description: Steel screw steamer.
Machinery description: Triple expansion 3 cylinders. 2 single ended boilers. 188 nominal horse power.
Career and ownership: 1915 owned by Finn Friis, Drammen, as *Fornjot*. 1916 owned by J B Stang as *Stanton*. 1917 owned by Chr. Nielsen & Company, Larvik, as *Trudvang*. 1918 owned by Herman Jacobsen & Company, Sarpsborg, as *Braatt II*.
Armament: Unarmed.
Destination and cargo: Newport for Rouen via Falmouth with a cargo of 2780 tons of coal.
Date sunk: 7 March 1918.
How sunk: Torpedoed by *UB-30*.
Reported position of loss: 7 miles south west by south of St Catherine's, and 50° 32′ north, 001° 22′ west.
Actual position of wreck: 50° 30.00′ north, 001° 19.37′ west.
Orientation/height: Lies 045°/225°. Stands 6 metres in 40 metres on shingle and rocky seabed, bows to the north east.
How identity of wreck proved: Bridge steering position recovered. Serial number checked against archives and found to have been sold to A/S Fornjot (Finn Friis and Company) in 1914.

SS *Tweed*
Torpedoed 13 March 1918

SS *Tweed*. Courtesy Glasgow University Archives.

On his next patrol off the Isle of Wight, Kapitänleutnant Erwin Wassner in *UB-59* sank a number of ships, the first of which was the steamer *Tweed,* a handsome looking ship. *Tweed* had departed Newhaven bound for Cherbourg, and in the early morning of 13 March 1918 she was off St Catherine's Point. At 0.45am, in convoy and escorted by vessels from the Auxiliary Patrol, she was steering a course of south west by south ½ south at 7½ knots. Although the ships in the convoy had been zig-zagging as required by their orders, *Tweed* had to reduce speed to allow another ship to take up her proper place in the convoy. It was at that moment that *UB-59*, on the surface, attacked.

Wassner recorded in his war diary, "During the night of 13 March, 5 nautical miles south of St Catherine's Point, we successfully torpedoed and sunk an unknown 2500 ton steamer which carried cargo and was armed, and en route to Le Havre." In the darkness, Wassner had misinterpreted what he saw; *Tweed* was not, in fact, armed, and her tonnage was 1025 tons gross, not 2500 tons.

Her master, Captain Archibald McMillan, reported, "*Tweed* was being convoyed and was exhibiting only a stern light when she was torpedoed just abaft the engine room on the starboard side. She commenced to sink and was down in 3 minutes except the bows which were visible for another 5 minutes. Four men were killed by the explosion and three went down with the vessel. The survivors escaped in No 4 lifeboat."

The Admiralty noted, "From his statements it would appear that he had slowed down to 7½ knots from 12 knots, his ordinary full speed, to allow the other ship in company with him to pick up his station. He had switched on his navigation lights, dimmed, for 5 minutes, some 20 minutes before the torpedo hit the ship. Had he continued zig-zagging while slowed down he would not have been torpedoed, in all probability."

Seven men lost their lives in the sinking, and 13 survived after rescue by one of the escorting trawlers.

The wreck of the *Tweed* lies in 40 metres of water south of St Catherine's Point. The wreck is upright, though some wreckage has collapsed to starboard, some lying close to the wreck while more lies out on the seabed. The engine lies over to starboard. Her engines and boilers are the highest parts of the wreck.

Name: *Tweed.* **Former name(s):** None.
Vessel type: Steam ship.
Builder: D J Dunlop & Company, Port Glasgow.
When completed: September 1892.
Machinery built by: D J Dunlop & Company, Port Glasgow.
Tonnage: 1025 tons gross.
Dimensions: Length: 230′. **Breadth:** 32′ 1″.
Depth of holds: 15′ 5″.
Official number: 99845. **Yard number:** –
Signal letters: MSBN. **Last port of registry:** Glasgow.
Ship description: Steel screw steamer. 2 decks. Well deck. Fitted with electric light. Schooner rigged.
Machinery description: Triple expansion 3 cylinders. 2 single ended boilers. 223 horse power.
Career and ownership: Owned by W Sloan & Company. Under government charter at the time of loss. *Tweed* had been utilised for the cross Channel supply service.
Armament: Unarmed.
Destination and cargo: Newhaven for Cherbourg with 1378 tons of general station coal, 877 tons of furnace coal, and 600 tons of government stores comprising 1000 drums of cresol oil, stowed in the well deck forward; the alleyways aft were stowed full of case goods.
Date sunk: 13 March 1918.
How sunk: Torpedoed by *UB-59.*
Reported position of loss: About 8 miles south west of St Catherine's, and 50° 25′ north, 001° 18′ west, later amended to 50° 30′ north, 001° 18′ west.
Actual position of wreck: 50° 28.26′ north, 001° 18.25′ west.
Orientation/height: Lies about 090°/270°, bows to the west. Stands 7 metres in 40 metres on shingle seabed.
How identity of wreck proved: Builder's nameplate, nameplate from stern steering boss and engraved capstan cover recovered.

SS *Tweed.* Courtesy Bristol's Museums Galleries & Archives.

SS *Londonier*
Torpedoed 13 March 1918

SS *Londonier*. Courtesy National Maritime Museum, Antwerp.

While *UB-59* had just sunk the Tweed, the *UC-71* was also active in the same area, and this time a Belgian steamer would be the victim. This was the 1870 ton *Londonier*, which had departed Calais for the Bristol Channel for orders.

Under charter to the French government, *Londonier* had crossed the Channel and was steering a course in the direction of the Needles at 9½ knots. The Admiralty noted, "It would appear the vessel was silhouetted seaward by St Catherine's Point which had been passed 10 minutes three miles distant. This fact may have some bearing on the ship being a target." Whether or not this was so is not recorded in the war diary of *UC-71*, this time under the command of Oberleutnant zur See Warzecha. In a calm sea he executed a surface attack, torpedoing the *Londonier* at 2am on 13 March.

According to Sven Degryse, the ship's master, "I had a lookout on the fo'c'sle head and an officer on the bridge. We were altering course but not zig-zagging and we were in company with another steamer and two trawlers. A submarine, apparently, had been spotted on the surface immediately before the explosion, 200 yards away. I presume two torpedoes were fired, both of which hit; they struck the fore side of the engine room on the port side." *Londonier* was abandoned straight away as the vessel sank immediately. 13 men managed to reach the ship's boats and rafts, but 12 men lost their lives. In the darkness, the survivors saw the conning tower of *UC-71* as it submerged and disappeared.

The wreck of the *Londonier* lies in 40 metres of water. She is upright but has collapsed to starboard. Her engine is the highest part of the wreck. The propeller shaft stands clear of wreckage. In the stern the gun lies on its side. The bow section is broken and low to the ground.

Name: *Londonier.* **Former name(s):** *Vrijhandel.*
Vessel type: Steam ship.
Builder: Irvines Ship Building & Dry Dock Company.
When completed: 1911.
Machinery built by: Richardsons, Westgarth & Company Ltd, Hartlepool.
Tonnage: 1870 tons gross.
Dimensions: Length: 279′. **Breadth:** 40′ 1″.
Depth of holds: 18′ 5″.
Official number: – **Yard number:** –
Signal letters: MBPV. **Last port of registry:** Antwerp.
Ship description: Steel screw steamer.
Machinery description: Triple expansion 3 cylinders. 2 single ended boilers. 175 nominal horse power.
Career and ownership: Owned by Scheepvaart Maats Gylsen (Brys & Gylsen Ltd, managers).
Armament: 1 × 12 pounder stern gun.
Destination and cargo: Calais for Bristol Channel for orders in ballast.
Date sunk: 13 March 1918.
How sunk: Torpedoed by *UC-71.*
Reported position of loss: 50° 31′ north, 001° 19′ west.
Actual position of wreck: 50° 28.59′ north, 001° 23.07′ west.
Orientation/height: Stands 7 metres in 40 metres on hard chalk seabed covered with shingle.
How identity of wreck proved: Ship's crockery recovered. Brass nameplate from the gun indicates it is a 12 pounder.

SS *Venezuela*
Torpedoed 14 March 1918

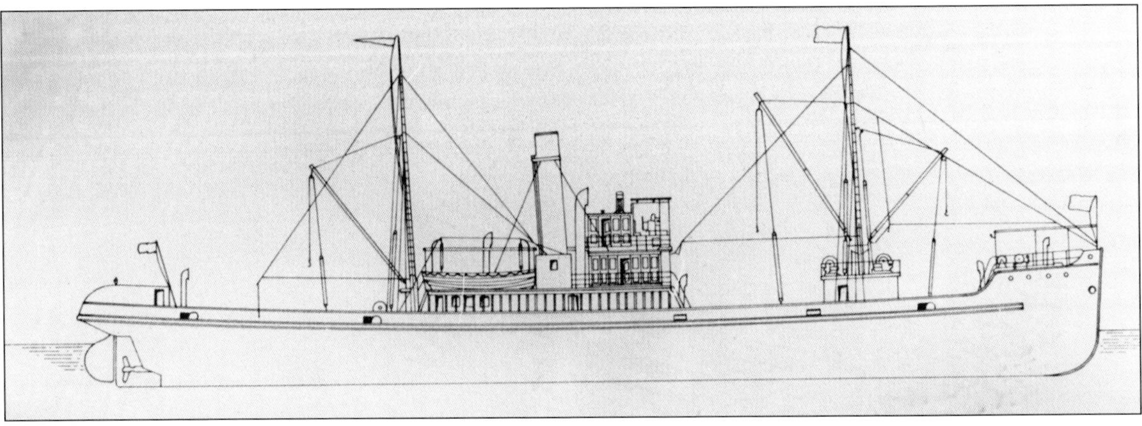

SS *Venezuela*. Author's collection

The day after he had despatched the *Tweed,* Erwin Wassner and *UB-59* were patrolling off the Needles, on the lookout for more ships to sink. He wrote in his war diary, "During the night of 14 March at the Needles Lighthouse, we successfully torpedoed and sunk an unknown steamer – at least 3000 tons – which was laden and armed. Steamer was making for Southampton. The explosion was followed by a tongue of flame, and then a second explosion." The ship, he added, sank "at once." She was the steamer *Venezuela,* not of 3000 tons but 730 tons; but Wassner was right that she was armed and fully laden. Although he fired only one torpedo, the second explosion is most likely explained by the ignition of coal gas from her cargo.

Wassner continued, "The sea in which we were working was frequently, but at irregular intervals, bombed with water bombs (depth charges)" but *UB-59* slipped away unseen and unmolested.

There were no survivors when the *Venezuela* sank. Later, some wreckage came ashore, and it was assumed the victim had been her.

The wreck of the *Venezuela* lies in 27 metres of water. She is upright, her two boilers and twin triple expansion engines being the highest parts. Her stern is almost buried. Her stern gun has been recovered.

Name: *Venezuela*. **Former name(s):** None.
Vessel type: Steam ship.
Builder: Bow, McLachlan, Paisley.
When completed: 1907.
Machinery built by: Bow, McLachlan, Paisley.
Tonnage: 730 tons gross.
Dimensions: Length: 211′ 2″. **Breadth:** 34′ 1″.
Depth of holds: 10′ 8″.
Official number: – **Yard number:** –
Signal letters: – **Last port of registry:** Le Havre.
Ship description: Steel twin screw river steamer. 1 deck. Fitted with electric light.
Machinery description: Twin triple expansion, 6 cylinders. 2 single ended boilers. 84 nominal horse power.
Career and ownership: Owned 1910 by cia Argentina de Nav (Nicolas Michanovich) Ltda and registered in Buenos Aries. 1917 owned by Dodero Huos. December 1917 owned by SA De Navigation Havriasc, Le Havre.
Armament: 1 × 90mm stern gun (recovered).
Destination and cargo: Swansea for Rouen via Falmouth with a cargo of coal.
Date sunk: 14 March 1918.
How sunk: Torpedoed by *UB-59*.
Reported position of loss: German position, "Needles Lighthouse."
Actual position of wreck: 50° 35.78′ north, 001° 43.39′ west.
Orientation/height: Lies 160°/340°. Stands 6 metres in 27 metres on shingle seabed.
How identity of wreck proved: Ship's name and former port of registry in brass letters on stern.

SS *South Western*
Torpedoed 16 March 1918

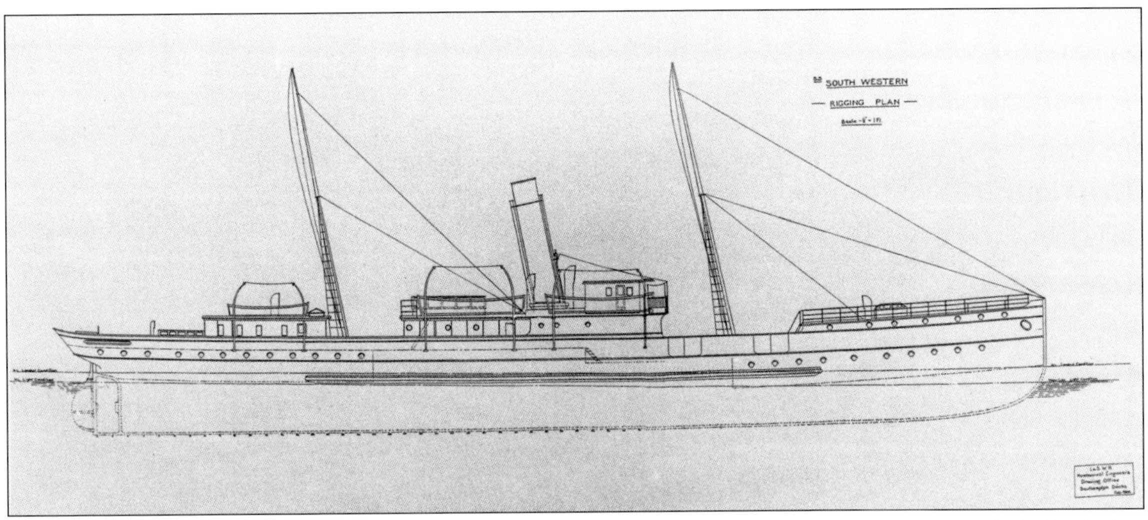

SS *South Western*. Author's collection.

The steamer *South Western* was an old ship; built in 1874 she was 44 years old. Her master was Captain John Alfred Clark, and he reported to the Admiralty, "The ship proceeded from Southampton on 16 March 1918 at 7.15pm. It was low water and the weather was fine and clear with a light easterly breeze. We were bound for St Malo. On the voyage nothing of note occurred, the vessel zig-zagging, approximate course from Dunnose Point being south west by west magnetic. At 11.30pm the *South Western* was struck by a torpedo on the starboard side, fore side of the bridge. The submarine was seen for the first time at 11pm close to the ship. Being too close for action it dived before we could fire. At 11.30 the submarine was seen again on the starboard beam five cables away. I immediately gave orders to open fire, but before the gun could be fired a torpedo struck the ship. The gun was never fired."

Kapitänleutnant Erwin Wassner in *UB-59* recalled, "During the night of 16 March, attack launched against a ferry which looked suspicious; ... it had a funnel in the middle and the two ends of the ship were tall. When we came nearer we realised that the ship was very small. Stopped the attack. Around midnight, torpedo against a 3000 ton steamer which was en route to Cherbourg. Unsuccessful; after 2 minutes the torpedo exploded on the seabed. After midnight, 5 nautical miles south of St Catherine's Point and on the surface, successful calibre 3 torpedo strike against the same steamer. The whole fo'c'sle exploded. After 20 minutes the steamer sank."

Captain Clark continued, "I was flung to the deck from the bridge by the wash and wreckage caused by the explosion. The amidships lifeboats were jammed and could not be launched. The two after boats were launched but capsized with people in them. The rafts were thrown overboard. The side of the ship was blown out and the bridge destroyed. The vessel sank in about 10 minutes, going down by the head with a heavy list to port."

Frank Gleadhill was an AB aboard the *South Western*; he was also trained as one of the gun crew. He said, "I laid awake in my bunk until about 11.30pm when I felt a jar throughout the ship which caused me to get up and put on my lifebelt and go on deck. I enquired what was the matter, and was told there was something suspicious about. Then I heard the captain shout out to keep a sharp lookout on both sides of the ship. I was on the port side of the boat deck and about 10 minutes after I heard the captain give the order, I heard him shout, "Submarine on the port beam!" As I was one of the gun's crew, I immediately ran aft onto the gun platform and took the training wheel, which was my station. Both No 1 (gunlayer) and No 2 (breechworker) were at the gun. I saw the submarine about 200 yards away from us. The order was given, "Close the breech!" and No 2 reported, "Ready!" I trained the gun and saw the submarine through the gunsights. Just at this moment the torpedo struck our ship on the starboard side, fore part of the bridge, and when I looked round after the explosion No 1 and No 2 had disappeared from the platform and I never saw anything of them afterwards, neither did I see anything of the submarine as our vessel was enveloped in smoke for more than a minute after the explosion."

South Western had a crew of 28 and she carried four passengers. From these 32 souls, only six survived

The wreck believed to be that of the *South Western* lies in just under 40 metres of water. When I first dived on her, one of the boilers, the engine and much of the wreck was buried in sand. This has shifted, and now most of the wreck including the engine and boilers is exposed. She is upright, there being a great deal of wreckage poking out of the sand. The bows are low to the seabed and comprise not much more than a pile of chain. It is likely that the wreck covers and uncovers with sand.

Name: *South Western.* **Former name(s):** None.
Vessel type: Steam ship.
Builder: J & W Dudgeon, London.
When completed: September 1874.
Machinery built by: Earles & Company Ltd, Hull.
Tonnage: 674 tons gross.
Dimensions: Length: 222′ 3″. **Breadth:** 27′ 1″. **Depth of holds:** 13′ 5″.
Official number: 72341. **Yard number:** –
Signal letters: NRCK. **Last port of registry:** Southampton.
Ship description: Iron screw steamer. Schooner rigged.
Machinery description: Triple expansion 3 cylinders. 2 single ended boilers. 225 nominal horse power.
Career and ownership: Built for and owned by the London & South Western Railway Company.
Armament: 1 × 13 pounder stern gun.
Destination and cargo: Southampton for St Malo with 12½ tons of general cargo and 4 passengers.
Date sunk: 16 March 1918.
How sunk: Torpedoed by *UB-59.*
Reported position of loss: 50° 25′ north, 001° 27′ west.
Actual position of wreck: 50° 31.33′ north, 001° 32.08′ west.
Orientation/height: Stands about 6 metres in 40 metres on seabed of shifting sand of variable height.
How identity of wreck proved: Not proved but almost certainly the wreck is the *South Western*, deduced through a process of elimination, and because the wreck is of the right size and description in the right locality.

SS *Luxor*
Torpedoed 19 March 1918

Luxor was a new ship, just completed, and on 18 March 1918 following her maiden voyage, she departed Cherbourg in ballast. She should have called at Weymouth Roads for orders before proceeding to Barry, Wales. Had it not been for the fact that she was delayed in leaving Cherbourg, and then, when in convoy, had to reduce her speed to maintain her position in the convoy, she might very well have escaped the fate which was to befall her. Her master, Roger Greenlees Muir, complained, "There was considerable delay in leaving Cherbourg. 8.15pm was the time ordered and at 8.15pm *Luxor* rounded the breakwater, but vessels were not punctual and *Luxor* was waiting from 8.20pm until 9pm. Our number in the convoy was not clear to me; I was to take up the same position as orders given to me the previous night, i.e. No 6. At 9.20pm escort trawlers went ahead and at 9.40pm we followed. Constantly through the night we had to reduce speed. One of the vessels in the convoy was the tug *Knight Templar*, towing the schooner *Jean* at a speed of 6½ knots."

When the convoy reached a position in mid Channel, it was past 2am on 19 March. The ship was steering north west ½ west at 6 knots, and she must have presented as a large target for any U-boat in the area, at that time finding herself leading the convoy. *UB-57*, under the command of Oberleutnant zur See Johannes Lohs, had sighted the *Luxor,* described as, "colourfully painted, of at least 4000 tonnes. Calibre 3 torpedo – a hit. A longer time after the sinking an unsuccessful bombardment of our position with depth charges took place. Return to St Catherine's Point."

UB-57's torpedo struck *Luxor's* starboard side either just abaft the engine room or abreast number 4 hold. The chief officer on watch had heard the approach of the torpedo at a distance of 500 yards, and had ordered the helm, "Hard a'port!" in a futile attempt to steer clear. Immediately the ship flooded and was quickly abandoned, there being no time to transmit an SOS, and the entire crew of 40 hands took to the boats. All were safely picked up by one of the escorting trawlers, the *Sea Monarch*.

The wreck of the *Luxor* lies in 60–62 metres of water in an area of rock gullies. The bow has broken off and rests against a cliff face, with parts of the hull projecting above it. The boilers and engine are the highest parts but the stern is largely buried. Forward of the boilers and bridge steering position there is a great deal of sand and lost fishing gear.

Name: *Luxor*. **Former name(s):** None.
Vessel type: Steam ship.
Builder: J Blumer & Company, Sunderland.
When completed: March 1918.
Machinery built by: North East Marine Engineering Company Ltd.
Tonnage: 3571 tons gross.
Dimensions: Length: 356′ 3″. **Breadth:** 48′ 7″.
Depth of holds: 23′ 9″.
Official number: 140560. **Yard number:** –
Signal letters: JSKC. **Last port of registry:** Liverpool.
Ship description: Steel screw steamer. 1 deck. Fitted with electric light.
Machinery description: Triple expansion 3 cylinders. 2 single ended boilers. 394 nominal horse power.
Career and ownership: Owned by Moss Steam Ship Company, Liverpool. Collier transport No 2027.
Armament: 1 × 4″ quick firing stern gun.
Destination and cargo: Cherbourg for Barry via Weymouth for orders in ballast.
Date sunk: 19 March 1918.
How sunk: Torpedoed by *UB-57*.
Reported position of loss: 50° 13.50′ north, 001° 44.50′ west.
Actual position of wreck: 50° 16.89′ north, 001° 36.60′ west.
Orientation/height: Stands 7 metres in 60–62 metres in rough, rocky ground with sand.
How identity of wreck proved: Ship's crockery recovered.

SS *Azemmour*
Torpedoed 20 March 1918

SS *Azemmour*. Author's collection.

UB-59's last victim before she returned to base was the French steamer *Azemmour*. *Azemmour* had departed London for Nantes on 18 March 1918, and by the early hours of 20 March, she was in a position roughly south of the Needles when *UB-59* moved in to attack. Her commander, Kapitänleutnant Erwin Wassner, wrote in his war diary, "20 March. 5am. Launched calibre 3 torpedo against a 1500 ton steamer but were unsuccessful; the gun sight had worked loose and shifted. Pursued the steamer and, 8 nautical miles south of St Catherine's Point, fired torpedo. Hit and sunk. The steamer had been armed and laden."

Azemmour's master, Captain Jean Pierre Guillaume, reported, "We were 28 in number. At 4.30am there was a loud noise which the crew believed was a torpedo scraping under the hull, but I felt a severe shock to the ship 15 minutes before sighting the submarine, as if struck by something but no explosion." He continued, "We were steering south 88° west at 8 knots, and were zig-zagging for at least an hour before the attack. About ½ minute before we were hit, the officer on watch reported seeing a submarine on the surface about 200 metres away. I ordered the helm be put hard a'starboard, but we were hit and the explosion ruptured the hull between the bulkhead and number 3 hold. There was no time to transmit a distress call on the wireless. The ship was abandoned very quickly. I was unable to ensure the complete evacuation of the ship before I left it due to the damage caused and her sinking condition. Five men are missing." *Azemmour* had disappeared in 4 minutes. The survivors were quickly rescued by the Auxiliary Patrol vessel, *Maid of Honour*.

The wreck of the *Azemmour* lies in 40 metres of water. She is upright and reasonably intact from her engine forward to the bow, though this is peeling back towards the seabed. Her part cargo of steel pipes is still stacked in her forward holds. Her engine is the highest part of the wreck. Aft of the engine the wreck slowly disappears into the seabed, though her stern gun is still in the open.

Name: *Azemmour.* **Former name(s):** *Wistaria.*
Vessel type: Steam ship.
Builder: Short Brothers, Sunderland.
When completed: February 1909.
Machinery built by: Short Brothers, Sunderland.
Tonnage: 897 tons gross.
Dimensions: Length: 205′ 3″. **Breadth:** 33′.
Depth of holds: 11′ 9″.
Official number: 125763. **Yard number:** 346.
Signal letters: HKWD. **Last port of registry:** St Nazaire.
Ship description: Steel screw steamer. 1 deck. Well deck. Fitted with electric light.
Machinery description: Triple expansion 3 cylinders. 2 single ended boilers. 143 nominal horse power.
Career and ownership: 1910 built for and owned by Mower Cotterell & Company Ltd as *Wistaria.* 1912 owned by British Burmah Petroleum Company Ltd. December 1912 purchased by C H Pile for Shipping Investments Ltd who sold her in 1914 to Cie Generale Transatlantique. Renamed *Azemmour.*
Armament: 1 × 90mm stern gun.
Destination and cargo: London for Nantes with 716 tons of general cargo and 500 tons of steel.
Date sunk: 20 March 1918.
How sunk: Torpedoed by *UB-59.*
Reported position of loss: 50° 25′ north, 001° 35′ west.
Actual position of wreck: 50° 28.95′ north, 001° 38.43′ west.
Orientation/height: Stands about 6 metres in 40 metres on shingle seabed.
How identity of wreck proved: Ship's crockery recovered.

Steam drifter *New Dawn*
Mined 23 March 1918

The *New Dawn* was an Admiralty drifter utilised as a minesweeper with the Auxiliary Patrol Force. On 23 March 1918, she was operating a few miles off the Needles where she reported the presence of a minefield.

Lieutenant Grant Rougvie, RNR, in command of the drifter *Jeannies,* reported, "While sweeping a supposed mined area in latitude 50° 35′ north, longitude 1° 38′ west, with *Unity,* the *New Dawn* reported a minefield south west by south ½ south 3 miles from the Needles. I immediately slipped and informed *Unity* when his wire was in to proceed in after us. I observed 5 mines on the surface about 100 yards between each mine and 2 to the south east about one mile distant."

"I ordered all drifters to open fire on them; one was sunk so I decided as the flood was on to sweep them with *New Dawn* before they submerged. I told off *Unity* to drop a Dan at the eastern end of the new minefield as several mines were showing by this time. *New Dawn* and *Jeannies* commenced sweeping at 1.30pm. After getting 4 mines in the sweep I made a signal 16 points to starboard, being then 300 yards to the eastwards of the western field on the point of turning. The *New Dawn* was struck about the stern and immediately afterwards amidships; four other explosions occurred in the sweep. The *New Dawn* sank in about 2 minutes time after being struck."

Commander Harrold, officer in charge of HMS *Magpie*, based at Yarmouth, Isle of Wight, reported to the Admiralty on 24 March, "I have the honour to forward herewith the report of Lieutenant Grant Rougvie, RNR, with reference to the finding of a minefield ... and the subsequent loss of the drifter *New Dawn*. In my opinion Lieutenant Rougvie was quite justified in deciding to sweep up these mines before they submerged and . . . considering the number of mines . . . he and the crews of HM Drifters *Jeannies* and *New Dawn* acted in a very gallant and praiseworthy manner."

"Also, the fact that 10 of the crew of *New Dawn* were rescued after such a violent explosion proves that every precaution had been taken to save life in the event of a vessel being sunk and that assistance was most promptly rendered by the crew of *Jeannies* who after the event instead of hoisting out their boat, lifted it and launched it by hand. Considering that six mines had just exploded simultaneously their morale was splendid and I cannot speak too highly of them. Nothing was saved from the *New Dawn* and the Skipper and two hands, as already reported, went down with her."

A fourth man died from his injuries one week later.

The minefield had been laid three days earlier by the German U-boat *UC-17*, under the command of Oberleutnant zur See Erich Stephan. Two small mine barrages were laid a few miles south of the Needles.

The wreck of the *New Dawn* lies in about 33 metres. She is quite broken. Her boiler is the highest part.

Name: *New Dawn*. **Former name(s):** None.
Vessel type: Steam drifter.
Builder: Mackie & Thomson Ltd, Glasgow.
When completed: March 1908.
Machinery built by: W V V Lidgerwood, Glasgow.
Tonnage: 93 tons gross.
Dimensions: Length: 86′ 4″. **Breadth:** 18′ 5″.
Depth of holds: 8′ 8″.
Official number: 127148. **Yard number:** –
Signal letters: – **Last port of registry:** Aberdeen.
Ship description: Steel screw steam drifter. 1 deck.
Machinery description: Compound 2 cylinders. 1 single ended boiler. 39 horse power.
Career and ownership: Owned by the Steam Herring Fleet Ltd and registered in Aberdeen, port no. A.221. Hired by the Admiralty for the Auxiliary Patrol Force as a minesweeper in November 1914, based at Poole. Admiralty No 774. Tender to HMS *Magpie*.
Armament: 1 × .45″ machine gun (recovered).
Destination and cargo: Poole for the Needles, minesweeping.
Date sunk: 23 March 1918.
How sunk: Mined by *UC-17*.
Reported position of loss: South west by south ½ south, 3 miles from the Needles.
Actual position of wreck: 50° 36.54′ north, 001° 36.36′ west.
Orientation/height: Lies 080°/260°. Stands about 4 metres in 33 metres on shingle seabed.
How identity of wreck proved: Builder's nameplate recovered. Ship's name in brass letters on bows.

SS *War Knight*
Collision, mine and gunfire 24 March 1918

SS *War Knight* ablaze after collision. Courtesy National Maritime Museum, Greenwich.

Although Kapitänleutnant Erwin Wassner in the *UB-59* had sunk four steamers on this patrol, he would not add to his score before returning to the Flanders Flotilla at Bruges. However, he was remarkably well placed to witness a terrible disaster which took place off the Isle of Wight in the early hours of 24 March 1918. In his war diary, Wassner wrote, "During the night of the 24th, on the surface, proceeded to attack a steamer which, in the mist, seemed to be very large. Later, when we got nearer, we found that it was only about 1000–1200 tons. Launched a calibre 3 torpedo but were unsuccessful. It seemed to have undershot. The track of the torpedo must have been seen on board the steamer; she changed course and started firing at us with her gun."

He continued, "3am. Heard in our immediate vicinity and repeatedly, the sound of a whistle. Carefully turned towards the sound. Visibility poor. 3.50am. There is a big explosion, with a high, blood red sheet of flame which grew higher and higher, and spread out in all directions. We were able to see two steamers, and both were in a blaze of fire, and several destroyers and steamers moved past them. According to radio messages which we overheard, a collision had taken place. Apparently, one of the steamers was a tanker. For hours it was possible to see two large burning spots on the water."

He added, "4.35am. Unsuccessfully attacked a 5000 ton tanker. We did not manage to get the stern torpedo tube ready in time and we could not fire at her again. Towards dawn, there was a further radio message about a second collision."

Wassner had witnessed the demise of the 7951 ton steamer *War Knight*, which had departed Philadelphia for New York and London on 5 March 1918. She formed part of a convoy comprising 16 merchant ships escorted by seven destroyers. After midnight on 24 March, the convoy was approaching the Isle of Wight but, at about 0.30am, two explosions and a flash of light were observed some miles off (this was probably the action in which *UB-59* was engaged). As a result, the convoy was ordered to alter course. This was carried out at 1.15am, but some vessels in the convoy did not receive the signal and carried on their course. A second signal was sent about 2.15am, ordering the convoy to alter course again, and still some vessels did not receive the signal. The unintended consequence was that the convoy split into two groups.

Efforts were made by one of the escorting destroyers to bring the convoy back into proper order, but while this was being done, both the *War Knight* and the tanker *O B Jennings* steered onto a collision course. Attempting to avoid each other, the *War Knight* turned to starboard but struck the tanker at right angles. The impact ruptured the tanks of the *O B Jennings* and her cargo of naptha poured like a torrent down the length of the *War Knight's* deck. Two seconds later it ignited, instantly incinerating the men on deck. From the crew of about 47, only seven or eight men, mostly engineers, survived.

One of the survivors was third officer George Brown. He said, "About 2.30am I was awakened by a violent impact. Jumping out of my bunk I rushed to the door and looked out on deck and found the whole ship to be in flames. At this time I heard the signal on the engine room telegraph to abandon the engine room, and the signal given on the steam whistle for all hands to take to the boats. Turning back to my room to put on a few clothes I observed Captain Holroyd hurrying past in the direction of the boats and at the same time the chief officer rushed out of his room and made in the same direction. I followed on as soon as possible, the ship then being one mass of flames from stem to stern. On arriving on the boat deck I found that both lifeboats had been burned away. The boat deck being unbearable with smoke and flames, I hurried over to the after end of the boat deck and took shelter in the engineer's alleyway, where I found the second, third, fourth and fifth engineers, one fireman, messroom steward and chief cook."

The ship's cook, named Hagarty, said, "I was awakened by a jarring sound. Thinking we had been torpedoed I slipped out of bed . . .. In about a minute I was out in the alleyway. This was already a mass of flames and smoke. One or two men were rushing about on fire. One of them brushed against the steward's boy and, I think, set him on fire. In company with a man

SS *War Knight* burnt out and aground in Watcombe Bay. Author's collection.

who proved to be Mason, I rushed through the galley into the starboard alleyway. This was also full of smoke, which I think was really gas, generated by the naptha. In this alleyway were gathered all the men who, up to now, are the only survivors. One or two went down, overcome by fumes; I heard them moaning. I can't say how the other men saved their lives; this is how I saved mine. I had got a cloth somewhere, and had it over my mouth and nose, but it was of very little avail. I went down but managed to get up again. I staggered into somewhere which proved to be the lavatory. Several men here were also suffocating like myself. Someone had an axe and attacked the alleyway door, but it was no good. I went down again, as I thought, for good. I could not breathe. As I fell my hand caught something which proved to be a flush lavatory. I pushed my face in there and threw salt water over it. I am positive this saved my life. I gasped, 'water boys' and the other fellows who heard me did the same. We were all nearly mad about now; some made a rush and got through some skylight or something on to the boat deck. I was the last man to escape. We ran across to the port side; it was red hot here. When we got on deck we saw a lifeboat in the water, just a piece of charcoal. One of the survivors said he saw four dead bodies on the boat deck, but could not recognise them."

After the survivors had jumped into the sea and were rescued, the fire on *War Knight* died down, and the ship was taken in tow later the next morning by a Portsmouth tug. The tug, despite warnings not to do so, towed the burning ship through a known, dangerous area. In fact, he towed her directly across the remnants of the minefield sown by *UC-17* which had accounted for the loss of the *New Dawn* the day before. Two mines exploded underneath *War Knight*, and a third exploded in contact with the towing wire. She was then beached in Watcombe Bay and sunk by gunfire to extinguish the fires. Although it was hoped the ship could be raised and repaired, this was never done.

The wreck of the *War Knight* lies in 13 metres of water, her three boilers being the highest parts. She is a large wreck but only the chain locker and her boilers stand up more than a few metres. She was extensively salvaged in the late 1960's for her non-ferrous metal fittings.

Name: *War Knight*. **Former name(s):** *Southerner*.
Vessel type: Steam ship.
Builder: Union Iron Works, Alameda, USA.
When completed: May 1917.
Machinery built by: General Electric Company, New York.
Tonnage: 7951 tons gross.
Dimensions: Length: 410′. **Breadth:** 56′.
Depth of holds: 38′.
Official number: 140335. **Yard number:** –
Signal letters: JPTD. **Last port of registry:** London.
Ship description: Steel screw steamer. 2 decks. Fitted with electric light.
Machinery description: One geared steam turbine. 3 single ended boilers.
Career and ownership: 1917 owned by the Shipping Controller (Furness Withy & Company Ltd, managers).
Armament: 1 × 6″ stern gun (since recovered but lost under tow in the western Solent).
Destination and cargo: Philadelphia and New York for London in convoy NH53 with 999 tons of fuel oil in her double bottom, and general cargo including foodstuffs, bales of rubber and drums of chemicals.
Date sunk: 24 March 1918.
How sunk: Collision with the SS *O B Jennings*, mined by *UC-17*, finished off with gunfire from own forces.
Reported position of loss: Watcombe Bay, Isle of Wight.
Actual position of wreck: 50° 39.96′ north, 001° 31.12′ west.
Orientation/height: Lies 157°/337°. Stands 6 metres in 13 metres on rocky seabed interspersed with shingle.
How identity of wreck proved: Contemporary reports identify the *War Knight* in this position. In addition she is the only merchant ship wreck known to have a steam turbine engine, which can be seen in the wreck.

SS *Isleworth*
Torpedoed 30 April 1918

SS *Isleworth*. Courtesy E N Taylor collection.

Isleworth was a British steamer engaged in general trading. She departed Bilbao on 24 April 1918, fully laden with a cargo of iron ore and a crew of 33 men, bound for Middlesbrough. The voyage had been uneventful and her master, Captain Robert Douglas, had followed his route instructions by keeping his ship close to land and zig-zagging up Channel. About 1.30pm on 30 April 1918, *Isleworth* reached St Catherine's Point, steaming at about 8 knots. Captain Douglas had posted lookouts in the crow's nest, on the bridge and one of the gunners was at the stern gun. When the ship was about three miles south west of Ventnor pier, disaster struck.

No-one on board *Isleworth* had any idea a U-boat was in the vicinity as nothing suspicious was seen, but the German U-boat *UC-17* was lying hidden, submerged at periscope depth. *UC-17's* commanding officer, Oberleutnant zur See Erich Stephan, judged the speed and direction of *Isleworth* and fired a torpedo. Captain Douglas later remarked, "We were hit on the starboard side by number 3 hatch or the engine room. I estimate the whole side of the ship was blown away."

Isleworth sank like a stone, the only survivors being the captain, third officer and two gunners. All the others had either been killed by the explosion or drowned.

The wreck of the *Isleworth* lies in 70 metres of water in St Catherine's Deep. She is completely upright and is fairly intact from her boilers to the stern. The bow section is much more broken. The wreck lies in a trench or valley and is protected by the presence of steep underwater cliffs to the immediate south. Great care is needed when diving on high water. When the tide turns divers decompressing and drifting with the tide will be carried towards a reef which rises from 70 metres to about 18 metres. Spring tides should be avoided and the dive planned to ensure divers have completed their deeper stops by the time they reach the reef.

Name: *Isleworth*. **Former name(s):** *Eversley*.
Vessel type: Steam ship.
Builder: R Thompson & Sons, Sunderland.
When completed: October 1896.
Machinery built by: Blair & Company Ltd, Stockton.

Tonnage: 2871 tons gross.
Dimensions: Length: 320′. **Breadth:** 46′.
Depth of holds: 21′ 3″.
Official number: 106607. **Yard number:** –
Signal letters: PMHN. **Last port of registry:** London.
Ship description: Steel screw steamer.
Machinery description: 2 single ended boilers. New donkey boiler 1911.
Career and ownership: Owned as *Eversley* by Scholefield Steam Shipping Company Ltd (H Scholefield & Son, managers) to 1917, then owned by Britain Steam Ship company Ltd (Watts, Watts & Company, London, managers).
Armament: 1 × 12 pounder, 12 cwt stern gun.
Destination and cargo: Bilbao for Middlesbrough with a cargo of 4200 tons of iron ore.
Date sunk: 30 April 1918.
How sunk: Torpedoed by *UC-17*.
Reported position of loss: 3 miles south west of Ventnor pier.
Actual position of wreck: 50° 33.65′ north, 001° 13.82′ west.
Orientation/height: Lies roughly 070°/250°. Stands 9 metres in 70 metres on hard chalk rock seabed with shingle.
How identity of wreck proved: Not proved but position of wreck is within 1 mile of position reported in 1918. In addition, size and description of wreck fits that of the *Isleworth*.

SS *Kyarra*
Torpedoed 26 May 1918

SS *Kyarra*. Courtesy Glasgow University Archives.

Oberleutnant zur See Johannes Lohs in the *UB-57* recorded in his war diary, "During the night of 25 May, we followed 3 tankers which had a large escort. After a long pursuit we launched, near Portsmouth, a torpedo against the first tanker (about 5000 tons) but missed. During dawn, we tried once more to launch an attack against the steamers. Missed the tanker *Madrono* (5874 tons) which sighted us, sent radio signals and attacked us with gunfire. In good conditions it is likely we would have managed to launch an attack against all 3 tankers. During the night of 26 May we left this zone and moved to the area of St Catherine's Point and St Alban's Head."

"On 26 May, near St Alban's Head, at 9.43am, fired torpedo and hit a 6000 ton passenger ship which was armed with 10.2cm gun. On each side, the ship had many lifeboats; they lowered 10 of them. The ship capsized to its starboard side although it was hit on the port side."

"At 10.10am, near St Alban's Head, sighted English submarine which had surfaced. At 11.35am, 6 depth charges were dropped in the direction of our previous position from where we had launched the attack; but now we were at a safe distance."

Lohs had sunk the large steamer *Kyarra* with a single torpedo. She had departed Tilbury, London, two days earlier, bound for Devonport, with a large crew of 112, 34 passengers and a pilot. As if to confirm the notes made by Lohs, *Kyarra's* master, Albert John Gladstone Donovan reported, "We were torpedoed on the port side of the fore stokehold and sank in 19 minutes. The track of the torpedo was seen." The concussion from the explosion shattered her steering gear and stopped both engines and *Kyarra* sank by the stern.

Kyarra had been steaming on a west-south-west course at 12½ knots, zig-zagging as she made her way down Channel. The morning was clear and the weather good with a light westerly breeze and a smooth sea. *UB-*

57, in a submerged position at periscope depth, had *Kyarra* in its sights, and the track of the torpedo was spotted when it was just 70 yards away from her side. The ship's boats were lowered, and all but six of those on board survived.

In the aftermath, patrol vessels reported sighting a periscope in position 50° 34′ north, 001° 58° west, and *Torpedo Boat 21*, the drifter *Flo Johnson* and seaplanes from Portland dropped depth charges. They reported, "Oil and bubbles seen. Results uncertain." By that time, as Lohs recorded, *UB-57* was already at a safe distance.

The wreck of the *Kyarra* is probably the most popular and easily accessible wreck in the country. Lying in no more than 30 metres of water on her port side, she is gradually breaking up, the depth of water over her increasing as the years go by. Despite being heavily dived since the late 1960's, divers continue to recover a wide variety of items from the wreck, including perfume bottles and gold watches.

Name: *Kyarra*. **Former name(s):** None.
Vessel type: Steam ship.
Builder: William Denny, Dumbarton.
When completed: May 1903.
Machinery built by: William Denny, Dumbarton.
Tonnage: 6953 tons gross.
Dimensions: Length: 415′ 5″. **Breadth:** 52′ 2″. **Depth of holds:** 28′ 6″.
Official number: 115755. **Yard number:** –
Signal letters: TWSC. **Last port of registry:** Freemantle.
Ship description: Steel twin screw steamer. Fitted with electric light and wireless. Accommodation for 125 first class, 136 second class and 250 third class passengers.
Machinery description: Twin triple expansion 8 cylinders. 4 single ended boilers. 770 nominal horse power.
Career and ownership: Originally owned by the Australian Steam Navigation Company Ltd. In 1914 she was taken over by the British government and converted into a hospital ship but on arrival in the UK she was used as a troop ship. In May 1918 she was returned to service as a hospital ship. Her final voyage was to steam to Devonport to board wounded Australian soldiers and return them home.
Armament: 1 × 4.7″ quick firing Japanese stern gun.
Destination and cargo: London for Devonport with 2600 tons of general cargo.
Date sunk: 26 May 1918.
How sunk: Torpedoed by *UB-57*.
Reported position of loss: 50° 34.50′ north, 001° 56.33′ west.
Actual position of wreck: 50° 34.90′ north, 001° 56.59′ west.
Orientation/height: Lies 090°/270°. Stands about 9 metres in 30 metres on rough seabed covered with shingle.
How identity of wreck proved: Ship's bell and ship's name in brass letters on bows recovered.

SS *Kong Guttorm*
Torpedoed 11 July 1918

SS *Kong Guttorm*. Courtesy Norwegian Maritime Museum/Nylands verksted.

The Norwegian steamer *Kong Guttorm* was to be the last Norwegian steamer sunk in the area. During the First World War as a whole Norway lost almost half its entire merchant fleet through enemy action; *Kong Guttorm* was the tenth Norwegian ship to sink in the area.

Kong Guttorm was part of a convoy of ships on voyage from Le Havre for Weymouth, escorted by trawlers from the Auxiliary Patrol Force. The convoy left Le Havre and steamed into a moderate gale from the west-southwest. In misty conditions and heavy seas, the convoy approached the mid Channel area; some ships in the convoy were finding it difficult to maintain station; and had gradually dropped astern, only *Kong Guttorm* and *Channel Trader* maintaining their courses and speeds. By 3pm, the escorting trawler, *Christopher Dixon*, had reduced speed to 7 knots, with much of the convoy several miles astern.

At 5.55pm, an explosion was heard and *Christopher Dixon's* Lieutenant W Meldrum, RNR, said, "At the moment of the explosion I was below getting my tea and as I rushed on deck the 2nd hand reported a vessel torpedoed. As I gave the order to port, she sank. I proceeded full speed towards where she had been and in the wreckage picked up four survivors, which unfortunately were all that could be seen. The water was discoloured in the same way as though ashes had been dumped. The survivors stated she had been blown in two. At 6.30 I proceeded on my course."

He added, "I do not think a submarine could have operated without being seen. The ship sank in one minute from the time of my hearing the explosion." In fact, *Kong Guttorm* had been torpedoed in a submerged attack by the large coastal U-boat, the *UB-103*, under the command of Kapitänleutnant Paul Hundius.

Only four men from a crew of 15 survived the sinking, and these men were later interviewed. One man, sailor Ingvald Wangberg, said, "The ship arrived at Caen on 6 July, and discharged her cargo of coal and finished on Wednesday 10 July, and hatches were replaced. French workmen and German prisoners were employed discharging, the latter being under guard working in the hold. No strangers were seen on board except clerks with papers connected with the Gas Company, to whom the cargo was consigned ... the ship left Caen and arrived Le Havre on the evening of 10th July and joined the convoy ... and sailed at 6am on the 11th with the convoy bound north." He continued, "I was due to relieve the helmsman at 6pm. About 5.30pm I went forward and the captain and the second mate were on the bridge ... Suddenly there was a crashing noise which appeared to come from amidships. I was the last person to get out from where I was. ... I could see nothing from the bridge because of the smoke, but I managed to climb up on to the fo'c'sle before the ship started to keel over and I was washed into the sea, being dragged under by the sinking ship."

Sailor Thorolf Hansen said, "There was a violent explosion which shook the whole ship. I ran up on deck but the ship was already leaning substantially over to starboard, and I saw a great hole had appeared in the port side of the ship. The bridge and deck had been destroyed." One other survivor, fireman Johannes Kruse, believed the ship had broken in two as he saw the stern in the air and the ship had listed heavily to starboard immediately after the explosion.

A wreck which is almost certainly that of the *Kong Guttorm* lies in 55 metres of water. The wreck is in two separate, upright pieces. The bow section lies more or less at right angles to the stern area joined by a debris field. Her engine and boiler are the highest parts. An electric motor and spare propeller lie at the back of the engine.

Name: *Kong Guttorm* **Former name(s):** None.
Vessel type: Steam ship.
Builder: Nylands Vaerksted, Christiania.
When completed: March 1901.
Machinery built by: Nylands Vaerksted, Christiania.
Tonnage: 731 tons gross.
Dimensions: Length: 191′ 5″. **Breadth:** 30′ 1″.
Depth of holds: 13′ 7″.
Official number: – **Yard number:** –
Signal letters: HDJQ. **Last port of registry:** Christiania.
Ship description: Steel screw steamer. 1 deck. Fitted with electric light.
Machinery description: Triple expansion 3 cylinders. 1 single ended boiler and donkey boiler. 97 nominal horse power.
Career and ownership: Owned by A/S Det Söndenfjelds-Norske Dampskibsselskap.
Armament: Unarmed.
Destination and cargo: Caen via Le Havre for Weymouth in ballast.
Date sunk: 11 July 1918.
How sunk: Torpedoed by *UB-103*.
Reported position of loss: 50° 20′ north, 001° 35′ west.
Actual position of wreck: 50° 17.21′ north, 001° 40.45′ west.
Orientation/height: Lies 070°/250°. Stands 6 metres in 55 metres on shingle/stony seabed.
How identity of wreck proved: Not proved. Description of wreck very closely fits that of the *Kong Guttorm*. Position is within a few miles of reported position of loss. An unmarked fo'c'sle bell has been recovered which has been judged to be of Norwegian design, and the engine room telegraph is of identical design to that of another Norwegian ship built by the same company.

Steam trawler *Michael Clements*
Collision 8 August 1918

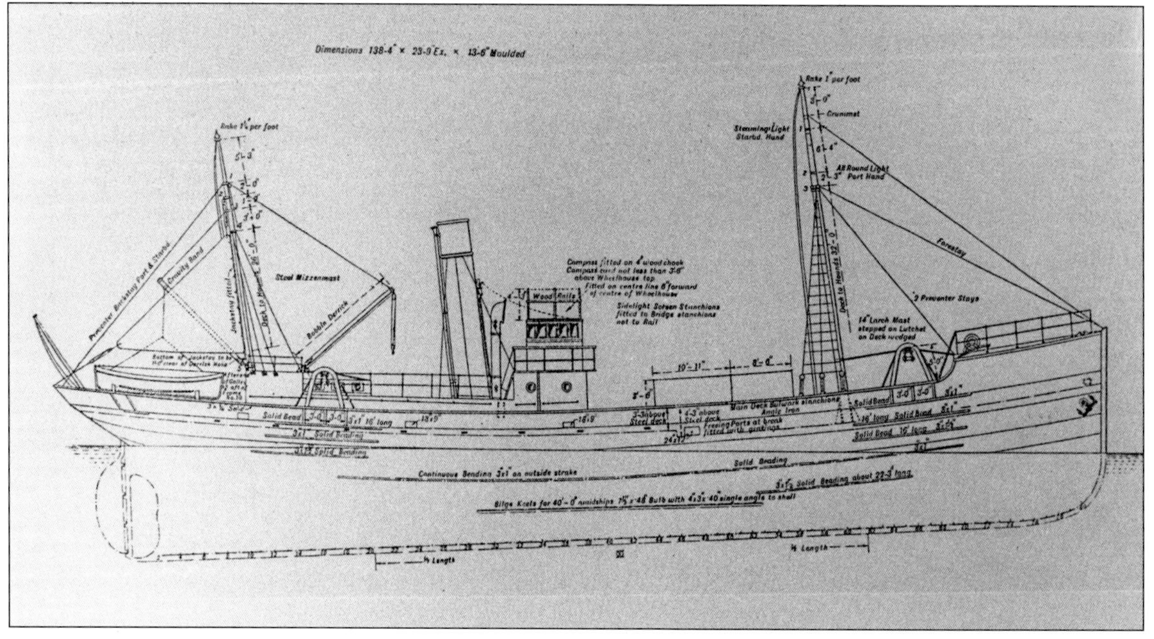

Plan of Mersey class Admiralty trawlers (HM steam trawler *Michael Clements*). Courtesy National Maritime Museum, Greenwich.

The Admiralty trawler *Michael Clements* was launched on 21 August 1917, and upon completion she was pressed into service with the Auxiliary Patrol Force based at Portland. On the night of 7/8 August 1918, *Michael Clements* was on duty off St Catherine's Point under the command of Lieutenant T W Logan, RNR. Although the U-boat offensive was in decline, the U-boat still posed a threat to shipping, and the trawler was engaged in listening duties, probably by using hydrophones.

Exactly what happened to the vessel is not known. Although a Court of Enquiry was held, it does not appear to have survived. However, the records for the Auxiliary Patrol Force (Portland) for 1918 show, "On the night of 7 August, *Michael Clements* was rammed and sunk by the (trawler) *John Cattling* while on listening patrol south of the Isle of Wight. There were no casualties. All the crew were saved and taken to Portland by 2 other trawlers of the Division." *John Cattling* was another member of the Auxiliary Patrol Force

Admiralty trawlers constructed under the war programme in the First World War took their names from the muster rolls of HMS *Victory* and HMS *Royal Sovereign* at the Battle of Trafalgar in 1805. Michael Clements was a carpenter on board HMS *Victory*, and he received a government grant of £26 6/s and £10 14/s as "Trafalgar prize money." This was the proportion of proceeds due for the capture of four French and Spanish ships seized on 21 October 1805, with Bounty Bill for ships destroyed.

The wreck of the *Michael Clements* lies in about 48 metres of water. She is upright with her bow gun being prominent, standing in the wreck. Her single boiler and engine are the highest parts.

Name: *Michael Clements.* **Former name(s):** None.
Vessel type: Steam trawler.
Builder: Cochrane & Sons Ltd, Selby.
When completed: Launched 21 August 1917.
Machinery built by: Either by C D Holmes & Company Ltd, or Amos & Smith Ltd, Hull.
Tonnage: 324 tons gross.
Dimensions: Length: 148′. **Breadth:** 23′ 9″.

Depth of holds: 12′ 9″.
Official number: – **Yard number:** 821.
Signal letters: – **Last port of registry:** –
Ship description: Steel screw steam trawler. Admiralty "Mersey" class trawler.
Machinery description: Triple expansion 3 cylinders. 1 single ended boiler. 590 indicated horse power.
Career and ownership: Served in the Auxiliary Patrol Area XIII (Portland), under Admiralty no 3561.
Armament: 1 × 6 pounder gun.
Destination and cargo: Portland for the Isle of Wight on submarine listening duties.
Date sunk: 8 August 1918.
How sunk: Collision with the Auxiliary Patrol trawler *John Cattling*.
Reported position of loss: Off St Catherine's Point.
Actual position of wreck: 50° 21.49′ north, 001° 29.09′ west.
Orientation/height: Lies roughly 090°/270°. Stands about 5 metres in 48 metres on shingle seabed, bows to the east.
How identity of wreck proved: Ship's bell recovered.

SS *Clan Macvey*
Torpedoed 8 August 1918

SS *Clan Macvey*. By J H Isherwood, from the collection held in Southampton Archives.

The *Clan Macvey* was a large, brand new ship, having been completed just one month before she was sunk. Her maiden voyage took her from Newcastle, where she had loaded 6,700 tons of government coal, consigned for the Naval Transport Officer in Port Said. The first part of the voyage passed without incident, but when the ship had reached the vicinity of Littlehampton on 7 August 1918 at 12.33pm, she was attacked by a submerged U-boat. The ship's lookouts had spotted a periscope and then a torpedo was seen to pass under *Clan Macvey's* stern. Responding with gunfire and manoeuvring so as to present a smaller target, the ship managed to escape, and continued down Channel.

By 7.50am on the morning of 8 August 1918, *Clan Macvey* was approaching Anvil Point. When she was about a mile south east of the point, the second officer reported, "Periscope abeam port side!" The periscope was sighted about ¼ mile away. Immediately afterwards the track of the torpedo was seen and though attempts were made to steer the ship clear of danger, the torpedo struck and exploded amidships under the funnel. The master, Captain Richard Caradoc Jones, said, "The ship heeled right over and took on a list of 35–45°, sufficient that it was not possible to stand on deck. The torpedo had struck right in line with the funnel and the vessel immediately lost way and came to a stop. A hole 80′ in length had been caused and the damage was very extensive."

Oberleutnant zur See Johannes Lohs in *UB-57* had successfully executed what was to be his final attack. The ship was abandoned and the survivors were rescued by one of the Auxiliary Patrol's drifters. Other Admiralty trawlers in the area, alerted by the explosion, headed for the *Clan Macvey*. One was the *Arthur Cavanagh* commanded by Captain George Irvine, RN, and the other was the *Vera Grace*. Captain Jones informed them his ship would float for days but declined to re-board her, but advised his ship should be towed to Swanage Bay or Poole Bay to be beached. Taking the ship in tow, the trawlers tried to pull *Clan Macvey*, but then the tugs *Vulcain* and *Pilot* arrived and took over the tow.

There followed an extraordinary exchange between Captain Jones and Captain Irvine, when they became embroiled in a heated dispute, but the towing of *Clan Macvey* carried on. She proved to be almost unmanageable; her helm was jammed hard to port and she had taken on a huge amount of water. Nevertheless, the tow proceeded at full speed, her decks awash, until suddenly the towing hawser parted as she broke her back and sank in Poole Bay, her two ends showing above water.

From the 55 men on board, seven men were killed in the explosion. Six days later, *UB-57* was lost with all hands in the Scheldte estuary on the Dutch coast. The body of Johannes Lohs and some of the crew were washed ashore. In recognition of Lohs' service and achievements, the U-boat Fleet Lohs, Kiel, was named after him.

The wreck of the *Clan Macvey* was later dispersed, and her remains lie in 18 metres of water. Her propeller shaft and stern steering machinery are recognisable, and one of her guns lies on the seabed off the port side of the wreck. Elsewhere, much wreckage pokes up from the sand, spread over a wide area. The site has a tendency to be silty.

Name: *Clan Macvey*. **Former name(s):** None.
Vessel type: Steam ship.
Builder: Northumberland Shipbuilding Company, Willington on Tyne, Newcastle.
When completed: July 1918.
Machinery built by: North East Marine Engineering, Newcastle.
Tonnage: 5818 tons gross.
Dimensions: Length: 400′ 1″. **Breadth:** 53′.
Depth of holds: 26′ 1″.
Official number: 141884. **Yard number:** 245.
Signal letters: – **Last port of registry:** Glasgow.
Ship description: Steel screw steamer. Fitted with electric light. 1 mast.
Machinery description: Triple expansion 3 cylinders. 3 single ended boilers. 569 nominal horse power.
Career and ownership: Owned by Cayzer, Irvine & Company Ltd (Clan Line).
Armament: 1 × 4″ stern gun and 1 × 15 pounder.
Destination and cargo: Newcastle for Port Said via Falmouth with a cargo of 6,700 tons of coal.
Date sunk: 8 August 1918.
How sunk: Torpedoed by *UB-57*.
Reported position of loss: Poole Bay.
Actual position of wreck: 50° 39.70′ north, 001° 46.82′ west.
Orientation/height: Stands no more than 2 or 3 metres in a dispersed condition on a seabed of sand.
How identity of wreck proved: The *Clan Macvey* is the only large steamer known to have been lost here. Contemporary reports state the ship broke in half in Poole Bay.

SS *Clan Macvey* after being torpedoed. Author's collection.

SS *Ohio*
Collision 12 October 1918

SS *Ohio*. Author's collection.

The 40-year-old steamer *Ohio* departed Le Havre at 6am on Saturday 12 October 1918, in convoy with other ships, bound for Glasgow. *Ohio's* position was in the centre of the convoy as the lead vessel, there being a line of ships on each side of her. Throughout the day a course of "north west by north ¾ north by compass, ¼ point easterly" was maintained. About 5pm the ship's navigation lamps were illuminated but screened, ready to be displayed at a moment's notice. Masthead lights were not permitted to be shown. At the time a northerly breeze was blowing but the weather was fine and visibility was good.

On the bridge was the ship's master, Captain Johan Sundberg, who said, "I was on the bridge continuously from 5pm … the ship was making 7 knots. About 6.45pm a white light and a green light were observed or possibly slightly off the port bow about a mile distant. The lights passed eastwards. When I saw these lights I ordered able seaman Ahnell to show our port light, which he did. … I then observed the green light from a patrol vessel which passed us, astern on our port side and cut across our course. Shortly afterwards a crash was heard from the stern, port side, and I saw that two steamers had collided. One of the vessels belonged to our convoy."

He continued, "I then saw a green light about 4 points off the port side, around half a mile distant. Our port light was then shining clearly as the lookout had just checked it. The vessel which was showing her green light veered to starboard and passed astern of *Ohio*. At the same time that this vessel passed astern, I observed the green light from a vessel which was later identified as the *Lady Plymouth* around ½ a minute's distance from our port bow. We kept our course and speed … *Lady Plymouth* gave a short blast on her steam whistle. This convinced me she had seen our red light. I expected that she would veer to starboard at any moment. She sounded her whistle 3 times when she was very close to *Ohio* approaching our port side forward of the bridge."

"I gave immediate orders to change our course to starboard and to the engine room 'full steam ahead' in order to avoid the *Lady Plymouth* striking *Ohio* amidships … she collided with considerable speed … a little aft of our mainmast, with her bow and starboard quarter. On board *Ohio* the water immediately started appearing and she appeared to be sinking. I gave the order to lower the lifeboats."

The *Ohio* had been unlucky; two convoys, mainly unlit, happened to cross each other in the darkness. It was remarkable there were not more casualties as the convoys criss-crossed each other.

Ohio's crew, comprising five officers, 11 men and two women, all escaped as the ship sank. The stewardess, 34 year old Svea Sundberg, later contracted pneumonia as a result of being exposed in the open lifeboat, and died several days later.

As far as is known, the wreck of the *Ohio* has not been located and identified.

Name: *Ohio.* **Former name(s):** *Duo* ex *Circassia*
Vessel type: Steam ship.
Builder: William Gray, West Hartlepool.
When completed: June 1878.
Machinery built by: T Richardson & Son, Hartlepool.
Tonnage: 1332 tons gross.
Dimensions: Length: 241′. **Breadth:** 33′ 3″.
Depth of holds: 18′ 2″.
Official number: 4440. **Yard number:** –
Signal letters: JPHS. **Last port of registry:** Sundsvall, Sweden.
Ship description: Iron screw steamer. 1 deck. Well deck.
Machinery description: Compound 2 cylinders. 2 single ended boilers. New donkey boiler 1901.
Career and ownership: Built as *Circassia* for the builder, William Gray. 1905 sold to Rederi AB Uno (C G Wickberg) Sundsvall and renamed *Duo.* In 1910 when previous company went bankrupt, ship sold at auction under a writ of execution and renamed *Ohio*, owned by Rederi Aktieb Othello (E A Enhörning, manager).
Armament: Unarmed.
Destination and cargo: Le Havre for Glasgow in ballast.
Date sunk: 12 October 1918.
How sunk: Collision with the SS *Lady Plymouth.*
Reported position of loss: 50° 20′ north, 002° 00′ west.
Actual position of wreck: Not known.
Orientation/height: –
How identity of wreck proved: –

SS *Spyros*
Foundered 20 December 1920

The *Spyros* was a 40-year-old Greek steamer. Not much is known about her, other than on 20 December 1920 she was on her voyage from Newcastle for St Ives. When in a position off the Isle of Wight, according to a newspaper account, "*Spyros* sprang a leak and foundered about 11 miles south of St Catherine's Point. The crew of 11 took to the ship's boats and after rowing about in the Channel landed at Hurst Castle in the early hours of Monday. Having rowed for some 35 miles they were somewhat exhausted. They were made comfortable by the coastguards and left later in the day for London."

The wreck of the *Spyros* lies in 30 metres of water. She is upright and reasonably intact, but breaking up. Her single boiler is the highest part of the wreck. Known locally as the *Reindeer*, it was thought the wreck might have been the *Albion* or *Clyde* until her identity was proved.

This was established by marine archaeologists who took accurate measurements of the wreck. They recorded the length at 155 feet, and the beam of 24 feet, compared to *Spyros'* length of 153′ 2″ and beam of 24′ 1″.

Name: *Spyros.* **Former name(s):** *Citos* ex *Nacka* ex *Jyden.*
Vessel type: Steam ship.
Builder: Rostocker Act. Ges. Rostock.
When completed: 1880.
Machinery built by: Rostocker A G Rostock.
Tonnage: 387 tons gross.
Dimensions: Length: 153′ 2″. **Breadth:** 24′ 1″.
Depth of holds: 13′ 4″.
Official number: 72844. **Yard number:** –
Signal letters: JVRD. **Last port of registry:** Chios, Greece.
Ship description: Iron screw steamer. 1 deck.
Machinery description: Compound 2 cylinders. 51 nominal horse power.
Career and ownership: 1914, as *Jyden,* owned by Det Forenede DampskibsSelsk, registered Odense, Denmark. 1917 owned by Rederiaktieb S Uman, registered Stockholm as *Nacka.* 1918 renamed *Citos*, and owned by Rederiaktieb. Ivar (T Ohlsson, manager), registered Malmo. Owned 1920/21 by P G Lemos & G F Andreadis as *Spyros.*
Destination and cargo: Newcastle for St Ives, cargo of coal.
Date sunk: 20 December 1920.
How sunk: Sprang a leak and foundered.
Reported position of loss: 11 miles south of St Catherine's Point.
Actual position of wreck: 50° 36.71′ north, 001° 34.84′ west.
Orientation/height: Lies 070°/250°. Stands 4 metres on seabed of shingle.
How identity of wreck proved: Badly worn bell recovered – only the date 1880 clearly visible. Length and breadth of wreck measured by archaeologists. Dimensions exactly fit the *Spyros.*

Steam trawler *Lois*
Ran aground 12 May 1921

Steam trawler *Lois*. Courtesy Peter Horsley collection, Fleetwood Museum.

Dense fog once again played its part in the loss of another vessel in the shallows of Chale Bay, Isle of Wight. This time it was a steam trawler which came to grief. On 12 May 1921, men living on the cliff top near St Catherine's Point heard the sound of a ship's whistle being blown. The signals sounded too close to the shore for comfort, and so it proved to be as the ship, which turned out to be the Fleetwood trawler *Lois,* tried to go astern as she headed for the beach. *Lois* slid on to the beach and stuck fast, rolling in the swell.

The next day, it was reported that her after deck was under water, and her propeller had gone. A report from Lloyd's said, "Trawler *Lois*: End on beach west Rocken End, apparently sitting on an old submerged wreck, holed in way of the engine." An inspection by a diver five days later revealed that *Lois* was listing heavily to port, and fractures had appeared in her hull. However, by 24 May, she had been patched up and refloated and with her head to the sea, it looked as though she would be saved. Work continued on the vessel, but because of the crosstides affecting that part of the coast, and because the diver was unable to stop up the leaks, all salvage was abandoned and she was left to the sea.

The wreck of the *Lois* lies mixed with many other pieces of wreckage in Chale Bay and it is not possible to say with any certainty which piece belongs to which wreck. Most winters, chunks of debris and wreckage move along the bay.

Name: *Lois.* **Former name(s):** None.
Vessel type: Steam trawler.
Builder: Cochrane & Sons, Selby.

When completed: February 1910.
Machinery built by: Amos & Smith, Hull.
Tonnage: 310 tons gross.
Dimensions: Length: 135′. **Breadth:** 24′.
Depth of holds: 12′ 4″.
Official number: 127577. **Yard number:** –
Signal letters: HTBV. **Last port of registry:** Fleetwood.
Ship description: Steel screw steam ketch trawler.
Machinery description: Triple expansion 3 cylinders. 1 single ended boiler. 91 registered horse power.
Career and ownership: In 1915 *Lois* was hired as a minesweeper for the Admiralty, No 961. She was paid off in 1919 and she was then owned by the Fleetwood Steam Fishing Company Ltd, port number FD 113.
Destination and cargo: Not known.
Date sunk: Ran aground 12 May 1921 and abandoned as a total loss on 25 June.
How sunk: Ran aground in dense fog.
Reported position of loss: West of St Catherine's Point and west of Rocken End.
Actual position of wreck: Impossible to determine with any accuracy.
Orientation/height: –
How identity of wreck proved: Not proved.

Steam trawler *Lois* wrecked in Chale Bay.
Courtesy Gordon Wheeler.

Auxiliary motor vessel *Imogene*
Foundered 31 October 1921

The *Imogene* was owned by a Mr E Willows, and he was on board his ship when she ran into trouble. Described by the local newspaper as, "better known in the aviation world than as a ship owner, he was the first to fly an airship in England, making a notable trip from Cardiff to London in August, 1910, was the first Englishman to fly an airship across the Channel, and, during the war, was in charge of the balloon anti-aircraft defences in London." Venturing into the shipping business, Mr Willows purchased the *Imogene*. He said, "In breasting the Needles on the run up Channel we encountered an exceptional tide set, which carried us on to the shingle bank almost before we were aware of the danger."

On 31 October 1921, *Imogene* was seen from the shore to be aground on the Shingle Bank close to the Elbow Buoy, but as the weather was calm no action was taken. By the next morning, however, the wind had freshened and the vessel was seen to be labouring heavily in the swell. Totland lifeboat was launched and succeeded in reaching the stranded ship, returning with her crew.

The next day a tug arrived to recover the *Imogene*, and some of her crew and some local boatmen returned with the intention of lightening the ship by jettisoning her cargo. At first the sea was calm, but when the tide turned, the wind freshened and a heavy swell began to run. "In spite of their warnings the others refused to leave the ship, and whilst the local men were endeavouring to persuade them to change their minds the sea dashed their motor boat against the vessel and damaged her side. The local men immediately left and despite the damage to their boat, reached Totland in safety after a hazardous trip."

"The others remained but the ship's boat was soon smashed and they signalled to the tug for assistance. The tug's boat was unable to approach them, however, owing to the broken water, and she put into Totland towards evening and asked that the lifeboat might be sent out again. The lifeboat got away at about 6.10pm in tow of the tug *Glenmore*. She returned at 10.30pm and reported that although she had searched in all directions she could not find the ship in the darkness. At dawn on Thursday the vessel could still be seen on the bank with huge seas breaking over her. The lifeboat crew were assembled for the third time … and considering the moderate wind extraordinarily heavy seas were running in the shallows on the bank. Eventually, the stranded men were rescued in a very exhausted state, as a result of their miserable experience in their waterlogged ship."

One week later, *Imogene* had broken up, only her stern showing, but that too was breaking up and the vessel became a total loss.

There is no information concerning the wreck of this vessel.

Name: *Imogene*. **Former name(s):** *Strathendrick*.
Vessel type: Auxiliary motor vessel.
Builder: Troon Shipbuilding company, Troon.
When completed: June 1882.
Machinery built by: Ruston & Hornsby Ltd, Lincoln.
Tonnage: 189 tons gross.
Dimensions: Length: 113′ 1″. **Breadth:** 22′ 2″.
Depth of holds: 11′ 9″.
Official number: 86666. **Yard number:** –
Signal letters: WKPS. **Last port of registry:** London.
Ship description: Wooden twin screw auxiliary motor vessel.
Machinery description: Twin 2 cycle single acting oil engines, 4 cylinders.
Career and ownership: Owned by E T Willows.
Destination and cargo: Poole for Antwerp with a cargo of China clay.
Date sunk: Stranded 31 October 1921, total loss one week later.
How sunk: Ran aground on the Shingle Bank.
Reported position of loss: Close to the Elbow Buoy, Shingle Bank.
Actual position of wreck: Not known.
Orientation/height: –
How identity of wreck proved: –

German U-boats of the First World War Scuttled after the Armistice in 1921

In the central part of the English Channel south of St Catherine's Point lie a number of First World War German U-boats. Five or six of these vessels were reported to have been among very many which were surrendered after the Armistice in 1918 and interred in various UK ports. Although their presence caused considerable interest at the time, by the early 1920's it was decided they had to be disposed of. Accordingly, a number were taken to the mid Channel position and scuttled. Exactly how this was done is not clear, but it appears some were used to test British gunfire against German steel. Taking information supplied by the Hydrographic Office, a number of these U-boats have been dived, but none positively identified. They are:

1. Unidentified German U-boat, supposed *U-122.*
Diving information: some damage evident to pressure hull, as if rammed. Intact wreck.
Name: *U-122.*
Vessel type: U-boat.
Builder: Blohm & Voss.
When completed: 1917.
Machinery built by: Probably Blohm & Voss or Vulcan.
Tonnage: 1164 tons displacement surface, 1512 tons displacement submerged.
Dimensions: Length: 81.5 metres. **Breadth:** 7.4 metres. **Draught:** 4.2 metres.
Description: Steel U-boat, minelayer.
Machinery description: 2 × 1200 horse power diesel engines, 2 × 600 horse power electric motors.
Armament: 4 × bow torpedo tubes for 12 × 50 cm torpedoes. 1 × 15cm deck gun. 42 mines plus 30 more in deck containers.
Date sunk: 1 July 1921.
How sunk: Reported as "scuttled."
Actual position of wreck: 50° 12.21′ north, 001° 26.27′ west.
Orientation/height: Lies 085/265°. Stands 8 metres in about 58 metres (very close to supposed *UC-II* minelayer).
How identity of wreck proved: Not proved.

2. Unidentified German U-boat, supposed *U-123.*
Name: *U-123.*
Vessel type: U-boat.
Builder: Blohm & Voss or Vulcan.
When completed: 1917.
Machinery built by: Probably Blohm & Voss or Vulcan.
Tonnage: 1164 tons displacement surface, 1512 tons displacement submerged.
Dimensions: Length: 81.5 metres. **Breadth:** 7.4 metres. **Draught:** 4.2 metres.
Description: Steel U-boat, minelayer.
Machinery description: 2 × 1200 horse power diesel engines, 2 × 600 horse power electric motors.
Armament: 4 × bow torpedo tubes for 12 × 50 cm torpedoes. 1 × 15cm deck gun. 42 mines plus 30 more in deck containers.
Date sunk: 28 June 1921.
How sunk: Reported as "scuttled."
Actual position of wreck: 50° 11.15′ north, 001° 18.32′ west.
Orientation/height: Lies 060/240°. Stands 5 or 6 metres in about 70 metres.
How identity of wreck proved: Not proved.

3. Unidentified German U-boat, supposed *U-152.*
Name: *U-152.*
Vessel type: U-boat. U cruiser.
Builder: Reiherstieg & Flensburger.
When completed: 1917.
Machinery built by: not known.
Tonnage: 1512 tons displacement surfaced, 1875 tons displacement submerged.
Dimensions: Length: 65 metres. **Breadth:** 8.9 metres. **Draught:** 5.3 metres.
Description: Steel U-boat built as a cargo boat but converted for war use.
Machinery description: 2 × 400 horse power diesel engines, 2 × 400 horse power electric motors.
Armament: 2 × bow torpedo tubes for 18 50cm torpedoes. 2 × 15cm guns and 2 × 8.8cm guns.
Date sunk: 30 June 1921.
How sunk: Reported as "scuttled."
Actual position of wreck: 50° 12.43′ north, 001° 18.97′ west.

Orientation/height: Lies 170°/350°. Stands 7 metres in 75 metres.
How identity of wreck proved: Not proved.

4. Unidentified German U-boat, supposed *U-153*.
Diving information: Large boat, upright with 3 guns evident. Bows blown off revealing torpedo tube bow cap. Two deck mounted torpedo tubes starboard side amidships. Twin screws.
Name: *U-153*.
Vessel type: U-boat. U cruiser.
Builder: Reiherstieg & Flensburger.
When completed: 1917.
Machinery built by: Not known.
Tonnage: 1512 tons displacement surfaced, 1875 tons displacement submerged.
Dimensions: Length: 65 metres. **Breadth:** 8.9 metres. **Draught:** 5.3 metres.
Description: Steel U-boat built as a cargo boat but converted for war use.
Machinery description: 2 × 400 horse power diesel engines, 2 × 400 horse power electric motors.
Armament: 2 × bow torpedo tubes for 18 50cm torpedoes. 2 × 15cm guns and 2 × 8.8cm guns.
Date sunk: 30 June 1921.
How sunk: Reported as "scuttled."
Actual position of wreck: 50° 14.48′ north, 001° 12.05′ west.
Orientation/height: Lies 030°/210°. Stands 7 metres in 60 metres. Depth of 65 metres nearby.
How identity of wreck proved: Not proved.

5. Unidentified German U-boat, supposed *UB-122*.
Diving information: Very large, substantial wreck. Possibly one of the large Deutschland class boats.
Name: *UB-122*.
Vessel type: UB-III series U-boat.
Builder: A G Weser.
When completed: 1918.
Machinery built by: Probably A G Weser.
Tonnage: 516 tons displacement surface, 651 tons displacement submerged.
Dimensions: Length: 55.3 metres. **Breadth:** 5.8 metres. **Draught:** 3.7 metres.
Description: Steel U-boat for coastal and Mediterranean use.
Machinery description: 2 × 550 horse power diesel engines, 2 × 394 horse power electric motors.
Armament: 4 × bow torpedo tubes, 1 × stern tube, for 10 × 50cm torpedoes. 1 × 8.8cm deck gun.
Date sunk: 30 June 1921.
How sunk: Reported as "scuttled."
Actual position of wreck: 50° 12.19′ north, 001° 18.32′ west.
Orientation/height: Lies 060°/240°. Stands 10 metres in 78 metres.
How identity of wreck proved: Not proved.

6. Unidentified German U-boat. Minelayer, probably UC-II or UC-III series, possibly *UC-110*.
Diving information: Twin screw minelayer. 6 mine chutes seen; empty, no covers. Bow section rotted away or blown off.
Vessel type: U-boat.
Builder: UC-II and UC-III series built by Blohm & Voss, Vulcan, GW, KWD or AG Weser.
When completed: 1915/16 for UC-II series, 1918 for UC-III series.
Machinery built by: Blohm & Voss, Vulcan, GW, KWD or A G Weser.
Tonnage: UC-II series: 417 tons displacement surfaced, 493 tons displacement submerged. UC-III series: 474 tons displacement surfaced, 560 tons displacement submerged.
Dimensions: Length: UC-II: 49.4 metres, UC-III: 56.1 metres. **Breadth:** UC-II: 5.2 metres, UC-III: 5.5 metres. **Draught:** UC-II: 3.7 metres, UC-III: 3.8 metres.
Description: Steel minelayer U-boat.
Machinery description: UC-II: 2 × 250 horse power diesel engines, 2 × 230 horse power electric motors. UC-III: 2 × 300 horse power diesel engines, 2 × 385 horse power electric motors.
Career: Not known.
Armament: UC-II series: 2 × bow torpedo tubes and 1 × stern tube with 7 × 50cm torpedoes. 1 × 8.8mm deck gun. 18 mines carried in 6 mine chutes. UC-III series: 2 × bow torpedo tubes, 1 × stern tube with 7 × 50cm torpedoes. 18 mines carried in 6 mine chutes.
Date sunk: Probably 1921.
How sunk: Probably sunk by own forces as a target.
Actual position of wreck: 50° 12.38′ north, 001° 26.05′ west.
Orientation/height: Lies 140°/320°. Stands 5 or 6 metres in 60 metres on shingle seabed (lies very close to wreck supposed to be *U-122*).
How identity of wreck proved: Not proved.

SMS *Nürnberg*
Scuttled 7 July 1922

Light cruiser *Nürnberg*. Courtesy Imperial War Museum.

The German light cruiser *Nürnberg* was completed in November 1916. Following the severe bruising suffered by both the British Grand Fleet and the German High Seas Fleet at the Battle of Jutland in May 1916, *Nürnberg* never saw action, but remained in port with the remainder of the German High Seas Fleet.

When the Armistice was signed in November 1918, *Nürnberg*, together with the remainder of the German Imperial Navy's main battle fleet, surrendered and proceeded to Scapa Flow. There, they were interned while their fate was decided. The U-boats were accepted at various ports in England. The German crews felt a sense of humiliation at being interned because the war had ended, and a plan was developed by them to scuttle the entire fleet at its moorings. On a predetermined signal, the plan was put into effect and the ships began to sink. Responding to this action, the British authorities were able to save a number of ships before they sank, but most were successfully scuttled. One of the beached ships was the *Nürnberg*, which had drifted ashore after her mooring chains parted. Patched up and refloated, she was taken to Portsmouth for use as a target.

On 7 July 1922 *Nürnberg* was taken to a position in mid Channel where her armour was tested against British gunfire from the battle cruiser HMS *Repulse*. Struck by more than thirty 6″ shells, the damage was inspected by the Royal Naval authorities and photographs taken. At least nine shells had struck the ship along the waterline, and *Nürnberg* eventually filled and sank.

The wreck of the *Nürnberg* lies in about 63 metres of water. She is very substantial, standing some 10 metres off the seabed, leaning over to port and lying across the tide. Some of her guns lie on the seabed.

Name: *Nürnberg.* **Former name(s):** None.
Vessel type: German light cruiser.
Builder: Howaldtswerke, Kiel.
When completed: November 1916.
Machinery built by: Howaldtswerke, Kiel.
Tonnage: About 4200 tons displacement.
Dimensions: Length: 450′. **Breadth:** 43′ 6″.
Draught: 16′.
Ship description: Königsberg class steel screw German light cruiser or "small protected cruiser." Fitted with armour belt and 10 guns.
Machinery description: Probably "marine type" geared turbines. Schulz-Thornycroft boilers.
Armament: 8 × 5.9″ 50 calibre semi-automatic guns, 2 or 3 × 22 pounder anti-aircraft guns, 4 × 19.7″ torpedo tubes, 2 above water and 2 submerged.
Destination: Portsmouth for mid Channel to test armour against British gunfire.
Date sunk: 7 July 1922.
How sunk: Gunfire from HMS *Repulse.*
Reported position of loss: 50° 07′ north, 001° 43′ west.
Actual position of wreck: 50° 08.17′ north, 001°41.74′ west.
Orientation/height: Lies 140°/320°. Stands 10 metres in 63 metres.
How identity of wreck proved: Not proved but wreck is of a large warship close to the position reported in 1922.

SS *El Kahira*
Foundered 8/9 July 1922

SS *El Kahira.* Courtesy Glasgow University Archives.

The Times newspaper carried a report on Friday, 7 July 1922 headed, "Violent summer storm. Gale and heavy rain. Widespread damage." The report continued, "The gale was due to an extremely deep cyclonic disturbance which passed north easterly from Cornwall across central England to the North Sea." This was followed, on 10 July, by another report, "The deep depression which was approaching Ireland from the Atlantic on Friday evening passed directly over the British Isles during the weekend occasioning rough and very unsettled weather generally. Gales were widespread especially in the south … and considerable damage to shipping and property resulted."

Into these storm conditions, the steamer *El Kahira* sailed, but she should not have been out at all; she was unfit to be at sea. From August, 1920, the ship was moored on the Thames, where she remained until July 1922. She was overdue a survey. It was known by her owners that her boilers were defective, that the equipment for raising and lowering the lifeboats was perished and that only two of the ship's six lifeboats were in a serviceable condition. Her owners also allowed her to proceed to sea without being equipped with a wireless installation, as was then required by law.

In late June 1922, *El Kahira* was chartered to carry a cargo of sugar to various Italian ports. Having loaded, she prepared to put to sea, but a leak developed in one of the boilers which delayed her departure. Repairs were effected but the boilers again gave trouble though the voyage continued. On 7 July, *El Kahira* passed Dover, and steamed into a freshening south west wind. The next day, the weather worsened; by midnight it was blowing a heavy gale which persisted until noon on 9 July, when the winds moderated.

On 1 August 1922 a body was washed up on the French coast. It was identified as that of Captain W N Pepperell, master of the *El Kahira*. A second body came ashore nearby later that month; it was the body of one of the greasers. There was then no doubt that the overdue ship had been lost somewhere in the English Channel, with no survivors. Twenty-nine men had disappeared with the ship. The location of the *El Kahira* was unknown.

At the Court of Enquiry held in September 1923, the court ruled that, "When the ship sailed she was an unsafe ship for the following reasons: 1. She was not provided with a wireless installation as required by law, 2. Her boats' falls were in such a condition that the boats could not be readily launched or easily handled and, 3. She had been so long laid up in the Thames and such a length of time had elapsed since she was last thoroughly surveyed, that it was highly improper to send her to sea without first causing her to be dry-docked and thoroughly overhauled."

The court added, "The court concludes … the owners … had already made several attempts to sell her and were, the court believes, sending her to Greece in the hope of disposing of her to purchasers who would be less exacting in their requirements than British shipowners. In their anxiety to avoid expense they were prepared to take the risk of the vessel being unseaworthy in respect of hull and machinery."

The managing owner, Ernest Olivier, was judged to be "primarily responsible for all the circumstances which made the investigation (into the loss) necessary and for the consequent large expenditure of public money, the court orders him to pay the sum of 200 guineas towards the expenses of the investigation."

The wreck of the *El Kahira*, lies in 60 metres of water. Her boilers and engine are broken and displaced, but are the highest parts of the wreck. She is an excellent dive.

Name: *El Kahira.* **Former name(s):** None.
Vessel type: Steam ship.
Builder: Robert Napier & Sons, Glasgow.
When completed: 1892.
Machinery built by: Robert Napier & Sons, Glasgow.
Tonnage: 2034 tons gross.
Dimensions: Length: 300′. **Breadth:** 37′ 5″.
Depth of holds: 15′ 8″.
Official number: 110140. **Yard number:** 427.
Signal letters: RFSC. **Last port of registry:** London.
Ship description: Steel screw steamer. Fitted with electric light. 2 decks, spar deck and promenade deck.
Machinery description: Triple expansion 3 cylinders. 4 single ended boilers. 510 nominal horse power.
Career and ownership: Owned and worked by the Khedivial Mail Steamship Company until 1919. Then purchased by the Transport & Trading Company. In 1920 sold to the Franco-British Steamship Company Ltd. In 1922 she was taken over by the Hydra Steamship Company and then sold to the Trading & Coaling Company. Ernest Olivier was the principal shareholder in the last three companies.
Destination and cargo: London for various Italian ports with a cargo of 1301 tons of bagged sugar.
Date sunk: 8 or 9 July 1922.
How sunk: Foundered in storm conditions.
Reported position of loss: None.
Actual position of wreck: 50° 15.65′ north, 001° 54.84′ west.
Orientation/height: Stands about 7 metres in 60 metres on shingle/gravel seabed, bows to the north east.
How identity of wreck proved: Builder's nameplate and ship's crockery recovered.

Steam drifter *Excelsior*
Foundered 5 September 1924

Steam drifter *Excelsior*. Courtesy Peter Jenkins.

Lloyd's Weekly Casualty Report for 12 September 1924 published an entry, "Needles, September 6. Following from the coastguard, Keyhaven: Master and crew of steam drifter *Excelsior*, of Lowestoft, Portsmouth for Newport, cargo scrap iron, have landed here. Master states vessel foundered 10 minutes after springing a leak at 11.15pm on September 5th; approximate position 5 miles west of Needles lighthouse. Weather at the time calm, fine, misty; visibility good."

There is no information as to whether the *Excelsior* has been located and identified. A search around a position provided by the Hydrographic Office revealed an isolated rock patch which had the appearance of wreckage and though there were readings on the magnetometer, no wreck has been found.

Name: *Excelsior*. **Former name(s):** None.
Vessel type: Steam drifter.
Builder: John Chambers, Lowestoft.
When completed: 1904.
Machinery built by: Elliot & Garrod, Beccles.
Tonnage: 62 tons gross.
Dimensions: Length: 74′. **Breadth:** 17′ 8″.
Depth of holds: 8′ 5″.
Official number: 119364. **Yard number:** –
Signal letters: – **Last port of registry:** Lowestoft.
Ship description: Wooden steam drifter.
Machinery description: Compound 2 cylinders. Probably 1 single ended boiler. 15 horse power.
Career and ownership: 1904 owned by Peter Baxter. 1912 owned by Robert Leeds. 1915–18 owned by E Catchpole & others, Kessingland. 1920 owned by A J Blaker, Southwick. Port No. 698.
Destination and cargo: Portsmouth for Newport with a cargo of scrap iron.
Date sunk: 5 September 1924.
How sunk: Sprang a leak and foundered.
Reported position of loss: 5 miles west of the Needles lighthouse. Hydrographic Office position: 50° 40.50′ north, 001° 44.93′ west.
Actual position of wreck: Not known.
Orientation/height: –
How identity of wreck proved: –

SS *Hartley*
Foundered 27 November 1924

Second Engineer Charles Cuthbert, SS *Hartley*. Courtesy Roger Wilson.

The steamer *Hartley* was a new ship which had completed only seven voyages when she fell foul of appalling weather on 27 November 1924. She had departed Barry bound for Ghent with a cargo of coal on Wednesday 24 November. The voyage proceeded normally until midnight on the 26th/27th when the ship was off Start Point. During the early hours, a strong wind blew up from the south east, said by a survivor, sailor F Adams, to be "blowing half a gale about 3 points on the starboard bow." Towards dawn the wind backed to the south-south-west at force 7, increasing force 8, on *Hartley's* starboard quarter. About 4.30am, Adams was sent to look around and make sure everything on deck was in order. He found everything, "all right" but the vessel was shipping heavy water both on the fore deck and on the after deck. With the wind on the starboard beam, *Hartley* was riding well, pitching a little but not rolling.

At 6.30am, things began to go wrong. Heavy cross seas carried onto the ship and the master, Captain William Pearson, decided to heave to. Attempting to steer in a southerly direction to meet the seas head on, Captain Pearson found the wind and sea too much and the manoeuvre had to be abandoned. Extra lashings were put on number 3 hatch and the fore hatches were re-lashed.

Between 8am and 9am, it was discovered that the tarpaulin on number 3 hatch had been torn. Further efforts were made to re-lash it and nail it into place, but soon after 9am with the gale blowing from the south west, one of the hatch boards became dislodged and went overboard. When a replacement was found, it would not fit. With heavy seas continuing to break across the well deck, more hatch covers were washed away and water poured into number 3 hold and from there, into number 4 hold. The ship took on a list to starboard and Captain Pearson ordered all hands to stand by on the boat deck. At 9.35am Captain Pearson ordered a wireless signal to be transmitted, "Stand by, about to abandon ship." Five minutes later, all the crew, except one man who had fallen overboard, boarded the lifeboat and abandoned *Hartley*.

Captain Pearson's SOS was picked up by the 7807 ton steamer *Machaon*. She was close at hand and immediately went to assist. Coming alongside the lifeboat, strenuous efforts were made to rescue the crew, but just at the wrong moment a large swell passed along the *Machaon's* side, capsizing the lifeboat and throwing everyone into the water. One man was hauled up to the poop by means of a lifebuoy with line attached, but the others struggled with their upturned boat. Conditions were, according to *Machaon's* master, Captain Arthur Dodd, very bad, with "the sea very rough and confused at times and too bad to lower a boat." Only sailor Adams was eventually rescued from the water; 20 other crew drowned. The *Hartley* finally went to the bottom at 11.12am, listing to starboard and sinking by the stern.

At the Court of Enquiry, the court found "that the loss of the vessel was due to the tarpaulins covering number 3 hatchway becoming damaged by the heavy water shipped on board and the washing away of the wooden hatch covers thus opening the hatchways to the sea. Number 3 and 4 holds were soon full of water and the ship foundered."

The wreck believed to be that of the *Hartley* lies in 40 metres of water. The wreck lies on its starboard side with the amidships section the highest part.

Name: *Hartley*. **Former name(s):** None.
Vessel type: Steam ship.
Builder: Smith's Dock, South Bank on Tees.
When completed: Launched 31 July 1924.
Machinery built by: Smith's Dock, South Bank on Tees.
Tonnage: 2147 tons gross.
Dimensions: Length: 280′. **Breadth:** 41′ 6″.
Depth of holds: 20′ 1″.
Official number: 148090. **Yard number:** 797.
Signal letters: – **Last port of registry:** Newcastle.
Ship description: Steel screw steamer. Self trimming collier. 1 deck. Schooner rigged.
Machinery description: Triple expansion 3 cylinders. 2 single ended boilers. 228 nominal horse power.
Career and ownership: Built for the Sharp Steam Ship Company but when lost owned by the Hartley Steamship Company (Messrs Richley, Halvorsen & Semple, managers).
Destination and cargo: Barry for Ghent with a cargo of coal.
Date sunk: 27 November 1924.
How sunk: Foundered in heavy weather.
Reported position of loss: 50° 26′ north, 001° 50′ west.
Actual position of wreck: 50° 23.94′ north, 001° 48.65′ west.
Orientation/height: Stands about 6 metres in 40 metres on shingle seabed.
How identity of wreck proved: Not proved. Wreck is of an unarmed steamer of about 2000 tons about 2 miles from the reported position of *Hartley's* loss.

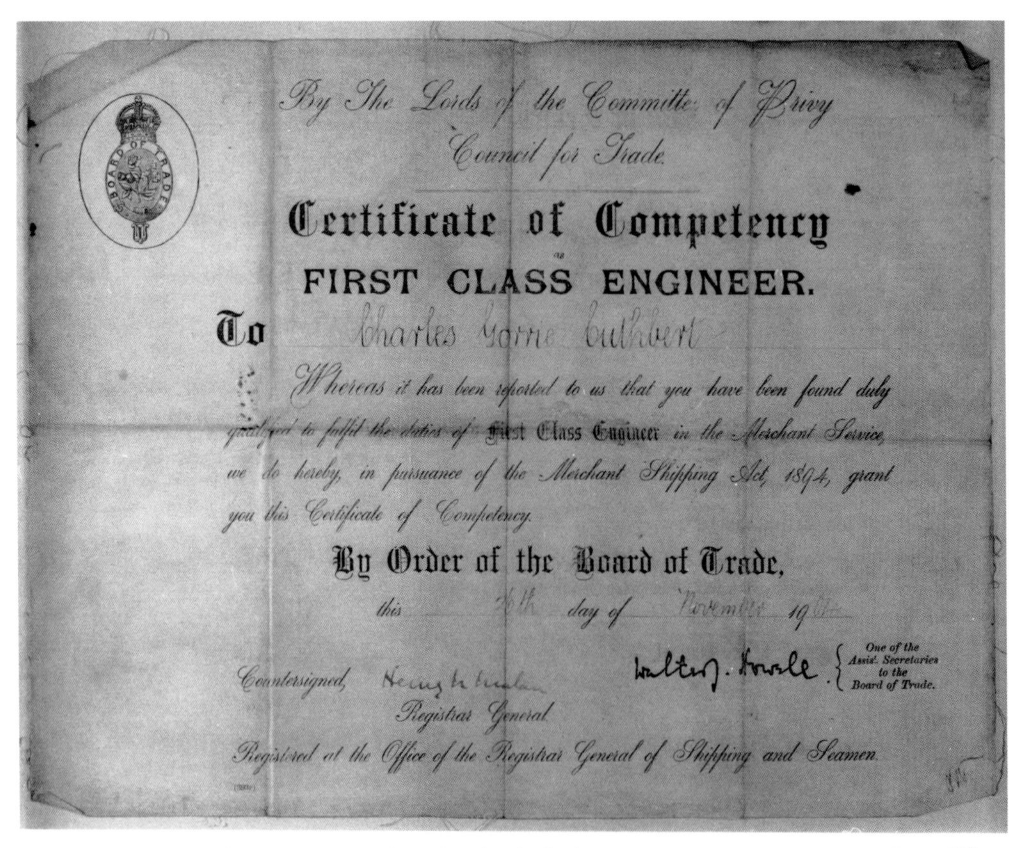

By The Lords of the Committee of Privy Council for Trade.

Certificate of Competency

as

FIRST CLASS ENGINEER.

To Charles Yorne Cuthbert

Whereas it has been reported to us that you have been found duly qualified to fulfil the duties of First Class Engineer in the Merchant Service, we do hereby, in pursuance of the Merchant Shipping Act, 1894, grant you this Certificate of Competency.

By Order of the Board of Trade,

this [illegible]th day of November 19[illegible]

Countersigned, [illegible] Registrar General

[illegible] One of the Assist. Secretaries to the Board of Trade.

Registered at the Office of the Registrar General of Shipping and Seamen.

Charles Cuthbert's First Class Engineer's Certificate, found on his body. Courtesy Roger Wilson.

SS *Castlereagh*
Foundered 22/23 February 1925

SS *Firth Fisher*, later renamed *Castlereagh*. Courtesy E N Taylor collection.

"Mysterious Channel disaster" was the headline in a local newspaper published on 7 March 1925 when it reported "that a Belfast steamer, the *Castlereagh,* with a crew of 10, was lost somewhere in the vicinity of the Needles during the fierce gales on Sunday and Monday February 22 and 23." The report was prompted by the discovery of two bodies recovered from the sea in the western Solent; they were identified as being members of the crew of the *Castlereagh,* but "the cause of the disaster, however, remains a mystery, as there were no survivors."

When the bodies were recovered they were wearing lifebelts, securely fastened; both had drowned. The examining doctor was of the opinion that the bodies had been in the water about three days, which was consistent with the ship sinking in the gales earlier in the week. The Coroner added, "Long experience has shown me that the Isle of Wight coasts were a dumping ground of Channel wreckage, and it seemed extraordinary that nothing but these two bodies have been found. When similar disasters have occurred to vessels of that size, hatchways, boats or other gear has invariably been washed up, but in this case there was nothing but these two bodies. That seemed to point to a sudden overwhelming of the ship; yet the crew evidently had time to don their lifebelts."

Former crewman, William Irwin, gave evidence at the inquest, and said, "The *Castlereagh* was a good sea boat. I have been round the west coast of Ireland in her in bad weather, and I would have gone anywhere with her under Captain Smythe, who was an exceedingly careful and experienced master, who, I am certain, would never run any unnecessary risk. The captain was born at sea and had been on ships all his life." Captain Smythe held what was known as a "square rigged" certificate, the highest possible credentials, rarely held by masters of coasting vessels.

Ten days after the supposed loss of the ship, a lifebelt, lifebuoy and a timber hatchway came ashore in the Solent, but that was all. *Castlereagh* had disappeared and all hands were lost.

The wreck of the *Castlereagh* lies in about 33 metres of water. She is upright but breaking up. Her forward hold is full of coal covered with mussel shells. Her single boiler and engine are the highest parts of the wreck.

Name: *Castlereagh*. **Former name(s):** *Firth Fisher*.
Vessel type: Steam coaster.
Builder: J Fullerton & Company, Paisley.
When completed: October 1898.
Machinery built by: Ross & Duncan, Glasgow.
Tonnage: 443 tons gross.
Dimensions: Length: 168′. **Breadth:** 25′ 1″. **Depth of holds:** 9′ 6″.
Official number: 99944. **Yard number:** –
Signal letters: QLDJ. **Last port of registry:** Belfast.
Ship description: Steel screw steam coaster. Well deck.
Machinery description: Compound 2 cylinders. 1 single ended boiler. 88 registered horse power. Machinery fitted aft.
Career and ownership: Owned in 1910 by J Fisher & Sons as *Firth Fisher*. At the time of loss owned by John Kelly (S Kelly, manager) as *Castlereagh*.
Destination and cargo: Ayr for Shoreham with a cargo of 481 tons 15cwt of coal.
Date sunk: 22 or 23 February 1925.
How sunk: Overwhelmed in heavy seas and foundered.
Reported position of loss: None.
Actual position of wreck: 50° 34.84′ north, 001° 56.16′ west.
Orientation/height: Stands about 5 metres in 33 metres on rough ground.
How identity of wreck proved: Ship's bell recovered.

SS *Betsy Anna*
Foundered 12 October 1926

SS *Betsy Anna* under way. Courtesy Memory Lane Photo Galleries, Hull.

The *Betsy Anna* was a Dutch steamer on voyage from Fleetwood for Amsterdam. Rounding Land's End, she steamed up Channel. What happened next is open to question, but it is certain she ran aground at Prawle Point. The ship's mate reported the vessel ran aground in dense fog. Locals, however, reported the weather clear, and *Betsy Anna* had been seen circling before running aground. She was, they were convinced, "an insurance job." It was 17 August 1926.

Whatever the truth, the ship was wedged between two projecting rocks, her stern working from side to side scraping across boulders and stripping her propeller, while the crew walked ashore. Although hardly damaged, it was expected the ship would become a total wreck. Her owners regarded salvage as hopeless and abandoned her, but sold her to an enterprising salvage company from the Isle of Wight.

In the weeks which followed, the ship was patched up. By continuously using three powerful pumps worked by two 40 horse power petrol motors, the ship was pumped out and the leaks stopped up with wood and cement. *Betsy Anna* was refloated and towed to Millbay, Salcombe, where she was beached for further temporary repairs. On 11 October 1926 she was fit enough to be towed back to Cowes where she would be properly repaired. The tow was conducted by the tug *Trustee*, with *Betsy Anna* being handled by a crew of 14.

The tow made good progress, with Portland Bill being passed about 7.30pm. Towards midnight, however, the weather turned very nasty when a fierce gale sprang up, and the situation worsened when the towing hawser parted. Heavy seas broke over *Betsy Anna* and it was impossible in the stormy seas to attempt to secure another hawser. Eventually, pumping had to be discontinued, and with water rising in the ship, it was obvious there was no hope of saving her. When the water had practically reached her deck level, she was finally abandoned, her crew being rescued by the *Trustee*.

The wreck of the *Betsy Anna* lies in about 25 metres of water. She is upright, though rotting through. Her stern leans over to port, her bows have broken and point upwards, and her engine has gone over. The highest parts of the wreck are her main and donkey boilers. The petrol motors still lie in the wreck.

Nameplate from donkey boiler. Author's collection.

Name: *Betsy Anna.* **Former name(s):** *Ashington.*
Vessel type: Steam ship.
Builder: W Dobson & Company, Newcastle.
When completed: May 1892.
Machinery built by: J Dickinson, Sunderland.
Tonnage: 880 tons gross.
Dimensions: Length: 206′ 7″. **Breadth:** 30′ 1″.
Depth of holds: 14′ 1″.
Official number: – **Yard number:** 51.
Signal letters: NGWR. **Last port of registry:** Amsterdam.
Ship description: Steel screw steamer. 1 deck. Well deck.
Machinery description: Triple expansion 3 cylinders. 1 single ended boiler. New donkey boiler 1912 (date can be seen on photograph of boiler nameplate). 120 nominal horse power.
Career and ownership: Owned as *Ashington* by Ashington Coal Company (W Millburn & Company, managers). From 1906 as *Betsy Anna* owned by Naamloze Vennotschap Exploitatie van SS Betsy Anna (W H Berghuys Coal Trade). Sold 1926 to Cowes Salvage Company.
Destination and cargo: Salcombe for Cowes for repairs.
Date sunk: 12 October 1926.
How sunk: Foundered in heavy weather.
Reported position of loss: 5 miles west of the Needles.
Actual position of wreck: 50° 36.98′ north, 001° 49.98′ west.
Orientation/height: Lies 080°/260°. Stands about 6 metres in 25 metres on gravel seabed.
How identity of wreck proved: Nameplate from donkey boiler recovered.

SS *Betsy Anna* undergoing repairs at Salcombe. Courtesy Fairweather collection, Cookworthy Museum, Kingsbridge.

Sailing barque *Eugène Schneider* Collision 25 December 1926

Sailing barque *Eugène Schneider*. Courtesy National Maritime Museum, Greenwich.

"An examination of these papers clearly shows that the English steamer was responsible for the accident in question. As a matter of fact, the watch on this vessel was inadequate. On the other hand, after the accident the captain of the English vessel did not have the necessary presence of mind to keep his vessel in the breach made in the *Eugène Schneider* which would have delayed the sinking of the sailing ship and would have allowed the crew to get on board the *Burutu*." These were the views of the French Marine Department following the loss of the large sailing ship *Eugène Schneider*, together with 24 lives.

Eugène Schneider departed Manoka in the Cameroons on 8 October 1925, bound for Ghent. She had made an excellent passage of 79 days and on Christmas night, 1925, she was taking full advantage of the strong wind blowing from the north east as she tacked back and forth in a broadly easterly heading in the central part of the English Channel. About 4.15pm, as darkness beckoned, all the ship's navigation lamps were illuminated and checked that they were in full working order.

About 11.30pm, nine of *Eugène Schneider's* crew were on deck. One said, "We were hoisting more sail to set, as the weather was getting fairer. It was, at that time, quite bright and calm. About half an hour before the crash we saw the lights of the British steamer, but we took little notice of them until we saw her bearing down upon us. We rang our bell and shouted for all we were worth, but we could not get out of her way and she struck us amidships." He continued, "The ringing of the bell and the crash awakened our shipmates who were sleeping below, and everybody ran on deck. The captain shouted 'You must try to save yourselves!' We did not think that our ship would sink so quickly and there was no rush to leave her, but suddenly, without any warning, she heeled over and plunged like a stone.

Four of us managed to jump and reached the deck of the British boat. The others must have been sucked down." The ship had been rammed starboard side adjacent to the crew's quarters. The ship sank by the head in 2 or 3 minutes.

When the four survivors gave evidence to the French authorities, they all agreed that when they boarded the *Burutu*, no-one was on watch. An apprentice was the first man they saw and he "could hardly stand upright. Later on he endeavoured to get into a whale boat (to look for survivors); the others pushed him away because he was very drunk; amongst the crew some of the men were no longer able to stand up; the officer tossed up to decide which out of those who were more sober should get into the two boats that had been let down." They added, "The officer on watch did not appear to be drunk but he ought not to have been at his post, for he asked us whether the ship that had been struck was a steamer or a sailing vessel."

Eugène Schneider had been rammed and sunk by the 5275 ton steamer *Burutu*, which was steaming down Channel under the command of her master, Captain William R Jones. He declared, "I did not notice any lights of the sailing vessel when I descended from the bridge a quarter of an hour before the collision took place. If the sailing vessel had been carrying any lights I ought to have seen them." The chief officer, Clifford Summers, stated, "I did not see the lights of the sailing vessel at all."

It seems extraordinary that the *Burutu* did not see the *Eugène Schneider*. Had she done so, she was under a duty to give way to the sailing ship. Clearly some of *Burutu's* crew were drunk, and there was a suggestion that the officer of the watch must have been negligent in not seeing the large sailing ship. If it is accepted that the *Eugène Schneider* was showing her navigation lights, then it was obvious no proper watch was being kept; perhaps more interest was shown in partaking of the Christmas festivities in the saloon.

The French Inspector of Shipping concluded, "The evidence given by Captain Jones in which he alleges that it was his vessel that was struck by the *Eugène Schneider* leads one to think that this experienced mariner ... is gifted with a particularly peculiar mentality. It is in defiance of common sense, showing evident bad faith on his part. One is justified in asking how much importance can be attached to similar affirmations so manifestly contrary to the truth."

To add to this, when news of the disaster was published, a former third officer from the *Burutu* made allegations against Captain Jones that he, Jones, was a "drunken fart," and was known throughout the whole fleet as "Beery Bill." Citing a number of occasions when Captain Jones was drunk and incapable, an investigation was carried out. However, witnesses were reluctant to back up the allegations and no action was taken. The British authorities declined to hold an enquiry into the sinking of the *Eugène Schneider*, adding that "if the French want to hold one that is up to them."

The wreck of the *Eugène Schneider* lies in about 66 metres of water. She is more or less upright but the stern, which stands 8 metres, leans over to starboard. Amidships she is more broken but a distinctive vertical donkey boiler can be seen. The bow section stands 6 metres and lies over to starboard.

Name: *Eugène Schneider*. **Former name(s):** None.
Vessel type: Sailing ship.
Builder: Chnt. Nantain de Constr. Ma. At Nantes.
When completed: 1902.
Machinery built by: –
Tonnage: 2218 tons gross.
Dimensions: Length: 277′ 3″. **Breadth:** 40′ 4″.
Depth of holds: 22′ 7″.
Official number: – **Yard number:** –
Signal letters: OGVH. **Last port of registry:** Nantes.
Ship description: Steel 3 masted sailing barque.
Machinery description: –
Career and ownership: Owned by Société. Générale d' Armament (G Belot, manager).
Destination and cargo: Manoka for Ghent with a cargo of 3000 tons of railway sleepers.
Date sunk: 25 December 1926.
How sunk: Collision with the SS *Burutu*.
Reported position of loss: 30 miles south west of St Catherine's Point and 50° 08′ north, 001° 40′ west.
Actual position of wreck: 50° 06.67′ north, 001° 40.99′ west.
Orientation/height: Stern stands 8 metres and bows stand 6 metres in 66 metres on hard chalk seabed with a covering of shingle. Bows to the south west.
How identity of wreck proved: Not proved, but position of wreck is very close to reported position of loss, and comparison of a donkey boiler on the wreck with a photograph of the ship shows the donkey boiler is similarly placed.

SS *Ioannis Fafalios*
Collision 4 May 1928

SS *Ioannis Fafalios*. Courtesy Adrian Ponchaud.

The steamer *Ioannis Fafalios* began life in 1907 as the *Bitinia*, under Italian owners, being sold in the mid 1920's to Greek owners and renamed. She departed Huelva on 28 April 1928 bound for Dunkirk. On 4 May, she was steaming up Channel fully laden with a cargo of iron ore shipped from the Spanish port. Just before noon she was in a position in mid Channel, groping her way through thick fog. It was, said survivor Dimitrios Fafalios, the second mate, so dense that "we could not see more than a ship's length away. I was on the bridge with the captain. The first I heard was several ships whistling. Our ship was sounding fog signals every half minute." He continued, "We were going slow, about 3 knots. After 5 to 7 minutes I heard a ship signalling on our port bow and we stopped engines. I heard two short blasts and we exchanged blasts. I could not see another ship; their ship kept on the same course."

Asked what happened next, Fafalios said, "In about ½ a minute I heard a short blast again. Then I saw a steamer half to one ship's length to our port. A collision occurred in a few seconds. She struck us a slightly glancing blow. Then the captain ordered the lifeboats. I got a lifebuoy from the bridge and I jumped into the water when I saw the ship was sinking." Asked what speed the other ship was going, Fafalios replied, "As far as I could see I think she was going fast."

The other ship was the Royal Fleet Auxiliary ship *Bacchus,* of comparable size to *Ioannis Fafalios*. *Bacchus* was steaming down Channel making for Gibraltar. Her officer in charge, Captain Banbury said, "We were sounding fog signals. I was on the bridge. When I first heard the whistle we were travelling at half speed, about 5 knots. I altered course to port and gave two short blasts … she was steady on that course when I heard the short blast of the whistle of a vessel on my starboard bow. Just after that a vessel loomed in sight out of the fog, 50 to 100 yards away … about 15° on my starboard bow. I immediately went full speed astern … we came in contact between 3 and 4 hatches. I stopped the engines, steadied my helm – with the idea of remaining alongside to check the inflow of water as much as possible, but she pulled away from me, pulling *Bacchus* round with her as well, and proceeded on and foundered about 150 yards ahead of us." He added, "The other vessel was crossing my bow with excessive speed for a fog."

As the collision occurred, 12 crew of the *Ioannis Fafalios* leaped or were flung by the force of the impact into the sea, where their cries of distress were heard; they were soon rescued by boats from the *Bacchus.* However, some were injured and killed by flying spars, hatch covers and other debris, flung up as the ship sank. Captain Theodorus Tsatsaronis and chief officer Pandalis Indreadis both died in this way. Others could not have escaped from inside the ship in time, sinking as she did in 1 ½ minutes. In all, ten men survived, but 12 were lost.

Meanwhile, *Bacchus* herself was in a sinking condition. Most of her crew left the ship with the survivors from the *Ioannis Fafalios* and taken aboard the steamer *Manchester Commerce*, which stood by while *Bacchus* steamed astern, later reaching Portland safely.

At a Court of Enquiry, the crew of *Ioannis Fafalios* were exonerated; not so Captain Banbury of the *Bacchus.* The judge announced, "I have come to the conclusion that the *Bacchus* alone was responsible for the collision. Her case is a hopelessly bad one. She seems to have broken every rule of navigation I can think of. She was travelling much too fast in a dense fog. She did not stop when whistles were heard ahead. She altered course for vessels whose courses and positions she did not know, and she made no attempt to reduce speed until a very short time indeed before the collision, and then it was too late."

The wreck of the *Ioannis Fafalios* lies in about 62 metres. She is upright and is a substantial wreck, her boilers and engines being the highest parts.

Name: *Ioannis Fafalios.* **Former name(s):** *Bitinia.*
Vessel type: Steam ship.
Builder: John Readhead & Sons, South Shields.
When completed: December 1900.
Machinery built by: John Readhead & Sons, South Shields.
Tonnage: 3125 tons gross.
Dimensions: Length: 323′ 5″. **Breadth:** 47′ 1″. **Depth of holds:** 23′ 7″.
Official number: – **Yard number:** 350.
Signal letters: JBQG. **Last port of registry:** Chios.
Ship description: Steel screw steamer. 1 deck. Fitted with electric light and wireless.
Machinery description: Triple expansion 3 cylinders. 2 single ended boilers.
Career and ownership: As *Bitinia*, owned by Betinia SS Co Ltd (L Kosovic & D Tripcovich). 1924 owned by Soc. Italiana di Nav. "G. Rossi". 1928 owned by S & D Fafalios as *Ioannis Fafalios.*
Destination and cargo: Huelva for Dunkirk with a cargo of iron ore.
Date sunk: 4 May 1928.
How sunk: Collision with the Royal Fleet Auxiliary ship *Bacchus.*
Reported position of loss: 20 miles south of St Alban's Head,
Actual position of wreck: 50° 08.02′ north, 001° 53.74′ west.
Orientation/height: Lies 065°/245°. Stands 8 metres in 62 metres on hard seabed covered with shingle.
How identity of wreck proved: Ship's bell recovered.

SS *Braedale*
Foundered 16 October 1932

SS *Bessie Barr*, later renamed *Braedale*. Courtesy E N Taylor collection.

The *Braedale* was a steam coaster which was bound down Channel for Bristol. Steaming west in the vicinity of the Isle of Wight on the night of 15/16 October 1932, the ship was being buffeted by rough seas and about 11.30pm, it was discovered the ship was leaking. Her master, Captain A W Dennis recalled, "Desperate pumping had little effect on the inrushing water, and though the crew worked like Trojans at the pumps the vessel was in imminent danger of sinking when the crew took to the two lifeboats at 2am."

"About half an hour after we left her she sank, and fearing that the boats would become separated in the darkness all eight men got into one boat and cast the other adrift. Heavy seas were encountered and the boat was soon half full of water. With some bailing while the others took the oars, we managed to keep her afloat, and providentially, the wind fell as daylight came and the seas became quieter."

On the afternoon of 16 October, the ship's boat came ashore through the breakers at Brighstone, Isle of Wight. Helped through the surf and heavy groundswell by coastguards, a local farmer and others, the exhausted crew from the *Braedale* reached safety. Two men were "so exhausted they almost fell back into the breakers, but willing hands seized them and dragged them up the beach."

Second engineer T Pinion said, "The foundering of the *Braedale* was apparently due to a fracture of the stern tube. This allowed water to flood the engine room and caused the engines to stop. Immediately the pumps were manned and it was a strenuous fight in the darkness for several hours in the rising water. We kept the *Braedale* going as long as we could, but when we saw our efforts were of no avail and the ship had developed a decided list we took to the rowing boat and stood by until the vessel sank, stern first."

The wreck of the *Braedale* lies in about 35 metres of water. She lies on her starboard side and her bow section is almost upside down and full of holes. Her single boiler is the highest part.

Name: *Braedale.* **Former name(s):** *Bessie Barr.*
Vessel type: Steam coaster.
Builder: Murdoch & Murray, Port Glasgow.
When completed: October 1894.
Machinery built by: Muir & Houston, Glasgow.
Tonnage: 406 tons gross.
Dimensions: Length: 142′ 2″. **Breadth:** 25′.
Depth of holds: 11′ 1″.
Official number: 104581. **Yard number:** 125.
Signal letters: NPBM. **Last port of registry:** Newcastle.
Ship description: Steel screw steam coaster. 3 masts. 1 deck and well deck.
Machinery description: Triple expansion 3 cylinders. 1 single ended boiler. 60 registered horse power. Machinery fitted aft.
Career and ownership: As *Bessie Barr* owned by R B Ballantyne & Company. 1914 owned by T M Collier. 1915 renamed *Braedale.* 1922 owned by S Thubron. 1932 owned by J Gillespie.
Destination and cargo: Dieppe for Bristol with a cargo of apples.
Date sunk: 16 October 1932.
How sunk: Developed a leak and foundered in heavy weather.
Reported position of loss: 15 miles south west of the Needles.
Actual position of wreck: 50° 33.37′ north, 001° 45.41′ west.
Orientation/height: Lies 130°/310°. Stands 5 metres in 35 metres on shingle seabed. High bank exists close to the east of the wreck.
How identity of wreck proved: Not proved, but a comparison of the wreck with a photograph of the ship shows very similar features. Wreck is of a small coaster, machinery aft, which fits the *Braedale.*

SS *Meandros*
Collision 12 February 1934

SS *Willaston*, later renamed *Meandros*. Courtesy National Maritime Museum, Greenwich.

The *Meandros* was a ship of 4309 tons, and her master, Captain Constantine Chandras said, "We left Madeira on February 3rd, for Amsterdam . . .. Proceeding on our way we encountered fog yesterday afternoon. The ship was rolling heavily and between 3 and 4 o'clock the fog increased in density. It was so thick that we could not even see other men on board standing within a few yards of us. We had to proceed dead slow." He went on, "For the next two hours we received several directional signals, and all of a sudden about 7.30 another ship loomed up on our port side. Without any warning the bows of the other ship struck us opposite the chart room and nearly cut us in half. Immediately the *Meandros* took on a very heavy list. There was a violent inrush of water which flooded our engines. I ordered the men to the starboard side with the hope of launching a lifeboat but the list prevented the men taking to the boat, I immediately ordered them to the port side. I was hauled off just in time."

Meandros had come into collision with the steamer *Dartford*, 4076 tons. Her master, Captain J Day, said, "From 3.40am on Monday until 2.30am today I only left the bridge once, and that was for 5 minutes. Until this morning, in fact, I have not had a wink of sleep since leaving the Tyne. At 7.30pm last night we were stopped in the hope of picking up a signal from St Catherine's Lighthouse. We had been stationary for roughly 10 minutes and had been keeping our siren blowing . . .. Suddenly we saw lights in our direction through the fog and heard a faint whistle. The vessel was the *Meandros* and just as we commenced to go astern the vessel, bound from the River Plate for Amsterdam with grain, dragged across our bow."

The two vessels were soon lost from view in the fog, but, in a dramatic rescue, a crewman from *Meandros* was saved. *Dartford's* fourth officer, Evan Rowlands, without hesitation, jumped overboard with a line and swam to the sound of cries in the water. There he found Theodor Mellis, numb with cold and on the point of drowning, tied the line around him as well as himself and both were hauled aboard the *Dartford.*

About 3.30am, 27 of the crew were rescued by the crew of the coaster *Eleth,* but two men were presumed lost.

It is not known if the wreck of the *Meandros* has been located and identified.

Name: *Meandros.* **Former name(s):** *Willaston.*
Vessel type: Steam ship.
Builder: W Dobson & Company, Newcastle.
When completed: October 1914.
Machinery built by: North East Marine Engineering Company Ltd, Newcastle.
Tonnage: 4309 tons gross.
Dimensions: Length: 400′ 5″. **Breadth:** 52′. **Depth of holds:** 25′ 1″.
Official number: 30879. **Yard number:** –
Signal letters: JHVP. **Last port of registry:** Chios.
Ship description: Steel screw steam ship. 1 deck. Fitted with electric light and wireless.
Machinery description: Triple expansion 3 cylinders. 3 single ended boilers. 427 nominal horse power.
Career and ownership: As *Willaston* owned by Wirral Transport Company Ltd (J Edgar & Company, managers). At the time of loss owned by Livanos Brothers (N G Livanos, manager) as *Meandros.*
Destination and cargo: Rosario, Argentina, for Madeira and Amsterdam with a cargo of linseed.
Date sunk: 12 February 1934.
How sunk: Collision with the SS *Dartford.*
Reported position of loss: About 13½ miles south-south-east of St Catherine's Lighthouse.
Actual position of wreck: Not known.
Orientation/height: –
How identity of wreck proved: –

HMS *Bruce*
Expended as a torpedo target 22 November 1939

HMS *Bruce*. Courtesy National Maritime Museum, Greenwich.

HMS *Bruce* was a Scott class destroyer completed towards the end of the First World War. She was engaged in escorting convoys while based at Harwich but after the war she was attached to various Flotillas through the 1920's and 1930's. In 1937 she was placed in reserve at Chatham before moving to Portsmouth. In 1939 it was decided she would be disposed of.

Later in 1939, *Bruce* was stripped of her armament and stores and on 22 November she was taken to a position off the Isle of Wight to be expended as a target. Aerial tests were conducted and *Bruce* was attacked with an 18″ aerial torpedo fitted with a magnetic pistol. The torpedo struck the ship amidships, sending smoke and debris up her funnels. She buckled and lifted up before sinking.

It is not known if the wreck of HMS *Bruce* has been located and identified.

Name: HMS *Bruce*. **Former name(s):** None.
Vessel type: Destroyer.
Builder: Cammell Laird, Birkenhead.
When completed: May 1918.
Machinery built by: Parsons.
Tonnage: 1530 tons displacement.
Dimensions: Length: 332′ 5″. **Breadth:** 31′ 9″. **Draught:** 12′ 3″.
Official number: – **Yard number:** –
Signal letters: – **Last port of registry:** Portsmouth.
Ship description: Steel twin screw destroyer. Scott class leader, No F48.
Machinery description: All geared steam turbines producing 40000 shaft horse power attaining 36.5 knots on her trials. Yarrow boilers.
Career and ownership: Royal Navy destroyer commissioned for service with 10th Destroyer Flotilla. Then served with 7th Flotilla at Rosyth, the 4th Flotilla (Home Fleet) at Harwich and Portsmouth. Became Flotilla leader for the 9th Flotilla and then 8th Flotilla in late 1923. In 1927 she served on the China station.
Armament: 5 × 4.7″ guns, 1 × 3″ anti-aircraft guns,

2 × 2 pounders. 1 × machine gun and × 4 Lewis guns. 6 × 21″ torpedo tubes in × 2 triple mountings (removed before ship was expended).
Destination and cargo: Paid off from Portsmouth and expended as a target off the Isle of Wight.
Date sunk: 22 November 1939.
How sunk: Aerial torpedo from own forces.
Reported position of loss: Off the Isle of Wight and off the Needles.
Actual position of wreck: Not known.
Orientation/height: –
How identity of wreck proved: –

HMS *Bruce* being expended as a torpedo target. Courtesy National Maritime Museum, Greenwich.

MV *Prinses Juliana*
Mined 12 June 1940

MV *Prinses Juliana*. Courtesy Roel Zwama collection.

Upon the outbreak of the Second World War in September 1939, life seemed to carry on as normal until the small Dutch steamer *Prinses Juliana* was destroyed by a mine. She was the first of some 13 ships which would be lost by enemy action by the end of 1940.

On the night of 8 June 1940, the Luftwaffe laid mines in the approaches to various south coast ports including Poole. The authorities became aware that the Swash Channel just outside the entrance to Poole Harbour had been mined and Navy divers from Portland were called in to deal with them. Whatever their success, some mines remained undetected.

The *Prinses Juliana* departed Poole on 12 June and was on her way through the Swash Channel under the watchful eye of her pilot, George Brown. Suddenly the ship struck an unseen mine, resulting in a huge explosion. The force was so great that the 198 ton ship was blown completely clear of the water, turning over in the process and landing in such a way that witnesses thought there could be no survivors. Fortunately, she did not sink immediately, and there was just time for Ivor Holloway, following behind in a pilot boat, to dive overboard and rescue George Brown and three Dutch crew. Two other crewmen died.

The *Prinses Juliana* settled in the seabed at the side of the Swash Channel on the Hook Sands, and after she had been joined the next day by the *Abel Tasman*, the two wrecks were largely dismantled.

The machinery and parts of the lower hull of the *Prinses Juliana* remain on the Hook Sands next to similar wreckage from the *Abel Tasman*. They are very close together and both can be seen quite easily in a single dive. The diesel engine of the *Prinses Juliana* stands 2 metres or so off the seabed. The wreckage has a thick encrustation of marine organisms. The upper works, after removal, were dumped near Handfast Point in a place known as The Yards.

Name: *Prinses Juliana.* **Former name(s):** None.
Vessel type: Motor coaster.
Builder: J Vos & Zoon, Groningen.
When completed: 1929.
Machinery built by: Appingedammer Brons Motorenfb, Appingedammer.
Tonnage: 198 tons gross.
Dimensions: Length: 106′ 3″. **Breadth:** 20′ 4″. **Depth of holds:** 8.2″.
Official number: – **Yard number:** –
Signal letters: PGVO. **Last port of registry:** Groningen.
Ship description: Steel screw motor coaster. 1 deck.
Machinery description: 4 cycle single acting oil engines, 3 cylinders. Machinery fitted aft.
Career and ownership: Owned in 1939 by P J Balk.
Armament: Unarmed.
Destination and cargo: Poole for Plymouth in ballast.
Date sunk: 12 June 1940.
How sunk: Mined by the Luftwaffe.
Reported position of loss: Swash Channel, near Poole Harbour entrance.
Actual position of wreck: 50° 40.54′ north, 001° 56.09′ west. Area of wreckage, The Yards: 50° 38.58′ north, 001° 55.41′ west.
Orientation/height: Stands 2–3 metres in about 6 metres on a seabed of sand.
How identity of wreck proved: Not proved, but contemporary reports state the *Prinses Juliana* and *Abel Tasman* were lost on the edge of the Swash Channel.

MV *Abel Tasman*
Mined 13 June 1940

MV *Abel Tasman*. Courtesy Noordelijk Scheepvaartmuseum, Groningen.

The day after the *Prinses Juliana* had been destroyed, another Dutch vessel came to grief at about the same spot. This was the 314 ton coaster, *Abel Tasman*. She too was blown up by a German mine, presumed to have been laid by the Luftwaffe. It was a sad end for the ship, as she had been engaged in Operation Dynamo in the rescue of British forces at the evacuation of Dunkirk only six weeks earlier. Despite having endured an air attack which killed two men and injured her commanding officer, *Abel Tasman* boarded 200 troops and 20 French staff officers and brought them safely back to England. The records concerning the loss of *Abel Tasman* do not appear to have survived, and little is known about her. However, witnesses reported that she was heading into Poole along the Swash Channel, one of a line of ships, four of which preceded her. How the other ships avoided disaster is not known exactly, but a mine exploded beneath Abel Tasman with a tremendous roar. The ship disappeared amid a welter of water, sand and spray, taking her entire complement of 11 Naval Reservists with her. The next day, a thorough search was conducted and a third, magnetic mine was located.

The wreck of the *Abel Tasman* lies with that of the *Prinses Juliana*, though it is difficult to determine which is which. The wreckage lies in about 6 metres of water on the edge of the Swash Channel on the Hook Sands. Apart from at least one oil engine, a boiler is also present as well as the wooden ribs of a ship's hull. Like the *Prinses Juliana*, much of the upperworks was removed in 1945 and dumped at The Yards, Handfast Point.

Name: *Abel Tasman*. **Former name(s):** None.
Vessel type: Motor coaster.
Builder: Sanders Brothers, Delfzijl.
When completed: 1937.

Machinery built by: Appingedammer Brons, Motorenfb, Appingedammer.
Tonnage: 314 tons gross.
Dimensions: Length: 126′ 5″. **Breadth:** 24′ 1″. **Depth of holds:** 8′ 4″.
Official number: – **Yard number:** –
Signal letters: PCBO. **Last port of registry:** Groningen.
Ship description: Steel screw motor coaster. 1 deck. Cruiser stern.
Machinery description: 4 cycle single acting oil engine. 220 horse power. Machinery fitted aft.
Career and ownership: Owned by J Bonninga.
Armament: Unarmed.
Destination and cargo: For Poole in ballast.
Date sunk: 13 June 1940.
How sunk: Mined by the Luftwaffe.
Reported position of loss: Swash Channel, Hook Sands, entrance to Poole Harbour.
Actual position of wreck: 50° 40.54′ north, 001° 56.09′ west. Area of wreckage, The Yards: 50° 38.58′ north, 001° 55.41′ west.
Orientation/height: Stands 2–3 metres in 6 metres on sand seabed.
How identity of wreck proved: Not proved but contemporary reports state the *Abel Tasman* was mined on the edge of the Swash Channel.

MV *Caroline Susan*
Presumed mined 13 June 1940

Hardly anything is known about the motor vessel *Caroline Susan*, other than during the late afternoon of 13 June 1940, military observers at the Needles Battery reported seeing a vessel blow up. Later, it was revealed that the vessel was the *Caroline Susan*. It is presumed she blew up on a mine, but this is by no means certain.

It is not known if the wreck of this small vessel has been found and identified. However, a fisherman's net was fouled in the position given below, and pulled up a heavy and substantial piece of ship's hull with frames. It is in the right position to be part of the *Caroline Susan*.

Name: *Caroline Susan*. **Former name(s):** Not known.
Vessel type: Motor yacht.
Builder: Not known.
When completed: Not known.
Machinery built by: Hyland, 1938.
Tonnage: 26 tons gross.
Dimensions: Length: 50′ 8″. **Breadth:** 11′.
Depth of holds: 16′ 1″.
Official number: 166171. **Yard number:** –
Signal letters: – **Last port of registry:** Poole.
Ship description: Wooden twin screw motor yacht.
Machinery description: 2 × 4 cylinder paraffin motors.
Career and ownership: Known to have been owned 1938/39 by Geoffrey McI Thomas, c/o National Bank of India Ltd, 26 Bishopsgate, London, EC2. Believed to have been a former Naval pinnace (no details known) which was converted in Southampton in 1938 to a motor yacht.
Armament: Unarmed.
Destination and cargo: Poole for an unknown destination.
Date sunk: 13 June 1940.
How sunk: Blown up, presumed to have been mined.
Reported position of loss: On the Dolphin Bank.
Actual position of wreck: 50° 40.24′ north, 001° 39.87 west.
Orientation/height: Position is very close to an isolated outcrop of rock in about 24 metres depth.
How identity of wreck proved: Not proved.

Steam trawler *Crestflower*
Bombed 19 July 1940

Steam trawler *Crestflower*.

Courtesy Memory Lane Photo Gallery, Hull.

The *Crestflower* was requisitioned by the Admiralty in August 1939 for use as a minesweeper. Like other vessels lost in 1940, records about her sinking do not appear to have survived. It is known that she was south of St Catherine's Point on 19 July 1940 under the command of Skipper G H Goodison, RNR, when she came under air attack from German warplanes.

Crestflower was struck by at least one bomb which killed two Naval ratings, and the vessel sank. She was accompanied by another trawler, the *Righto*, and an Admiralty comment later said, "Neither ship appears to have taken warning from the first aircraft sighted. If ships had gone to action stations then more rounds of 12 pounder could have been fired."

The wreck of this trawler lies in 38 metres of water. She is more or less upright, though the stern is fairly buried in shingle. The bow section lies on its port side, the bow gun lying on the seabed. Her boiler and engines are the highest parts of the wreck.

Name: *Crestflower*. **Former name(s):** None.
Vessel type: Steam trawler.
Builder: Cochrane & Sons, Selby.
When completed: May 1930.
Machinery built by: Amos & Smith Ltd, Hull.
Tonnage: 367 tons gross.
Dimensions: Length: 150′ 3″. **Breadth:** 24′ 5″.
Depth of holds: 13′ 2″.
Official number: 160894. **Yard number:** –
Signal letters: GJMZ. **Last port of registry:** Hull.

Ship description: Steel screw steam trawler. 1 deck. Fitted with wireless, direction finding equipment and an echo sounding device.
Machinery description: Triple expansion 3 cylinders. 1 single ended boiler. 96 registered horse power.
Career and ownership: Owned by the Yorkshire Steam Fishing Company Ltd (A Turgoose, manager). Requisitioned by the Admiralty in August 1939 for use in minesweeping duties.
Armament: 1 × 12 pounder bow gun.
Destination and cargo: Not known, presumably on Admiralty business.
Date sunk: 19 July 1940.
How sunk: Bombed by German aircraft.
Reported position of loss: 50° 29.6′ north, 001° 17.8′ west.
Actual position of wreck: 50° 27.75′ north, 001° 18.68′ west.
Orientation/height: Stands about 5 metres on hard chalk seabed with a covering of shingle.
How identity of wreck proved: Builder's nameplate recovered.

SS *Terlings*
Bombed 21 July 1940

SS *Terlings* on trials. Courtesy Glasgow University Archives.

The steamer *Terlings* departed Southampton on 4 July 1940 as part of convoy OA178. Reaching the vicinity of Cherbourg, the convoy came under a sustained air attack from German warplanes. Although not directly hit, salvoes of bombs exploded very close to the ship, and, according to her master, Captain Charles Earl, "lifted the ship right out of the water." The chief engineer reported that bearings and castings had been broken and the propeller shaft had been lifted. Following instructions, *Terlings* limped north and anchored off Poole, subsequently steaming to Southampton for repairs.

Repairs were carried out and the ship was returned to service, in time to sail again in the early hours of 21 July. Departing Southampton at 3.30am, she was heading for Sydney via Milford Haven in ballast, in convoy with other ships. About 3.20pm, the convoy reached a position south west of St Catherine's Point, steering a westerly course at about 7 knots. Suddenly, and with hardly any warning, numerous German warplanes appeared and began to bomb the convoy. They had attacked from astern and seem to have taken the convoy by surprise. The aircraft were a Gruppe of Do-17 bombers with fighter escort and dive bombing Me-110's from the Fifth Gruppe, Lehrgeschwader 1.

Interviewed later, survivors reported, "We were attacked by 36 aircraft. Many bombs were dropped all around and we were hit 9 times. There was a burst of machine gun fire from each plane." The report continued, "5 men were killed on the ship, and another 3 died in the water, and 2 were wounded. Our ship sank immediately after the first attack. All the survivors were in the water. We were picked up by destroyers."

Captain Earl, three engineers, the donkeyman, two firemen and two others died in the attack. Eighteen survivors were later landed at Portland including four stretcher cases, three walking wounded and ten uninjured crew.

The wreck of the *Terlings* lies in 40 metres of water, though in the scour amidships 45 metres can be found. From the stern to the boilers, the wreck is upright, the boilers and engines being the highest parts. The gun is still in the stern. The bow section is lying over on its port side and is largely buried in shingle.

Name: *Terlings*. **Former name(s):** None.
Vessel type: Steam ship.
Builder: Lithgows, Glasgow.
When completed: June 1937.
Machinery built by: Rankin & Blackmore Ltd, Greenock.
Tonnage: 2318 tons gross.
Dimensions: Length: 283′ 5″. **Breadth:** 44′ 4″.
Depth of holds: 21′ 6″.
Official number: 165469. **Yard number:** 897.
Signal letters: MMJM. **Last port of registry:** London.
Ship description: Steel screw steamer. 1 deck. Cruiser stern. Fitted with direction finding equipment.
Machinery description: Triple expansion 3 cylinders. 2 single ended boilers fitted with superheaters. 179 nominal horse power.
Career and ownership: Owned by Lambert Brothers Ltd (Ministry of Shipping).
Armament: 1 × 4″ stern gun and 1 × Lewis gun.
Destination and cargo: London via Southampton for Milford Haven and Sydney in ballast.
Date sunk: 21 July 1940.
How sunk: Bombed by German aircraft.
Reported position of loss: 10 miles south west of St Catherine's Point.
Actual position of wreck: 50° 28.26′ north, 001° 33.75′ west.
Orientation/height: Stands about 6 metres in 40–45 metres on shingle seabed.
How identity of wreck proved: Ship's bell recovered.

SS *Ajax*
SS *Coquetdale*
SS *Empire Crusader*
HMS *Borealis*
Bombed 8 August 1940

SS *Elbe*, later renamed *Ajax*, under way. Courtesy National Maritime Museum, Greenwich.

The tale of convoy CW9 is one of seven lost ships, others damaged, and lives lost. It began when the convoy – UK coastal (Channel coast) – departed Southend on 7 August 1940. Among the convoy was the Dutch steamer *Ajax*, the prize ship – formerly German, now British – *Empire Crusader,* and the barrage balloon motor vessel HMS *Borealis. Borealis* led the starboard column, though it is not clear whether she sailed with the convoy from Southend or joined it from Portsmouth.

The first indication of trouble occurred during the darkness of the early hours of 8 August when the convoy was off the Sussex coast. Ambushed by fast, surface raiding German E-boats, the convoy suffered a severe mauling. In the attack, the ships *Holme Force, Fife Coast* and the *Ouse* were sunk. The convoy proceeded on its way, reaching the eastern end of the Isle of Wight by dawn on 8 August. Joining them was the British steamer *Coquetdale*, which had sailed from Southampton to Portsmouth to form up with the convoy and *Ajax,* which had put into St Helens Roads, came out to rejoin the convoy as it approached St Catherine's Point.

The convoy stood out from the Isle of Wight as it steamed west, and headed for Falmouth. About 9am, however, a most alarming sight came into view; numerous enemy aircraft. Waves of aircraft continued to fly over the convoy for the next few hours, and it came in for a terrible beating. At this time, *Ajax* was about 10 miles west of St Catherine's Point, *Coquetdale* about 15 miles south west of St Catherine's Point, *Empire Crusader* about 10 miles south of St Catherine's Point and HMS *Borealis* somewhere nearby off to starboard.

Captain J Lits of *Ajax* said, "We were attacked by enemy aircraft. At the time I was endeavouring to raise the kite a little, as I thought it was rather too low, when the chief officer, who was on the bridge, cried out that 50 enemy planes were making towards us. I immediately ran to the bridge. I could not actually see the planes which attacked us due to the bridge protection, but I understand that 3 enemy aircraft appeared on our port beam, two bombers and one fighter; they flew

SS *Elbe*, later renamed *Ajax*, under way. Courtesy Prof Theodor Siersdorfer, Essen.

athwartships and the bomber dropped a salvo of 3 high explosive bombs. I saw the first bomb fall on the foredeck in the fo'castle, the other two fell almost instantly on number 2 hatch, also forward." Captain Lits added, "The ship shuddered violently and listed about 25° to port – I think the whole of the port side forward was blown out." Concluding, Captain Lits said, "We lowered the port boat after we had been hit … we pulled away and the ship sank within 5 minutes of being struck." Four men died in the attack.

On board *Coquetdale*, her master, Captain William Harvey said, "Nothing untoward happened until 9.10am at which time I was on the bridge which is amidships. We were … travelling at about 8 knots, visibility was good and the sea fine with west-north-west wind. I had just given instructions to the engine room and as I glanced up I caught sight of a number of planes very high up on my starboard bow approaching from the west-north-west." He went on, "The planes swooped down on us, almost vertically, and all three gunners opened fire immediately but I do not think they registered any hits. The bombs, some of which made a whistling sound, were numerous, started dropping all round us, and many of them struck the ship. Not knowing what damage had been caused we stopped the ship. There was a few seconds lull in the bombing and we saw the *Ajax* sinking very quickly. I started the engines up again and put her hard to starboard … but before we could get her round there was another attack, and the planes circled all around us. Bombs were still dropping and some of the splashes rose to a height of 50–60 feet. The water was very black. Some of the bombs hit us right amidships about 170 feet back from the bow and the whole of the port side was blown out. Three of the bombs dropped aft and blew the gun to smithereens."

Soon after this attack, *Coquetdale* was abandoned, and the ship went down.

The *Empire Crusader* was next to go. Ironically, she was a German ship which had been captured by HMS *Isis* off the coast of Spain in 1939, taken as a prize and renamed *Empire Crusader*. Her chief engineer on 8 August was J Cowper, who gave an account of what happened to the ship. He said, "We proceeded until 9.15am when in position about 10 miles south of St Catherine's; there was a heavy explosion on our star-

SS *Coquetdale*. Author's collection.

Ice covered SS *Leander*, later renamed *Empire Crusader*. Courtesy Prof Theodor Siersdorfer, Essen.

board bow approximately 3 miles away. I could see bombs falling but the attack was too far away to see what was really happening." Continuing, he said, "At 12.15 we were ordered to action stations again. I was having lunch in the saloon at the time with the second mate and a Naval rating when there was a terrific explosion forward as a bomb struck the foredeck ... just as I got to the engine room there was another violent explosion, approximately 2 or 3 feet from the ship on the port side, which lifted the ship in the air. A huge column of black water was thrown up about 60 feet into the air and completely deluged the ship."

Describing the damage, Mr Cowper added, "The engine room skylights were broken and the steam pipes burst. The whistle pipe was broken and there was general pandemonium. Bombs were falling astern of us in all directions ... the mainmast had gone, the paravanes had gone, the hatches had been stripped off and there was a crater amongst the coal which was on fire. The front of the bridge had been blown in." Amid all this destruction, men were being machine gunned by their attackers as the crew began to abandon ship. Mr Cowper said, "I went to the chart room but I could not see anybody there. The whole front of the chart room had caved in and there were papers, books and drawers all lying in a heap. As I came out of the chart room I saw two Naval ratings; one of them was dead and the other was so seriously injured that I knew I could do nothing for him."

In the meantime the fire was travelling to the front of the ship. The bridge had caught fire and the ship seemed to be going down by the head. The ship was finally abandoned and five men were left dead. Later *Empire Crusader* capsized and was completely abandoned, still burning. She was not seen to sink but a search the next day failed to find her.

HMS *Borealis*, the last vessel to sink, was a barrage balloon vessel. As she steamed past St Catherine's Point about 12.20pm, her balloon was flying at about 3250 feet, but it did not deter the attack. The balloon was immediately shot down, bursting into flames, and a bomber closed on *Borealis*, dropping a bomb which scored a direct hit on the ship. It first struck the fore mast, bringing it down over the starboard side of the bridge before being deflected to the deck which it pierced halfway between the bridge and the stem, burst below the deck and blew a hole in the starboard bow on the water line. The sea entered and flooded the forward compartment. Lieutenant Hague, RNR, said, "The explosion wrecked the bridge entirely, destroyed the gun positions which were on top of the wheelhouse and demolished the upper steering position. No trace could be found of the chart table, chart and convoy orders. The concrete protection around the wheelhouse was demolished." He continued, "I stopped the engine and the vessel fell out of line as the bridge steering gear was no longer effective."

Soon after, attempts were made to tow the vessel to safety, but about 5pm another attack took place, and, with the ship unmanageable and undefended, her crew left in one of the boats. After the final wave of bombers had been driven off, *Borealis* was boarded again, but it was found she had taken further hits and was listing heavily to port and was abandoned. Twenty minutes later, she listed more heavily to port and went down by the bows.

The RAF did everything possible to defend the convoy, and on that day of 8 August 1940, not less than ten Hurricane fighters were shot down, while the RAF accounted for eight Junkers Ju97's, ten Messerschmitt's and one Heinkel He59.

The wrecks of all four ships sunk on 8 August 1940 have been located and identified.

The *Ajax* lies in 40 metres of water. Her bow section lies over to port, as do her boilers, the port boiler being almost buried in gravel. The engine stands clear and is the highest part of the wreck.

Name: *Ajax*. **Former name(s):** *Ceuta* ex *Elbe*.
Vessel type: Steam ship.
Builder: Hamburger Elbe Schiffswerke, Hamburg.
When completed: 1923.
Machinery built by: Gutte Hoffnungshütte, Oberhausen.
Tonnage: 942 tons gross.
Dimensions: Length: 221′ 1″. **Breadth:** 34′ 5″.
Depth of holds: 13′ 4″.
Official number: – **Yard number:** –
Signal letters: PCFQ. **Last port of registry:** Amsterdam.
Ship description: Steel screw steamer. Well deck.
Machinery description: Triple expansion 3 cylinders. 2 single ended boilers. 126 nominal horse power.
Career and ownership: Built as *Elbe* for Rederei A Kirksten, Germany. 1925 sold to Reed, Rochling, Menzell & Company, Germany. 1927 sold to Oldenburg

Portugesische, Dampfsh, Rhed, Germany and renamed *Ceuta*. Sold 1927 to Koninklijke Nederkandsche Stoomboot Maatschappij and renamed *Ajax*.
Armament: Armed, probably with a Lewis gun mounted on the bridge.
Destination and cargo: Left Southampton for Portsmouth to join convoy CW9 for Falmouth, in ballast.
Date sunk: 8 August 1940.
How sunk: Bombed by the Luftwaffe.
Reported position of loss: 10 miles west of St Catherine's Point.
Actual position of wreck: 50° 30.54′ north, 001° 32.64′ west.
Orientation/height: Lies 020°/200°. Stands about 6 metres in 40 metres on gravel seabed.
How identity of wreck proved: Ship's bell recovered.

The wreck believed to be the *Coquetdale* lies in 40 metres of water. The wreck leans half over to port and has collapsed in that direction. Her hull plating amidships, starboard side, has blown outwards, consistent with internal explosions from exploding bombs. Her boilers are the highest part of the wreck.

Name: *Coquetdale*. **Former name(s):** None.
Vessel type: Steam ship.
Builder: J Priestman & Company, Sunderland.
When completed: July 1923.
Machinery built by: G Clark Ltd, Sunderland.
Tonnage: 1597 tons gross.
Dimensions: Length: 245′. **Breadth:** 37′.
Depth of holds: 18′ 3″.
Official number: 146925. **Yard number:** 285.
Signal letters: MLPG. **Last port of registry:** Sunderland.
Ship description: Steel screw steamer, designed for the coal and timber trade, with self trimming cargo holds.
Machinery description: Triple expansion 3 cylinders. 2 single ended boilers. 186 nominal horse power.
Career and ownership: Built for and owned by Enfield Steamships Company Ltd (S Marshall & Company, managers).
Armament: 4 × Lewis guns and 1 × rifle.
Destination and cargo: Portsmouth for the Clyde via Falmouth in ballast.
Date sunk: 8 August 1940.
How sunk: Bombed by the Luftwaffe.

Belgian pilot boat *Pilote No 15*, later renamed HMS *Borealis*. Courtesy Captain J F van Puyveld, Brussels.

Reported position of loss: 15 miles south west of St Catherine's.
Actual position of wreck: 50° 25.56′ north, 001° 42.17′ west.
Orientation/height: Stands about 6 metres in 40 metres on gravel seabed.
How identity of wreck proved: Not proved but wreck is within 2 miles of reported position of loss. In addition, damage to the hull is consistent with bomb damage as her plating has been blown outwards. This fits with the survivor's description of bombs landing in the ship.

The wreck of the *Empire Crusader* lies in 40 metres of water. It lies on its port side. The engines are covered with hull plating but the boilers stand up one on end and are the highest parts of the wreck. The gun lies partly buried at the stern. The propeller has been salvaged.

Name: *Empire Crusader.* **Former name(s):** *Leander.*
Vessel type: Steam ship.
Builder: Atlas Werke A G Bremen.
When completed: 1925.
Machinery built by: Atlas Werke A G Bremen.
Tonnage: 1042 tons gross.
Dimensions: Length: 225′. **Breadth:** 33′ 3″.
Depth of holds: 13′ 7″.
Official number: 167405. **Yard number:** –
Signal letters: DOGQ. **Last port of registry:** London.
Ship description: Steel screw steamer. 1 deck. Equipped with submarine signalling apparatus and electric light.
Machinery description: Triple expansion 3 cylinders. 2 single ended boilers. 127 nominal horse power.
Career and ownership: Built as *Leander* for Dampfschiffahrts Ges Neptun, Germany. November 1939 captured as a prize by HMS *Isis* off Vigo, Spain. Allocated to the Ministry of War Transport (Joseph Constantine Steam Ship Line Ltd, managers) and renamed *Empire Crusader.*
Armament: 1 × 12 pounder stern gun, 4 × Lewis guns.
Destination and cargo: Seaham for Devonport with a cargo of 1020 tons of coal.
Date sunk: 8 August 1940.
How sunk: Bombed by the Luftwaffe.
Reported position of loss: 10 miles south of St Catherine's Point when abandoned.
Actual position of wreck: 50° 27.03′ north, 001° 27.10′ west.
Orientation/height: Lies 090°/270°. Stands 6 metres in 40 metres on hard chalk seabed with a covering of gravel.
How identity of wreck proved: Bridge steering pedestal recovered manufactured by the shipbuilder.

The wreck of HMS *Borealis* lies in 40 metres of water. She lies half over on her starboard side. Her amidships area containing her diesel engine is the highest part. The propeller has been salvaged.

Name: HMS *Borealis.* **Former name(s):** *Pilote No 15.*
Vessel type: Motor ship.
Builder: Not known, but in Emden, Germany.
When completed: 1930.
Machinery built by: Not known.
Tonnage: 451 tons gross.
Dimensions: Length: – **Breadth:** –
Depth of holds: –
Official number: – **Yard number:** –
Signal letters: OTEB. **Last port of registry:** Ostend.
Ship description: Steel screw motor ship, former Belgian pilot boat.
Machinery description: Diesel engine.
Career and ownership: Owned by the Belgian Marine Administration. Hired by the Admiralty in June 1940 for service as a barrage balloon vessel and based at Portsmouth. Renamed *Borealis.*
Armament: 2 × Hotchkiss anti-aircraft guns.
Destination and cargo: Escorting convoy and towing barrage balloon, Southend for Falmouth.
Date sunk: 8 August 1940.
How sunk: Bombed by the Luftwaffe.
Reported position of loss: 4½ miles 173° from St Catherine's Lighthouse.
Actual position of wreck: 50° 29.07′ north, 001° 18.97′ west.
Orientation/height: Stands about 5 metres in 40 metres on hard chalk seabed covered with shingle.
How identity of wreck proved: Process of elimination and wreck is within one mile of reported position of loss. Comparison of the wreck with a photograph of the ship as a pilot boat shows a close likeness.

HMS *Warwick Deeping*
Shelled 11 October, sunk 12 October 1940
HMS *Listrac*
Shelled 11 October 1940

Steam trawler *Warwick Deeping*. Courtesy Hull Daily Mail Publications Ltd.

The *Listrac* and the *Warwick Deeping* were commissioned into the Royal Navy for use as anti-submarine and anti-invasion vessels. They were not purpose built but adapted for their new roles, *Warwick Deeping* from 1939 and *Listrac* after she was seized at Portsmouth in July 1940.

The two ships left in company on the night of Friday 11 October 1940 and proceeded to carry out an anti-invasion patrol to the south of the Isle of Wight. About 11.35pm, *Listrac* was 10 miles south of St Catherine's Point, and *Warwick Deeping* a few hundred yards off her starboard quarter. The conditions were good with a calm sea and bright moon. At this time the lookout on *Warwick Deeping* sighted some ships off the port quarter, reporting what he had seen at once to the officer of the watch. Simultaneously, gun flashes were seen and gunfire heard on the port side and splashes of shells appeared around the ships.

At first, it was thought the ships might have been our own destroyers, and Lieutenant Kirkup, RNR, officer commanding *Listrac*, called all his men to action stations, ordered her recognition signal be lit but that fire

HM steam trawler *Warwick Deeping.* Courtesy of Alec Gill & Jim Fuller.

SS *Listrac.* Courtesy Captain J F van Puyveld, Brussels.

was not to be opened. *Warwick Deeping* was also being shelled by the mystery ships and she was compelled to zig-zag and alter course. No order for action stations had been given but the crew were alerted by the gunfire and rushed on deck.

The attacking ships were German torpedo boats, and they had crept up to the coast of the Isle of Wight in search of targets. They were later identified as the *Falke, Wolf, Greif, Kondor* and *Seeadler*, part of the 5th Torpedo-Boote Flotilla. They pressed home their attack and continuously shelled the two British ships. *Listrac* was hit in the boiler room and the force of the explosion seemed to have broken her back. One of the mess rooms was next to the boiler room and it was assumed the damage caused was responsible for the deaths of most of the senior ratings. *Listrac* was hit again and she began to fill with water.

On *Warwick Deeping* things were better, but not by much. She had been struck by two shells, one of which disabled the bow gun, while the other holed the ship below the water line. There was so much gunfire that skipper John Bruce, RNR, captain of *Warwick Deeping*, thought our own destroyers had engaged the enemy, and he gave orders to retire to the northward. It became clear, however, that *Warwick Deeping* was in a bad way. She was down by the head and commencing to list heavily to port. Skipper Bruce thought there might be a chance she could be beached but within 20 minutes of the attack, however, she was labouring and her engines were running hot. The decision was taken to abandon her, and all her crew escaped in the ship's boats. There were no casualties. Later, unseen, *Warwick Deeping* slipped beneath the waves.

On the *Listrac,* the enemy continued to pour gunfire into her, shelling her until she sank. A torpedo had been fired at her but missed. Lieutenant Kirkup ordered the vessel to be abandoned, taking to some rafts since one of the ship's boats was smashed and the other could not be lowered in time. Eleven men died in the attack, five in the action and six later from their wounds.

The Admiralty held an enquiry into the loss of these two ships, as well as into the losses of two Free French submarine chasers, *CH6* and *CH7,* which also fell victim to the German destroyers after *Listrac* and *Warwick Deeping* had been sunk. Although it was concluded that the vessels had been taken by surprise, it was acknowledged that *Listrac* and *Warwick Deeping* were endangered through the failure of the Admiralty to install proper alarm systems in the ships, through which the gun's crews could have been called quickly to action stations. In addition, due to the demands placed on these vessels since they had been commissioned, they had received inadequate training in gunnery and "This outer patrol was instituted as a warning patrol; the vessels used were never thought capable of giving battle to destroyers or torpedo boats, and E-boat attack would be a high test for such inexperienced crews." The report went on, "to take minesweeping and anti-submarine vessels off their normal duties and expect them to become efficient as fighting units was asking for the impossible."

The wreck of the *Warwick Deeping* lies completely upright and remarkably intact in 36 metres of water. Some depth charges lie off the stern on the seabed. She makes an excellent dive.

Name: *Warwick Deeping.* **Former name(s):** None.
Vessel type: Steam trawler.
Builder: Cochrane & Sons Ltd, Selby.
When completed: December 1934.
Machinery built by: C D Holmes Company Ltd, Hull.
Tonnage: 445 tons gross.
Dimensions: Length: 155′ 8″. **Breadth:** 26′ 1″. **Depth of holds:** 14′ 1″.
Official number: 163958. **Yard number:** 1130.
Signal letters: GWWR. **Last port of registry:** Hull.
Ship description: Steel screw steam trawler. Cruiser stern.
Machinery description: Triple expansion 3 cylinders. 1 single ended boiler. 111 nominal horse power.
Career and ownership: Owned by Newington Steam Trawling Company Ltd. Purchased by the Admiralty in August 1939 for use as an anti-submarine vessel.
Armament: 1 × 4″ fo'c'sle gun, 1 × .5″ twin barrelled machine gun fitted on the wheelhouse roof (recovered in recent years).
Destination and cargo: Portsmouth for anti-submarine patrol off the Isle of Wight and return.
Date sunk: 12 October 1940.
How sunk: Shelled by German destroyers *Falke, Wolf, Greif, Kondor* and *Seeadler.*
Reported position of loss: Not seen to sink.
Actual position of wreck: 50° 34.25′ north, 001° 27. 82′ west.
Orientation/height: Lies 150°/330°. Stands 6 metres in 36 metres on shingle seabed.

How identity of wreck proved: Ship's bell and builder's nameplate recovered.

The wreck of the *Listrac* lies in about 38 metres of water. She has settled over to starboard and is breaking up. The engines are broken, but the large single boiler is in place and this is the highest part of the wreck. One of the guns is on the seabed next to the port side of the wreck and two smaller guns are in the wreck near the fo'c'sle.

Name: *Listrac.* **Former name(s):** None.
Vessel type: Steam coaster.
Builder: Forges & C de la Mediterrane, Havre.
When completed: 1907.
Machinery built by: Forges & C de la Mediterrane, Havre.
Tonnage: 778 tons gross.
Dimensions: Length: 196′. **Breadth:** 27′ 8″.
Depth of holds: 14′ 6″.
Official number: – **Yard number:** –
Signal letters: JWQS. **Last port of registry:** Le Havre.
Ship description: Steel screw steam coaster. 3 masts.
Machinery description: Triple expansion 3 cylinders. 1 single ended boiler. 72 nominal horse power. Machinery fitted aft.
Career and ownership: Owned by Worms & Cie. 1917 detained in Hamburg. Taken into Admiralty service in July 1940 and used as an anti-submarine vessel from August 1940.
Armament: 2 × 37mm guns on the fo'c'sle, 2 × 100mm guns in the waist of the ship and 2 × Hotchkiss anti-aircraft guns.
Destination and cargo: Portsmouth for anti-submarine patrol off the Isle of Wight and return.
Date sunk: 11 October 1940.
How sunk: Shelled by German destroyers *Falke, Wolf, Greif, Kondor* and *Seeadler.*
Reported position of loss: 10 miles south of St Catherine's Point.
Actual position of wreck: 50° 25.92′ north, 001° 19.77′ west.
Orientation/height: Stands about 6 metres in 38 metres on hard chalk seabed covered in shingle.
How identity of wreck proved: Number and location of guns and location and description of wreck exactly fits the *Listrac.*

HM Submarine *Swordfish* Mined 7 November 1940

HM Submarine *Swordfish*. Courtesy Wright & Logan collection, Royal Naval Museum.

The British submarine *Swordfish* was completed in November 1932. After successful trials she was based with the 5th Submarine Flotilla at Portsmouth. She later transferred to the 2nd Flotilla and at the outbreak of the Second World War, she saw active service in the North Sea and off the Norwegian coast. In the process, she was bombed by mistake by our own aircraft and had three torpedoes fired at her by HM Submarine *Sturgeon*. As the autumn of 1940 approached, *Swordfish* returned to home waters and was in action off Cherbourg where she attacked a convoy of eight ships – some camouflaged – claiming a hit on one of these at a range of 8800 yards.

On 7 November 1940 *Swordfish* sailed from Portsmouth under the command of Lieutenant Michael Langley for an operational patrol off Brest and to relieve HM Submarine *Usk*. Nothing more was heard from her and the Admiralty sent a signal ordering her to leave her patrol area on 14 November. Neither the boat nor her complement of 39 were seen again, and it was assumed she must have been lost in her patrol area, possibly off Ushant.

In the 1980's a previously unknown wreck was located south of St Catherine's Point and when dived upon it was found to be a submarine. Some brass letters had fallen from the rotted wooden mounting board on the side of the conning tower, and from these it was determined that the submarine must be the *Swordfish*. Comparison of the wreck with photographs of *Swordfish* helped to confirm the wreck was her. It is likely she struck a mine laid by the Luftwaffe or surface craft – the 10th Fliegerkorps made hundreds of minelaying operations in the Channel in 1940 and 1941.

The wreck is broken in two just forward of the conning tower, and one of the escape hatches is open. The damage to the boat is consistent with her having struck a mine. She lies in about 36 metres of water in an area of rough ground. It is not clear who laid the mine or when it was laid.

Name: *Swordfish*. **Former name(s):** None.
Vessel type: Submarine.
Builder: Chatham Dockyard.
When completed: November 1932.
Machinery built by: Chatham Dockyard.
Tonnage: 737 tons displacement surfaced, 927 tons displacement submerged.
Dimensions: Length: 202′ 6″. **Breadth:** 24′. **Draught:** 10′ 6″
Official number: – **Yard number:** –
Signal letters: – **Last port of registry:** Based in Portsmouth.
Ship description: Steel twin screw "S" class submarine.
Machinery description: 2 × 1550 horse power diesel engines and 2 × 1300 horse power electric motors.
Career and ownership: Vessel authorised in the programme for 1929. Launched 10 November 1931. Attached to the 5th Submarine Flotilla at Portsmouth and then, after a tour of duty in Gibraltar she transferred to Devonport in the 2nd Flotilla. In the autumn of 1940 she returned to Portsmouth with the 5th Flotilla. Awarded the battle honour "English Channel 1940".
Armament: 1 × 3″ gun, 1 × .303 Lewis gun, 5 × rifles and 6 × bow torpedo tubes for 12 torpedoes.
Destination and cargo: Portsmouth for Brest on war patrol and return.
Date sunk: Presumed 7 November 1940.
How sunk: Presumed struck a mine.
Reported position of loss: Not reported.
Actual position of wreck: Not disclosed to prevent further unauthorised interference with the wreck.
Orientation/height: Stands about 6 metres in 36 metres on hard ground.
How identity of wreck proved: Boat's name in brass letters from side of conning tower.

HMS *Acheron*
Mined 17 December 1940

HMS *Acheron*. Courtesy Wright & Logan collection, Royal Naval Museum.

HMS *Acheron* was an Acasta class destroyer, built by Thornycroft's at Woolston in 1931. Upon completion she was attached to the Home Fleet but in 1932 served on the Mediterranean station. After four years she returned to Portsmouth where she was held in reserve. At the outbreak of the Second World War she was back in service based in Portsmouth, but on 24 August the Luftwaffe conducted an air raid over the city in broad daylight. In the attack, *Acheron,* tied up alongside HMS *Bulldog*, was severely damaged when a bomb exploded on her quarter deck, killing several men. The bombing put her out of action; some of her guns were damaged, and her main structure was demolished to the level of the lower deck.

Working all night, her crew emptied the ship of all ammunition; she was feared to be in a sinking condition and it was expected she would have to be dry-docked. When the unloading was complete, *Acheron* underwent extensive repairs in Portsmouth Dockyard which carried on until mid December. She had been virtually rebuilt aft; so extensive had been the damage. Upon completion of repairs, it was necessary for the ship to undergo trials to ensure she was fit to be classed as a fighting ship. Accordingly, she was made ready and, with a full complement of 190 men and 25 dockyard workers, she put to sea intending to put herself to the test off St Catherine's Point.

About 6.40am on 17 December 1940, *Acheron* was steaming between the Needles and St Catherine's Point having successfully conducted the first run. The morning was bitterly cold with a strong wind from the north east. According to one of the few survivors, *Acheron* was about to turn to make another run, this time to the east, when, "I heard a muffled roar and a sudden unfamiliar hiss. The blackness of the night was transformed by a brilliant light. I was horrified to see the ship on fire;

great flames were leaping skyward completely enveloping the bridge." He continued, "The deck was now tilting alarmingly and the ship was completely submerged forward of the 3″ gun deck, so it was an easy thing to slide down the sloping deck . . .. Looking over my shoulder some 200 yards behind me I saw the gaunt stern poised vertically above the sea and then accompanied with a tremendous gurgle it slid into the dark waters."

After the sinking, the survivors were able to save themselves by clinging on some overcrowded rafts; there had been no opportunity to lower any boats. Some could not survive the intensity of the cold, and overcome with exhaustion, slipped away and were lost. In the morning, an escort vessel came on the scene and 19 men from a total of 215 were rescued.

It is presumed *Acheron* fell victim to a mine. Her sinking was not claimed by a U-boat. It is highly likely that *Acheron* struck a mine laid by the Luftwaffe, since the 10th Fliegerkorps carried out hundreds of minelaying operations in the Channel during 1940 and 1941.

The wreck of the *Acheron* lies in two separate pieces. The bow section is completely vertical, the stem pointing to the surface, while the stern section is upright but largely buried in the shifting sand and gravel. Depths are about 40 metres.

Name: HMS *Acheron*. **Former name(s):** None.
Vessel type: British destroyer.
Builder: Messrs J Thorneycroft and Company Ltd, Woolston.
When completed: October 1931.
Machinery built by: Parsons Marine Steam Turbine Company.
Tonnage: 1350 tons displacement.
Dimensions: Length: 323′. **Breadth:** 32′ 3″. **Draught:** 8′ 5″.
Official number: – **Yard number:** –
Signal letters: – **Last port of registry:** Based in Portsmouth.
Ship description: Steel twin screw Acasta class destroyer.
Machinery description: Steam turbines geared onto 2 shafts giving 34000 shaft horse power. 3 drum boilers "Thorneycroft specials." 35 knots recorded on trials.
Career and ownership: Royal Navy destroyer based with the Home Fleet to 1932. Then served with the Mediterranean Fleet until 1936, when she was returned to Portsmouth and placed in reserve. Recommissioned 1937 for service with HMS *Vernon* (Torpedo School). 1939 to the time of loss based in Portsmouth.
Armament: 4 × 4.7″ guns, 2 × 2 pounder anti-aircraft guns and 8 × 21″ torpedo tubes.
Destination and cargo: Portsmouth for south of the Isle of Wight for high speed trials and return.
Date sunk: 17 December 1940.
How sunk: Presumed to have struck a mine.
Reported position of loss: 50° 31′ north, 001° 31′ west.
Actual position of wreck: Not disclosed.
Orientation/height: Bow stands 8 metres in 40 metres, stern stands 3 metres in 40 metres on sand seabed.
How identity of wreck proved: Ship's hooter marked *Acheron* recovered.

HMS *Sona*
Bombed 4 June 1942

Sona as a private yacht. Author's collection.

HMS *Sona* began life in 1922 as a private motor yacht. She had several owners including the Earl of Dunraven, Sir William Berry and Baron Camrose, but in 1939 she was taken into Admiralty service initially as an anti-submarine vessel, but latterly as an accommodation ship.

On the night of 3/4 June 1942, *Sona* was tied up alongside Poole Quay when an air raid was mounted by the Luftwaffe. About 90 German bombers flew over the town and it was estimated 77 bombed their respective targets. When the raid was over, *Sona,* which had been hit and suffered very extensive damage, sank at her mooring, resting on the soft mud of the harbour bottom.

The wreck was obstructing the quay and she was later raised by salvage vessels and taken out to Handfast Point, where her remains were dumped in the same area as those of the *Prinses Juliana* and *Abel Tasman.*

The general area where wreckage was dumped is known as The Yards. It is shallow, not more than 4 or 5 metres deep, and any remaining wreckage is likely to be heavily encrusted with marine growth.

Name: HMS *Sona.* **Former name(s):** *Sona.*
Vessel type: Motor yacht.
Builder: Camper & Nicholson Ltd, Southampton.
When completed: July 1922.
Machinery built by: Vickers-Petters Ltd, Ipswich.
Tonnage: 555 tons gross.
Dimensions: Length: 169′ 8″. **Breadth:** 27′.
Draught: 11′ 8″.
Official number: 145389. **Yard number:** –
Signal letters: KMPH. **Last port of registry:** Southampton.
Ship description: Steel twin screw motor yacht. Schooner rigged.
Machinery description: 2 oil engines, 2 stroke cycle single acting.
Career and ownership: Built for the Earl of Dunraven. Owned 1927 by Sir William Berry, baronet. 1930 owned by Baron Camrose, Long Cross, Surrey. Taken into Admiralty service in September 1939 as an

Plan of *Sona*.

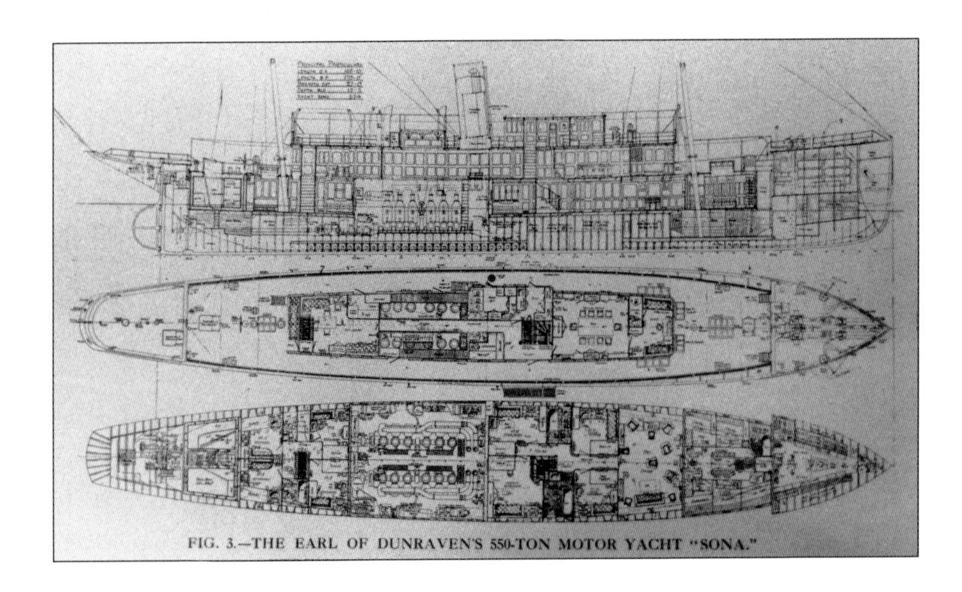

Author's collection.

anti-submarine yacht. From September 1940 she was used as an accommodation ship.
Armament: Not known.
Destination and cargo: None.
Date sunk: 3/4 June 1942.
How sunk: Bombed by the Luftwaffe.
Reported position of loss: Poole Quay, but later raised and dumped at Handfast Point in position (corrected) 50° 38.61′ north, 001° 55.63′ west.
Actual position of wreck: Close position 50° 38.58′ north, 001° 55.41′ west.
Orientation/height: Nothing much stands more than 1 metre in 4–5 metres on sand seabed.
How identity of wreck proved: Not proved.

HMS *Sona*, bombed alongside Poole Quay.

Courtesy The Ian Andrews Collection.

MV *Leny*
Mined 23 June 1942

MV *Leny*.

Courtesy Roal Zwama collection.

The *Leny* was another Dutch coaster which came to an untimely end near Poole, in 1942. She had been part of convoy WP175 – Bristol Channel for Portsmouth – and one of her two survivors, able seaman W H Hopkins said, "We sailed from Swansea at 10am on the 21st June proceeding to an anchorage where we joined convoy WP175. We continued without incident on our voyage to Poole until about noon on the 23rd when we left the convoy and proceeded independently to go into Poole Harbour, with a small Belgian vessel from the convoy, the SS *Marcel*, following us about a mile astern."

"The weather was fine with good visibility, calm sea and light airs; we reduced speed to slow as we were a little too early and had to wait for the tide, then increased to 6 knots, steering approximately 280°. At 1239pm … when in position 114° from Poole Bar Buoy 2 miles, there was a violent explosion right aft which must have blown off the entire stern of the vessel. I was kneeling on the deck abreast the mast at the time and was flung back against the bulwarks as the ship heeled over on her port side. I looked aft and almost immediately the after part of the ship was under water as far as amidships; the fore side of the bridge was left standing but I think the after part was blown away."

"The vessel turned on her side with the bows out of the water. A terrific column of water was thrown up by the explosion, which descended on top of me, the vessel hung for a second or two, then sank within 2 minutes in 9 fathoms, with the balloon still flying above the water. When I came to the surface I saw another man in the water not far away, who shouted to me to hold on to an object something like a lifebuoy which was floating near me. I did not like the look of this object, which I thought might be part of a mine, and later the Poole Naval Authorities informed me they thought it was a buoyancy chamber from an acoustic mine. There was plenty of wreckage nearby so I hung on to a piece of wood and after a few minutes a local fishing vessel, which had witnessed the explosion, came along and took both of us on board. We were the only survivors from the crew, who were all aft at the time and must have been blown to pieces." Eight men from the crew of ten died when *Leny* sank.

The mine which sank the *Leny* was almost certainly dropped by a German aircraft.

The wreck which is probably that of the *Leny* lies in 16 metres of water close to the wreck of the *Ferncliff*. Nothing much stands more than 1 or 2 metres, with most of the wreck buried in mud.

Name: *Leny*. **Former name(s):** None.
Vessel type: Motor coaster.
Builder: Gebr. van Diepen Brothers, Waterhuizen.
When completed: 1937.
Machinery built by: Humboldt Deutzmotoren, A G Köln-Deutz.
Tonnage: 343 tons gross.
Dimensions: Length: 136′ 3″. **Breadth:** 24′ 6″. **Depth of holds:** 9′ 7″.
Official number: – **Yard number:** –
Signal letters: PFOK. **Last port of registry:** Kampen.
Ship description: Steel screw motor coaster. 1 deck. Cruiser stern.
Machinery description: Oil engine, 4 stroke cycle single acting, 6 cylinders. 300 horse power. Machinery fitted aft.
Career and ownership: Owned by G de Groot.
Armament: 1 × Twin Marlin, 1 × Lewis gun, 2 × Savage Lewis guns and 2 × PAC rockets.
Destination and cargo: Swansea for Poole with a cargo of 440 tons of coal.
Date sunk: 23 June 1942.
How sunk: Struck a mine.
Reported position of loss: 114° from Poole Bar buoy, 2 miles.
Actual position of wreck: 50° 38.84′ north, 001° 53.04′ west.
Orientation/height: Stands 1–2 metres in 16 metres on mud seabed.
How identity of wreck proved: Not proved but position of wreck fits the *Leny*. Ammunition of .303 calibre recovered from the site is dated 1940.

HMS *Sargasso*
Mined 6 June 1943

HMS *Sargasso*.

Wright & Logan collection, Royal Naval Museum.

HMS *Sargasso* was another motor yacht requisitioned for Admiralty service in 1939 and she was used as a Dan layer, attached to the 9th Minesweeping Flotilla. In that capacity she was on operational duties south west of the Needles on the afternoon of 6 June 1943. The day before, the area had been swept for mines and three had been located and detonated in the sweeps. It is likely the mines were laid by torpedo boats of the 5th TB Flotilla comprising *T-22*, *Mowe*, *Falke*, *Greif* and *Kondor*.

Sargasso was under the command of Lieutenant Francis Knight, RNVR, who told what happened to his ship. "We were heading the Flotilla pointing to each Dan as they came up to it. I was on the bridge. I asked them to send a signal to (HMS) *Blyth* to tell them what we were doing, but before the signal could be sent the explosion occurred, just knocking me off my feet. I immediately went to the port side of the bridge as the ship was listing that way, and saw that she was sinking very quickly. It was then reported to me by the 1st Lieutenant that the chief engineer was down in the engine room. There was no sense in remaining on the bridge as the noise of escaping air and steam from the engine room made it impossible for orders to be heard . . .. I gave orders for the rafts to be thrown overboard and the Dans to be cut adrift … on leaving the bridge I joined the 1st Lieutenant (Robert Shaw Fraser, RNVR) by the engine room hatch when the chief engineer appeared half way up the ladder. He was helped out of the engine room and left in charge of the 1st Lieutenant."

"After that I gave orders to abandon ship … when I was in the water I saw that the chief engineer and the 1st Lieutenant had not yet left and I ordered them to do so. The 1st Lieutenant threw the chief engineer into the sea and followed immediately to assist him. I swam back and joined them … at that moment the ship sank by the stern when we were approximately a few feet from her."

Lieutenant Robert Fraser said, "I realised immediately that we had been hit by a mine and I rushed out on deck making for the bridge when I encountered the captain who stated that he had ordered 'abandon ship' … I then ran back to the engine room where there appeared to be a great deal of steam and you could hear a lot of water swirling below. I realised there must be someone down there and I was just trying to muster enough courage to go and do something about it when a hand appeared which I grabbed hold of. This was the chief engineer who was badly dazed. I staggered to the side of the ship with him on the upper deck, which by this time was awash. I then seized the Dan which was just near. The ship then sank and I grabbed the chief engineer and that was the last I saw of the ship. The whole incident seemed to me to take something like 2 minutes."

From her complement that day of three officers and 20 men, two men were lost. *Sargasso* was sunk by a German mine, almost certainly dropped by aircraft, but whether it was a contact, magnetic or acoustic mine was not discovered.

The wreck of the *Sargasso* lies in about 43 metres of water. She is broken amidships. Her stern section is upright, complete with twin bronze propellers, while her bow section lies half over on its port side.

Name: HMS *Sargasso*. **Former name(s):** *Atlantis* ex *Mingary*.
Vessel type: Motor yacht.
Builder: Alexander Stephens & Sons.
When completed: June 1926.
Machinery built by: Sulzer.
Tonnage: 216 tons gross.
Dimensions: Length: 123′. **Breadth:** 20′ 6″. **Draught:** 8′ 3″.
Official number: 148910. **Yard number:** –
Signal letters: MBWX. **Last port of registry:** Portsmouth.
Ship description: Steel twin screw motor yacht. 1 deck. Schooner rigged. Fitted with electric light.
Machinery description: 2 × oil engines, 2 stroke cycle, single acting, 4 cylinders.
Career and ownership: Built as *Mingary* in 1926 and owned by Kenneth Clark, Argyllshire. 1929 owned by Hugh Tevis and registered in Southampton. 1930 owned by Dr Alfred Berliner, registered Travermonde. 1933 owned by Lord Michelham, registered Portsmouth. 1937 owned by Loel Guiness MP, registered Portsmouth. 1939 requisitioned by the Admiralty as a Dan layer for the 9th Minesweeping Flotilla. Took part in Operation Dynamo, in 5 daily trips bringing back 605 troops from the beaches of Dunkirk.
Armament: Not known.
Destination and cargo: Engaged in minesweeping activities off the Needles.
Date sunk: 6 June 1943.
How sunk: Mined.
Reported position of loss: 50° 31.54′ north, 001° 42.18′ west (corrected).
Actual position of wreck: 50° 31.18′ north, 001° 42.50′ west.
Orientation/height: Stands about 5 metres in 43 metres on shingle seabed, bows to the south.
How identity of wreck proved: Location and description of wreck exactly fits that of *Sargasso*. A number of Dan markers remain in the wreck. Small arms ammunition is of Second World War vintage.

Carentan
Foundered 21 December 1943

Chasseur similar to *Carentan*.

Author's collection.

Carentan was a French submarine chaser originally known as *Chasseur No 5*. After the fall of France in 1940, *Chasseur No 5* took part in Operation Dynamo, during which she engaged with the enemy and brought back French and English officers to England from Dunkirk. She came to the UK as part of the Free French Navy when France was occupied by the Germans, and it was in Portsmouth harbour that she and other French vessels were seized by the Admiralty and taken into service. She was renamed *Carentan* in 1941.

Like other Chasseurs, *Carentan* was used on anti-submarine patrols and other duties. Her final voyage began on the morning of 21 December 1943, when she set sail from Portland in company with HMS *Rorqual*, a British submarine. It was perhaps unwise to have commenced the journey; the weather was moderate but deteriorating and a gale warning had been issued of west or south west gales reaching force 8 or 9, imminent. Chasseurs were not intended for use in the English Channel; they had been designed more for use in the Mediterranean Sea, and their sea keeping abilities were not well suited to the chops of the English Channel. However, there was evidence that they were excellent sea-boats, though their steering was very poor in a following sea, and their stability tests reached only the bare minimum standard.

Despite the imminent gale, *Carentan* and *Rorqual* proceeded to the east, making about 8½ knots, and all seemed to be well. However, they were approaching St Alban's Head and Anvil Point, both of which produced very dangerous seas in bad weather. In the event, St Alban's Head was passed in steep seas, but no undue difficulty was experienced. *Rorqual's* commanding officer noted that *Carentan* seemed to be steering a zig-zag course, and that this was almost certainly caused by the effects of the following sea, which lifted her stern and overtook her, causing her to swing from side to side.

By the time the vessels were off Anvil Point, an ebb tide had set in, and with the gale now blowing, a very rough sea sprang up, wind against tide, producing wave heights of 4–5 metres. One of the survivors was Leading Signalman Charles Koelsch, who said, "I was on the bridge … we had a sea from starboard and a big wave took us right around to starboard and she took a heavy list and she seemed to wait and then she turned over." He went on, "The compass, on the bridge, is marked to 45° on each side and for a while I watched it and it came over to 50° both sides. The ship went rolling over just to the edge and we were wondering if it would come up again or not … it was not very quick. We had time to realise what was happening and when I saw she was turning over I saw the captain gripping the compass and when I looked back the bridge was about 2 yards from the water so I jumped into it … I was caught in the mast and rigging and taken right down … I managed to get out and I saw light … I swam to that part and then I had some difficulty to get out of the railings and then I managed to get up to the surface."

Rorqual, responding to the capsized escort, reported sighting seven persons in the water, three of whom were rescued quickly, and another three were sitting on the upturned hull. By the time *Rorqual* reached the seventh man, he had drowned. Swanage lifeboat was called out, and they saved the men on *Carentan's* hull, but no others were found. However, the survivors on the upturned hull reported that some of the crewmen were alive inside the wreck, as they were tapping on the hull. *Rorqual's* commanding officer Lieutenant Commander Clarabut even considered submerging *Rorqual* under the *Carentan* in the hope of supporting her, but it was decided this might result in the loss of his boat as well, and the idea was abandoned.

Carentan, still buoyant, drifted slowly inshore, and it was hoped that some survivors might yet be rescued from her. However, about 2 hours after capsizing, she sank lower in the water and finally disappeared. Twenty-one men died, many of whom were unable to escape the ship before she turned over.

The wreck of the *Carentan* lies in about 31 metres of water. She has rotted, and lies on her port side. Her twin diesel engines are the most prominent parts of the wreck. Both propellers have been salvaged. The shell of the wheelhouse was made of brass.

Name: *Carentan.* **Former name(s):** *Chasseur No 5.*
Vessel type: French submarine chaser.
Builder: F et C de la Mediterranee.
When completed: April 1939.
Machinery built by: MAN.
Tonnage: 107 tons displacement.
Dimensions: Length: 121′ 4″. **Breadth:** 16′ 6″. **Draught:** –
Official number: – **Yard number:** –
Signal letters: – **Last port of registry:** –
Ship description: Steel twin screw motor submarine chaser.
Machinery description: Twin diesel engines producing 1100 horse power at 16 knots.
Career and ownership: In service of the French Navy until she escaped to the UK in 1940, where she was seized at Portsmouth and put to Admiralty use.
Armament: 1 × 75mm (3″) bow gun (since recovered), 1 × 2 pounder pom-pom fitted aft, 2 × 20mm Oerlikons, one each side of the bridge, 2 × .303 vickers machine guns and 2 × .5″ Browning machine guns and 2 × racks of depth charges.
Destination and cargo: Portland for the Needles escorting HM submarine *Rorqual.*
Date sunk: 21 December 1943.
How sunk: Capsized in heavy weather.
Reported position of loss: 3.5 miles 098° from St Alban's Head.
Actual position of wreck: 50° 34.99′ north, 001° 56.21′ west.
Orientation/height: Stands about 4 metres in 31 metres on rocky seabed with shingle.
How identity of wreck proved: *Carentan* reported capsized in the position given. Wreck is that of a twin diesel engine chasseur. Only *Carentan* was lost in the area.

Tank Landing Craft
Presumed foundered June 1944

Landing craft (tank) similar to those lying near St Catherine's Point. Wright & Logan collection, Royal Naval Museum.

The wrecks of at least four landing craft are known to lie in the sea area covered by this book. Three are tank landing craft, and they lie close to each other off St Catherine's Point, one with damage consistent with gunfire. It is likely they were lost after the D-Day invasion and after the Normandy beachhead had been consolidated. There is a strong probability that all three were being towed back to the Solent when they sank, but the causes remain unknown. For the purposes of identification, each is marked as "Unknown" followed by a number, which is the depth of water in which they lie in metres.

Name: *Unknown 58.* **Former name(s):** –
Vessel type: Tank landing craft.
Ship description: Steel twin screw tank landing craft.
Machinery description: Twin diesel or petrol engines, fitted aft.
Career and ownership: Presumed to be the Royal Navy (Ministry of Defence).
Armament: Not known.
Destination and cargo: Probably Normandy for the Solent.
Date sunk: Presumed June 1944.
How sunk: Not known.
Reported position of loss: Not reported.
Actual position of wreck: Close position: 50° 33.20′ north, 001° 21.30′ west.
Orientation/height: Stands 6 metres in 58 metres, completely upright, with wheelhouse standing, damaged apparently by gunfire.
How identity of wreck proved: Unidentified.

Name: *Unknown 51.* **Former name(s):** –
Vessel type: Tank landing craft.
Ship description: Steel twin screw tank landing craft.
Machinery description: Twin diesel or petrol engines, fitted aft.
Career and ownership: Presumed to be the Royal Navy (Ministry of Defence).
Armament: Not known.
Destination and cargo: Probably Normandy for the Solent.

Date sunk: Presumed June 1944.
How sunk: Not known.
Reported position of loss: Not reported.
Actual position of wreck: 50° 33.27′ north, 001° 21.73′ west.
Orientation/height: Lies 090°/270°. Stands 6 metres in 51 metres completely upright on stony/gravel seabed. Wheelhouse still standing. Some 4″ pipes lie in the wreck forward of the wheelhouse. Twin propellers in place. Great care should be taken when diving this wreck on low water slack. When the tide starts to flood, a vortex is created over the wreck as it sweeps down to deeper water which has the effect of preventing ascent. Until the effect weakens, divers have to be carried east with the tide before commencing ascent.
How identity of wreck proved: Not identified.

Name: *Unknown 28.* **Former name(s):** –
Vessel type: Tank landing craft.
Ship description: Steel twin screw tank landing craft.
Machinery description: Twin diesel or petrol engines, fitted aft.
Career and ownership: Presumed owned by the Royal Navy (Ministry of Defence).
Armament: Not known.
Destination and cargo: Probably Normandy beaches for the Solent.
Date sunk: Presumed June 1944.
How sunk: Not known.
Reported position of loss: Not reported.
Actual position of wreck: 50° 33.52′ north, 001° 22.27′ west.
Orientation/height: Stands about 5 metres in 28 metres, completely upright on gravel seabed. Gravel has heaped up on the sides of the wreck. Interior contains much sand, but ladders and other parts of the structure can be seen disappearing into the sand. Both engines are exposed as is a very large stern capstan. Wheelhouse has disintegrated.
How identity of wreck proved: Not identified.

Name: *Unknown 30.* **Former name(s):** –
Vessel type: Landing craft.
Ship description: Steel twin screw landing craft, probably a store carrier or similar.
Machinery description: Twin diesel or petrol engines.
Career and ownership: Presumed to be the Royal Navy (Ministry of Defence).
Armament: Not known.
Destination and cargo: Unknown.
Date sunk: Not known.
How sunk: Not known.
Reported position of loss: Not reported.
Actual position of wreck: 50° 33.55′ north, 001° 57. 56′ west.
Orientation/height: Lies 000°/180°. Stands 3–4 metres in 30 metres, completely upright on stony/shingle seabed. Vertical boiler stands up on the deck starboard side forward. Vessel is not a tank landing craft but has a deck preventing access to the interior, and is thought, therefore, to be a store carrier or similar. At least one of the propellers has been recovered.
How identity of wreck proved: Not identified.

SS *Dungrange*
Torpedoed 10 June 1944
MV *Ashanti*
Torpedoed 10 June 1944

The steamer *Dungrange* and the motor vessel *Ashanti* were part of a convoy heading for the D-Day landing beaches in Normandy, in support of the invasion forces. The convoy departed the Isle of Wight on 9 June as part of convoy ETC4W, which at first comprised six ships, though more joined the convoy later. *Dungrange* was the last ship. One of her crew was senior ordinary seaman E Ludlam, who said, "I came on duty at 3am on the 10th and joined two other members of the crew who were standing in the stern watching a tanker which had dropped 3 miles astern of the convoy. At 3.30am there was a loud explosion and she immediately caught fire (this was almost certainly the destruction of the *Ashanti*). At 3.55am I went to the bridge and at 4am on the 10th June, when about 25 miles from the French coast, steering a southerly course at 5 knots, the SS *Dungrange* was struck by one torpedo. The explosion occurred on the starboard quarter and the whole of the stern was blown high into the air. The engines, which were situated aft, were completely shattered, and the boilers exploded."

"I heard the captain shouting 'Jump over the side' and saw several of the crew preparing to jump over the port wing of the bridge. I climbed from the bridge onto the ammunition locker on the fore deck, which was already under water, and then stepped off the locker into the water, swam over the forward well deck and clear of the ship, pushing my way with difficulty through the wreckage which lay thickly on the water." He continued, "When I turned round the vessel had disappeared and therefore must have sunk in approximately 2½ minutes . . . I switched on my lifejacket light, which was seen by gunner Lashater, who was on a raft. He also switched on his light and paddled towards me and I climbed on board the raft after being in the water for half an hour. He stated that the vessel rolled over to starboard as she sank by the stern."

Dungrange had been ambushed by a German E-boat. Eighteen men were lost, with only Mr Ludlam and Mr Lashater surviving.

The *Ashanti* was, like *Dungrange,* a coaster, and she was in a similar position in mid Channel heading for the Normandy beaches. An E-boat attacked her too, and she disintegrated in a huge explosion as the torpedo ignited her cargo of cased petrol. There were no survivors from her crew of 17.

There is no information concerning whether these two wrecks have been located and identified.

Name: *Dungrange.* **Former name(s):** *Yewbank* ex *Okehampton* ex *Aberdale.*
Vessel type: Steam coaster.
Builder: J Fullerton & Company, Paisley.
When completed: May 1914.
Machinery built by: Fishers Ltd, Paisley.
Tonnage: 621 tons gross.
Dimensions: Length: 175′. **Breadth:** 28′ 1″.
Depth of holds: 10′ 4″.
Official number: 135580. **Yard number:** –
Signal letters: –
Last port of registry: Grangemouth.
Ship description: Steel screw steam coaster. 1 deck. Well deck. 3 masts.
Machinery description: Triple expansion 3 cylinders. 1 single ended boiler. 90 registered horse power. Machinery fitted aft.
Career and ownership: Owned at the time of loss by the Dungrange Steam Ship Company Ltd (Buchan & Hogg Ltd, managers).
Armament: 1 × twin Oerlikon, 2 × single Oerlikons, 1 × Lewis gun, 4 PAC rockets.
Destination and cargo: Isle of Wight for the Normandy beaches with a cargo of ammunition.
Date sunk: 10 June 1944.
How sunk: Torpedoed by E-boat.
Reported position of loss: 25 miles north of the Normandy beaches, and 35 miles north of assault area, south of St Catherine's Point.
Actual position of wreck: Not known.
Orientation/height: –
How identity of wreck proved: –

Name: *Ashanti.* **Former name(s):** None.
Vessel type: Motor coaster.
Builder: Goole Shipbuilding and Repairing Company Ltd, Goole.
When completed: May 1936.
Machinery built by: Nydqvist & Holm A/B, Trollhättan.
Tonnage: 534 tons gross.
Dimensions: Length: 183′ 6″. **Breadth:** 27′ 1″.
Depth of holds: 8′
Official number: 164622. **Yard number:** –
Signal letters: MLLB.
Last port of registry: London.
Ship description: Steel screw motor coaster. 1 deck. Cruiser stern.
Machinery description: 2 × oil engines, 2 stroke cycle single acting, 6 cylinders. 102 nominal horse power. Machinery fitted aft.
Career and ownership: Owned at the time of loss by T E Evans & Company Ltd.
Armament: Not known but 7 gunners were on board.
Destination and cargo: Isle of Wight for Normandy beaches with a cargo of cased petrol.
Date sunk: 10 June 1944.
How sunk: Torpedoed by E-boat.
Reported position of loss: 25 miles north of the Normandy beaches, and 35 miles north of assault area, south of St Catherine's Point.
Actual position of wreck: Not known.
Orientation/height: –
How identity of wreck proved: –

SS *Albert C Field* Torpedoed 18 June 1944

SS *Albert C Field.* Author's collection.

The *Albert C Field* was a Canadian steamer which left Penarth on 16 June 1944, bound for the Normandy beaches. She carried 2500 tons of ammunition as well as 1300 bags of US mail. Joining up with convoy EBC14 (an eastern "feeder" for operation Neptune) in Barry Roads, she proceeded on her voyage until about 11.40pm on 18 June. At that time her chief officer, Mr Robson, was alerted by the sound of an aircraft. Looking around, he saw an aircraft flying only 20 feet off the water at a distance of 700 or 800 feet off the starboard bow. He said, "We were steaming approximately east, and the plane was flying from east to west, parallel to the ship. As we had received no warning of enemy aircraft I thought this was an allied plane hunting for submarines. None of the ships in the convoy opened fire."

Mr Robson continued, "HM trawler *Herschell* was between our ship and the aircraft at the time, and I presume that the plane dropped the torpedo when clear of the trawler. The aircraft, which I believe was a JU 88, did not alter course, but flew straight on and was out of sight within a matter of seconds … we were struck by one torpedo from an aircraft. No-one saw the track of the torpedo which struck on the starboard side amidships, on the bulkhead separating our two holds. The explosion was dull, like a very heavy depth charge. No water was thrown up and no flash seen. The ship listed slightly to starboard and the bags of mail stowed amidships in number 2 hold caught fire immediately. Both lifeboats, which were on the poop aft, were blown out of their davits and were seen floating upside down in the water."

"Half the crew jumped overboard immediately as they were under the impression the ship would blow up at any moment ... within 3 minutes of the torpedo exploding the ship hogged amidships, broke in two and sank. Although explosions had not previously been heard, two explosions of ammunition took place immediately the ship broke in two. As I could not swim I did not jump overboard, and was taken down with the ship. On surfacing I was able to reach a raft and climb on to it. Other survivors were clinging to mail bags and wreckage in the vicinity."

As *Albert C Field* sank, the trawler *Herschell* came to the rescue, and commenced to pick up survivors, but the master and three men went down with the ship. In all likelihood, the ship had been sunk by a German night bomber of Kampfgeschwader (KG)26, whose Groups II and III were operating that night.

The wreck of the *Albert C Field* lies in two pieces in 38 metres of water. There is a debris field amidships where a quantity of damaged ammunition lies, shining up green in torchlight. The only parts of the wreck which stand up are the bow and stern sections, some 70 or 80 metres apart.

Name: *Albert C Field.* **Former name(s):** None.
Vessel type: Steam ship.
Builder: Furness Ship Building Company, Haverton Hill on Tees.
When completed: 1923.
Machinery built by: MacColl & Pollack, Sunderland.
Tonnage: 1764 tons gross.
Dimensions: Length: 252′ 5″. **Breadth:** 43′ 3″. **Depth of holds:** 17′ 8″.
Official number: 147767. **Yard number:** –
Signal letters: KPFN. **Last port of registry:** St Catherine's, Ontario.
Ship description: Steel screw steamer.
Machinery description: Triple expansion 3 cylinders. 111 nominal horse power.
Career and ownership: One of 20 ships built for the Eastern Steamship Corporation (G C Leitch, manager) between 1923 and 1926, all in British yards. Intended for canal work by transhipping cargo from "lakers" to the ports on the St Lawrence River. Owned 1939 by Upper Lakes & St Lawrence Transportation Company Ltd, Toronto.
Armament: 5 × Oerlikons, 2 × PAC's, 2 × PAC's (J).
Destination and cargo: Penarth for the invasion beaches of Normandy with 1300 bags of US mail and 2500 tons of ammunition.
Date sunk: 18 June 1944.
How sunk: Aerial torpedo from German aircraft.
Reported position of loss: 50° 28.50′ north, 001° 46′ west.
Actual position of wreck: 50° 28.24′ north, 001° 45.37′ west.
Orientation/height: Stands about 4 metres in 38 metres on shingle seabed, the boilers being the highest parts.
How identity of wreck proved: Large quantity of exploded ammunition lies on the seabed of Second World War vintage. The vessel was of such an unusual and distinctive design i.e. bridge at the bows, accommodation and machinery at the stern, which is what the wreck is like.

SS *Ashmun J Clough*
Torpedoed 26 August 1944

Following the D-Day Normandy landings in June 1944, allied merchant ships continued to bring in stores and supplies to the beachhead in support of the invasion force. One of those ships was the one-year-old American built steamer, *Ashmun J Clough*, 1791 tons. The ship left Barry Dock on 24 August and the next day she joined a convoy comprising four ships. A number of Liberty ships joined the convoy at Swansea; some went on different routes when the convoy reached Falmouth. There were six ships left as it proceeded up Channel bound for Utah Prairie Beach. Escorted by the corvette HMS *Azalea*, by the morning of 26 August 1944, the convoy had reached mid Channel, estimated to be about 23 miles north of Cherbourg.

Her chief officer, P M Coyne, reported, "The convoy proceeded as routed until 0830 ... we were steering a southerly course at 8 knots in 32 fathoms when there was a violent underwater explosion ... on the starboard side amidships and the vessel immediately settled by the stern. When I arrived on deck about 5 seconds after the explosion there were clouds of black smoke everywhere, but I do not think any water was thrown up as the decks were dry."

He continued, "It was impossible to ascertain the full extent of the damage as the vessel was settling so rapidly; the engine room was holed and the engines stopped immediately. The chief engineer, who was on watch, must have been killed instantly. All hatches were blown off ... all rafts were thrown clear of the ship whilst the starboard lifeboat was smashed and thrown over onto the port boat, which appeared undamaged ... there were several others on the boat deck with me and I shouted to them to go forward, the fore part of the ship still being well above water. No sooner had I spoken, however, than the vessel sank beneath us approximately 2½ minutes after the explosion."

Chief Officer Coyne suffered many cuts and bruises from cases and debris whirling around as he was dragged under with the ship and caught up in ropes, but amazingly he managed to gain the surface only to find the *Ashmun J Clough* had completely disappeared. He commented, "As the ship sank beneath us I saw the master, second officer and radio officer on deck, but there was no sign of them when I surfaced. Most of the men who were taken down with the ship wore lifejackets, but when I last saw the master he was carrying his. I think many of the missing men were fouled by ropes and debris, and never came to the surface."

The survivors were rescued soon after by a motor launch and transferred to HMS *Azalea*. Sixteen men lost their lives.

The *Ashmun J Clough* had been torpedoed following a submerged attack by the type VIIC German U-boat *U-989*, under the command of Kapitänleutnant Rodler von Roithberg.

The wreck of the *Ashmun J Clough* lies upright and fairly intact in about 63 metres of water. She is a substantial wreck. Her holds are full of war cargo including tank tracks, tyres and other military stores. The wreck is heavily fished and a huge amount of angling gear fouls the wreck. This is not as dangerous as it might seem, as the strength of the tides ensures that fishing lines are woven together in great swathes, up to a metre thick, while many weights and lures chafe through and fall into the wreck and on the surrounding seabed. Diving on this wreck is not recommended in other than good water clarity. The wreck lies in the westbound shipping lane, but most – not all – traffic passes to the north.

Name: *Ashmun J Clough*. **Former name(s):** None.
Vessel type: Steam ship.
Builder: Walter Butler Shipbuilders Incorporated, Superior, Wisconsin, USA.
When completed: 1943.
Machinery built by: Prescott Company, Menominee, Michigan, USA.
Tonnage: 1791 tons gross.
Dimensions: Length: 250′ 6″. **Breadth:** 41′ 3″. **Depth of holds:** 18′ 4″.
Official number: 169602. **Yard number:** –
Signal letters: BHTG. **Last port of registry:** London.
Ship description: Steel screw steamer, electric welded. 1 deck. Cruiser stern.
Machinery description: Triple expansion 3 cylinders.

Presumed 2 single ended boilers.
Career and ownership: Owned by the Ministry of War Transport on bare boat charter from WSA (owners), (Stephenson, Clarke & Associated Companies, managers).
Armament: 1 × 12 pounder stern gun, 4 × Oerlikon guns, 2 × Strip Lewis guns and 2 × F.A.M.S.
Destination and cargo: Barry Dock for Utah Prairie Beach, France, via Falmouth, with 1200 tons of military stores.
Date sunk: 26 August 1944.
How sunk: Torpedoed by *U-989*.
Reported position of loss: 23 miles north of Cherbourg, and 50° 10′ north, 001° 41′ west.
Actual position of wreck: 50° 11.00′ north, 001° 43.00′ west.
Orientation/height: Stands 8–9 metres in 63 metres.
How identity of wreck proved: Not proved but wreck lies close to reported position of loss and its size and description of cargo strongly indicates this is the *Ashmun J Clough*.

SS *Dumfries*
Torpedoed 23 December 1944

SS *Dumfries*. Courtesy National Maritime Museum, Greenwich.

The activities of German U-boats in the Channel in the Second World War are in marked contrast to the First World War, when they ranged far and wide and with far greater success. The allies had developed better detection methods and made much greater use of aircraft, and as a result, life for the U-boat became very difficult. However, one of their successes was in sinking the *Dumfries*, a valuable ship carrying important raw materials in the form of iron ore.

Dumfries and her crew of 67 and two passengers, under the command of her master, Captain R Blakey, departed Gibraltar in convoy MKS71 (Mediterranean – UK) bound for St Helens Roads. The voyage had progressed as expected until the ship was in a position in mid Channel about 8.20am on 23 December 1944. Steaming at about 7 ½ knots, Captain Blakey reported, "there was a violent explosion which appeared to be underneath number 1 hatch. A great deal of water was thrown up on both sides, right over the bridge. The bow of the ship lifted with the explosion. No flash was observed. The hatches of number 1 hatch were blown off, also the beams and the iron ore was thrown up but the decks were not torn. The derricks were lying horizontally on the decks and the starboard derrick had fallen on top of the raft and smashed it completely. No damage to the ship's side was visible. Number 1 hold had flooded but number 2 was quite dry, and the forepeak also was dry. The wireless aerial came down."

Dumfries had been struck by a single torpedo fired from the type VIIC U-boat, the *U-772*, under the command of Kapitänleutnant Ewald Rademacher.

Captain Blakey continued, "We had a Lascar crew and they started to panic, so I told the chief officer to put them into a boat, and I would go slow ahead and try to beach the ship. The engines were in perfect working order. The wireless (signal) was got away on an emergency aerial but we could not receive back. There was nobody to steer as the officers were looking after the boats, so I took the wheel myself. The ship was going slow ahead, but the compass had gone and there was nothing to steer or guide by. We proceeded like this for about 3 or 4 minutes. I then went out to the wing of the bridge and noticed the ship had eased down and was well down by the head."

Captain Blakey added, "There were ten men left on board and no means of escape, and the number 1 bulkhead was starting to creak, so I considered I could not risk going on without some means of escape for these ten men. I then signalled to the corvette who was escorting the convoy and asked for assistance, explaining the position to the commanding officer, and asked him to stand by while we tried to get the vessel in. All the men on board volunteered to stand by and were very angry when told to get off. The commanding officer of the corvette said he had not time to wait as he was the only escort with the convoy which he would have to catch up, so he told us to get on board."

On the way in, the corvette came across a deep sea tug, and Captain Blakey and his ten men transferred to her with the intention of locating the *Dumfries* and towing her in. Despite searching into the night, however, *Dumfries* could not be found and after contacting a motor torpedo boat at 10pm, they were informed she had sunk at 5.30pm. A week later *U-772* herself was lost with all hands.

The wreck of the *Dumfries* lies in 57 metres of water. She is a very substantial wreck, leaning to starboard, standing some 11 or 12 metres, but is showing signs of breaking up. At her stern, the gun lies on the seabed just in the wreck. Her engine is exposed but her boilers are still beneath decking. The highest part of the wreck is her entire port side, covered with lost fishing gear.

Name: *Dumfries*. **Former name(s):** None.
Vessel type: Steam ship.
Builder: Hawthorn, Leslie & Company Ltd, Newcastle.
When completed: July 1935.
Machinery built by: North East Marine Engineering Company Ltd, Newcastle.
Tonnage: 5149 tons gross.
Dimensions: Length: 416′ 3″. **Breadth:** 55′ 2″. **Depth of holds:** 26′.
Official number: 161585. **Yard number:** –
Signal letters: GYLT. **Last port of registry:** Newcastle.
Ship description: Steel screw steamer. 1 deck. Cruiser stern. Fitted with direction finding equipment.
Machinery description: Quadruple expansion 4 cylinders. 3 single ended boilers. 442 nominal horse power.
Career and ownership: Owned by B Sutherland & Company Ltd. 1941 owned by Gdynia America Shipping Lines (London) Ltd.
Armament: Armed with a stern gun, details not known, and probably Oerlikons amidships. Stern gun seen on the wreck and other gun pedestals seen amidships, but details are not recorded in the archives.
Destination and cargo: Gibraltar for St Helens Roads with a cargo of 8258 tons of iron ore.
Date sunk: 23 December 1944.
How sunk: Torpedoed by *U-772*.
Reported position of loss: Abandoned close to 50° 22.84′ north, 001° 42.68′ west (corrected).
Actual position of wreck: 50° 19.77′ north, 001° 44.42′ west.
Orientation/height: Stands 12 metres in 57 metres on seabed of rock and shingle.
How identity of wreck proved: Ship's bell recovered.

SS *Dumfries*. Courtesy R A Snook/F W Hawks collection.

Motor tanker *Y48*
Foundered 11 January 1945

The only information about this vessel comes from the Hydrographic Office, which details the sinking of an American tanker, the *Y48*. The vessel was reported to have been in a sinking condition and was sunk by gunfire from our own forces as it was a hazard to navigation.

The wreck of this vessel lies in about 58 metres. She stands 8 or 9 metres and is almost upright with a slight list to starboard. She has a small bow gun, and equipment for delivering fuel of the type commonly found in petrol service stations. A spare propeller is on the deck partly covered in wreckage. Although her bridge telegraph, steering position, compass, clock, barometer and portholes were recovered, all of American origin, nothing has been found to positively identify the ship.

Name: *Y48*. **Former name(s):** None.
Vessel type: Motor tanker.
Builder: Lancaster Iron Works, Perryville, Maryland, USA.
When completed: 1944.
Machinery built by: Not known.
Tonnage: 633 tons gross.
Dimensions: Length: 183′. **Breadth:** 30′.
Depth of holds: 14′.
Official number: – **Yard number:** –
Signal letters: – **Last port of registry:** –
Ship description: Steel twin screw motor tanker.
Machinery description: Twin diesel engines, 700 horse-power.
Career and ownership: Thought to be US Army Transportation Service.
Armament: Details not known, but the wreck has a small bow gun, probably a 2 pounder, but may be smaller.
Destination and cargo: Not known.
Date sunk: 11 January 1945.
How sunk: Gunfire by own forces as the vessel was in a sinking condition and a hazard to navigation.
Reported position of loss: 50° 14′ north, 001° 17′ west.
Actual position of wreck: 50° 14.52′ north, 001° 17.28′ west.
Orientation/height: Lies 100°/280°. Stands 8 metres in 58 metres on shingle seabed.
How identity of wreck proved: Wreck is clearly that of a small tanker, and the position of the wreck is very close to the reported position of loss of the *Y48*.

U-480
Presumed mined soon after 24 February 1945

The Type VIIC German U-boat, the *U-480*, under the command of Oberleutnant zur See Hans-Joachim Förster, sailed from Bergen, Norway, on 6 January 1945 to conduct operations in the English Channel. She was assigned to the 11th U-boat flotilla, having been commissioned at Kiel on 6 October 1943.

U-480 was the first German U-boat to be coated with a 4mm thick layer of "Alberich", a rubber coating designed to neutralise the effects of Asdic, which the Germans regarded as the most dangerous British development for detecting submerged submarines. *U-480* reported that the results were positive following her patrol in the Channel in August 1944.

According to German records, among her last known movements she was "cruising grid AM33" off north-west Scotland. A final report from her, noted as 24 February 1945, was to inform the German authorities that she had sunk the British streamer *Oriskany*, 1644 tons, in position 50° 05′ north, 005° 51′ west, off Land's End.

U-480 never returned from her patrol. She was lost with all hands sometime after 24 February 1945, presumed having been mined in a deep minefield identified as "Brazier D2".

The wreck of the *U-480* lies in about 58 metres of water. She is damaged at the stern, consistent with being mined, and her rubber coating is still evident on the hull.

Name: *U-480*. **Former name(s):** None.
Vessel type: U-boat.
Builder: –
When completed: Commissioned at Kiel 6 October 1943.
Machinery built by: Schmidt/Hartmann.
Tonnage: 761 tons displacement surfaced, 865 tons displacement submerged.
Dimensions: Length: 67.1 metres. **Breadth:** 6.2 metres. **Draught:** 4.8 metres.
Ship description: Steel twin screw Type VIIC U-boat.
Machinery description: 2 × 1400 horse power single drive Schmidt/Hartmann diesel engines and 2 × 375 horse power electric motors.
Career and ownership: Owned by the German Imperial Navy.
Armament: 4 × bow torpedo tubes, 1 × stern torpedo tube for 14 torpedoes. 1 × 8.8 cms and 1 × 2 cms deck guns.
Destination and cargo: Operational war patrol in the English Channel.
Date sunk: Soon after 24 February 1945.
How sunk: Presumed mined in a deep minefield.
Reported position of loss: Not reported.
Actual position of wreck: 50° 22.14′ north, 001° 44.24′ west.
Orientation/height: Stands about 6 metres in 58 metres on shingle seabed.
How identity of wreck proved: Through serial number engraved on conning tower range-finder.

SS *Everleigh*
Torpedoed 6 February 1945

SS *Everleigh*. Courtesy National Maritime Museum, Greenwich.

The *Everleigh* has the dubious distinction of being the last ship lost in the area due to enemy action. Her master, Captain William Gould, had a crew of 48 men. He said, "We left Southend at 10am on the 5th February and proceeded in convoy without incident until, through easing down to transfer our pilot off the Nab, we fell astern of the convoy and were still about 2 miles astern when at 2.40pm on the 6th, in position 50° 29′ north, 001° 47′ west, an explosion occurred. At the time of the explosion I was not on the bridge but in my own room. It was a double explosion, i.e. a deep thud at first, she shook, and then in about 2 seconds the explosion occurred. It was rather muffled, and contained terrific shaking power. It was not as loud as I expected – I had been torpedoed 3 times previously – in view of the amount of damage done."

The damage had been done by the type VIIC U-boat, the *U-1017*, under the command of Oberleutnant zur See Werner Riecken who had unleashed a single torpedo at *Everleigh*. *U-1017* herself was destroyed 11 weeks later off the Irish coast.

Captain Gould added, "The actual damage I saw was the main mast was looking aft, the deck was buckled and bulwarks split amidships on the port side, the hatches were gone from number 5 hatch, and her poop was soon awash. The bulkheads between number 4 and 5, I think had gone, and the engine bulkhead must have gone eventually. She went down so rapidly I did not have time to observe more, but I think the explosion must have occurred on the port side in view of the damage amidships being on this side. Also, the men missing were blown out of their quarters on 'tween decks in number 5 hold port side, while those on the starboard side 'tween decks were not injured."

In concluding his report, Captain Gould said, "She went down in about 4 minutes, stern first, and we left her standing perpendicular with about 60 feet of her bow out of the water in 23 fathoms. We saw nothing of a submarine, or the track of a torpedo. We were picked up by a small landing craft and landed at Portland at 5.50pm." Six men died when *Everleigh* was torpedoed.

The wreck of the *Everleigh* lies in about 40–42 metres of water. She is a substantial wreck, more or less upright, her boilers being the highest parts.

Name: *Everleigh*. **Former name(s):** None.
Vessel type: Steam ship.
Builder: Furness Ship Building Company.
When completed: January 1930.
Machinery built by: Richardsons & Westgarth & Company Ltd, Sunderland.
Tonnage: 5222 tons gross.
Dimensions: Length: 406′ 3″. **Breadth:** 56′.
Depth of holds: 26′ 9″.
Official number: 161347. **Yard number:** –
Signal letters: GLSV. **Last port of registry:** London.
Ship description: Steel screw steamer. 1 deck. Fitted with electric light and wireless.
Machinery description: Triple expansion 3 cylinders. 3 single ended boilers. 527 nominal horse power.
Career and ownership: Owned by Atlantic Shipping & Trading Company Ltd (W J Tatem Ltd, manager).
Armament: Armed but details of how many guns and what they were are not recorded in the archives.
Destination and cargo: Southend for Barry Roads and New York in ballast.
Date sunk: 6 February 1945.
How sunk: Torpedoed by *U-1017*.
Reported position of loss: 50° 29′ north, 001° 47′ west.
Actual position of wreck: 50° 29.31′ north, 001° 47.14′ west.
Orientation/height: Lies 075°/255°. Stands 8 metres in 40–42 metres on shingle seabed.
How identity of wreck proved: Ship's bell recovered and position of wreck is remarkably close to the position reported at the time of loss.

SS *Everleigh* in the Panama Canal. Courtesy Tom Rayner collection.

Steam tug *Security*
Foundered 8 December 1946

Steam tug *Security* — Courtesy of Bristol's Museums Galleries & Archives

On 18 November 1946, three tugs, the *Contest, Watercock* and *Security* departed the Thames together bound for Falmouth, where they were to take in tow the tanker *Kelletia* and take her to the Tyne. They did not know it but they would head into some persistently stormy weather. So bad was the weather that the tugs were forced to shelter first at Dover, secondly at Newhaven and finally at Portsmouth, dodging in and out as the weather moderated or worsened. But that was not the main threat to these tugs, and *Security* in particular. There were a number of factors which had rendered her unseaworthy, and these would cause her to founder in a storm off the Isle of Wight.

Earlier in 1946 *Security* had passed her survey. This is surprising, since two weeks later, while the crew were engaged in chipping away rust and repainting, one of the chipping hammers penetrated the hull below the water line. The hull plating was found to have wasted away to the thickness of paper and urgent repairs were carried out, but no further examination of the hull was made. In addition, the steering gear was of an unusual design, and was prone to jam, and one of the bilge pipes was wasted and holed rendering it useless for the purpose of pumping out the compartment beneath the crew space. In short, the *Security* was in "ripe" condition, yet she was at sea in this unsafe state.

The tugs eventually reached Falmouth, but not before a quantity of water, estimated at 3 tons, was discovered under *Security's* crew space. The water was pumped out by using a salvage pump, probably because it was known the bilge pipe was defective, but it was not discovered how the water came to be there.

On 7 December, shortly afer noon, despite a very bad weather forecast, the *Kelletia* was taken in tow and the procession steamed up Channel. By 11am the next day a south easterly gale was blowing and the flotilla, in effect, hove to. There was heavy rain with hard squalls; in fact a low and intense secondary depression supervened on a primary depression causing the wind to back and increase in an entirely unpredicted fashion.

When they were to the south of Anvil Point, water was again discovered under *Security*'s crew space and this time the salvage pump could make no impression on the depth of water. The presence of this water was going to affect *Security*'s stability. About 4pm, the weather worsened still further and *Watercock's* tow line parted. Her master, skipper Arthur Couves said, "We were towing the *Kelletia* when our tow rope parted. It was while we were getting out of trouble that I saw the other tug, *Security*, in trouble. She suddenly turned over and sank in less than 5 minutes. We searched around for survivors and picked up five. The seas were so bad it was impossible to launch a boat and we had to throw handlines."

Roy Coomer, a crewman of the *Security*, said, "I know very little of what actually happened. I had just come out of the cabin on the deck when I was washed overboard. I was in the water for about an hour, clinging to a piece of wood with Mr Dix for the whole of that time." Another survivor, Harry McKee, said, "We ran into some particularly heavy weather and without warning our vessel suddenly turned over on her side. She went down by the bows in a matter of a couple of minutes. We had been hit by one heavy sea after another which gave the vessel no time to right herself."

Security's master and three men drowned when the tug sank, but five men were rescued.

There is no information concerning whether the *Security* has been located and identified.

Name: *Security*. **Former name(s):** *Stoke* ex *Security* ex *Diligence* ex *Kingfisher*.
Vessel type: Steam tug.
Builder: J P Rennoldson & Sons, South Shields.
When completed: June 1904.
Machinery built by: J P Rennoldson & Sons, South Shields.
Tonnage: 189 tons gross.
Dimensions: Length: 102′. **Breadth:** 23′ 1″.
Depth of holds: 12′.
Official number: 118084. **Yard number:** –
Signal letters: MNTC. **Last port of registry:** London.
Ship description: Steel screw steam tug and salvage vessel.
Machinery description: Triple expansion 3 cylinders. 1 single ended boiler.
Career and ownership: 1904/5 owned by Liverpool Steam Tug Company Ltd. 1946 owned by Elliott Steam Tug Company Ltd (J Pager, manager).
Destination and cargo: Falmouth for the Tyne towing the tanker *Kelletia*.
Date sunk: 8 December 1946.
How sunk: Foundered due to stress of weather.
Reported position of loss: 8 miles south west of St Catherine's and 12½ miles south east of Anvil Point.
Actual position of wreck: Not known.
Orientation/height: –
How identity of wreck proved: –

SS *Varvassi*
Ran aground 5 January 1947

SS *Moscha D Kydoniefs*, later renamed *Varvassi*. Courtesy E N Taylor collection.

Quite how the Greek steamer *Varvassi,* 3863 tons, ran onto the Bridge Reef close to the Needles remains something of a mystery, though the combination of currents and wind were said to have been responsible. About 6.55am on Sunday 5 January 1947, the *Varvassi,* under the command of Captain George Coufopandelis, was approaching the entrance to the Needles Channel where a pilot cutter was waiting for her to guide her in and lead her to her destination of Southampton. It was seen that she was steering the wrong course and the pilot boat made every effort to warn her of the danger ahead. All her signals were in vain, however, and *Varvassi* ran firmly aground close to the Needles Lighthouse.

Witnesses to the event reported that the ship was making about 3 knots at the time she struck, about an hour before high water, and that on the top of the tide the vessel remained firmly wedged. Captain Coufopandelis declined assistance from Yarmouth Lifeboat, confident his ship would refloat with the assistance of a tug which had arrived from Southampton. However, the weather began to deteriorate with the wind increasing from a moderate south-easterly breeze to half a gale and a heavy sea. As the tide fell *Varvassi* began to work herself closer to the Needles Lighthouse and efforts were made to run out her anchors to hold her in place. The ship began to take on water and it became clear in the rough conditions that any attempt at salvage would have to wait until daylight.

Twenty-four hours later, Yarmouth Lifeboat was back alongside the *Varvassi*, where seas were breaking clean over her and threatening to wash her officers from the bridge. She had 10 feet of water in her holds. In a tricky and dangerous operation, the entire crew of 35 was taken off safely and brought to Yarmouth.

In a lull in the weather, *Varvassi* was boarded and the seven live heifers kept in a pen on deck were fed and watered, and the ship's cats and canaries were saved. All the crew's possessions were recovered. However, the weather soon deteriorated again, and the prospect of saving the ship diminished. The heifers were eventually despatched by a slaughterman. By 18 January, all the ship's boats, hatches, rudder and part of the bridge had been washed away and *Varvassi* became a total wreck, the water surrounding her stained orange from her cargo of tangerines.

The wreck of the *Varvassi* is well known but seldom dived as she lies within an area which contains the protected wrecks of HMS *Assurance* and HMS *Pomone* on Goose Rock and a licence is needed to dive the site. The *Varvassi's* remains lie scattered on the Bridge Reef in about 6 metres, some of it in deeper water on the north eastern part of the reef. Two of her boilers can sometimes be seen awash at low water spring tides.

Name: *Varvassi.* **Former name(s):** *Moscha D Kydoniefs* ex *Lady Charlotte* ex *Noelle* ex *Bronze Wings.*
Vessel type: Steam ship.
Builder: Northumberland Shipbuilding Company Ltd, Newcastle.
When completed: March 1915.
Machinery built by: North East Marine Engineering Company Ltd, Newcastle.
Tonnage: 3863 tons gross.
Dimensions: Length: 375′ 2″. **Breadth:** 51′ 9″. **Depth of holds:** 23′ 7″.
Official number: 242. **Yard number:** –
Signal letters: JKHN. **Last port of registry:** Piræus.
Ship description: Steel screw steamer. 1 deck. Fitted with electric light.
Machinery description: Triple expansion 3 cylinders. 3 single ended boilers. 371 nominal horse power.
Career and ownership: Built 1915 as *Bronze Wings* and owned by Wing Steamship Company Ltd. 1918 named *Noelle* and owned by Universal Steam Navigation Company Ltd. 1922 named *Lady Charlotte* and owned by Redcroft Steam Navigation Company Ltd. 1937 named *Moscha D Kydoniefs.* 1946 named *Varvassi* and owned by Mrs Evgenia J Crandris.
Destination and cargo: Algiers for Southampton with a cargo of 6000 tons of iron ore, wine and tangerines.
Date sunk: 5 January 1947.
How sunk: Ran aground.
Reported position of loss: On the Bridge Reef close to the Needles Lighthouse.
Actual position of wreck: 50° 39.73′ north, 001° 35.65′ west.
Orientation/height: Boilers stand about 3 metres on seabed of rock in 6 metres of water.
How identity of wreck proved: Contemporary reports and photographs clearly show the wreck in the position stated.

SS *Varvassi* aground on the Bridge Reef. Courtesy Gordon Wheeler.

Steam tug *Carbon*
Broke loose and ran aground 10 November 1947

Steam tug *Carbon*. Author's collection.

The *Carbon* was a small steam tug of about 50 tons. On 10 November 1947, having been sold by the Admiralty, she was being towed in the Channel when she broke adrift while off St Alban's Head. No-one was on board. In gale force winds and rough seas she was blown towards the Isle of Wight, running aground on a long finger of rock in Compton Bay. She filled with water but at first appeared to be undamaged, and hopes were entertained that she would be refloated. However, continuing rough weather prevented salvage operations from taking place, and she became a total wreck.

The wreck of the *Carbon* is exposed at low water, and on very exceptionally low tides it is possible to walk around her. She rests on a sand seabed with her starboard bows almost touching the reef.

Name: *Carbon*. **Former name(s):** *John Hollway*.
Vessel type: Steam tug.
Builder: R Craggs & Sons, Middlesbrough.
When completed: December 1896.
Machinery built by: J Stewart & Sons Ltd, London.
Tonnage: 185 tons gross.
Dimensions: Length: 74′ 5″. **Breadth:** 17′ 7″.
Depth of holds: 9′.
Official number: 108125. **Yard number:** –
Signal letters: – **Last port of registry:** –
Ship description: Steel screw steam tug. 1 deck.
Machinery description: Compound 2 cylinders. 1 single ended boiler. 65 registered horse power.
Career and ownership: Owned by the Admiralty from 1900 and used as a dockyard berthing tug, number C150. Sold 1947 and lost.
Destination and cargo: –
Date sunk: 10 November 1947.
How sunk: Broke her tow and was blown ashore.
Reported position of loss: Compton Bay.
Actual position of wreck: Close position 50° 39.62′ north, 001° 28.64′ west.
Orientation/height: Wreck stands about 2 metres on sand seabed.
How identity of wreck proved: Contemporary reports identify the wreck as the *Carbon*.

MV *Volkerak*
Ran ashore 15 March 1951

MV *Volkerak*. Courtesy Bristol's Museums Galleries & Archives.

The presence of thick fog continued to be a hazard off the south coast of the Isle of Wight, but this time it was accompanied by heavy rain and a strong wind. Early on the morning of Saturday 15 March 1951, the Dutch motor vessel *Volkerak* ran aground in Chale Bay to the west of Rocken End.

A team of rescuers arrived on the spot and a line was made fast to the ship from the shore. Yarmouth lifeboat arrived, but the crew refused to be taken off, they eventually coming ashore with all their possessions and personal effects by way of breeches buoy. Later that day, a heavy sea worked up and the *Volkerak* was driven further onshore. She was finally abandoned as her hatches, lifeboat and deck house were washed away and she became a total loss.

The remains of the *Volkerak* lie scattered along Chale Bay with the remains of other ships. Although her remains were dry at low water in 1951, as the cliffs have receded due to erosion and the beach has advanced, they now lie in 5 or 6 metres of water.

Name: *Volkerak*. **Former name(s):** *Kortenaer* ex *Albatros*.
Vessel type: Motor ship.
Builder: C v d Giessen & Zonen, Krimpen.
When completed: 1904.
Machinery built by: Deutz A G Köln.
Tonnage: 337 tons gross.
Dimensions: Length: 129′ 6″. **Breadth:** 24′ 6″.
Depth of holds: 9′ 6″.
Official number: 80766 **Yard number:** –
Signal letters: PIID. **Last port of registry:** Rotterdam.
Ship description: Steel twin screw motor coaster.
Machinery description: 2 stroke single acting 4 cylinder oil engines. Machinery fitted aft.
Career and ownership: Owned by H K v d Meer (J Vermaas Scheepv Dedr, managers).
Destination and cargo: Fowey for Amsterdam with a cargo of china clay.
Date sunk: 15 March 1951.
How sunk: Ran shore in thick fog.
Reported position of loss: Ship Ledge, Brighstone, then amended to ¾ mile west of Rocken End.
Actual position of wreck: Approximately 50° 35.45′ north, 001° 19.40′ west.
Orientation/height: Scattered in 5 to 6 metres of water.
How identity of wreck proved: Not proved but contemporary reports identify the wreck in this position.

Motor vessel *Albatros*
Struck wreckage in fog 22 December 1952

MV *Albatros* lying across the wreck of MV *Volkerak*. Courtesy St Catherine's Quay Museum, Blackgang Chine.

The Dutch coaster *Albatros* became yet another victim of thick fog off the south coast of the Isle of Wight, but in somewhat more remarkable circumstances. She had departed Mounts Bay, Penzance, in December 1952, where she had loaded a cargo of scrap from HMS *Warspite*, then being broken up in the bay. Her master, Captain H Meertens, had navigated the vessel up Channel bound for Hull. He had last made landfall off Start Point, but thereafter became disorientated in thick fog. Reaching the vicinity of the Isle of Wight on 22 December 1952, and by a bizarre coincidence, *Albatros* struck the mast of the wreck of the *Volkerak*, lost in 1951, and came to rest lying across it. Captain Meertens said, "I had heard no warning signals and as my ship had been in deep water only a few minutes before I thought she was all right." *Albatros* soon had a list to starboard and seas began to wash over her. The next day her holds were flooded, and the hatches, wheel-house, steering gear and rudder were gone. Although some of her gear was saved she became a total loss.

The remains of the *Albatros* lie with those of the *Volkerak*, though it is impossible to determine which is which. Like other wrecks along this coast, much lies scattered in the shallows along the bay in 5 to 6 metres of water.

Name: *Albatros*. **Former name(s):** None.
Vessel type: Motor vessel.
Builder: W Rubertus, Groningen.
When completed: 1913.
Machinery built by: J & K Smit's Mfb, Kinderlijk.
Tonnage: 131 tons gross.
Dimensions: Length: 91′ 1″. **Breadth:** 19′ 5″. **Depth of holds:** 8′ 7″.
Official number: – **Yard number:** –
Signal letters: PCGD. **Last port of registry:** Delfzijl.
Ship description: Wooden screw motor vessel, former sailing ship.
Machinery description: 2 stroke cycle single acting 2 cylinder oil engines.
Career and ownership: Owned by H Meertens N V Scheepv. Bedr "Gruno" managers.
Destination and cargo: Penzance to Hull with a cargo of scrap metal.
Date sunk: 22 December 1952.
How sunk: Struck a wreck in thick fog.
Reported position of loss: About a mile west of Rocken End.
Actual position of wreck: Approximately 50° 34.45′ north, 001° 19.40′ west.
Orientation/height: Lies in 5 or 6 metres of water on shingle seabed.
How identity of wreck proved: Not proved but contemporary reports state the *Albatros* struck the wreck of the *Volkerak*.

HM Submarine *Upstart*
Scuttled 29 July 1957

The *Upstart* was a British submarine built in the early 1940's and upon completion she was engaged on operational patrols in the Mediterranean. When the Second World War came to an end many submarines were laid up, some were sold to other navies, and others scrapped. *Upstart* survived until 1957 when it was decided she should be expended as a sonar target.

On 29 July 1957, *Upstart,* stripped of her armament, stores and propellers, was taken to a position south of the Needles and scuttled.

The wreck of the *Upstart* lies in about 38 metres of water. She is more or less upright. Some diving reports suggested the vessel had an unusual circular design of conning tower; in fact the entire bridge of the *Upstart* had fallen from the wreck and was lying nearby on the seabed. On each side the name *Upstart* was riveted on in large brass letters.

Name: HMS *Upstart.* **Former name(s):** *P65.*
Vessel type: "U" class submarine.
Builder: Vickers Armstrong, Barrow.
When completed: 1943.
Machinery built by: Admiralty or Davey Paxman.
Tonnage: 648 tons displacement surfaced, 735 tons displacement submerged.
Dimensions: Length: 195′ 6″. **Breadth:** 15′ 9″. **Depth:** 15′ 10″.
Ship description: Steel twin screw submarine.
Machinery description: 2 × diesel engines and 2 × General Electric motors.
Career and ownership: Owned by the Royal Navy.
Armament: 4 × 21″ torpedo tubes for × 8 torpedoes. 1 × 3″ 50 calibre deck gun. 3 × .303 machine guns (removed).
Destination and cargo: Portsmouth for the Isle of Wight for scuttling.
Date sunk: 29 July 1957.
How sunk: Scuttled.
Reported position of loss: 9 miles south of the Needles.
Actual position of wreck: 50° 30.42′ north, 001° 32.78′ west.
Orientation/height: Lies 090°/270°. Stands 5 metres in 38 metres on seabed of shingle.
How identity of wreck proved: Vessel's name in brass letters on both sides of the bridge.

HM Submarine *Upstart.* Courtesy Wright & Logan collection, Royal Naval Museum.

MV *Augustenburg*
Collision 18 April 1962

MV Augustenburg. Courtesy Fotoflite, www.fotoflite.com.

On 18 April 1962, a number of signals were picked up by Niton Radio reporting that a collision had taken place between the Danish motor vessel *Colorado* and the German motor vessel *Augustenburg* in the English Channel. Among the messages received was one from the *Colorado* at 1.20pm which said, "Collided with *Augustenburg,* position 50° 16′ north, 000° 54′ west. We are intact but German vessel sinking." At 1.30pm another signal reported, "All crew on board Danish vessel." Fifteen minutes later, the captain of the *Augustenburg* requested a salvage vessel as the ship was still afloat.

The Admiralty despatched the duty destroyer HMS *Dundas* to the scene to render whatever assistance it could. On arrival, she took on board the master and some of the crew of *Augustenburg,* who reported their ship badly holed aft and unsafe to board. Before the salvage tug reached the scene, *Augustenburg* sank at 5.35pm.

The British authorities were not interested in holding an enquiry between foreign vessels in international waters, but the German authorities certainly were and they held one in June 1962. The findings were that *Augustenburg* left Buenos Aries for Hamburg with a cargo of apples and on the morning of 18 April 1962, she was entering the English Channel when she ran into cloudy, murky weather, with visibility at about 4 miles. The ship's radar had broken down on the previous voyage and had not been repaired due to lack of spares. About midday, the captain handed over the watch to the second officer and went to lunch in the saloon. Not long after, visibility had reduced drastically as the vessel entered thick fog. Reducing speed to "ahead, very slow" a man was sent to the bow to act as lookout. The captain became aware that something was amiss and returned to the bridge to resume command.

The faint outline of another ship appeared off the starboard bow and the captain made a slight alteration to port when suddenly the other ship, which turned out to be the 5510 ton Danish motor vessel *Colorado,* turned to starboard and headed directly for the *Augustenburg.* The captain ordered, "Stop engines! Full speed astern!" It was too late to avoid a collision, and the *Colorado* struck *Augustenburg* on her starboard side aft between number 3 and number 4 hold. *Colorado*'s bow drove through *Augustenburg's* deck almost half way across the ship, striking at an angle of 60°or 70°. By this time the captain had already ordered "all crew to assemble on deck and don lifejackets."

After the collision, *Colorado* withdrew from *Augustenburg* and came alongside and rescued all the crew. The doomed ship had already gained a list of 15° to 20° and her captain reported that at 5.20pm she sank in position 50° 14′ north, 001° 04′ west.

The German enquiry concluded that the Danish ship was entirely responsible for the loss of the *Augustenburg.*

The wreck of the *Augustenburg* lies in 75 metres of water on her starboard side, bows to the south west. She stands about 15 metres off the seabed and is very much intact. She is a large, substantial wreck.

Name: *Augustenburg.* **Former name(s):** *Washington Express.*
Vessel type: Motor ship.
Builder: A/B Götaverken.
When completed: September 1933.
Machinery built by: Kieler Howaldtswerke AG.
Tonnage: 3639 tons gross.
Dimensions: Length: 352′. **Breadth:** 47′.
Depth of holds: 21′ 3″.
Official number: – **Yard number:** –
Signal letters: DINA. **Last port of registry:** Hamburg.
Ship description: Steel screw motor ship. 1 deck.
Machinery description: Twin 2 stroke single acting 7 cylinders oil engines.
Career and ownership: Owned by M S Augustenburg (H Schuldt).
Destination and cargo: Buenos Aries for Hamburg with a cargo of apples.
Date sunk: 18 April 1962.
How sunk: Collision in fog with the Danish motor ship *Colorado.*
Reported position of loss: 50° 14′ north, 001° 04′ west.
Actual position of wreck: 50° 14.18′ north, 001° 03.44′ west.
Orientation/height: Lies 065°/245°. Stands 15 metres in 75 metres.
How identity of wreck proved: Accurate position given by the German captain at the time of loss. Comparison of features on the wreck with photographs of the ship show a close likeness.

Motor tug *Witte Zee*
Struck rocks and foundered 23 February 1964

Motor tug *Witte Zee*. Courtesy Smit International, Rotterdam.

In the early hours of Sunday 23 February 1964 in thick fog, the Liberian registered ship *Brother George* ran aground on Brook Ledge on the south coast of the Isle of Wight and stranded. As the tide was low at the time, it was expected the ship would refloat at high water, but as a precaution tugs were summoned to stand by in case they were needed to pull her clear. One of those which responded was the Dutch ocean going tug *Witte Zee*.

Witte Zee's master was Captain Johannes Kleyn, who told what happened next. "We attempted to put a line aboard the *Brother George*. We moved in and fired a line-carrying rocket across the stranded steamer when we struck a rock and were holed. We were unable to deal with the terrific inrush of water. I decided to make for the sheltered waters of the Solent and beach the tug but, after covering less than 2 miles, I was compelled to radio for assistance." Responding to Captain Kleyn's call for help, the Yarmouth lifeboat and the tug *Gatcombe* answered and reached the *Witte Zee* in time to rescue all the crew.

A witness from the shore put a slightly different perspective on the incident, reporting that he "saw the tug struck by a huge wave which broke over her stern. She rolled heavily to port under the blow and, instead of righting herself immediately, there was an appreciable delay before she returned to an even keel. I assume she was holed on the port side."

Captain Kleyn added, "When I abandoned my tug

the deck was awash and it was far too dangerous to leave anyone on board." Shortly before 11pm that night he learned that another tug had taken the *Witte Zee* in tow, but when 4 miles off Compton she had finally sunk. The *Brother George* was eventually refloated.

The wreck of the *Witte Zee* lies upright and almost intact in 33 metres of water. She is a popular dive site, though there are signs she is beginning to break up.

Name: *Witte Zee.* **Former name(s):** None.
Vessel type: Motor tug.
Builder: J & K Smit's Scheeps, Kinderdijk.
When completed: 1943.
Machinery built by: J & K Smit's Mach, Kinderdijk.
Tonnage: 328 tons gross.
Dimensions: Length: 131′ 10″. **Breadth:** 25′ 1″.
Depth of holds: 13′ 1½″.
Official number: 37244. **Yard number:** –
Signal letters: PIRD. **Last port of registry:** Rotterdam.
Ship description: Steel screw motor tug.
Machinery description: 4 stroke cycle single acting 6 cylinder oil engine.
Career and ownership: Owned by N V L Smit & Company, Sleepdienst.
Destination and cargo: Brook Ledge for the Solent after failed attempt to salve the *Brother George.*
Date sunk: 23 February 1964.
How sunk: Holed while attempting to salve a stranded steamer. Later filled and sank in deep water.
Reported position of loss: 4 miles off Compton.
Actual position of wreck: 50° 35.85′ north, 001° 28.44′ west.
Orientation/height: Lies 000°/180°. Stands about 6 metres in 33 metres on shingle seabed.
How identity of wreck proved: Wreck lies 4 miles south of Compton and agrees with contemporary reports. Wreck is of a large tug and *Witte Zee* is the only one known to have been lost in the area.

Motor vessel *Guernsey Coast*
Collision 6 August 1964

MV *Guernsey Coast.* Courtesy Fotoflite www.fotoflite.com.

The *Guernsey Coast* was a small coaster of 646 tons gross, operating on the UK–Channel Islands service. She was under contract to carry cargoes of tomatoes. On the evening of 5 August 1964, she departed St Peter Port bound for Shoreham. As the vessel reached a position in mid Channel south of the Isle of Wight, visibility deteriorated and the vessel reduced speed. About 1am, however, visibility improved and the vessel gained speed, making about 10½ knots. However, the fog came down again and *Guernsey Coast* sounded her whistle as she groped her way on an east-north-east heading. By 2am, the fog was dense and the master, Captain John Healy, was on the bridge keeping watch on the radar. The ship maintained her speed; captain Healy was relying on his radar.

About 2.30am Captain Healy noticed an echo appear on his radar set and altered *Guernsey Coast's* heading to clear the other ship. However, he noted that the other ship was still heading on a parallel course, and as the vessels approached fog signals could be heard from forward of the beam. When the two ships were about ¾ mile apart it became apparent that the other vessel was on a collision course and *Guernsey Coast's* helmsman was ordered to put the helm "hard to starboard." When only 200 yards distant, *Guernsey Coast* altered course "hard to port" in a final effort to avoid a collision, but it was too late.

The other ship was the steamer *Catcher*, 7238 tons, on voyage from Antwerp for Puerto Rico. She crashed into the *Guernsey Coast*, striking her at right angles on her port side aft, cutting her down almost half way through. The smaller ship heeled right over to starboard and began to settle at once. All the crew assembled on deck with their lifejackets while the *Catcher's* bows, still embedded in their ship, towered above them. The obvious route of escape was to board the *Catcher* and all the crew except the captain and the acting chief engineer Frank Frew managed to reach safety in this way. Then, quite suddenly, *Guernsey Coast* sank, going down rapidly by the head, throwing Captain Healy and Mr Frew into the water. Although Captain Healy was soon picked up, no sign could be found of Mr Frew and he was presumed to have drowned.

The Court of Enquiry held in May 1965 concluded that, "The navigation of the *Guernsey Coast* was deplorable. She was proceeding at an excessive speed in fog and failed to make any reduction in speed at any time even though she heard the fog signals of the *Catcher*. The master was relying on his radar and even if his observations of the echoes he saw on the radar screen were accurate, he must have failed to detect the near approach of the *Catcher* on a dangerous course." The Court continued, "In the opinion of the Court this collision was contributed to by the wrongful act and default of Captain Healy in navigating his vessel at excessive speed in fog and not stopping the engines on hearing a fog signal forward of the beam." His certificate was suspended for 12 months.

The wreck of the *Guernsey Coast* lies upright and intact in 63 metres of water, standing some 14 metres off the seabed. Her aft accommodation still stands as does her amidships deckhouse, though the upper bridge has collapsed forward and hangs over the forward hold. There is a large V shaped hole in her hull on the port side aft, extending from her keel to the upper deck, where she was struck by the *Catcher*.

Name: *Guernsey Coast*. **Former name(s):** *Welsh Coast*.
Vessel type: Motor coaster.
Builder: Ardrossan Dry Dock Company Ltd.
When completed: January 1938.
Machinery built by: J G Kincaid & Company Ltd, Greenock.
Tonnage: 646 tons gross.
Dimensions: Length: 209′ 7″. **Breadth:** 33′ 1″. **Depth of holds:** 13′ 7½″.
Official number: 164349. **Yard number:** –
Signal letters: GDGY. **Last port of registry:** London.
Ship description: Steel screw motor coaster. 1 deck.
Machinery description: 4 stroke cycle single acting 6 cylinders oil engine fitted aft.
Career and ownership: 1963 owned by British Channel Island Shipping Company Ltd (manager Montague Robinson, Liverpool).
Destination and cargo: St Peter Port for Shoreham with 46800 trays of tomatoes of 292 tons.
Date sunk: 6 August 1964.
How sunk: Collision in fog with the SS *Catcher*.
Reported position of loss: Variously as 30 miles off Cherbourg, 38 miles north east of Cap de la Hague, and wreckage and oil slick spotted between positions 50° 09′ north, 001° 17.30′ west, and 50° 08′ north, 001° 28′ west.
Actual position of wreck: 50° 07.31′ north, 001° 38.87′ west.
Orientation/height: Lies 045°/225°. Stands 14 metres in 63 metres on shingle seabed.
How identity of wreck proved: Location, size and description of wreck fits *Guernsey Coast* exactly, as does the description of damage where the collision took place, which is exactly as described by the survivors.

Motor trawler *Zeemansblik*
Ran aground 19 February 1965

Motor trawler *Zeemansblik* aground at Atherfield Point. Courtesy St Catherine's Quay Museum, Blackgang Chine.

The *Zeemansblik* was a Belgian trawler which was on her way back to her home port of Zeebrugge following 16 days' trawling in the Bristol Channel. She had had a successful trip, with about 7 tons of fish packed in ice in her hold. Soon after 10pm on the night of Friday 19 February 1965, a "Mayday" message was picked up by Niton Radio from the *Zeemansblik* reporting she had run aground on Atherfield Ledge on the south coast of the Isle of Wight. Her message added, "We require lifeboat. Listing badly. Have lost liferaft."

The coastguard was alerted to the incident and Yarmouth Lifeboat was sent to the scene. Distress flares were fired from the stranded trawler and assistance arrived from rescuers on the coast and from the sea. Then, the lost liferaft drifted back to the trawler, and the crew of five abandoned ship, leaving the vessel with her engine and bilge pumps running and all her lights, radio and navigation equipment left switched on.

One of the vessels which answered the Mayday call was the small coastal tanker *Esso Jersey*, which arrived in time to pick up the crew from their liferaft. As for the *Zeemansblik*, she was rolling and bumping heavily as a ground swell was breaking over the ledge, causing her to work her way closer inshore. Eventually, she came to rest on the northern edge of the Mixen, the central part of Atherfield Ledge which comprises three distinct ledges. It was later found she was badly holed and that her decks were strained.

It proved impossible to save the vessel, and she was largely dismantled where she lay. The lower parts of her hull, some machinery and tanks, spare propeller and masts were not recovered and parts can still be seen at low water lying among the rocks. Some wreckage has moved and has spread along the beach.

Name: *Zeemansblik*. **Former name(s):** None.
Vessel type: Motor trawler.
Builder: Not known.
When completed: Not known.
Machinery built by: Not known.
Tonnage: 83 tons gross.
Dimensions: Length: – **Breadth:** –
Depth of holds: –
Official number: – **Yard number:** –
Signal letters: – **Last port of registry:** Zeebrugge.
Ship description: Wooden screw motor trawler.
Machinery description: Diesel engine.
Career and ownership: Port number Z539.
Destination and cargo: Zeebrugge for fishing in the Bristol Channel and return.
Date sunk: 19 February 1965.
How sunk: Ran aground.
Reported position of loss: Atherfield Ledge.
Actual position of wreck: 50° 36.50′ north, 001° 21.72′ west.
Orientation/height: Very low to the ground and scattered in about 3 metres of water at high tide on a rock and gravel seabed. Not really a dive site.
How identity of wreck proved: Contemporary reports and photographs of the time clearly identify the vessel as the *Zeemansblik*, and the author recalls visiting the wreck.

Motor vessel *Gorizont*
Collision 27 November 1975, sank 1/2 December 1975

MV *Gorizont*. Courtesy Deutsches Schiffahrtsmuseum, Bremerhaven.

One of the more unusual shipping losses concerned the sinking of the Russian ship *Gorizont*; not in her manner of loss but relating to the activities in which she was engaged. Ostensibly she was a fishing factory ship, operating in support of Russian trawlers. In 1975 the Cold War was at its height, and both the West and the East were engaged in spying operations against each other. Although there is no confirmation, it was rumoured at the time that the *Gorizont* was a spy ship, as were the trawlers which operated with her.

On 27 November 1975 *Gorizont* was in a position in mid Channel south of the Isle of Wight when she collided with the motor vessel *Ifni*. The circumstances are unknown, but *Gorizont* was severely damaged.

The Times reported, "Despite a clear message that no help was wanted the Royal Navy kept a close watch yesterday on the wreck of the 4374 ton Soviet fishing factory ship *Gorizont* after she had been in collision the previous evening with a new Moroccan cargo ship in the Channel 21 miles off the Isle of Wight."

"The first ship sent to search for survivors was the guided missile destroyer HMS *London*. Captain Peter Nicholl found seven or eight Soviet trawlers round the wreck of the *Gorizont,* the bows of which projected about 50 feet above the water . . .. The first news of the accident came in an SOS message in Russian at 7.48pm on Tuesday. Offers of help from the Bembridge coastguard were politely rejected. HMS *London* was warned off by the Soviet trawlers which had rushed to the scene, but stood by all night to warn shipping of the hazard. The frigate HMS *Penelope* took over yesterday morning when the spot was marked and buoyed."

"The Moroccan ship involved in the collision was the 6700 ton *Ifni,* which was holed but was able to proceed to Le Havre for repairs. An oil slick at the scene of the collision was found to consist of light fuel oil which is non-pollutant and no threat to the British coastline."

Gorizont slowly sank in deep water, disappearing on the night of 1/2 December 1975. After the scene had been abandoned by the Russians, Royal Navy divers inspected the wreck and reported it to be lying upside down.

The wreck of the *Gorizont* lies in about 72 metres of water, but stands an impressive 23 metres off the seabed. Far from being upside down, she is upright and divers report seeing "unusual" fittings on her.

Name: *Gorizont.* **Former name(s):** None.
Vessel type: Motor ship.
Builder: Schiffswerft Neptun-Ros.
When completed: 1961.
Machinery built by: Masch Augsburg-Nurnberg.
Tonnage: 4404 tons gross.
Dimensions: Length: 344′. **Breadth:** 47′ 4″.
Depth of holds: 27′ 11″.
Official number: – **Yard number:** –
Signal letters: UYOC. **Last port of registry:** Odessa.
Ship description: Steel screw fishing factory ship, built as a motor training ship, ice strengthened.
Machinery description: 2 cycle single acting 6 cylinders oil engines.
Career and ownership: Owned by the USSR.
Destination and cargo: Not known.
Date sunk: Night of 1/2 December 1975 following collision on 27 November 1975.
How sunk: Collision with the MV *Ifni.*
Reported position of loss: 21 miles off the Isle of Wight.
Actual position of wreck: 50° 13.45′ north, 001° 13.25′ west.
Orientation/height: Lies 085°/265°. Stands 23 metres in 72 metres.
How identity of wreck proved: Position fixed by the Royal Navy at the time of sinking.

Motor vessel *Margaret Smith*
Capsized 28 June and foundered 29 June 1978

MV *Margaret Smith*.

"Navy men save four" ran the headlines in the Southern Evening Echo, reporting the dramatic rescue of the crew of the motor dredger *Margaret Smith*. The vessel had been engaged in dredging for gravel on 28 June 1978 in the vicinity of Cowes when she lost power and radioed that she was drifting off Gurnard Ledge and was taking in too much water for the pumps to handle. Drifting east on the flood tide, she reached a spot just off Cowes seafront when a Royal Navy rescue helicopter arrived on the scene.

Lowered down the helicopter's highline was Royal Navy diver Loz Coleman, who reached the ship and cleared the vessel's liferaft moments before the *Margaret Smith* capsized. One of her crew, 19-year-old Gordon Thompson, said, "If the diver had delayed cutting the rope another 30 seconds we would all have been in the drink and would not have stood much chance in the freezing water." He added, "I was first in the raft before the rest got on and had to hang on to the rope to stop the liferaft drifting away. The rotor blades of the helicopter were churning up the water like mad and nearly capsized the raft."

Loz Coleman said, "I was winched down on to the ship where one man was already in the liferaft and another was getting in. I asked the third man and the skipper to put on lifejackets and they got in. I was still on the ship and the list to starboard was getting worse. It was obvious she was going to sink or turn over so I cut the rope between ship and raft, jumped in the water and towed the liferaft clear. Then the ship turned turtle. Another couple of seconds and we would all have gone under with the ship."

Margaret Smith remained afloat and began to drift west on the ebb tide, chased by the tugs *Kolas* from Cowes and *Calshot* from Southampton. Eventually the wreck was towed to an Admiralty mooring in Yarmouth Roads. The next day the vessel sank in 15 metres of water.

The wreck of the *Margaret Smith* remains substantially intact. She lies on her starboard side.

Name: *Margaret Smith*. **Former name(s):** *Sand Wren* ex *Pen Adur* ex *Lerryu* ex *Morton Cobbett*.
Vessel type: Motor dredger/sand carrier.
Builder: J Harker Ltd, Knottingley.
When completed: 1943.
Machinery built by: Crossley Brothers Ltd.
Tonnage: 309 tons gross.
Dimensions: Length: 42.98 metres. **Breadth:** 6.41 metres. **Depth of holds:** 2.286 metres.
Official number: 167140. **Yard number:** –
Signal letters: MCNP.
Last port of registry: Southampton.
Ship description: Steel screw motor dredger/sand carrier (suction). 1 deck. Converted to general cargo.
Machinery description: Oil engine, 5 cylinders.
Career and ownership: Owned at the time of loss by T J Bowen and P D Caines.
Destination and cargo: Southampton for dredging in the Solent.
Date sunk: 29 June 1978.
How sunk: Gravel cargo shifted, vessel took on water and capsized.
Reported position of loss: Yarmouth Roads.
Actual position of wreck: 50° 42.96′ north, 001° 28.15′ west.
Orientation/height: Lies across the tide, standing 6 metres in 15 metres on shingle seabed.
How identity of wreck proved: Vessel known to be in this position after sinking at her mooring.

Motor vessel *Pool Fisher*
Foundered 6 November 1979

MV *Pool Fisher*. Courtesy J & M Clarkson, Longton.

On 3 November 1979, the British coaster *Pool Fisher* arrived at Hamburg from Norway in ballast to load a cargo of 1250 tons of muriate of potash – a salt – in bulk. She had a crew of 14 hands and one passenger – the wife of the chief engineer – under the command of her master, John Stewart. Departing Hamburg at 1pm, *Pool Fisher* commenced her voyage towards the English Channel. The weather forecast was for winds to veer south to south west, force 6 or 7, occasionally gale 8, with rain at times. By about 8.30pm that night, the ship was in the southern North Sea experiencing force 7 winds and heavy seas. She was pitching and proved difficult to steer. Two days later, she was sighted south of Brighton, steering erratically and appearing to be down somewhat by the head, taking heavy seas.

In the early hours of 6 November 1979, *Pool Fisher* was south of St Catherine's Point steering 265° in a westerly gale. Wave heights were from 3½ to nearly 5 metres. She could have hardly been in a worse place; the geographical nature of the seabed caused sea conditions to be worse than elsewhere. At 5.47am, a "Mayday" was sent by the *Pool Fisher*. It said, "Mayday anyone hear me Mayday going over position south west of St Catherine's Point." Niton Radio requested a better position but there was no response. *Pool Fisher* had gone.

Only two men survived from the 15 souls on board, both deck hands who had been asleep in their berths. Woken by the boatswain, who was wearing a lifejacket, he said, "Quick lads, get up on deck; she's going down by the head." Reaching the starboard side forward of the officer's mess room, the boatswain shouted, "she's going." One deck hand named Crane was swept into the sea, while the other, named Fook managed to reach the boat deck. Mr Fook said, "We went through our mess room; then we went through the galley and the galley is on the starboard side. The ship took another roll over to port and we tried the door from the galley to the starboard side but with her leaning over to port we could not open it so we went – it came back upright again – so we went through the officer's pantry and she took another big one to her port and that is when I fell through on to the sink in the pantry. She came upright again. She was rolling pretty heavily at this time back and forward. She kind of went dead slow over to port, very slow, and we had to walk out ...."

Alerted by the Mayday call, the Royal Navy search and rescue helicopter from Lee on Solent searched the sea south west of St Catherine's Point. Lieutenant Bill Sample, her pilot, said, "It seemed that for hours we were flying up and down a 25 mile square stretch of water, looking down at the masses of debris and hoping to see someone hanging on. Then, all of a sudden, we saw two men waving to us. Our diver, Leading Aircraftsman John Taylor, went into the water to hold onto them and ensure they were not swept away." After saving Crane and Fook, who were holding on to a baulk of timber, Lieutenant Sample said, "They told us that at one stage there were three others holding on to the lump of wood. But, gradually, they died one by one and dropped off into the sea to be washed away. They said they had no time to put on lifejackets. They just jumped into the sea in T shirts. They were beginning to give up when we found them. They were freezing to death."

Late in 1980 a Court of Enquiry was held to determine the cause of loss of the *Pool Fisher*. Their finding was that, "the said casualty was probably caused by entry of water into the fore part of the *Pool Fisher's* hold following a failure of the aftermost section of her hatch boards on her No 1 hatch, which failure was caused or contributed to by the wrongful act or default of her master, John Maclaren Stewart and her mate, Francis William Cooper." The Court said, "The master is responsible for his vessel in all respects and at all times; the mate is particularly responsible for battening down of hatches. The sinking occurred, as we find, because the hatches were not properly battened down. With great reluctance therefore in view of the high esteem in which the officers concerned were held, and because they could not come to court to defend themselves, we nevertheless feel bound to find that they were responsible for the failure which led to the loss of the *Pool Fisher*."

The wreck of the *Pool Fisher* lies upside down, with her bows broken, in 40 metres of water.

Name: *Pool Fisher*. **Former name(s):** None.
Vessel type: Motor vessel.
Builder: N V Schpsw "Foxhol" Foxhol.
When completed: February 1959.
Machinery built by: Klockner-Humboldt-Deutz.
Tonnage: 1028 tons gross.
Dimensions: Length: 66.30 metres. **Breadth:** 10.32 metres. **Depth of holds:** 4.414 metres.
Official number: 187980. **Yard number:** –
Signal letters: GXLL. **Last port of registry:** Barrow.
Ship description: Steel screw motor vessel, general cargo ship.
Machinery description: 4 stroke cycle single acting 6 cylinders oil engines.
Career and ownership: Owned by James Fisher & Sons.
Destination and cargo: Hamburg for Runcorn with a cargo of potash.
Date sunk: 6 November 1979.
How sunk: Foundered in storm conditions.
Reported position of loss: South west of St Catherine's Point.
Actual position of wreck: 50° 27.46′ north, 001° 26.59′ west.
Orientation/height: Lies 000°/180°. Stands about 6 metres in 40 metres on hard chalk seabed with shingle covering.
How identity of wreck proved: Wreck located and dived on in 1980, and name of ship painted on bows was seen.

Unidentified wrecks

Although there are a number of named wrecks where the true identity is uncertain, but where, in good faith, a name has been attributed, there remain others where it has not been possible to even make a reasonable suggestion as to their possible identity. Some of these wrecks are included here, but with one or two exceptions, they do not include wrecks which lie in the west bound shipping lane in the area covered by this book.

Wreck in position 50° 05.44′ north, 001° 48.82′ west. Lying in about 64 metres on LW neaps, this is a small wreck, compound engine fitted aft, with a long boiler of a type fitted vertically in steam drifters, estimated tonnage no more than 100 tons, and no more than 30 metres in length. There is a possibility this could be the wreck of the *Badger.*

Wreck in position 50° 10.54′ north, 001° 21.53′ west. Lying north/south and standing 5 metres, with a 4 metre high ridge close to the west, this is the wreck of another unidentified U-boat lying in 95 metres.

Wreck in position 50° 10.93′ north, 001° 42.10′ west. Known by anglers as one of 'The Legs' (the other 'Legs' being the *Ashmun J Clough*) so called because they both lie on the 50° 11′ west position. ('Legs' refers to bingo slang – 'Legs Eleven.') This is a large, upright wreck, but because no cargo is evident, there are large empty spaces between sections of the wreck. Amidships, there are two boilers and a triple expansion engine, thickly covered in lost angling gear. Depth to the seabed is 60–62 metres on HW. Seabed comprises sand and shingle. As the wreck is heavily fished, and is in the westbound shipping lane (though most shipping passes to the north) it is not recommended as a dive.

Wreck in position 50° 11.32′ north, 001° 22.77′ west. Lying 028°/208° and standing about 9 metres in about 93 metres, this wreck was originally thought to be the Norwegian *Borgsten*, but is in fact an unidentified U-boat.

Wreck in position 50° 11.80′ north, 001° 39.28′ west. Lying upright, across the tide, bows to the north, is what appears to be a steam trawler. There is a small triple expansion engine and single boiler, and a large winch fitted immediately forward of the boiler. Coal in the form of large briquettes is tightly packed in the wreck forward of the winch. Wreck stands about 4 metres on a shingle, uneven seabed in about 62 metres. Wreckage has collapsed off the wreck to port. Wreck lies in the westbound shipping lane, though most shipping passes to the north.

Wreck in position 50° 30.13′ north, 001° 31.07′ west. Lying more or less east/west in about 42 metres, this is the wreck of a motorised steel barge. Completely upright, both the bow and stern sections are upright and intact, though the hull amidships has collapsed. The steering position aft is in place. Wreck has a small diesel engine and single screw. Two lifebelts were seen stowed beneath the deck port side aft, which could well bear the name of the vessel. Estimated dimensions: 30 metres x 5 metres maximum.

Wreck in position 50° 13.46′ north, 000° 59.54′ west. Lying 050°/230° on a sloping seabed, bows to the north east, standing about 6 metres. Depth to the seabed on HW springs about 70 metres. Estimated 2000 tons. Wreck has a compound engine, two single ended boilers and barrels of cement in forward holds.

Wreck in position 50° 16.11′ north, 001° 39.38′ west (stern) and 50° 16.12′ north, 001° 39.58′ west (bows). Bow section of a fairly substantial wreck, largely upside down, though the forward mast can be seen disappearing into the sand. Some railings and other debris lies among rocks close to the port side. Quantities of coal seen, either cargo or bunker fuel. Depth on HW is about 60 metres. Seabed is sand and shingle in broad dunes. Stern section not investigated.

Wreck in position 50° 21.90′ north, 001° 05 03′ west. Lying 063°/245° in 56 metres on HW, this is a substantial, largely intact wreck lying on its starboard side, standing about 8 metres. There is a possibility this could be the *Meandros,* but other than the location there is no other evidence to support that view.

South Coast Shipwrecks
Index

Mingary as a private yacht, later renamed HMS *Sargasso*. Authors' collection

Steam trawler *Nemrod* wrecked in Chale Bay. Authors' collection

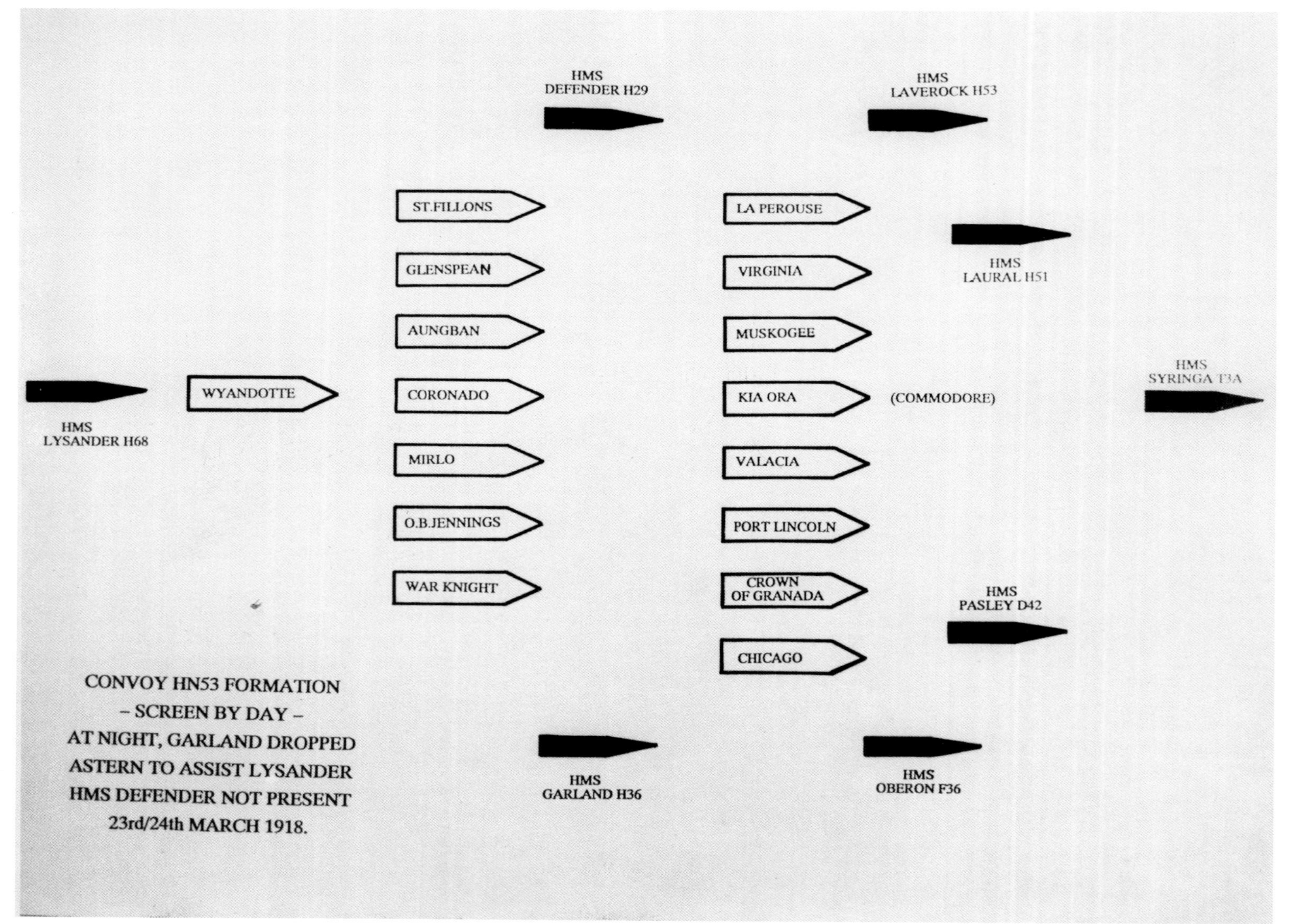

Convoy formation plan SS *War Knight*.

Authors' collection